Women, Language and Politics

Women, Language and Politics addresses the problem of the under-representation of women in politics by examining how language use constructs and maintains inequality in political institutions. Drawing on different political genres, from televised debates to parliamentary question times, and fifty interviews with politicians conducted between 1998 and 2018, the book identifies the barriers and obstacles women face by considering how gender stereotypes constrain women's participation and give women additional burdens. By comparing the UK House of Commons with newer institutions such as the Scottish Parliament, the National Assembly for Wales and the Northern Ireland Assembly, the book asks: how successful have newer institutions been in encouraging equal participation? What are the interactional procedures that can be thought of as making an institution more egalitarian? *Women, Language and Politics* also explores the workings and effects of sexism, fraternal networks, high visibility in the media and gendered discourses through detailed case studies of Theresa May, Julia Gillard and Hillary Clinton.

SYLVIA SHAW is Senior Lecturer in English Language and Linguistics at the University of Westminster. She is a sociolinguist who has conducted research projects in the House of Commons and the devolved political institutions of the UK. Her publications focus on gender, language and power in different types of political discourse.

Women, Language and Politics

Sylvia Shaw

University of Westminster

CAMBRIDGE
UNIVERSITY PRESS

CAMBRIDGE
UNIVERSITY PRESS

University Printing House, Cambridge CB2 8BS, United Kingdom

One Liberty Plaza, 20th Floor, New York, NY 10006, USA

477 Williamstown Road, Port Melbourne, VIC 3207, Australia

314–321, 3rd Floor, Plot 3, Splendor Forum, Jasola District Centre, New Delhi – 110025, India

79 Anson Road, #06-04/06, Singapore 079906

Cambridge University Press is part of the University of Cambridge.

It furthers the University's mission by disseminating knowledge in the pursuit of education, learning and research at the highest international levels of excellence.

www.cambridge.org
Information on this title: www.cambridge.org/9781107080881
DOI: 10.1017/9781139946636

© Sylvia Shaw 2020

First published 2020

Printed in the United Kingdom by TJ International Ltd, Padstow Cornwall

A catalogue record for this publication is available from the British Library.

Library of Congress Cataloging-in-Publication Data
Names: Shaw, Sylvia, 1969- author.
Title: Women, language and politics / Sylvia Shaw, University of Westminster.
Description: Cambridge ; New York, NY : Cambridge University Press, 2020. | Includes bibliographical references and index.
Identifiers: LCCN 2019058889 | ISBN 9781107080881 (hardback) | ISBN 9781107440265 (ebook)
Subjects: LCSH: Women--Political activity. | Women politicians. | Sex role--Political aspects. | Feminism--Political aspects. | Sexism in political culture. | Male domination (Social structure)
Classification: LCC HQ1236 .S48 2020 | DDC 320.082--dc23
LC record available at https://lccn.loc.gov/2019058889

ISBN 978-1-107-08088-1 Hardback

For my family, great and small

Contents

Contents

Figures

Tables

Acknowledgements

Many people have supported me in the research and writing stages of the work presented in this book. I would like to acknowledge the contribution of all the research participants in the House of Commons, the Northern Ireland Assembly, the National Assembly for Wales and the Scottish Parliament. I am extremely grateful for their time, good nature and willingness to participate in the interviews for the projects. I am also very grateful to Denis Oag in the Scottish Parliament and Elizabeth Connolly in the Northern Ireland Assembly for helping with practical arrangements in the institutions and for sharing their valuable insider knowledge and suggestions. The research in the devolved parliaments was also supported by Stephen Pihlaja, Irene Lucking and Lucy Dawson, who helped with the classification and enumeration of speaking turns, the transcription of interview data, administration and travel arrangements. Thanks also to Roshi Naidoo and Phil Cole for their hospitality while I was undertaking research in Cardiff.

Next, I would like to acknowledge the financial support I have received from the Economic and Social Research Council; from Middlesex University in the initial stages of writing this book; and from the School of Humanities, University of Westminster, for awarding me a research sabbatical to complete the book in 2018–19. Thanks also to colleagues who commented on drafts of the chapters: Jane Arthurs, Andrew Caink, Anna Charalambidou, Lucy Jones, Petros Karatsareas, Damien Ridge, and Louise Sylvester; to the anonymous US reviewer who made valuable suggestions, particularly about the Hillary Clinton case study in Chapter 7 and to Helen Barton at Cambridge University Press. Billy Clark has been present in my working life through all the stages of the twenty years of research discussed here, and I am very grateful for the positive advice and support he has given me over those years. Similarly, Deborah Cameron has been an inspirational, witty and knowledgeable supervisor, mentor and then co-author in this period. I have also been lucky enough to work in environments in which I have been encouraged by my colleagues, whether a quick conversation by the photocopier or more detailed advice about research and publications, and this is greatly appreciated.

Finally, I would not have managed to write this book without the kindness, encouragement and support of family and friends who have listened to me and kept my spirits up in times of need. Most importantly, to Rob and the boys, who have patiently shared the daily ups and downs of research and writing and who have lost me to multiple field trips and to the office in the loft for weeks on end – thank you.

Abbreviations

AL	Alliance Party (Northern Ireland)
AM	Assembly Member (National Assembly for Wales)
BAME	black, Asian and minority ethnic
CA	Conversion Analysis
CDA	Critical Discourse Analysis
CMP	current MP (the MP with the current 'legal' speaking turn)
Con	Conservative Party (UK)
CoP	community of practice
DQTs	departmental question times
DUP	Democratic Unionist Party (Northern Ireland)
EU	European Union
FM	first minister
FMQs	first minister's questions
HoC	House of Commons, Westminster, UK
HoR	House of Representatives (Australian National Parliament)
IMP	intervening MP (the MP intervening on the CMP, either legally or illegally)
LAB	Labour Party (UK)
LibDem	Liberal Democrats Party (UK)
LO	leader of the opposition
MLA	Member of the Legislative Authority (Northern Ireland Assembly)
MP	Member of Parliament (of the UK House of Commons)
MSP	Member of the Scottish Parliament
NAW	National Assembly for Wales, Cardiff, UK (to be renamed 'Welsh Assembly')
NIA	Northern Ireland Assembly, Belfast, UK
OR	official report
PC	Plaid Cymru (the national party of Wales)
PM	prime minister
PMQs	Prime Minister's Questions

SDLP	Social Democratic and Labour Party (Northern Ireland)
SF	Sinn Féin (Northern Ireland)
SNP	Scottish Nationalist Party (the national party of Scotland)
SP	Scottish Parliament, Edinburgh, UK
SRW	the substantive representation of women
U	an illegal utterance that is 'unattributable' to an individual speaker
UUP	Ulster Unionist Party (Northern Ireland)
VAW-P	Violence against women in politics

Transcription Conventions

[	beginning of an overlapping utterance with the line above/below
]	end of an overlapping utterance with the line above/below
CAPS	increased volume, shouting
underline	particular emphasis on word or syllable
(.)	micropause of under a second
(3)	pause in seconds
=	latching – one utterance runs straight on from the next without a pause
(laughter)	round brackets indicate noises such as cheering or laughter

1 Introduction

1.1 Overview and Aims

On 7 February 2017, Senator Mitch McConnell read the following statement in an attempt to justify the silencing of Senator Elizabeth Warren's earlier speech in the US Senate:

Senator Warren was giving a lengthy speech. She had appeared to violate the rule. She was warned. She was given an explanation. Nevertheless, she persisted.[1]

This statement and subsequent reactions to it encapsulate many of the issues raised in this study of women, language and politics. First, it is a statement made by a man in a political institution referring to invoking formal rules to justify the collective and institutional silencing of the speech of a woman politician, having already silenced her on the floor of the chamber by a series of interruptions. Second, it is about the interpretation and application of institutional rules as a controlling mechanism with which to silence someone. Elizabeth Warren's speech had criticised the appointment of Jeff Sessions as US attorney general by reading out previous objections to his appointment in 1986 as a federal court judge.[2] The citing of these objections to Sessions' appointment was deemed to have broken a rule[3] which prohibits ascribing to a senator any 'conduct or motive unworthy or unbecoming a senator'. However, the application of these rules is not clear-cut and involves subjective judgements, with this particular rule being conventionally viewed as an edict that is rarely enforced (Jacobson 2017). Further doubt about the enforcement of the rule rested on the fact that a male colleague of Warren's subsequently read out the same objections from 1986 on the floor of the Senate – in full and without censure.[4]

Third, it is about resistance, as Warren did not comply with the silencing but persisted in contesting it, and was only silenced after she had held the entire Senate to a vote on the matter. Even then, when the vote went against her, she persisted by delivering her speech outside the Senate building. Finally, the quotation signals resistance to silencing on a much larger scale. Video recordings of this banished speech were shared on social media millions of times

1

with hashtags like #Shepersisted, with #LetLizspeak being used first to protest against Warren's silencing before becoming more generalised as a meme that signalled resistance to the unfair silencing of *any* woman. 'Nevertheless, she persisted' also became a rallying cry of protests against injustice across a much broader range of issues. Feminist reactions to the quotation show how, in these times of both misogyny and transformation for women in politics (Dovi 2018), collective resistance to this silencing resulted in much more publicity for Warren's objection to Sessions (and for Warren's own political agenda) than would otherwise have been achieved if the speech had originally been delivered in the Senate. This book investigates the ways in which women politicians use language in parliaments; how they interact with other politicians on the debate floor; how they contribute to political discourse; how they are silenced; and how they resist. In this chapter I describe the main aims of and the academic background to the research, as well as a range of wider political contexts. In the chapter's final section I explain the organisation and structure of the book.

In 2018–19 women made some inroads into traditionally male-dominated and highly masculinised political institutions, both numerically and culturally. The United Kingdom had a second woman prime minister, Theresa May. In the United States a larger and more racially, ethnically and politically diverse group of women than ever before formed the 116th US Congress in January 2019 (Edmondson and Lee 2019), with Nancy Pelosi as the Speaker of the House. At the time of writing, six out of the twenty-four Democratic candidates for the US presidential election in 2020 are women, including experienced politicians like Tulsi Gabbard, Elizabeth Warren and Kamala Harris. In Denmark, Mette Frederiksen, and in New Zealand, Jacinda Adern, women perform the role of prime minister with both competence and confidence. Yet research shows that women are still experiencing a significant gender gap in candidacy, are disadvantaged by institutions and remain discriminated against by party elites (Medeiros et al. 2019).

In October 2017 the #MeToo hashtag encouraged women to share experiences of sexual assault in the wake of allegations against Hollywood producer Harvey Weinstein, which inspired women in the media and in politics to disclose a wide range of bullying, sexual harassment and sexual assault allegations. In the British parliament at Westminster, this led to the resignation of male senior ministers and members of Parliament (MPs) in the latter part of 2017 (described in more detail in Krook 2018). The Weinstein allegations and the #MeToo and #Timesup movements galvanised support for the victims of sexual harassment in the workplace in a way that had hitherto not been achieved.[5] Sexual assault and harassment had always occurred in these professional contexts, but with this movement it became more unacceptable to tolerate this behaviour as a normalised part of the established order of 'the way things are done' in political and other professional institutions. Alongside these events, which can be viewed as advances for women, this has also been a time of catastrophic events for women's representation in politics and more generally in public life. In the United States, the defeat of Hillary Clinton by Donald Trump in 2016, despite a recorded conversation in which he described sexually assaulting women (see further discussion in Section 7.2), and the appointment of Brett Kavanagh as a US Supreme Court justice, despite allegations of sexual assault against him, are both events that show the strength of hegemonic masculinity and its ability to subordinate women. The former event was possibly the catalyst for the #MeToo movement, which started a year after Trump's election win of 2016, but the latter occurred a year after the Weinstein allegations in 2017, showing the strength and persistence of masculinist practices to reinforce and cement the established gender order.

Within this rich and complex set of contemporary concerns for women in politics, this book seeks to investigate a specific range of parliamentary institutions and political contexts spanning twenty years, from 1998 to 2018. By examining the patterns of interaction within political discourse in relation to gender it addresses a fundamental social problem, the under-representation of women in politics and the ways in which language use constructs and maintains gender inequalities in political institutions. The following three sets of questions are addressed:

1. How do women in politics participate in debate forums, particularly in those that are historically male-dominated, and in which women are still vastly under-represented and men over-represented? What are the constraints and obstacles that they face in institutions such as the UK House of Commons (HoC), and how can this be illuminated by detailed linguistic analyses of the debate floor?
2. How successful have the 'new' devolved institutions of the United Kingdom been in encouraging equal participation of all members? What are the particular interactional procedures that can be thought of as making an institution more egalitarian?
3. What obstacles remain as barriers to women's participation in political forums? How do gender stereotypes constrain women's participation and give them additional burdens? What are the effects of sexism, fraternal networks, high visibility and gendered discourses of linguistic performance upon women politicians. Finally, how do successful politicians like Theresa May, Julia Gillard and Hillary Clinton attempt to resist and counter these effects?

While these research questions address the fundamental and global problem of the inclusion of women in politics and more generally in public life, this investigation is also highly selective and contextualised within UK political institutions together with case studies of three (white, Western) women political leaders from the United Kingdom, Australia and the United States (Theresa May, Julia Gillard and Hillary Clinton). In this chapter I explain this focus by situating the research theoretically and locating its position within the sociolinguistic field of gender and language studies. Although sociolinguistics is at the core of the enquiry, the particular context of politics means that I also draw on insights and perspectives from other disciplines, particularly political science, and these are reviewed in Section 1.3.

1.2   Language, Gender and Politics

1.2.1   Theoretical Approaches to Language and Gender

In this section I describe the theoretical basis of the study of language and gender in this investigation before considering the benefits of using a sociolinguistic approach to tackle issues of gender and power in workplace interaction, specifically in political contexts. Fundamental to the study of language and gender is the idea that identities are co-constructed in interaction. Gender is enacted and emerges performatively (Butler 1990) rather than being a biological, essential or inherent trait residing in individuals. However, the construction of identities through performance in interaction is also constrained by what Judith Butler describes as the 'rigid regulatory frame' (Butler 1990: 330). This refers to the restrictions placed on individuals by the conventional and routine communicative norms of a particular context, institution or group. Gender is therefore a variable and contested concept, being both a flexible category in which speakers' gender identities are constructed in their performance in interaction and a category partially fixed by institutional arrangements based on gendered communicative norms. Wider structural societal arrangements according to gender can also be considered as partly constituting these norms, and patriarchy can be thought of as one such embedded ideological framework based on male dominance and privilege. As the feminist Lynne Segal writes: 'It is only *particular* groups of men in any society who will occupy positions of public power and influence. But this is precisely what secures rather than undermines the hierarchical structuring of gender through relations of dominance: the *symbolic* equation of "masculinity" with power and "femininity" with powerlessness' (Segal 2006: 273, italics in original). While both men and women are not uniformly powerful or powerless, this dynamic remains a useful concept with which to examine the workings of gender and power in institutions.

This attention to both performative aspects of gender and the restrictive nature of gendered norms and ideologies envisages the enactment of gender as a contextually bound process, and this means that analysts have been encouraged to 'think practically and look locally' (Eckert and McConnell-Ginet 1992b). Further, moving away from focusing on gender *difference*, some analysts instead view the interaction of gender and language as rooted in the 'everyday social practices of particular local communities' with both gender and language being jointly constructed in those practices (Eckert and McConnell-Ginet 1992b: 462). By focusing on these 'communities of practice' (CoPs), detailed accounts of the specific terms of participation in a community according to different factors (including gender) can be identified, and for this reason a CoP approach was adopted for the analysis of political institutions in Chapters 3 and 4, and this is discussed in more detail in Chapter 2.

In addition to the local and the everyday aspects, broader social practices also need to be taken into account, as 'language should be seen as being produced within an ideological system that regulates the norms and conventions for "appropriate" gendered behaviour' (Mills and Mullany 2011: 41). Gender and power therefore also need to be viewed from a *macro* point of view and are part of the role of discourses to shape power relations and meaning as 'practices that systematically form the object of which they speak' (Foucault 1972: 49). While a focus on essential differences between women and men is therefore rejected by researchers in an attempt to recognise speakers' identities as 'fluid, multiple, multi-layered, shifting and often contradictory' (Baxter 2006: 16), it is also necessary to recognise the rather fixed gendered roles and expectations in particular contexts such as traditional male-dominated institutions. In other words, in many situations, such as the parliamentary debates analysed in this book, institutional status is fixed within a hierarchy and often a discursively employed 'general conception of fundamental gender difference is brought into play' (Mills and Mullany 2011: 165). Treading this line between the shifting, multiple, changing and contested ways in which gender is constructed in interaction and the fixity of how gender is conceived in traditional institutions is one of the challenges of investigating language and gender in these contexts. As Judith Baxter notes in relation to women and leadership, as long as gender difference is 'a key discriminating feature of leadership identity, it remains relevant as a topic of research' (2018: 8), and the same can be said of women in politics. Treading this line therefore means we need to focus not on gender difference but the difference gender makes (Cameron 1992), while recognising that discussions about gender are highly contextualised and do not automatically rest on static and essentialising categories and power relations.

The focus on women, language and politics in this book seeks to explore women's marginalisation and under-representation in the public sphere by combining theories, methods and findings from sociolinguistics and politics, but it does not do so by ignoring the role of men. It has been argued that in the study of gender and politics it is necessary 'to understand the nature of male dominance, the way that male power is wielded and perpetuated, and the negative effects this has for politicians of both sexes' (Bjarnegård and Murray 2018a: 264). For this reason, the linguistic behaviour of both women and men are examined in the examples, debates and interviews represented here. To the best of my knowledge, none of the politicians referred to in this book have expressed a trans- or non-binary gender identity, and so all would consider themselves as belonging to one of these two groups.

Theoretically, hegemonic masculinity (Connell 1995; Connell and Messerschmidt 2005) is seen as privileging the position of some men through the operation of masculine norms and practices, homosocial activity and fraternal networks that exclude all women and those men who do not fit particular norms of race, class, age, sexuality and so on. The data presented in Chapters 3 and 4 concur with this and lead to the identification of the 'old boys' club' as one of the major barriers that women (and some men) face in parliamentary contexts. Subsequent analyses of parliamentary and other political discourse in Chapters 6 and 7 explore the roles of women and men in creating and establishing these homosocial networks. Women are nevertheless still placed centrally in this investigation in recognition of the particular pressures and burdens that they face in political interaction and the fact that no sociolinguistic investigations exist to account for women's political participation in this way. This decision is undertaken critically, and with cautions in mind, that a 'focus on women's under-representation reinforces the view of men in politics being the norm and women being deviations from that norm' (Bjarnegård and Murray 2018b: 266).

Early work in the field of language and gender tended to orient to essentialising differences as a set of assumptions about men's and women's behaviour, presuming that there were fixed linguistic styles associated with gender (sometimes even referred to as 'genderlects') and that these had a straightforward relationship to power. One such essentialising belief particularly relevant to women in the public sphere is that women tend to be supportive or cooperative in their speech, and men competitive. This cooperative/competitive dichotomy relating to gendered speech styles disadvantages women in professional contexts that require them to perform in confrontational or adversarial ways. Politics is one such context and this 'different voice' ideology (Cameron and Shaw 2016), discussed in detail in Chapter 5, plays out in complex ways in political institutions and speech events. This includes the claim that a belief in women's 'cooperative style' can lead to additional burdens being placed on women entering professions in the form of an expectation that they will bring a 'civilizing difference' to hitherto male-dominated professions (Walsh 2001).

The linguistic analyses of language and gender in political contexts presented in this book are relevant to these claims and are discussed in the analysis of parliamentary data (Chapters 3 and 4) and the identification of barriers to women's progress in politics (Chapter 5). Overall, though, conceptions of men's and women's language as having fixed 'styles', or essentialised sets of differences, is now viewed as an early phase of research into language and gender because

[w]e invented notions like 'genderlect' to provide overall characterisations of sex differences in speech. The 'genderlect' portrayal now seems too abstract and overdrawn, implying that there are differences in the basic codes used by women and men, rather than variably occurring differences, and similarities ... genderlect implies more homogeneity among women, and among men – and more difference between the sexes than is, in fact, the case. (Thorne et al. 1983: 14)

This means that theoretical models of gender need to consider diverse intersections of gender with other characteristics such as race, social class, sexuality, national identity, age and so on. These elements can be thought of as 'multiple axes' where 'each aspect of identity redefines and modifies all others' (Pavlenko and Blackedge 2004: 15, see also Levon 2015 for a useful discussion of intersectionality in sociolinguistics and Section 1.4 for further discussion). It also rejects the idea that 'basic codes', or linguistic forms, can be routinely associated with gender (or any other characteristic). Instead, different ways of talking are culturally coded to indirectly index gender (Ochs 1992). Ochs notes that the relation between language and gender is rarely direct and only a few forms directly and exclusively index gender (for example pronouns *he/she* and some address forms such as *Mr* and *Mrs*). More commonly, gender is indexed indirectly, and this means it is non-exclusive (variable features of a language may be used by/for/with both women and men). Therefore, linguistic forms index other social information in addition to gender, and gender is constitutive where 'one or more linguistic features may index social meanings (e.g. stances, social acts, social activities), which in turn helps to constitute gender meanings' (Ochs 1992: 341).

As explained in more detail in Chapter 5, neither this notion of indirect indexicality of gender and language nor a lack of empirical evidence for monolithic male and female 'styles' of speech reduces the *ideological* significance of gender and difference with respect to language. Earlier findings in language in gender, while theoretically at odds with indexicality and the flexibility of gender as a category, can give us information about such views or offer us a 'window onto the deeply entrenched stereotypical norms of women's and men's speech styles' (Mills and Mullany 2011: 53). Here 'stereotype' can be defined as 'one noticeable form of behaviour that is afforded prototypical status' (Mills 2003: 184) through a process of simplification and generalisation. Views about such stereotypical and normative gendered behaviour are rooted in deeply held beliefs about the gender order and what Jane Sunderland describes as 'gender differences discourse' (2004: 52). This is the pervasive ideological position that there are fixed gendered differences in the behaviour of women and men, including in their communicative style. The linguistic behaviour of women and men therefore 'will be represented in ways congruent with the community's more general representation of the essential natures of the two groups'. Gendered ideologies also regulate participation in the gender order and are how people explain and justify that participation (Eckert and McConnell-Ginet 2013: 22). In this way, gendered ideologies relating to difference or opposites (such as the cooperative/competitive dichotomy and the 'different voice' ideology mentioned earlier) can be seen as 'a significant lens for the way people view reality, difference being for most people what gender is all about' (Sunderland 2004: 52, see also further discussion in Section 2.4.2).

Underlying these entrenched notions, and the sociolinguistic research questions listed earlier, is a feminist critique analysing the workings of these kinds of gendered ideologies as evidenced in different types of political discourse (from parliamentary debates, to media performances and representations, to ethnographic interviews with politicians themselves). One mainstay of these gendered ideological standpoints is the 'masculine voice of authority' or the notion that the norms of public interaction and other authoritative behaviours are expected to be performed by men, not women. Hillary Clinton explains this ideology, which also acts as a default assumption about women, men and politics, in her 2017 memoir:

It's men who lead. It's men who speak. It's men who represent us to the world and even to ourselves. That's been the case for so long that it has infiltrated our deepest thoughts. I suspect for many of us – more than you might think – it feels somehow *off* to picture a woman President sitting in the Oval Office or in the Situation Room. It's discordant to tune into a political rally and hear a woman's voice booming ('screaming,' 'screeching') forth. Even the simple act of a woman standing up and speaking to a crowd is relatively new. Think about it: we know of only a handful of speeches by women before the latter half of the twentieth century, and those tend to be by women in extreme and desperate situations. Joan of Arc said a lot of interesting things before they burned her at the stake. (Clinton 2017: 121)

As expressed in this quotation, this set of ideological positions is part of wider cultural norms relating to traditional gender roles and stereotypes, the gendered nature of the public/private divide and the evaluation of the linguistic behaviour of women and men, including their language and the sound of their voices. Therefore, these gendered beliefs about the 'masculine voice of authority' position women in impossible no-win situations often referred to as the 'double bind' of women in leadership. Women in politics are arguably more vulnerable to the effects of these double binds than women in other professions, because public speaking in 'high-performance' events (Coupland 2007) is a routine and frequent part of their daily professional life: Parliaments exist to enable talk and on election it is assumed that a politician has the capacity to speak publicly. Jamieson (1995: 121) names femininity/competence as a bind in which perceived 'female' characteristics such as being 'easily influenced, emotional and illogical' are at odds with the 'masculine' qualities of maturity and competence required of public figures. Double binds have many manifestations, not least in relation to constructions of femininity and appearance, emotions and authenticity.

Often, the management of these double binds and contradictory expectations hinges on language use, as shown in Chapter 7, when Julia Gillard and Hillary Clinton negotiate the knotty problem for a woman of being ambitious. Both these women politicians needed to carefully manage the negative perception that they were on a self-serving individual quest for success, which is deemed 'unfeminine'. However, it is quite clear that any successful politician must be ambitious to some extent, and this posed them with a problem that was resolved through the way they constructed themselves linguistically (see further discussions in Chapters 7 and 8). Therefore, in each instance of a double bind situation, woman politicians need to mitigate the adverse effects of being automatically perceived as behaving in counter-stereotypic ways simply because they are *woman* politicians. Both women UK prime ministers, Theresa May and Margaret Thatcher, have embodied this set of decisions symbolically in their choice of peripheral feminine accessories: the chunky necklaces, bracelets and fashion-statement shoes for May and the famous handbag for Thatcher. These accoutrements show how they carefully managed gender, politics and the double bind: to appear at once feminine enough to conform with normative notions of 'femininity', but not too feminine as to incur negative perceptions that they do not have the perceived 'masculine' leadership qualities of strength and toughness.

1.2.2   Women and Language in the Public Sphere and in the Workplace

Historically, women have been excluded from public spaces and confined to the domestic sphere. Karalyn Khors Campbell's (1989) study of the rhetoric of nineteenth-century women reformers in the United States and more recently the historian, Mary Beard's *Women and Power* (2017) both describe historical and classical depictions of women's silencing and eradication from public discourse. When discussing the *Odyssey*, both authors describe how Telemachus scolds his mother, Penelope, and tells her: 'Public speech shall be men's concern' (Homer 1980: 9, cited in Campbell 1989: 1[6]). However, Beard's descriptions of the silencing and persecution of women who dared to enter the classical male world of 'muthos' or authoritative public speech are intended to illustrate a contemporary point. She goes on to explain: 'I want to reflect on how it might relate to the abuse that many women who do speak out are subjected to even now' and that the 'long back-story' to antiquity can help us to understand 'the fact that women, even when they are not silenced, still have to pay a very high price for being heard' (Beard 2017: 8). Cultural constructions of gendered linguistic behaviour are not quite so uniform, with well-known linguistic studies showing that women's public speech *is* viewed positively in some cultures (for example, Kulick 1993) and other research showing that in different historical periods, some women have actually been encouraged to speak in public (Jones 1987 cited in Cameron 2003: 451). However, setting these exceptions apart, it is still overwhelmingly the case that women continue to face silencing and negative sanctions when they speak out publicly, and these can be viewed as linked to, but more extreme and damaging to women, than the effects of the double binds described in the previous section. The UK member of Parliament Jess Phillips observes there are several strategies used by men to silence women in the UK HoC, including 'shushing' them across the floor of the chamber (Phillips 2017: 3). More detailed examples of these behaviours are given in Chapter 3. Sanctions against women speaking out include increased levels of violence directed against women in politics (VAW-P) both internationally and in UK institutions (see for example Krook 2017, 2018) and vicious 'trolling' on social media. Mary Beard herself was subject to violent threats on Twitter along with extreme criticisms of her appearance, including being described as 'too ugly for TV' (Biressi and Nunn 2017: 42). In their account of the insults directed towards Mary Beard, Biressi and Nunn note that the catalogue of extreme criticisms of Beard's appearance function to

split the intellect from the female body and disparage the former by resorting to cliched insults about the latter, as though Beard's appearance and so-called lack of attractiveness could be deployed to discredit her voice. This practice highlights the all-too familiar way in which women are measured as purely body in public space. Men, in contrast, are accorded the metaphysics of presence associated with the intellectual, philosophical, reasoning and *reasonable* public voice. (2017: 42, italics in original)

These descriptions of attacks on the female body to undermine the intellect also make women visible in a way that men are not. This puts an emphasis on acceptable forms of feminine appearance (Puwar 2004a) and reminds us of reactions to earlier historical incursions of women into the public and political domains. Figure 1.1 shows the front of a postcard sent to Christabel Pankhurst on 23 August 1909. Its depiction of a suffragette as a monstrous caricature of femininity with broken teeth, a grotesque 'smile', unkempt hair and a pathetic attempt at a 'feminine' line of flowers in her hair could scarcely depict stronger contempt or more deeply held misogyny.

This postcard was sent to Pankhurst's London residence,[7] by an anti-suffragist who signed himself 'Yours, Joe' with the message: 'Dear Christie, Don't you think you had better sew a button on my shirt'. Although there are undoubtedly more violent anti-suffragist images, the fact that this 'hate mail' was sent directly

Figure 1.1 Anti-suffrage postcard sent to Christabel Pankhurst in 1909. (Source: © Museum of London.)

to Pankhurst and targeted her appearance together with the directive to fulfil her role as a man's domestic servant chimes with more contemporary verbal attacks and Twitter 'trolling'. Hillary Clinton was famously heckled by a man at a 2008 campaign rally who told her to 'iron my shirt' (Sheldon 2015), and there are clear parallels with the kinds of personal attack aimed at the appearance of women, particularly via social media, described earlier. Although this book cannot examine all such interactions, these historical and contemporary depictions and treatment of women in the public sphere are relevant contexts against which the linguistic analyses of gender and parliamentary discourse must be set. Indeed, the striking image of the suffragette in Figure 1.1 (once seen, never forgotten) frequently comes to mind in many of the detailed examples discussed throughout the parliamentary and political discourse represented here.

While these wider contexts of women's treatment in the public sphere form a fundamental background to the analysis of women, language and politics, this work draws more directly on sociolinguistic research into gender and language in the workplace. For example, early studies into the way women and men interact in meetings found that men spoke for longer than women and took more speaking turns (Eakins and Eakins 1976; Edelsky 1981; Kathlene 1995), and this is a recurrent finding born out in more contemporary studies (such as Karpowitz and Mendelberg 2014; Carter et al. 2018). This is relevant to the studies of gender and floor apportionment in parliaments described here and analysed in more detail in Chapters 3 and 4. Other sociolinguistic studies have sought to investigate a wider range of discursive norms in different workplace settings. Possibly the most influential of these is Janet Holmes' (2006) work on gender and language in the workplace. Drawing on a sizeable corpus of data from New Zealand workplaces, Holmes shows how women and men in differently gendered workplace settings draw on a wide range of linguistic features that are routinely and stereotypically associated with femininity and masculinity. These include women adopting humorous and 'queenly' personas to mitigate the effects of acting in authoritative roles (Holmes 2006). Similarly, Louise Mullany (2007) examines gendered discourses in the professional workplace, contributing to the field of interactional and critical sociolinguistics by using different discourse analytic approaches (discussed in more detail in Chapter 2). She adds empirical evidence to show that communicative workplace norms are changing towards more stereotypically female models of communication and, like Holmes (2006), finds that men and women draw on a range of styles conventionally coded masculine and feminine. Other relevant workplace studies investigate how women adapt to male-dominated workplaces by adjusting their communicative norms to perform different traditionally masculine professions, such as police officers (McElhinny 1998) and engineers (Angouri 2011). These studies show how women are disadvantaged in workplaces orientated to men and how these contexts 'dictate who is understood as best suited for different types of employment' (McElhinny 1998: 309). Further, when women adopt confrontational or authoritative language to embrace the discourse norms of a male-dominated workplace, they are often judged negatively for their behaviour as it is incongruent with gendered communicative norms relating to how women *should* speak. This has also been found to be the case for *men* who use normatively feminine speech styles in 'feminine' workplaces as they are often ridiculed (Holmes 2006).

In this way, it has been claimed that 'institutions are organised to define, demonstrate and enforce the legitimacy and authority of linguistic strategies used by one gender – or men of one class or ethnic group – whilst denying the power of others' (Gal 1991: 188). The reasons for this are complex and related in part to the 'fraternal networks' (Walsh 2001) that exist in parliamentary institutions and the high visibility of women in historically male-dominated workplaces (Bourdieu 1991). Parliaments can therefore be viewed as a 'linguistic habitus' in which 'silence or hyper-controlled language' is imposed on some people, while others are allowed the 'liberties of a language that is securely established' (Bourdieu 1991: 82). In my view, parliaments are 'gendered spaces' in which the setting and the communicative tasks together become an index of a gendered style (Freed 1996: 67). This is explored in Judith Baxter's work into gender, language and leadership (2010), which seeks to understand the possible role of language as a factor in explaining women's under-representation in business environments. Like Holmes (2006) she investigates 'differently gendered' organisations by developing Rosabelle Moss Kanter's classic 1977 work *Men and Women of the Corporation* in order to propose three 'prototypical' categories of gendered corporations 'each of which privileges a dominant gendered discourse: *Male-Dominated, Gender Divided, and Gender Multiple*' (Baxter 2010: 17). While she recognises that actual institutions are likely to have elements of all three categories, she suggests that one of the three types will 'figure more predominantly and characterise a woman leader's experience within it'. In the male-dominated corporation, Baxter claims that:

Men use speech to command and control, to get access to the floor, and once there, to keep it. They are likely to use language for display purposes, asserting their dominance through verbosity, name-dropping, subtle or overt boasting, and entertainment strategies such as jokes or anecdotes. Women on the other hand are expected to listen and be amused by men. On the whole they are expected to agree and support, and not to interrupt, challenge or question the authority of men. If they do challenge, they will need to do this in acceptable ways in order not to upset the status quo. (2010: 18)

These descriptions of the linguistic strategies certainly seem to concur with the descriptions of behaviour of MPs in the HoC (for example Childs 2000, 2004; Crewe 2014b; Lovenduski 2014b; Puwar 2004a, 2004b; Shaw 2000, 2006; Sones et al. 2005). However, Baxter notes that the male-dominated organisation is likely to be masked by 'gender-neutrality' (2010: 19) where tokenism (Kanter 1977) gives examples of minority members who have succeeded. Another strong characteristic of a male-dominated corporation is that there is a prevalent use of negative or sexist language to describe women leaders in disparaging ways (Brewis 2001). This description of negative and sexist language is identified as one of the main barriers to women's participation in politics in the analysis of the HoC and in political life more generally, and is the subject of further discussion in Chapter 5.

Baxter's work (2010, 2017, 2018), like that of Ilie and Schnurr (2017), explicitly engages in 'leadership' research. This is an interdisciplinary area of research, primarily drawing on theories and methods from psychology but also from business, management, economics and political science (Eagly and Heilman 2016). These studies offer useful empirical evidence about the behaviour, appraisal and treatment of women leaders which I draw upon throughout this book. Particularly useful are studies into gendered stereotypes: participation and volubility and measurable 'backlash effects' to women's agentic leadership roles (Brescoll 2011, 2016; Cunningham et al. 2017; Eagly and Carli 2007; Hoyt and Murphy 2016; Kanter 1977; Johnson et al. 2008; Kathlene 1995; Okimoto and Brescoll 2010; Vial et al. 2016; Vinkenburg et al. 2011). However, critical approaches to these studies have observed that they tend towards quantitative, positivistic approaches, and do not include contextualised studies of power and emergence (Robinson and Kerr 2018). It is also of note that studies of leadership offer metaphors for women's professional experiences, roles and situations which cross easily into popular discourse. In this way the 'queen bee' (the woman leader who distances herself from or is punitive towards other women) may face the glass or concrete ceiling – she may face visible or invisible barriers to higher levels of the professional hierarchy – or get stuck on a 'sticky floor' (held back in a low-paid position). If she does reach the higher levels, she may be teetering on the edge of a glass cliff (promoted to a precarious, undesirable and unstable senior position) in a 'chilly climate' (one that is hostile and unfair to women).

Other metaphors are used to describe women's roles as mothers and carers when they hit the 'maternal wall': on the 'mommy track' to promotion and experience the 'child penalty'. While it is helpful to identify these obstacles for women in the workplace, these metaphors can lead to overgeneralised explanations which overlook nuances and detailed contextual accounts of particular workplaces and professions (see Chapter 6 and the discussion of Theresa May and the 'glass cliff'). Certainly, these terms should not be used uncritically, especially as their existence in the absence of an equivalent set of metaphors for *men's* behaviour and roles in the workplace seems to further marginalise and problematise women's roles in disproportionate ways. Further, in many accounts, it is women who are seen as self-sabotaging their progress (Smith et al. 2012), which, as Mavin (2006) points out in relation to the 'queen bee' metaphor, perpetuates a 'blame or fix the women' perspective and fuels existing inequalities. Although more nuanced discussions of these metaphors exist (for example Derks et al. 2016), the terms themselves commonly tend to act as repositories for gendered discourses of differentiation such as 'women beware women' or 'women sabotage their own success' which are themselves sexist.

Research into language in *political* contexts is grounded in political discourse analysis which sets out analytical frameworks and approaches such as critical discourse analysis (CDA) (Fairclough 2000; Fairclough and Fairclough 2012; van Dijk 2000, 2004; Wodak 2009, 2014), cognitive approaches (Chilton 2004) and rhetorical studies (Charteris-Black 2014; Cockcroft et al. 2014; Martin 2014; Reisigl 2010). The adversarial nature of political discourse has led to a focus on linguistic im/politeness (Archer 2015, 2018; Bortoluzzi and Semino 2016; Bull 2013; Bull and Wells 2012; Harris 2001; Murphy 2014; Waddle et al. 2019). Studies into political discourse and *gender* include that of Ruth Wodak (2003, 2009, 2014), in which she combines her discourse historical approach to CDA with ethnographic-style investigations in the European Union (EU) Parliament. Like the analyses of the HoC data from 1998 to 2001 presented in Chapter 3 of this book, Wodak uses a CoP approach and draws on Bourdieu's (1991) theoretical notion of the 'habitus' in order to capture the conventions and 'rules of the game' of political institutions (Wodak 2009: 11). With respect to gender, Wodak finds that in the EU Parliament, women politicians differed from each other in their gender role constructions in which they were successful at 'doing politics'. She found the EU Parliament overall to be an institution which was characterised by greater complexity and flexibility than other public institutions, which 'allows for a wider range of identity constructions' (Wodak 2003: 692). Clare Walsh's (2001) research into gender and language in male-dominated institutions such as the HoC and the Church of England[8] offers many insights into the discursive norms of these CoPs. She finds that, on the one hand, women's increased presence in these institutions has 'called into question the unproblematized status of the implicitly masculinist belief systems, values and discursive practices that predominate in these domains' (Walsh 2001: 204). On the other hand, she notes that in some cases this has led to the 'defensive strengthening of traditional fraternal networks' and the fact that these networks 'transcend the boundaries of institutional discourses is one factor that has helped to ensure that women do not participate as equals' (2001: 204).

Other research on women, language and politics investigates the discursive construction of political leadership by focusing on particular leaders in context, such as Margaret Thatcher (Atkinson 1984; Bull and Mayer 1988; Wilson and Irwin 2015), Julia Gillard (Appleby 2015; Varney 2017; Walter 2017), Hillary Clinton (Bennister 2016; Romaniuk 2016; Sheldon 2015), Ellen Johnson Sirleaf (Jones 2015) and Helle Thorning-Schmidt (Millar et al. 2015). Work in different global contexts focuses on language and women's political leadership in Cameroon (Atanga 2010), Hong Kong (Feng and Wu 2015), Italy (Formato 2014, 2019), Japan (Shibamoto-Smith 2011), Latin America (Boxer et al. 2017; Cortès-Conde and Boxer 2015), Trinidad and Tobago (Esposito 2017), Tunisia (Kammoun 2015) and Uganda (Tamale 1998). Comparative work considers differences between two or more political cultures with respect to gender and language, such as Cornelia Ilie's (2013) study comparing the gendering of confrontational rhetoric in the British and Swedish parliaments. Others focus on particular genres of political discourse with respect to gender, such as televised political debates (Adams 1992, 2015; Cameron and Shaw 2016, 2020; Edelsky and Adams 1990), parliamentary debates (Bäck et al. 2014; Formato 2014; Ilie 2010, 2018; Shaw 2000, 2006, 2011; Wang 2014) and social media platforms such as Twitter (for example Rubtcova et al. 2018; Yoong 2019). Important contributions also include investigations into the relation of gender to specific aspects of political language, such as metaphor (Ahrens 2009; Boyd 2013; Charteris-Black 2009; Koller and Semino 2009; Lim 2009) or politeness (Christie 2003; Felice and Garretson 2018; Fracchiolla 2011; Harris 2001; Shibamoto-Smith 2011).

Overall, though, it is notable that there are far more studies of *media representations* of women politicians (see Baxter 2018; Carlin and Winfrey 2009; Formato 2019; Mavin et al. 2010; Ross 2017; Sensales and Areni 2017; Trimble 2017; Worth et al. 2016) than there are linguistic analyses of their *performances* in debates. For example, there are extensive analyses of media representations of Sarah Palin, the controversial US Republican politician who ran as a candidate for the vice presidency in 2008 (see Carlin and Winfrey 2009; Eberhardt and Merolla 2017; Loke et al. 2011; Schreiber 2016; Wasburn and Wasburn 2011). However, studies of her language use in political performances are rare (for example Acton and Potts (2014) on her use of demonstratives in televised interviews). The second notable feature of the literature is that research into gender and the linguistic style of *men* politicians is sparse. Until Donald Trump burst onto the global political stage in 2015, there were very few analyses of the linguistic performances of men politicians with respect to *gender*, with one notable exception being a comparison of Bill and Hillary Clinton's language use in televised media interviews in 2003 (Suleiman and O'Connell 2008). Analyses of Trump's language and his hyper-masculine style have only just begun (see for example Sclafani 2017, and further discussion in Chapter 7) and are likely to proliferate given his extreme behaviours, his unconventional communicative style and its successful influence over the US electorate. It remains to be seen whether linguistic performances of masculinity more generally in political contexts answer calls of sociolinguists and political scientists that 'a focus on men is a necessary complement to, rather than a substitute for, existing scholarship on women; both theoretically and empirically, researching both sexes in tandem has the potential to greatly enrich our knowledge and understanding of gender in politics' (Bjarnegård and Murray 2018a: 264).

1.3   Women, Men and Politics

Different theoretical and practical insights from political science have informed the analyses and discussions presented in this book. Foremost, the different conceptions of 'representation' and research by feminist scholars in political science on the position and influence of women in politics have been particularly useful. The under-representation of women in politics is important for 'symbolic' reasons (Pitkin 1967), as women symbolically 'stand for' the group they represent. Similarly, women in politics physically and numerically stand for other women, and this is commonly referred to as 'descriptive' or numerical representation. Descriptive representation or the 'politics of presence' (Phillips 1995) is seen as linked to and affecting the 'substantive representation of women' (SRW). This term is used to describe the ways in which women in political roles affect the processes of democratic decision-making by the inclusion of women's perspectives and interests (Mansbridge 1983, 1999; Phillips 1995; Wängnerud 2009). In this way, it has been suggested that the 'feminization' of politics (Lovenduski 2005) is likely to increase due to an increase in women's descriptive or numerical representation. This consideration of SRW, sometimes termed 'the difference women make' to political institutions, is controversial (Dodson 2006). This is because the proposition put forward by 'difference democrats' (Asenbaum 2019a) – that a monolithic grouping (women) will have predictable and democratically beneficial effects on a parliamentary system when elected – can be seen as essentialist and reductive. Certainly, the descriptive or numerical representation of all different groups of citizens will make it more *likely* that their interests are addressed, but it cannot ensure that this *will* happen and further, 'It is difficult to swallow whole the notion that one has to be one to represent one' (Reingold 2000: 34).

Earlier studies in politics, like those described earlier in sociolinguistics, were based on more static notions of gender and on the communicative 'style' of women than a performative or constructivist theoretical model of gender allows. Claims for women's presence in institutions based on difference are therefore not theoretically appropriate, and 'the argument for group presence *ought not* to be justified by expectations or hopes for different performance – the argument must be grounded in straightforward claims of justice and fairness' (Dodson 2006: 8). Acknowledgement of these theoretical problems, along with a recognition of differences between women (who may or may not represent women's interests), and the fact that *men* can act for women gave rise to a move away from asking 'What difference do women make?' when elected. Instead, political scientists asked questions such as 'Who claims to represent women?' 'Where, why, and how does substantive representation of women (SRW) occur?' (Celis et al. 2008: 99) and also 'To whom are representatives accountable?' and 'How effective is the (claimed) representation?' (Allen and Childs 2018: 3).

Connected to the discussion of the numbers of women in political institutions and the ways in which this will affect women's substantive representation is the concept of 'critical mass' (Dahlerup 1988). This apparently simple metaphor represents the idea that once the number of any minority group reaches a threshold level of about 30 per cent (Dahlerup 1988), a chain reaction (like that occurring in physics) will take place. At this point, women (or any other minority group) will have reached the level of representation which enables them to work together to promote policy change in favour of the interests of women and to ensure that male colleagues put forward and support legislation promoting women's interests (Childs and Krook 2006). This concept has been shown to be much more complex than the metaphor would suggest, however, as 'unlike science there is no magic in numbers in politics' (Allen and Childs 2018: 3; Beckwith 2007). There is also some evidence that an increase in the numbers of women in traditionally male-dominated institutions could actually galvanise male resistance to women's disruptive presence (Bjarnegård 2013; Murray 2014). Similarly, it has been suggested that the sudden influx of women MPs in the 1997 UK general election actually led to a gendered split within the public sphere (Walsh 2001). In this way, women's incursion into hitherto male-only spaces can lead to them being re-attached to stereotypically 'feminine' portfolios and responsibilities (such as health and education) and effectively bar them from more stereotypically 'masculine' fields (such as defence and finance). This also presents practical problems for those attempting to measure 'the difference women make' when representing women's issues in parliament. It is not clear whether women's involvement in particular topics is as a positive consequence of their 'women's interest' or as a negative consequence of limitations imposed by the narrowing of women's scope as part of this gendered split.

Certainly, some studies that have attempted to measure women's involvement in this way have found unexpected results, with one study finding that in the UK HoC, women's contributions overall focused more on 'women's issues', but this decreased as women's descriptive representation increased, particularly with the influx of women MPs into the institution in 1997 (Blaxill and Beelen 2016). This certainly needs further investigation, but it is clear that the critical mass theory is not nearly nuanced enough to account for empirical results which point to much more complex sets of causal effects of increasing the numbers of women in institutions where they have hitherto not been represented. To reflect these complexities of representation, it has been suggested that instead the focus for SRW should be on 'critical actors' (Childs and Krook 2006). These politicians are identified by their actions and can be men or women (Celis and Erzeel 2015) and are thought to be individuals who 'act for' women, regardless of the proportion of their numbers in an institution. More recently, research into SRW has shifted away from individual politicians and towards both elected and non-elected actors for women, operating in broader, collective contexts (Allen and Childs 2018; Celis and Lovenduski 2018). This research shows how groups like women's parliamentary organisations (in this case, the UK Parliamentary Labour Party's Women's Committee) display 'a broad and consistent set of women's issues over time that constituted the group's main agenda for change' (Allen and Childs 2018: 18).

The ways in which such agendas for change can be instigated and resisted have been a focus of research in feminist institutionalist scholarship (Celis and Lovenduski 2018). This branch of political science recognises that an account of gendered patterns of representation alone can only lead to a descriptive account of gender in institutions rather than an explanatory one (Krook and Mackay 2011). It cannot 'explain the persistence of inequality and permutations of exclusionary practices that operate within political institutions', nor capture the gender norms and discourses that underpin institutional dynamics (Mackay 2004: 111 cited in Krook and Mackay 2011: 3). To explain these relationships, feminist institutionalism recognises that parliaments can be gendered and that 'constructions of masculinity and femininity are intertwined in the daily culture or "logic" of political institutions' (Krook and Mackay 2011: 6).

This approach shares much with the focus of this book on gendered communicative norms in day-to-day parliamentary interaction. Like research in sociolinguistics, feminist institutionalism examines both formal and informal practices in the construction of inequality and gendered norms that frequently masquerade as neutral ones (Chappell 2006). Sociolinguistic accounts of gendered discourses and of 'micro' linguistic choices that can be linked to overarching political, social and exclusionary ideologies can help to identify such formal and informal gendered norms and practices. In this way, interactional features (such as turn-taking and floor apportionment – see Chapters 3 and 4), when considered alongside an awareness of the significance of the choice of a particular linguistic feature (such as an address form – see Chapters 5 and 6) and the identification of gendered discourses, can go some way towards making the 'invisibility' of gendered aspects of formal institutions (Waylen 2017: 5) more visible. It also offers additional ways of conceptualising both 'new' political institutions and the capacity for gendered change in existing state institutions (Krook and Mackay 2011; Mackay 2010, 2014; Mackay and McAllister 2012). These insights offer further contexts for the analyses of the HoC in Chapter 3 and of the 'new' devolved institutions of Northern Ireland, Scotland and Wales in Chapter 4.

The two disciplinary approaches also share theoretical ideas about gender, with both sociolinguists and political scientists acknowledging that gender is a category that can only be understood in relation to other characteristics. This intersectional turn in gender research (Collins 1990; Collins and Bilge 2016; Crenshaw 1989, 1991) identifies the ways in which experiences of domination and discrimination vary within the group 'women' as well as between women and men. Women are multiply disadvantaged and/or privileged in different ways from each other, and their lives are shaped not only by gender but by other intersecting elements of their identities such as race, ethnicity, social class, sexuality and place. The intersections of these aspects are mutually constituted and mutually constitutive in a dynamic relationship. This relationship demands that further questions about race, social class, sexuality and place be asked of 'gendered' acts and identities (Davis 2008; Levon 2015). While the focus of this book is on *gender*, language and political representation in a narrow, mainly Anglo-American context, it is also possible to acknowledge the persistent under-representation of politicians according to other categories, particularly race and ethnicity. This has been thought of as a 'double disadvantage' with some candidates likely to be punished by voters for their status as both women and racial minorities (Beal 2008; Dolan et al. 2017). However, in the United States, it has been more recently found that 'women of color constitute a larger share of elected officeholders within their racial group than do white women' (Dolan et al. 2017: 119). Although this varies greatly across different global contexts, the complex interplay of gender and ethnicity is shown in Celis et al. (2014), who examine how political gender quotas as a form of equality policy affect ethnic minority groups in a comparative study in Belgium and the Netherlands. They find that ethnic minority women are better represented than ethnic minority men, and this is also the case in Bejarano's (2013) study of Latina political candidates in the United States. This is thought to be because ethnic minority women are seen as more electable and, according to interviewees, are 'the softer face of the emancipation of ethnic minority candidates' whereas ethnic minority men were thought to promote 'voter rejection based on racist stereotypes about ethnic minority men being criminal' (Celis et al. 2014: 49). Women in this category were also thought to challenge the male elite groups in the institutions less than men from the same group where 'ethnic minority women, especially younger women, are seen as complementary to incumbents who are predominantly white, older, middle-class men' (Celis et al. 2014: 49).

With respect to media coverage, studies have found that race and gender can cause a double barrier for 'minority US Congresswomen' as they receive more negative and less frequent media coverage than all other representatives (Gershon 2012). Similarly, Ward's (2017) study found that the news coverage of black, Asian and minority ethnic (BAME) women in the 2010 UK General Election was negative and narrowly focused on their ethnicity and gender. Judith Baxter's analysis of media representations of Gina Miller[9] in 2016–2017 found that the 'online toxicity' generated by Miller's political actions can only be explained by the double threat posed by her gender *and* ethnicity (Baxter 2018: 154). However, Ward also finds that there are some advantages for some BAME women relating to their newsworthiness as BAME candidates, which meant that some of them 'enjoyed a visibility advantage' (Ward 2017: 43). Further studies have started to describe and explain variation among different women in relation to political recruitment and descriptive representation (for example Evans 2016; Smooth 2006; and for a comprehensive overview of intersectionality and its influence in political science, see Mügge et al. 2018).

While acknowledging that discrimination and under-representation can affect women in multiple, intersecting ways, it is also necessary to recognise that the politicians in this study (men and women) are overwhelmingly from privileged white, middle-class or elite social categories. This is a reflection of political representation in the institutions at the time they were studied. The overall lack of diversity in the institutions is also coupled with the fact that gender in politics continues to be performed and understood according to rather inflexible binary terms (Trimble 2017). At a time when gender itself is being perceived as an increasingly flexible category, in both politics and media representations of politicians, 'bodies, traits, skills and roles are perceived as male or female, masculine or feminine' and it has been noted that 'few elected politicians challenge the parameters of the sex/gender divides' (Trimble 2017: 10).

The parliamentary actors studied here therefore represent a particularly homogenous group of successful, privileged individuals who nevertheless have differential access to power and resources, as well as strategies for reinforcing and resisting dominant and unequal discourses. The factors that determine this access and the ability to resist or dominate others are highly contextualised within the political institutions and include not only gender, race and social class but also institutional and professional roles such as seniority, length of time in office and partisan attachments (particularly government versus opposition positionings but also less visible roles such as party whips, junior ministerial appointments and committee memberships). Gender is justified as a central concern, given the particular misogynistic and exclusionary practices affecting women in politics and the masculinist cultures of political institutions described earlier. However, the ethnographic methods and CoP approaches to describing the institutions in Chapters 3 and 4 and the case studies in Chapters 6 and 7 allow opportunities for fine-grained observations of performances, practices and norms related to a range of these other intersecting professional and social characteristics.

1.4   Summary and Structure of the Book

Chapter 2 situates this research within a critical sociolinguistic, feminist approach to the analysis of parliamentary discourse. It explains the mixed method framework that allows reflexivity and a sensitivity to the parliamentary and political contexts under scrutiny. This recognises that 'the point to doing feminist social research is not … to attain methodological purity, but to give insights into gendered social existence that would otherwise not exist' (Ramazanoglu and Holland 2002: 147). Ethnography is identified as a central method with which to describe and explain the interactional norms of parliamentary discourse. It also explains how the ethnographic approach, using the notion of the community of practice (CoP), is combined with applied conversation analysis (CA) and critical discourse analysis (CDA). The challenges of undertaking research in political institutions are discussed, such as problems of access into the closed, elite communities.

The analysis of parliamentary data starts in Chapter 3 with an ethnographic account of the HoC CoP when Tony Blair's Labour government came into power in 1997. In doing so, it seeks to address the first research question: How do women in politics participate in debate forums, particularly in those that are historically male-dominated and in which women are still vastly under-represented and men over-represented? The reason this parliamentary term is significant is that it showed the greatest increase ever in women MPs from one term to the next, and the newcomers' presence generates socio-spatial impact that brings into clear focus what has hitherto been taken for granted (Puwar

2004b: 77). In the context of this disruption in the institution, men's and women's participation is measured using a corpus of sixty hours of different types of speech events between 1998 and 2001. Ethnographic descriptions and analyses of the floor reveal differing behaviour relating to gender and 'legal' and 'illegal' turns, with some 'illegal' linguistic behaviours rarely performed by women politicians. In contrast, the ethnographic description and analyses of gender and participation in the 'new' devolved institutions of the United Kingdom in Chapter 4 shows a different pattern. Using similar ethnographic and discourse analytic methods to examine the third term of these institutions in 2009–11, the chapter seeks to answer the second set of research questions: How successful have the 'new' devolved institutions of the United Kingdom been in encouraging equal participation of all members? What are the interactional procedures and contexts that can be thought of as making an institution more egalitarian? The analyses of these institutions show that, unlike the HoC, women and men take part in the full range of linguistic practices. This leads to a discussion of the institutional and interactional factors that possibly contribute to making a political institution more egalitarian while also identifying continuing obstacles and barriers to women's participation and progress.

Chapter 5 aims to examine the workings of these continuing obstacles to women's political progress in more detail, as set out in the third set of research questions. Interviews with politicians and analytic observations point to the following interrelated barriers to women's participation and representation in politics:

1. stereotypical views of women and men, particularly in relation to their speech 'styles' or communicative norms;
2. how women are positioned in relation to the adversarial politics and the 'different voice' ideology;
3. sexism, with a focus on the ways in which sexist language is used against women;
4. homosocial bonding and fraternal networks as mechanisms that exclude women (and other minority groups) and that operate through humour and irony;
5. gendered media representations of women in politics.

Chapters 6 and 7 then explore these barriers from a different analytical perspective: through case studies of leading women politicians. Chapter 6 examines the ways in which Theresa May used adversarial language in Prime Minister's Question Time exchanges (PMQs); how she attempted to engage with 'humorous' homosocial and sexist exchanges in the HoC; how she represented herself in 'critical gendered moments' (defined in detail in Chapter 2); and how she was represented in the media. In Chapter 7, I focus on similar topics in relation to two other women leaders. First, Julia Gillard (prime minister of Australia, 2011–13), and the ways in which she resisted her sexist treatment in the Australian House of Representatives (HoR), and how this was subsequently represented in the media. Second, Hillary Clinton and her attempt to become the Democratic Party presidential candidate (in 2008) and her presidential bid (in 2015–2016), focusing in particular on critical gendered moments in her televised debates with Donald Trump and her representation in the media. Finally, in Chapter 8, I discuss the implications of the analyses presented in the book for understanding institutional change and women's progress within politics.

2   Gender and Language in Political Institutions

2.1   Introduction: Linguistic Research into Gender in Parliamentary Contexts

In this chapter I explain the different types of data and various methods used to address the research questions set out in Chapter 1. In order to assess the linguistic participation of men and women in parliamentary discourse, a combination of methods has been used. First, I undertake an assessment of the *amount* that women and men participate in different UK parliaments. This involves classifying and counting the different types of speaking turns in institutions using video recordings of debates (Chapter 3) and publicly available parliamentary reports (Chapter 4). However, this broad-brush approach, while giving a basic assessment of participation, is not detailed enough to give an understanding of the mechanisms of the debate floor or the informal rules that govern its occupation. As observed by Nirmal Puwar, 'if we are to move beyond banal versions of diversity which simplistically count the heads of "different" bodies in organisations, then our tools of analysis need to engage with in-depth ethnographic research in institutions' (Puwar 2004b: 77–8). The ethnographic method, viewing the parliaments as CoPs, is therefore the central and underlying approach. The ethnographic descriptions of the informal rules and practices of parliamentary interaction draw upon in situ observations of the parliaments, along with interviews with politicians and the use of different discourse analytic approaches to the microanalysis of debate interaction. These ethnographic descriptions, observations and analyses lead to the identification of the main obstacles and barriers to women's political participation (described in Chapter 5), which are then investigated in detail using case studies of prominent women political leaders in Chapters 6 and 7.

Carrying out research into parliamentary institutions with political actors presents the linguistic researcher with a number of challenges. On the one hand, it is relatively easy to scrutinise the frontstage view (Goffman 1959; Wodak 2009) of public parliamentary speech events. On the other hand, it can be extremely difficult to gain access to parliamentary institutions and there are unique difficulties involved in conducting research in the backstage (behind the scenes) of these closed, elite, political communities. Here I set out the characteristics of the parliamentary setting (and the political actors within it) that need to be considered when researching gender and linguistic behaviours in these institutions. On the frontstage, debates, question times and other parliamentary proceedings are televised and increasingly available to watch through official channels (such as BBC Parliament) and also through secondary broadcasting sources such as online news sites and social media. The 'Official Report' or 'Hansard' is another publicly available source of data, which gives a written record of all proceedings in the parliamentary chamber. Although the representation of speeches in these Official Reports (henceforth ORs) is partial and selective, and therefore not suitable for all types of analysis (for a full discussion, see Shaw 2018 and Section 2.4.1), the reports allow for the identification of some rhetorical features and open up possibilities for large-scale quantitative analyses of linguistic features or interactive phenomena. Several research projects have constructed corpora from ORs (including the publicly available Hansard Corpus)[1] and have published findings on diverse topics including the framing of political discourse (Willis 2017), linguistic change (De Smet 2016), semantics of labour relations over time (Demmen et al. 2018) and metaphor (Charteris-Black 2017; Alexander 2016).

Quantitative studies using large-scale data sets of political speech (either from ORs or from transcripts of interviews and political debates) have also been used to measure different aspects of women's representation and participation (Banwart and McKinney 2005; Bicquelet et al. 2012; Bird 2005; Blaxill and Beelen 2016; Catalano 2009; Jones 2016; Yu 2014). Such quantitative studies often run up against the anti-essentialist, highly contextualised and performative nature of the construction of gender in discourse within which the relation between gender and language is indirect, indexical and non-exclusive (as described in Chapter 1). While a full critique of these approaches is outside the scope of this chapter, it is worth considering some important principles that quantitative studies into sex differences in communicative political styles need to take into consideration.

The first principle is the establishment of a theoretical basis upon which the term 'gender' can be used. Is it in fact being conflated with 'sex' and is the basis of either of these terms centred on biological, cultural or performative assumptions? This theoretical position will affect all aspects of the research process, analysis and interpretation of results. A good example of how this can be established in quantitative studies is in Gleason's (2019) work on gender and oral arguments in the US Supreme Court, which examines the success of attorneys' arguments in relation to their conformity to gendered communicative norms, given a performative model of gender. Atheoretical claims about gender are much more common, however, and usually present gender as a bottom-line explanation for particular behaviours, as Harrington and colleagues put it: 'clearly because members of a social group do X, this does not in itself make X explicable by that group membership' (2008: 15).

The second underlying principle is the political nature of gender as a variable, as the identification of sex differences per se is an ideologically loaded process. Given the strength of *beliefs* about gendered differences in speaking styles mentioned in Chapter 1 (and discussed in more detail in Chapter 5) and the fact that gender differences can actually arise out of unequal gender relations, researchers need to meticulously examine the motivation and the evidence for the basis of their arguments before embarking on such research. It has been suggested that researchers should establish warrants, or reasons for carrying out research into language and gender (Harrington et al. 2008; Swann 2002), rather than undertaking research that reinforces difference for the sake of difference and perpetuates the ideological cycle of beliefs in gendered differences. These beliefs then feed expectations of gendered behaviour, which in turn possibly affect gendered performances themselves.

The third principle involves whether a particular quantitative study is balanced in its analyses. Often, quantitative studies into gendered differences in communication styles have been criticised for stressing differences – but ignoring similarities – between women and men on the one hand and yet ignoring intra-group differences on the other. Examples of these critiques include Janet Hyde's 'Gender Similarities Hypothesis' (2005); Deborah Cameron's critique of gender differences in communicative styles (2007); and empirical evidence for similarities in men's and women's styles, for example Larson (2016)).

As noted in Chapter 1, claims that there are identifiable, fixed, gendered speech styles have gained little traction within sociolinguistics, but these claims are common in some studies in political science. For example, Jones (2016) claims to show that Hillary Clinton's style has become more masculine over time. Using publicly available interview and debate transcripts from 1992 to 2013, Jones identifies features of masculine and feminine speaking styles, claiming that, based on previous studies: 'In general, and on average, women tend to use pronouns (especially first-person singular pronouns), verbs and auxiliary verbs, social, emotional, cognitive, and tentative words more frequently than men. In general, and on average, men tend to use nouns, big words (words greater than six letters), articles, prepositions, anger, and swear words more frequently than women' (Jones 2016: 625). She quantifies the presence of these features in Clinton's interviews and debates and finds that Clinton's use of 'masculine' linguistic features has increased over time.

However, while Jones's work contains some insightful discussions of the different factors affecting Clinton's popularity, this type of analysis is problematic because it gives no explanation of *why* any of these categories is associated with men or women, implying that gender is in fact the only explanation offered (women use first-person singular pronouns more because they are women).

A more fundamental problem is that these claims are overgeneralised and ignore both *context* and *genre*. These gendered linguistic features were identified in a range of texts, mostly written genres rather than spoken ones, and so they have little relevance to the use of the same features in the specific genres under consideration: political interviews and debates. Indeed, gendered differences may well disappear when the sample is narrowed to these specific genres (see for example Romaniuk's (2016) analysis of Clinton's style in political interviews). The claims also incur the difficulties associated with the form/function problem – in other words, one linguistic form cannot be reliably attributed to one function (as explained in the classic examination of the different functions of question tags by Cameron et al. (1988)). So, the question arises: Within any of these large linguistic categories, which specific function (or meaning) is the gendered one, or are all occurrences associated with either men or women? Taking the first-person singular pronoun 'I' as an example, it is possible to identify a range of uses and meanings of the pronoun in a particular genre of political discourse: UK House of Commons (HoC) debates, shown in Example 2.1.

Example 2.1 First-person singular pronouns occurring in HoC political discourse (Official Reports)

(a)   If **I** thought that Iraq was a threat to this country, **I** would have taken immediate action (Tony Blair 14/07/2004).

(b)   He can lead a protest, **I** am leading a country (Theresa May 01/02/2017).

(c)   **I** beg to move Government amendment (a) to Lords amendment (Stephen Pound 27/04/2016).

(d)   **I** beg to move, That the clause be read a Second time (Brandon Lewis 05/01/2016).

(e)   There is really nothing further to that point of order, but because it is the right hon. Lady, **I** feel **I** must take it (John Bercow (Speaker) 21/03/2016).

These examples, taken from a specific political genre, show the importance of context in determining the meaning and function of linguistic forms and the difficulties inherent in identifying style at a lexical level. Examples (c) and (d) have an 'illocutionary' force (Searle 1969) peculiar to this one context, which means that when performed by authorised people, the utterances achieve a non-verbal effect (in this case concerning the legal progression of a bill through parliament). The pronoun 'I' is an indivisible part of that speech act and, given the relative numbers of men and women in the HoC and across levels of seniority, it is unlikely that women perform this parliamentary function, and the pronoun 'I' in this sense more than men. Similarly, the rest of the examples have highly contextualised meanings and functions, from Blair's hypothetical formulation in (a) to Theresa May's adversarial one in (b) and including Bercow's rather patronising 'I feel' in (e), which could easily be mischaracterised as a feminine 'emotion word'.

This example illustrates that a much more fine-grained set of ethnographic and discourse analytic observations is required in order to understand the formal and informal rules and linguistic practices of political institutions. This means gaining access to the backstage of political institutions, and the problems in gaining access are multiple and arguably still reliant on disciplinary orientation and patronage. For example, political scientists are more likely than researchers from other disciplines to have access to existing contacts within political institutions. Entry into the institutions and to specific events (such as Prime Minister's Question Time [PMQs] in the UK HoC) requires sponsorship from MPs or others employed within the institution. Parliaments also vary greatly in their openness to researchers and the degree to which they facilitate research projects and agendas. However, access to the backstage is fundamental to the understanding of parliamentary interaction, gender and participation. The frontstage view clearly depicts the strict official rules about speaking (as set out in the institution's 'Standing Orders'),[2] including *what* can be said (participants need to avoid 'unparliamentary language', for example) and *how* it can be said (for example adhering to strict forms of address and strictly controlled speaking turns). However, it is only by going behind the scenes that researchers can begin to understand informal rules. These are not written down or even publicly acknowledged, but nevertheless they form part of political actors' knowledge about 'the way things are done'. At the same time, the political actors themselves pose unique challenges for the researcher. Politicians' elite roles exacerbate problems of access for them, especially as academic research agendas are rarely aligned to the pressing political concerns of a particular day in parliament. Therefore, it is extremely difficult to arrange to spend time with a politician, and these appointments are subject to last-minute postponement or cancellation.

Even if access to the closed communities of the parliamentary research site is gained, another set of challenges arises from the relationship of the researcher to the researched. The researcher is necessarily 'researching up' when conducting research with political elites, as politicians have more power and status than the researcher. This power differential, together with the access constraints to the backstage and the public nature of the frontstage, underlies the choice of research design and methodological approach for the analysis of gender and language in these contexts and is discussed in this chapter. These situations present certain challenges for the feminist analysis of political discourse (discussed in Section 2.2) and determine the choice of a mixed method approach (Section 2.6) and the selection of linguistic ethnography, Conversation Analysis (CA) and Critical Discourse Analysis (CDA) as part of that approach (Section 2.4). Section 2.5 explains the rationale behind the inclusion of case studies of international women political leaders in Chapters 6 and 7.

2.2   Feminist Linguistic Methodology

It has been claimed that feminist research, regardless of its discipline, can be distinguished from non-feminist research into the behaviour of women and men 'by having a critical view of the arrangement between the sexes' in which male–female differences need to be theorised and viewed as part of 'a larger picture' (Cameron 1997b: 21). Similarly, 'critical research' has been defined as that which is concerned with analyses of social inequalities and opposes other existing paradigms and theories that fail to address those social inequalities (Billig 2000: 291). Theoretical positions – such as the notion of 'women's language' being *constitutive of* and not simply *reflecting* social identities (Gal 1995) – contribute to the larger picture of critical feminist research that aims to examine the cultural significance of gendered ideologies that frame both linguistic behaviour and judgements about that behaviour. Measuring or accounting for the cultural significance of gendered behaviour necessitates the adoption of particular methods of enquiry that allow the description and scrutiny of the 'local contexts and belief systems within which language use is embedded' (Cameron 1997b: 29). Ethnography – in particular, the 'Ethnography of Speaking' (Hymes 1972b, 1974) – addresses these local contexts and allows the investigation of both gendered behaviour and ideologies. As described in more detail in Section 2.3, ethnography is particularly 'open to a wide variety of discourse analytic traditions' (Copland and Creese 2015: 25) and therefore forms the core of the mixed method approach adopted here.

While there are many different approaches to feminist research methods and there is no agreed-upon fixed set of procedures common to all research describing itself as 'feminist', there are some core feminist research principles that tend to be adopted by feminists researching language. In addition to the specific aims and focus of feminist linguistics to pursue 'explicitly political goals by criticising ruling linguistic norms' (Hellinger 1990: 12, cited in Wodak 1997: 8), feminist research also involves research principles that are seen as fundamental to its emancipatory aims. Firstly, feminist research aims to empower its subjects, recognising that research should be 'on, for and with' (Cameron et al. 1992) the members of the community under scrutiny. Secondly, feminist research tends to have an ontological commitment to valuing the subjective, lived experiences of individuals, and viewing those experiences as the most appropriate sources of knowledge relating to social behaviour. This is also linked to the epistemological commitment to recognise the multiplicity of human experience and to value the subjective and differing accounts of social actors. From this perspective, justifying one truthful account as being more objective or valuable than another is viewed as being a '"masculinist" position that identifies its own value system and politics as rational and superior' (Ramazanoglu and Holland 2002: 16). Feminist methodology has sought to challenge patriarchal knowledge and male-centred positivism (for example Daly 1977: 7), but the privileging of subjectivity is not commonly advocated. '[B]ecause of the social diversity of gender relations, and the variable interaction of gender relations with other power relations, feminist knowledge of women's lives cannot be assumed or generalized without qualification and empirical investigation' (Ramazanoglu and Holland 2002: 16). So, while recognising the important status of subjective and personal accounts of experience is core to feminist methodology, this is not done so at the expense or exclusion of empirical approaches.

A critical approach to research also recognises that the research process itself is a social process with its own attendant subjectivities and viewpoints. Research decisions reflect wider networks of disciplinary, political, ontological and epistemological positions, and much critical and feminist research recognises that these positions should be made as explicit as possible. In this way, the researcher needs to be *reflexive* about 'owning up' to theoretical and political affiliations (Heller et al. 2018). This reflexivity rests in providing clarity about theoretical and methodological decisions and a recognition that the researcher's perspective is itself subjective and that alternative descriptions, interpretations and claims may also be viable. This is considered in the research design presented here, as interviews give politicians opportunities to provide alternative interpretations of the researcher's analysis. Feminist research shares this core principle of reflexivity within ethnographic approaches, which are the subject of the following section.

2.3 Ethnography in the 'Community of Practice'

Ethnographic approaches emphasise that the contexts for communication should be investigated rather than assumed and that detailed analysis of linguistic data is essential to understanding its significance (Rampton 2007: 585). It has been claimed that this informal knowledge about 'what can be said when, where, by whom, to whom, in what manner and under what particular social circumstances' (Saville-Troike 2003: 8) has been overlooked in political accounts of institutions because mainstream comparative research in this area tends to analyse formal rules (Helmke and Levitsky 2004). Certainly, while ethnographic research is common in sociolinguistic accounts of workplace interaction (see for example Angouri 2011, 2018a, 2018b; Holmes 2006,

2017; Holmes and Marra 2002; Marra et al. 2017; Mullany 2007; Shaw 2000, 2006, 2013, in press; Wodak 2003, 2009), it has been less common in studies of politics, with Rhodes' (2005) 'Everyday Life in a Ministry' and Emma Crewe's anthropological studies of the House of Lords (2005, 2010) and the HoC (2015) being notable exceptions. The central role of ethnography in sociolinguistics is partly because of the influence of Dell Hymes, who devised a framework for the ethnographic observation of communication known as the 'Ethnography of Speaking' (Hymes 1972b, 1974). This framework allows for the communicative event to be broken down into different components (such as 'purposes', 'acts', 'keys' and 'norms') against which the interaction can be observed and described. This framework is used here as the basis for describing interactive events in the HoC and the devolved political institutions of the United Kingdom.

Hymes' approach to ethnography used the notion of a 'speech community' defined as 'any human aggregate characterised by regular and frequent interaction by means of a shared body of verbal signs and set off from similar aggregates by significant differences in language usage' (Gumperz and Hymes 1972). However, as noted in Chapter 1, I use Eckert and McConnell-Ginet's (1992a, 1992b) development of Wenger's (1998) model of 'Communities of Practice'. The CoP is defined as: 'An aggregate of people who come together around mutual engagement in an endeavour. Ways of doing things, ways of talking, beliefs, values, power relations – in short – practices – emerge in course of a mutual endeavour' (Eckert and McConnell-Ginet 1992b: 464). In this way, individuals belong to multiple, changing CoPs upon different terms of participation, and gender is seen as one of the factors that may affect an individual's membership in and participation within any given Community. The three aspects of practice that define a CoP are mutual engagement, a joint negotiated enterprise and a shared repertoire (Wenger 1998: 73). The CoP approach is therefore more flexible and less static than the notion of a speech community as it emphasises performance, change and the dynamic emergence of identities in interaction. This means it is compatible with the theoretical notion of gender as a social construct (Cameron 1996; Holmes and Meyerhoff 1999; Mullany 2007) and offers a connection between local practices and larger macro social structures in society (McElhinny 2003: 30). The CoP approach, together with a notion of the 'gender order' (Eckert and McConnell-Ginet 2013: 22–3), can therefore help to illuminate both the local gendered terms of participation in a CoP and the overarching ideologies which maintain and constrain gendered behaviour. Like Wodak (2009) I also find Bourdieu's notion of the linguistic 'habitus' (Bourdieu 1991) useful in conceiving of the daily and routine practices in this CoP (Shaw 2000). Bourdieu states: 'This linguistic "sense of place" governs the degree of constraint which a given field will bring to bear on the production of discourse, imposing silence or a hyper-controlled language on some people while allowing others the liberties of a language that is securely established' (Bourdieu 1991: 82).

This notion of sets of habitual and unconscious social structures and practices is therefore a useful theoretical construct with which to examine the *constraints* that are brought to bear on individuals within a CoP (see further discussion in Chapters 3 and 8).

Ethnographic observations, interviews and archival research formed the basis of the ethnographic descriptions and analyses of gendered norms in the different institutional CoPs examined in this book: the HoC (see Chapters 3 and 6), the Northern Ireland Assembly (NIA), the National Assembly for Wales (NAW) and the Scottish Parliament (SP) (see Chapter 4). As described in more detail elsewhere (Shaw in press), the archival research consisted of standing orders, the ORs, parliamentary publications and research documents, such as Erskine May's Treatise (Erskine May 2015). I observed the parliaments over several visits to the research sites where I watched the parliamentary proceedings from the public galleries in the different chambers (see Appendices A and B for details). This allowed a full view of the debating chambers, rather than the restricted view offered by video recordings. A view from the public galleries allows the observer to hear more of the interaction and get a better sense of the rapport or confrontation between speakers and to gain a sense of how the chamber operates. In situ observation also reveals peculiarities of the institutions related to their physical layout and membership composition: for example, the frequent informal conversations that occur in the SP because of the spacious horseshoe shape of the chamber, the amount of internet surfing conducted by the members of the WA (the only UK political institution that has this facility) and the strikingly small and compact layout of the WA with its sixty members. While many of these observations do not relate directly to gender, they nevertheless give a richer account of the contexts against which linguistic contributions such as heckling or 'sledging', interrupting or challenging the Speaker or Moderator may occur. However, sometimes these observations do give a sense of the gender order in these institutions. For example, in a debate in 2010 at the NIA at Stormont, it was possible to see Peter Robinson (the First Minister) sending the then DUP Minister Arlene Foster out of the chamber to fetch him a glass of water, rather than any of the other men front-bench Ministers sitting much nearer to him. The visits also allowed observation outside the debating chambers, which gave a broader impression of the culture of the institutions. For example, political divisions in the NIA at Stormont are also reflected in the seating arrangements in the Assembly's refectory. It operates under an informal but strict layout according to political affiliation and role so that members of one party sit in a designated area, as do the press and domestic assembly staff (and less stringent versions of this partisan segregation are visible in similar communal areas in the SP and the HoC). So, the ethnographer can observe that informal segregation together with formal power-sharing permeates all institutional arrangements of the NIA.

Traditional ethnographic research uses observation as 'the principle source of knowledge about social phenomena' (Gobo 2008: 190). However, much linguistic ethnographic research necessarily adopts an 'ethnographic perspective' (Green and Bloome 1997: 6) rather than a more orthodox ethnographic approach (Copland and Creese 2015: 30). This ethnographic perspective recognises that not all the elements of the research focus will emerge through observation alone, making 'formal interviews valuable data sources' (Copland and Creese 2015: 30). In my own research, I adopted an ethnographic perspective where formal, semi-structured interviews supplemented the observational data. The reasons for this were that I was seeking insights into politicians' own experience of communicative norms in relation to interpretations I was making about discourse analytic data (see the discussion on the mixed method approach and triangulation of data in Section 2.6), and also because, as mentioned above, I only had limited access to the research sites and so time spent in the field was restricted.

Interviewing politicians as part of an elite, closed and prestigious institutional CoP poses challenges for the ethnographic interviewer (see Shaw in press). The ethnographic researcher needs to recognise the participants as *political* actors who, as interviewees, often play out their professional roles according to party political and ideological allegiances. These actors can be expert interviewees with extensive experience of different types of interview contexts. As Williams notes of the experience of interviewing MPs for research purposes, 'habits bred in their daily conversations with constituents, journalists or lobbyists seem to persist in these quite different circumstances' (1980: 310). This has led to the observation that 'political interviews are themselves highly political' and that politicians as interviewees can shape the interview in different types of dominant and resistant behaviour that have been observed to 'range from monologues of speech, highly defensive off-hand behaviour, to a delivery of pre-scripted official speech' (Puwar 1997: 1.1).

The power dynamic between researcher (academic) and researched (politician) means that the researcher is 'researching up' from a position of less power and status than that of the interviewee. This power relationship can call into question some of the tenets of feminist research, which assume the researcher is in a more powerful position than the interviewee and in which it is nevertheless incumbent on the researcher to create a friendly, non-hierarchical and emancipatory environment (Gobo 2008: 58). A dilemma posed by this unusual power dynamic for feminist researchers is that 'the emphasis on power-sharing and the vulnerability of the researched (…) may not be transferable, indeed may be counter-productive to the development of feminist theory and practice in research with the "powerful"' (Luff 1999: 692). My experience of interviewing men and women politicians was very mixed, showing the difficulty inherent in making any global claim about the power of individuals in relation to the interviewer according to their professional role or gender. I experienced highly defensive and offhand treatment from some men and women interviewees and genuinely collaborative, friendly and constructive treatment from others. Politicians also varied greatly with respect to how able they were to reflect on their linguistic behaviour when asked: some could immediately provide examples of their own and other politicians' linguistic strategies and informal practices in debates; others struggled to conceive of their use of language outside normative notions of correct and incorrect, standard or non-standard varieties. The differential awareness and ability of interviewees to express the metadiscourse of language use remain an unexplored aspect of ethnographic interviewing for sociolinguistics.

2.4   Discourse Analytic Approaches

In political science, techniques for measuring participation include the 'Discourse Quality Index' (DQI) (Steenbergen et al. 2003; Steiner et al. 2004). This is a system for measuring the quality of discourse according to Habermas' discourse ethics in which the following six categories are used: participation, justification, consideration of the common good, respect, constructive politics and authenticity (Steenbergen et al. 2003: 27–30). The DQI works on the principle that these indicators of discourse quality can objectively and reliably be measured by a coding scheme to arrive at an overall score for discourse quality in political speech events. Many aspects of this system are problematic, however, as the coding does not allow for a sophisticated account of the context and related meanings of utterances; relies on subjective beliefs of the coders and treats them as objective facts; and does not recognise the complexity and multiplicity of the functions of language. To take one category as an example, the participation of politicians is only measured with respect to the amount they are interrupted, which leaves no room for the different types of speaking turns, and possible supportive and prompting functions of interruptions political debate (see further critiques of the DQI in for example King 2005). Linguistic approaches to discourse analysis such as Conversation Analysis and critical discourse analysis foreground the details of interactive events and the underlying ideological positions inherent in linguistic choices of speakers, and, for this reason, have been selected to be used alongside ethnography to analyse political interaction in the parliamentary data.

2.4.1   Conversation Analysis

The interviews and observations undertaken as part of the ethnographic approach described above were complemented by a close analysis of the debate floor. This can be viewed as a detailed way of accounting for the acts undertaken by participants in this CoP using Hymes' (1972b, 1974) 'Ethnography of

Speaking' framework described in Section 2.2. Applied conversation analysis (CA) was used for its formal tools for analysis, particularly in relation to turn-taking in spoken interaction (Sacks et al. 1974) rather than for its strict theoretical stance in its 'pure' form that gender can be enacted only by direct indexicality. Using applied CA is particularly compatible with ethnography (Copland and Creese 2015: 51) because the emphasis of the analysis is not solely on how the participants obey relevant rules but also 'on how they jointly construct the conversation and their shared understanding of what is happening within it' (Copland and Creese 2015: 51). Gaining the floor has been viewed by analysts as an 'economy' in which, depending on the context, 'turns are valued, sought or avoided' (Sacks et al. 1974: 201). Power in these microanalytic contexts is 'power as territory: gaining access to discursive space' (Thornborrow 2002: 27), where 'power can be construed as one participant's ability to affect what the next participant does in the next turn' (2002: 136). This notion of a competitive economy is particularly apt for the highly regulated debate floor where turns are sought for professional and political gain.

To distinguish between different types of simultaneous talk in conversations, researchers have often used the model of turn-taking proposed by Sacks et al. (1974). This model states that a turn can be a unit of any length, and at the end of a turn (a transition relevance place) a set of rules apply to how the turn-taking progresses: (1) the speaker selects another speaker (using a turn allocation component); (2) the next speaker selects her/himself to speak; or (3) if no next speaker is selected, the current speaker continues. This model provides the basis for discriminating between inadvertent overlap and interruptions that are dominant and violations of the turn-taking system in conversations. At rule (2) more than one speaker can select themselves to speak, giving rise to overlapping speech. A speaker may also simply misproject the transition relevance place (think someone has finished a turn when they have not), which will also result in overlapping speech. So the model allows for the classification of an instance of overlapping speech as an interruption when overlapping speech occurs at a point where there is no transition relevance place. However, there is a further problem with relying upon a purely structural explanation for the classification of interruptions and inadvertent overlaps. The work of Coates (1989) and Edelsky (1981) suggests that even if an interruption occurs in the middle of another speaker's turn, it does not necessarily have to be a marker of dominant behaviour, it may be a *supportive* intervention. Therefore, the classification of interruptions cannot rely on an analysis of turn structure alone but must also consider wider contextual factors such as the aims of the participants and the effects of the interruption upon the subsequent interaction.

The system for classifying overlapping speech as either inadvertent overlaps or interruptions devised by Sacks et al. (hereinafter SSJ) (1974) is not fully applicable to debates, because debates have a different turn-taking system than do conversations. According to SSJ's analysis of spoken interaction, debates are the most 'extreme transformation of conversation – most extreme in fully fixing the most important (and perhaps nearly all) of the parameters which conversation allows to vary' (1974: 731). SSJ use a conversation analytic approach to investigate the turn-taking system of conversations. The first step of this approach is to observe recurring patterns in naturally occurring data. Making such observations with respect to debates allows the identification of the components of the turn-taking systems which will be discussed in more detail in the analysis of the HoC data in Chapter 3.

Out of the fourteen facts that SSJ identify as pertaining to conversation (1974: 701), seven also apply to UK parliamentary debates. These are (1) speaker change occurs; (2) overwhelmingly one party talks at a time; (3) occurrences of more than one speaker at a time are common but brief[3]; (4) transitions (from one turn to the next) with no gap and overlap are common; (5) turn allocation techniques are used; (6) repair mechanisms exist for dealing with turn-taking errors; and (7) the number of participants can vary. The differences between conversations and debates in accordance with the facts identified by SSJ are (1) in conversations turn order is not fixed but varies, whereas in debates it is partially fixed; (2) turn size is not fixed in conversations but is sometimes limited in debates; (3) the length of a conversation is not specified in advance, whereas a debate does have time restrictions; (4) the relative distribution of turns is not fixed in advance in conversations, but some turns in debates are pre-specified; (5) in conversations, talk can be discontinuous, but in debates it must progress from one speech to another; (6) in conversations the topics are not specified in advance, but in debates they are specified; and (7) in conversations, turns (or 'turn construction units') vary from one word to much longer utterances, whereas in debates turns vary greatly but very rarely consist of one-word utterances. Finally, this comparison also identifies the role of the Speaker, or moderator in the HoC (also known as the 'Presiding Officer' in the Scottish Parliament and the National Assembly for Wales) as a participant within the debate with responsibilities for ensuring adherence to the rules. In relation to the debate floor, the Speaker is in control of turn order; the length of turns and debates; and the relative distribution of turns and often provides the turn allocation components and repair mechanisms.

The 'floor' in spoken interaction can be thought of as an interactional structure (Edelsky 1981: 383) related to the turn-taking mechanism of the interaction. The floor has been 'variously defined as a speaker, a turn, and control over part of conversation' (1981: 401). An analysis of which participant holds the floor often necessitates the attribution of a turn to one speaker. In her study of academic meetings, Edelsky notes that this 'one at a time' sequence is a conceptual prerequisite for much research into turn-taking, but that actual utterances may not be attributable to any one speaker (1981: 396). This leads Edelsky to define the floor as:

the acknowledged 'what's going on' within psychological time/space. What's going on can be the development of a topic or function (teasing, soliciting a response, etc.) or an interaction of the two. It can be developed or controlled by one person at a time or by several simultaneously or in quick succession. It is official or acknowledged in that, if questioned, participants could describe what's going on as 'he's talking about grades' or 'we're all answering her'. (1981: 405)

The 'what's going on' of legal speakers in debates can be described as 'the MP is giving a speech'. In the case of illegal speakers, the 'what's going on' can be described as 'an individual MP is responding to something that has been said' or 'a group of MPs are reacting to something that has been said'. In this sense, the illegal turns are contingent upon the legal ones. Edelsky's (1981: 405) definition of the floor means that a speaker can have a speaking turn without necessarily holding the floor. For example, requests for clarification, backchannels and hearing and understanding checks are not necessarily floor-holding speaking turns. In debates, collective illegal responses fall into this category and are therefore not floor-holding turns. However, individual illegal questions or comments that are responded to by the MP giving the speech can hold the floor. Although these comments are always made in response to something that is said in the legal speech of an MP, when the legal MP responds to the illegal intervention the 'what's going on' can be described as 'the MP is responding to the illegal intervention'. In this way the focus of the interaction shifts from the legal to the illegal speaker, and the illegal speaker can be said to hold the floor.

2.4.1.1   The Official Report(s) and the Transcription of Debates for the Analysis of 'the Floor'

To give an account of the interactional details of the debate floor and to make the most of readily available resources, it was necessary to make a number of practical decisions regarding the use of the parliamentary ORs and detailed transcriptions of debate discourse. The Official Reports such as the Hansard in the UK HoC are the official records of what is said in the chamber. They are the definitive and authoritative account of proceedings and are often quoted by MPs when referring to previous speeches, questions or statements. The official reports are referred to as 'verbatim' records and are defined as that which: 'though not strictly verbatim, is substantially the verbatim report, with repetitions and redundancies omitted and with obvious mistakes corrected, but which on the other hand leaves nothing out that adds to the meaning of the speech or illustrates the argument' (Hansard 4th Series 1907: 239).

The reports are therefore a valuable resource for discourse analysts for some types of analytical tasks. However, the partial and selective representation of the debate discourse means that many linguistic features from the event itself are omitted in the report, including out of order utterances or illegal interventions, and 'other obvious properties of spokenness' (e.g. intonation and stress), the 'correction' of repetitions, incomplete utterances, false starts, pauses, reformulations and 'grammatical slips'' (Slembrouck 1992: 104). In other words, much of what is significant for the analysis of spoken discourse is omitted from the official report, and therefore it is not a suitable source of data for many such analyses, in particular concerning floor apportionment and turn-taking (for a full discussion see Shaw 2018, and for accounts of the omissions and reductions in the ORs see Hughes 1996; Mollin 2007; Slembrouck 1992). Given the selectivity of the ORs, the transcripts used for the conversation analyses of turn-taking were taken from video recordings of debates. The transcription scheme (shown on page viii) is not as detailed as conventionally used for CA studies (see Atkinson and Heritage 1999), and the low-level scheme reflects the necessity of being detailed enough to show timed pauses in order to investigate the occupation of the floor with interruptions, while at the same time taking the practical considerations of time and the large amount of data to be transcribed into account. All the examples of parliamentary data used in this book are either labelled 'transcript' where they have been transcribed in this way from video recordings or labelled 'official report' in cases where the video recordings are not available or detailed transcriptions are not necessary for the analysis.

Politicians' comments *about* the OR form part of the ethnographic material relating to the formal and informal rules of the institution. According to interviewees in the HoC, MPs can check their speech for accuracy and ask for it to be changed if there has been an error, but only if it does not change the sense of their speech (Shaw 2002: Interview E). One MP I interviewed felt that corrections made to the 'verbatim' report did not accurately represent what she said:

I am having constant battles with Hansard I mean I go up when I have time and you can check your speech and they'll have me saying things like 'but has not the Minister realised that' you know and you think but I've never said that 'has not the Minister' you know, I don't say that, that is not what I say – 'I said "hasn't", can't you change it?' And they're like 'no, we have to have "has not"'. (Shaw 2002: Interview E)

Part of the reason for this MP's concern at the way she is represented in the Hansard is because of the perceptions of people who read the speech:

It is just really infuriating – I know that a lot of people will sometimes pull your speech off the internet or whatever it is and you sound like a complete raving upper-class nutter. But the problem is that there is no objective measure the only measure is the Member's word. (Shaw 2002: Interview E)

More recently, the Labour MP, Jess Phillips, has succeeded in getting the standard spelling of the word 'Mum' changed to 'Mom' in the official report to better reflect her Birmingham dialect (Walker 2016; and Hansard 28 May 2015, Column 264). This shows that the reporting practices may have some degree of flexibility and that there may be various other such changes as similar appeals by MPs are made.

2.4.2   Critical Discourse Analysis and Gendered Discourses

The analysis of the construction of politicians' gendered identities on the debate floor, in one-to-one ethnographic interviews and in relation to their representation in the media (see Chapters 5–7), draws upon the theories and categories associated with critical discourse analysis (CDA) (for example Fairclough 1992; Fairclough and Wodak 1997; van Dijk 2008; Wodak 2009). CDA is a particularly suitable approach for the study of political discourse as it has a commitment to examining inequalities and has been extensively used in institutional contexts. This critical study of discourse seeks to examine how power relations are created and negotiated (Fairclough and Wodak 1997: 258) and to conduct micro examinations of linguistic features in order to expose connections between language, power and ideology that are not otherwise apparent (Fairclough 1989: 5). Studies of political discourse using CDA are common and are carried out according to the different formulations of Critical Discourse Studies (van Dijk 2000, 2004, 2008, 2016), the Discourse Historical Approach (Wodak 2009) and Critical Discourse Analysis (Fairclough and Fairclough 2012; Fairclough 2000). While these multiple approaches mean that there is no single common version of CDA, they all share a view of language as social practice, in which language both shapes and is shaped by society. This 'implies a dialectal relationship between a particular discursive event and the situation(s), institution(s) and social structure(s) which frame it' (Fairclough and Wodak 1997: 258). In this way, a CDA approach allows the examination of elements of parliamentary discourse (for example interruptions, address terms or sexist jokes) in relation to the conventions of the speech event, the CoP in which it occurs, and overarching institutional and societal ideologies relating to male dominance and female subjugation and resistance.

The term 'discourse', apart from its conventional, structural use in linguistics to refer to 'the organization of language above the sentence or above the clause' (Stubbs 1983: 1), is also used in this book to refer to ideological positions or 'ways of seeing the world' (Sunderland 2004). This position stems from Foucault's theory of discourses as 'practices that systematically form the objects of which they speak' (1972: 49). Under this view, 'discourses' – sometimes used interchangeably with 'ideologies' (see Sunderland 2004: 6; Mills and Mullany 2011: 76) – are systematic 'ideas, opinions, concepts, ways of thinking and behaving' that are formed within a given context and that have particular, detectable effects (Mills 1997: 17). Sunderland established that specific 'gendered discourses' can be detected that act as a set of constraints through which men and women 'are represented or expected to behave *in particular gendered ways*' (Sunderland 2004: 21). As mentioned in Chapter 1, and discussed further in Chapter 5, the overarching gendered ideology is that of the 'gendered differences discourse' or the 'common sense' notion that difference between men and women is 'what gender is all about' (Sunderland 2004: 52). This concept of gendered discourses also allows the identification of more subtle, underlying ways in which assumptions and beliefs about gender operate in different texts and contexts. For example, in her analysis of a newspaper article describing the academic success of girls and boys, Sunderland notes how a 'battle of the sexes' discourse; a 'poor boys' discourse and a 'gender equality now achieved' discourse run alongside the overarching discourse of gendered difference (Sunderland 2004: 36–44). In common with CDA approaches, the criteria or 'warrants' (Sunderland 2004; Sunderland and Litosseliti 2008) for the identification of these discourses lie in the microanalytic detail of texts or linguistic 'traces' that can be found by the analyst. In this way, it is claimed that discourses can be empirically explored, identified and named in a principled way by using both textual and extratextual knowledge (Sunderland 2004: 29).

Judith Baxter's (2018) identification of gendered discourses in media representations of women leaders shows a commitment to explicating this process of discourse identification and naming. She also attempts to make this process more robust by the reflexive self-awareness of the researcher and an acknowledgement of the inevitable subjectivity of the process: 'Discourse identification, as well as the naming of discourses, are [*sic*] not considered to be neutral activities; rather they say as much about me, the "namer" as they do about the discourses themselves' (Baxter 2018: 10). As part of this nuanced, reflexive process, Baxter also advocates reading 'against the grain' or avoiding automatically identifying the more dominant gendered discourses by 'looking for gaps, ambiguities and contradictions' (Baxter 2018: 82). The concept of gendered discourses is used here to identify and name gendered discourses and sexist practices (and those resisting them) in parliamentary discourse and to do so in such a way that is reflexive and based on linguistic evidence.

The analyses in Chapters 5–7 draw attention to the clear role of intertextuality in the constitution of these discourses. As Sunderland explains 'a particular text can be seen as a reaction to previous texts and also a "drawing in" of those texts through the way it adopts comparable or oppositional styles' (2004: 30). The running jokes, homosocial bonding and in-group markers of collegial understanding found in political institutions (or at least, the UK ones analysed here) are developed *across* events and have effects on subsequent events. The fact that these types of discourses are gendered means that these intertextual mechanisms possibly play an important role in the marginalisation and exclusion of women and the maintenance of their position firmly *outside* the status quo. In Chapter 6, I explore how such discourses positioned the then prime minister Theresa May and how she attempted to negotiate them.

2.5   Case Studies

The case studies presented in Chapters 6 and 7 are directed towards addressing the third set of research questions: What are the effects of sexism, fraternal networks, high visibility and gendered discourses of linguistic performance upon women politicians, and how do successful politicians like Theresa May, Julia Gillard and Hillary Clinton attempt to resist and counter these effects? To address these questions, I conduct a detailed and highly contextualised analysis of the three individual leaders with respect to these barriers to their progress. The case study provides an in-depth 'multidimensional exemplification of a subject that can help to tell an important story but at the same time vividly encapsulate abstract principles as well' (Duff 2018: 306). Here, and in more detail at the beginning of Chapter 6, I explain why these leaders were chosen for the case studies and the main principles against which I selected texts and contexts for the analyses of the cases.

As the ethnographic and discourse analytic research in the first half of the book (Chapters 3 and 4) had been carried out in UK parliaments, the choice of Theresa May as the UK's second woman prime minister seemed an obvious one. The case study of May is more detailed than the other two because it draws extensively on the prior descriptions and analyses of floor apportionment, adversarial language and humour in the HoC and it is against this backdrop that her performances are appraised. For the other two case studies I wanted to focus on prominent, successful and powerful women leaders who nevertheless had certain characteristics in common, one being that they had faced challenges that have been attributed to the enactment of their roles as *women* leaders. It is for these reasons that I chose leaders from the Anglo-American political tradition with Julia Gillard (Australia's first premier, 2009–13) performing politics in a parliamentary context (the Australian House of Representatives) which is founded on the Westminster model of parliamentary democracy. Gillard is also well known for the misogyny she faced in her time in office, and so her case provides an opportunity to examine her strategies for managing and resisting these attacks. Similarly, the focus on Hillary Clinton in the final case study identifies some of the ways in which sexist beliefs about the enactment of her authority and her negative media representation may have contributed to the failure of her bid for the US presidency against Donald Trump in 2016 (and to a lesser extent her failed presidential bid in 2008).

For the most part, the selection of data with which to examine the leaders' political performances differs in each case. The Theresa May case study includes an assessment of her performances in Prime Ministers Question Time (PMQs) exchanges with Jeremy Corbyn, because this speech event and its adversarial norms are discussed in detail in Chapter 3. I also sought a common principle with which to select particular occasions of each leader's performances which were pertinent to the research questions. As I was unable to compare *parliamentary* performances in a comparative way (see further explanation in Chapter 6), I sought to identify 'critical gendered moments' that could be selected across different discourse types and contexts. By 'critical gendered moments' I mean the exact points in political performances in which gender or gender relations (including sexist and feminist discourses) are overtly and critically appraised by the women leaders. This allowed a common thread to the selection of material across the case studies and ensured the relevance of gender was to the fore in the data examined (see Chapter 6).

2.6   The Mixed Method Approach

The approach taken to the research questions in this book is best described as critical 'mixed method' research (see Table 2.1 showing the data and methods used in different parts of the book and the research questions they investigate). Although the term 'mixed method' is often used to refer to an equal mixture of quantitative and qualitative methods, here it is more accurate to represent this mixture as a combination of ethnography with different aspects of discourse analysis. This approach uses enumeration to guide interpretations according to theoretical principles set out in Chapter 1 and the methodological considerations set out in this chapter. Although the enumeration of linguistic features through the classification and counting of different types of spoken turns forms part of the research design, these findings guide the qualitative interpretations rather than providing statistical measurements or 'proofs' of the type conventionally associated with quantitative paradigms. Political scientists working within the 'feminist institutionalist' framework recognise the need for such mixed method research to elucidate the relationships between institutional rules and 'gendered outcomes' (Gains and Lowndes 2014: 526). This is echoed by sociolinguists who recognise the complex characteristics of workplaces as research sites, to which access is often difficult and in which the focus of the analyst's research is multifaceted social and institutional phenomena (Angouri 2018b; Holmes and Marra 2002; Mullany 2007; Stubbe et al. 2003).

One of the benefits of using this mixed method or 'pragmatist approach' (Dörnyei 2007) to the feminist linguistic analysis of political institutions is that it has empirical benefits relating to the examination of phenomena using evidence from different types of data and from different perspectives.

The term 'triangulation' is often used to describe this process and is a term that describes combining data sources to study the same social phenomena with the aim that 'methodological triangulation can help to reduce the inherent weaknesses of individual methods by offsetting them by the strength of another' (Dörnyei 2007: 43). The research projects described in Chapters 3 and 4 give different examples of the richness of the data offered by this kind of triangulation, particularly in relation to informal rules and the transgression of formal rules in parliamentary interaction (see also Shaw in press). On many occasions when conducting fieldwork in parliaments, I was present in the debating chamber and made field notes to record my observations. After watching the debates and question times, I carried out ethnographic interviews with politicians and was able to ask them directly about their impressions of the events I had just observed. On most occasions, the politicians had been participants in the prior events in the debating chamber, and that is why they were free to be interviewed at that time of the week. This gave me access to an immediate insider perspective on the observed events in the chamber(s). The speech event itself was video-recorded and transcribed as discussed above and was therefore available for the close analysis of different discursive features. This meant that the interpretation of any one event in the CoP could draw upon the combination of ethnographic field notes and impressions from direct observation; interview data from participants; and close, microanalytic observations from transcriptions.

A further benefit of triangulation in relation to investigating linguistic norms is when the data show divergent findings or interpretations, which can lead to an enhanced understanding by pointing to areas for further investigation (Dörnyei 2007: 165). This is certainly important when the interpretations of discourse analytic observations by the researcher are confounded by the participants' own perspectives. This occurred on a number of occasions in the course of the research projects. For example, when first investigating turn-taking in the HoC, I interpreted legal 'give way' interventions from political opponents as violative interruptions that were intended to wrest the floor from the legal speaker, and present interactive and substantive challenges to them. However, interviews with MPs revealed that 'give way' interventions (even from political opponents) were viewed positively by many MPs as an indicator of respect and interest in the speech they were delivering – one MP even commenting that 'at least it shows that everyone isn't asleep'. These divergent interpretations of events and norms therefore show that multiple data sources are important in these closed parliamentary institutions where it is not always possible for the researcher as 'outsider' to reliably interpret these interactive phenomena (Shaw in press).

In this way, mixed method approaches are 'an opportunity to better understand different ways of seeing, knowing and valuing' (Greene and

Table 2.1 *Summary of data and methods in the book*

Chapters	Political Institution/Case	Type and amount of Data	Date of Collection	Methods	Research Question Addressed
3	UK House of Commons	Sixty hours of video recordings (sub-corpus of detailed transcriptions of five debates); Sub-corpus of Prime Minister's Question Time (see Appendix A for full list) Ethnographic observation Six ethnographic interviews with politicians (Shaw 2002; Appendix A)	1998–2001	Ethnographic descriptions of norms and practices; Quantitative assessment of participation; Conversation Analysis; CDA and rhetorical analyses for the identification of adversarial features	(1) How do women in politics participate in debate forums, particularly in those that are historically male-dominated, and in which women are still vastly under-represented and men over-represented? What are the constraints and obstacles that they face in institutions such as the UK House of Commons, and how can this be illuminated by detailed linguistic analyses of the debate floor?
4	Northern Ireland Assembly (NIA)	260 hours of debate speaking turns quantified (official report);	2009–11	Quantitative assessment of participation	(2) How successful have the 'new' devolved institutions of the UK been in encouraging equal participation of all members? What are the particular interactional procedures that can be thought of as making an institution more egalitarian?
	National Assembly for Wales (NAW)	Sub-corpus of detailed analysis of turn-taking in NIA, NAW and SP		CA/CDA analysis	
	Scottish Parliament (SP) UK House of Commons	Forty-four interviews with politicians from the NIA, NAW and SP (see Appendix B for description of data)		Ethnographic descriptions of norms and practices	

5	All	Relevant academic literature and research findings; Relevant parliamentary examples and media texts	Up to 2018/2019	CDA and the identification of gendered discourses	(3) What obstacles remain as barriers to women's participation in political forums? How do gender stereotypes constrain women's participation and give them additional burdens? What are the effects of sexism, fraternal networks, high visibility and gendered discourses of linguistic performance upon women politicians?
6 and 7	UK Prime Minister Theresa May (House of Commons and UK press)	Twenty-four Prime Minister's Question Time (House of Commons: July 2016–July 2018, see Appendix C)	2015–18	CA/CDA analyses of texts/parliamentary interaction/TV debates;	(3) What obstacles remain as barriers to women's participation in political forums? How do gender stereotypes constrain women's participation and give them additional burdens? What are the effects of sexism, fraternal networks, high visibility and gendered discourses of linguistic performance upon women politicians, and how do successful politicians like Theresa May, Julia Gillard and Hillary Clinton attempt to resist and counter these effects?
	Australian Prime Minister Julia Gillard (House of Representatives and Australian press)	Examples of 'critical gendered moments' in the House of Commons, House of Representatives and in the 2016 US televised presidential debates	2010–13	Identification and analysis of gendered discourses and 'critical gendered moments'	
	Hillary Clinton 2008 and 2016 presidential bids	Examples from UK/US/ Australian press coverage of women leaders	2008–16		

Caracelli 2003: 107). Miles and Huberman warn about the dangers of falling into a monomethodological 'default' mode, characterised by an 'unquestioning, partisan frame of mind' (1994: 43 cited in Dörnyei 2007: 313). This is echoed by Billig's concern that critical research should 'beware of its own linguistic orthodoxies' and endeavour 'even to expose the self-interest and the political economy of the sign "critical"' (2000: 292). This last point is fundamental to the mixing of methods, a point that Louise Mullany also makes in relation to mixed method research: 'Detailed researcher reflexivity is crucial when one integrates approaches in order to ensure that researchers present a legitimately accountable case for combining discourse analytic frameworks' (Mullany 2012: 510). This chapter has aimed to explain the rationale for the mixing of methods in a reflexive, critical way to further our understanding of the gendered dynamic of political institutions, starting with the UK HoC in Chapter 3.

3 Women's Linguistic Participation in a Traditional Male-Dominated Forum – The UK House of Commons

3.1 The House of Commons as a Community of Practice (CoP)

In this chapter, I address the first set of research questions described in Chapter 1: How do women in politics participate in debate forums, particularly in those that are historically male-dominated, and in which women are still vastly under-represented and men over-represented? What are the constraints and obstacles that they face in institutions such as the UK House of Commons, and how can this be illuminated by detailed linguistic analyses of the debate floor? To answer these questions, I begin by describing the CoP of the House of Commons before using the mixed approach of ethnography and different types of discourse analysis to examine patterns of participation in relation to floor apportionment (3.2); adversarial language (3.3); and the use of humour and irony in parliamentary discourse (3.4).

The House of Commons (HoC) at Westminster can be described as a 'traditional' parliament because it is one of the oldest and is arguably the archetypal political legislature upon which many parliaments around the world are based. In relation to gender, it has always been male-dominated, with women first taking up seats in 1918 but their representation only rose to above five per cent in 1987, before almost doubling between 1992 to 1997 from 9 to 18 per cent (Cracknell and Keen 2014). This rose to 32 per cent by the 2017 General Election. This historical pattern of representation, and in particular the sudden influx of women MPs in 1997 into this CoP are of particular institutional significance. At that point of rapid change, the gender regime was disturbed and on entry to the HoC new women MPs were mistaken for MPs' wives and secretaries (Sones et al. 2005), characterised as 'Blair's Babes', and subjected to extraordinary levels of sexist media coverage. Additionally, many of the 1997 intake (of whom 65 were newly elected) claimed that they had a 'less combative and aggressive style' (Childs 2004) in the debating chamber. This connection between gender and the linguistic performance of political actors at this pivotal period in the 1997–2001 parliamentary term is the focus of this chapter.

Figure 3.1 shows the interior of the HoC debating Chamber, with two sets of green benches facing each other. The Speaker's (moderator's) chair, which

Figure 3.1 Image of the House of Commons debating chamber looking towards the Speaker's chair. (Source: Universal Images Group/Contributor/ Getty Images.)

resembles a throne, is at the head of the chamber with seat for two officials (clerks) in front of it. Between the benches at the head of the chamber is a table with two 'despatch boxes' on either side which function as lecterns – one for the Prime Minister (who sits on the front bench on the left of the image), and one for the leader of the Opposition (LO) who sits on the front-bench on the right of the image. The most senior members of the government (the Prime Minister and other Ministers) sit on the front bench and are sometimes referred to collectively as 'frontbenchers'. MPs with no additional responsibilities in the government sit behind them and are referred to as 'backbenchers', or junior MPs. This is mirrored on the opposition benches with front-bench 'shadow' ministers and more junior backbenchers.

As noted in Chapter 1, it has been claimed that 'institutions have been organised to define, demonstrate and enforce the legitimacy and authority of linguistic strategies used by one gender – or men of one class or ethnic group – whilst denying the power of others' (Gal 1991). The historical and continued numerical dominance of men MPs leads to the presence of women being 'out of place' in a context that is 'a brutal example of the dominance of a culture of traditional masculinity, and an unmistakeably masculine gender regime' (Lovenduski 2014a: 17). This is certainly the case in the House of Commons and is vividly described by Nirmal Puwar:

The position of an MP has been performed as a highly masculinist act. Relations are organised on the basis of patronage, hierarchical fraternising and competitive individual exhibitionism. Gangs, blocks and allegiances are formed to offer support in a system of patronage and combat. Displays of masculinity in the House of Commons are conducted in a spectacular, exaggerated and theatrical manner ... the hero of this performance is a white male … this is the template against which the speech, gestures and bodily movements of female and black and Asian bodies are measured. (Puwar 2004b: 74–5)

Gendered practices and patterns are therefore underpinned by assumptions of masculinity and constantly reinforced by the exclusion of women. In her detailed ethnographic account of the House of Commons (carried out in 2012–13), Emma Crewe characterises MPs identities and roles as 'endlessly diverse, navigating many complex, dynamic socio-political worlds' (2014b: 53). For this reason, as described in detail in Chapter 2, viewing the House of Commons as a CoP acknowledges that individuals belong to multiple, changing communities upon different terms of participation and that gender is seen as just one of the factors that may affect an individual's membership of, and participation within, any given community. The claim that an individual's membership of a CoP is 'peripheral' or 'core' depends upon 'how successfully an individual has acquired the shared repertoire, or assimilated the goal(s) of the joint enterprise' (Holmes and Meyerhoff 1999: 176). For women in a male-dominated institution the acquisition of the shared linguistic repertoire involves negotiating the 'socially ascribed nature of gender: the assumptions and expectations of (often binary) ascribed social roles against which any performance of gender is constructed, accommodated, or resisted' (Bergvall 1999: 281).

   The ethnographic description of the HoC using in situ observations of debates, interviews with MPs and formal records of proceedings, together with academic analyses of the HoC (for example Childs 2000, 2004; Puwar 2004a, 2004b; Crewe 2014b; Lovenduski 2005, 2014b) and suggestions about the linguistic style of 'male-dominated' institutions (for example Kanter 1977; Brewis 2001; Baxter 2010) all suggest that the distinctive linguistic practices thought to characterise the shared repertoire of institutions like the House of Commons CoP fall into three overlapping categories:

1. Occupying, holding and keeping the 'floor'.
2. Behaving in a verbally aggressive way, an 'adversarial style'.
3. Manipulating the serious 'key' of debates to a humorous or ironic one.

Each of these aspects will be examined in this chapter using empirical data and the mixed method approach identified in Chapter 2. In addition to the ethnographic data leading to a description of the CoP, the data are taken from a corpus of 60 hours of debate proceedings between 1998 and 2001,[1] allowing a description of the debate floor and the formal and informal rules and norms that govern its apportionment; an overall assessment of the participation of MPs in different types of speaking turn; and the detailed analysis of video transcripts for applied Conversation Analysis across smaller stretches of debate discourse.

3.2   Floor Apportionment in the House of Commons

The definition of the floor given in Chapter 2 views it as a way of gaining control over a scarce resource, an 'economy' in which, depending on the context, 'turns are valued, sought or avoided' (Sacks et al. 1974: 701). Although the metaphors of scarcity and a competitive economy may misrepresent the nature of ordinary conversations (Edelsky 1981), they seem appropriate for an adversarial debate in which the debate turns are strictly regulated and the debate floor is sought after for both political and interactional advantage. In the HoC, speaking turns are strictly controlled as MPs are called to speak by the Speaker. An MP must stand to speak, and they should be the only person standing in the chamber when they are speaking as it is not permitted to speak when sitting down, commonly referred to as 'a sedentary position'. When an MP speaks they must address all their comments to the Speaker (moderator) rather than addressing their political opponents directly, and they cannot refer to another MP directly (such as by using a pronoun 'you') but must address them by their title (The Right Honourable Lady, Gentleman etc). Other aspects of HoC interaction will be explained in relation to particular examples discussed below and also in terms of the definition of the debate floor proposed in Section 2.4.1.

It has been suggested that in formal public arenas men are more likely to gain and hold the floor and to speak for longer than women (for example Brescoll 2011; Karpowitz and Mendelberg 2014) – see also a more detailed discussion in Chapter 5, with some claims made that women 'leave the floor to men' (Holmes 1995: 193). Therefore, linguistic practices which involve taking, holding and yielding the floor may be one of the ways in which men's and women's terms of participation vary in this CoP. Other factors affecting MPs' access to the debate floor include their status within their party, with the Prime Minister having the most access to the floor as he/she has exclusive rights to respond in Prime Minister's Question Time (PMQs). Ministers and Shadow Ministers and those with particular departmental responsibilities occupy the floor more than back-bench MPs with no particular responsibilities other than representing their constituents. Apart from this distinction between Ministers and back-bench MPs, there are also less formal aspects of status that contribute to the amount individuals speak in debates. For example, some MPs who have been in office for several years have more opportunity to speak in debates than newly elected MPs. This is partly because MPs with more experience of debates understand the procedures better than newly elected MPs, and so may be able to use this knowledge to gain the Speaker's attention more effectively. The ability of an MP to secure a speaking turn may also rest on a number of factors including the relationship of the MP to the Speaker; their reputation as a particularly good orator; or the fact that they have previously held a position of high status.

As noted earlier, the HoC is a forum in which the contributions of Members are strictly controlled by rules about when they can speak. These are enforced both by the Speaker and through the vigilance of MPs in the chamber – who can draw the Speaker's attention to rule violations by shouting 'order' as an appeal to the Speaker to stop the debate on a 'point of order'. In their study of US televised political debates, Edelsky and Adams (1990) note that these debates consist of an 'ideal' form when the rules and procedures are adhered to and the debate offers participants an equal opportunity to speak. The comparison of the operational factors in the turn-taking systems for conversations and debates (see Section 2.3) identified the 'ideal' progression of turns in debates, devised in order to 'permit the equalization of turns' (Sacks et al. 1974: 730). Alongside this ideal or canonical form there also exists the 'real' event in which 'illegal' violations of the rules take place. In order to identify the extent to which women and men MPs have control over the debate floor it is necessary to attempt a description of the floor activities taking both the ideal and illegal turns into account.

The ideal progression of debates is restricted so that the system is as fair as possible – enabling speakers to express themselves without interruption and allowing every participant the opportunity to speak. Participants are allotted a speaking turn in advance of the debate if they have particular responsibilities in that specific debate for introducing or opposing a motion. If MPs are not allotted a speaking turn in advance of the debate, MPs must signal to the Speaker that they wish to contribute by standing up at the end of a speech. The Speaker then calls one of the standing MPs to speak in the debate. It will be shown below that this ideal is not adhered to in terms of the turn-taking system of debates and questions times in the HoC, and 'thus a speech event that should allow everyone an equal chance becomes an event in which prior inequalities (e.g. gender, age and ethnicity) can be re-enacted' (Edelsky and Adams 1990: 171). The interaction is prone to violations of the rules by MPs who aim to promote their own speech or to undermine the speech of another MP. Example 3.1 below shows a particularly disorderly extract from a PMQ session in July 1998.

Example 3.1 Jane Griffiths' Question to the Prime Minister (PMQs 01/07/98: Transcript – see transcription conventions on p. XI)

> SP = the Speaker; JG = Jane Griffiths (Labour); PM = Prime Minister; MPs = 'crowd' noises made by MPs; 1MP one MP speaking from a sitting position; (O) = Opposition; (L) = Labour; *Italics* = speech from a sitting position

1   SP   : ORDER order I must remind the Honourable Lady and the <u>Hou</u>se that
2   : the Prime Minister is responsible only for his own government's <u>poli</u>cies [(.) and
          MPs :   [*cheer*
3   SP   : not for the] the activities of the oppo<u>sit</u>ion (.) if she could rephrase her <u>ques</u>tion in
          MPs : *cheering--*]   [*cheering*]

4	SP	: some way of course I would <u>hear</u> it and I am sure that the Prime Minister is
5		: already <u>form</u>ing an answer [(.) where<u>by</u> ha ha ha ha whereby (.) he will enunciate
	MPs :	[*Laughter --------------------- Muttering---------*
6	SP	: his responsibilities in terms of] <u>pol</u>icy on these matters (.) Miss Griffiths it is
	MPs : *muttering----------------------*]
7	SP	: your <u>first</u> question in Prime Minister's question time (.) <u>could</u> you rephrase it in
	1MP :	*well done*
8	SP	: some way th that the Prime Minister is res[<u>pon</u>sible (4)]
	MPs :	[*Laughter ---------------Muttering-*
9	JG (L)	: <u>thank</u> you madam speaker I stand cor<u>rect</u>ed (1)
	MPs : *muttering-----------------------------------*
10	JG (L)	: would the would the Prime Minister agree with <u>me</u> that
	1MP(O) : *muttering---------------------------------------*
11	JG (L)	: if (.) the (.) party opposite [(2)]
	1MP (O):	[*NO NO no*]
	MPs :	[*JEERING-*
12	SP	: quiet QUIET (7)]
	MPs : *JEEring muttering*]
13	1MP (L) :	*pol*icy (1) *policy confirm <u>our</u> policy* (1) *policy*
14	JG (L)	: [would the would the Prime] Minister agree with me (.) w would he would he
	MPs : [*muttering--------------------*]
15	JG (L)	: share with me in con<u>fir</u>ming that <u>our</u> policy is to sup<u>port</u> the poor[est workers
	MPs :	[*cheering---*
16	JG (L)	: in this country (5)]
	MPs : *cheering-------CHEERING-----muttering*
17	SP	: well done that girl well done ha ha (4)]
	MPs : *muttering--------------------LAUGHTER---laughter*
18	PM	: my honourable friend is quite right [(.) quite right (.) no we (.)] the position of the
	MPs :	[*LAUGHTER-----muttering-----------------*
	1MP(O):	[GIVEN ENOUGH TIME]
19	PM	: government will remain that we sup<u>port</u> the minimum wage and we look forward t
20		to hearing a position from the party opposite

Example 3.1 starts with the Speaker intervening on a question asked by
Jane Griffiths, a Labour MP first elected in 1997 who is asking her first
parliamentary question. The main or 'legal' speaking turns are shown
as the numbered lines in the transcript, the indented, unnumbered lines
and italicised text show illegal interventions. Jane Griffiths' attempts to
ask a question of the Prime Minister Tony Blair, immediately before this
excerpt starts. Blair and Griffiths belong to the same 'ruling' Labour party
in government at the time. Griffiths starts her question with the formulaic 'Would the prime Minister agree with me ...', as she does not intend
to challenge the Prime Minister but to reinforce her party's position with
her question. Unfortunately, she formulates the question incorrectly and
adds 'that the party opposite'. The transcript above starts as the Speaker
explains (lines 1–8) that the parliamentary rules dictate that questions to
the Prime Minister must be directed towards an area for which the Prime

Minister is responsible and not, as in this case, towards the policies of the opposition parties (for which he is not responsible). The Speaker (a woman, Betty Boothroyd) enforces the rules by explaining to Griffiths that she must 'rephrase' her question (line 3), and the correction is notable for the ironic cheering from MPs that accompany it, and the rather patronising tone of the Speaker who underlines the fact that 'it is your first question' (line 7). The illegal and collective jeering, laughing and muttering occur throughout the extract, including when Griffiths starts to form her question a second time by first thanking the Speaker and pausing (line 9). Then she gives the formulaic 'would the Prime Minister agree with me' a second time (line 10), but also repeats her earlier error by saying 'if the party opposite' (line 11), thereby again asking the Prime Minster about an area for which he is not responsible. The reaction to this repeated error is immediate, with a single opposition MP shouting 'No no no' and sounds of jeering and shouting continuing for nine seconds, despite another intervention by the Speaker to quieten the chamber (line 12). A single MP from Griffiths' own party audibly prompts her to give the correct response and to say 'confirm *our* policy' before Griffiths finally produces the correct form for the question in her third attempt (lines 14–16). Collective, disruptive and ironic cheering accompany the correct completion of Griffiths' question, and the Speaker colludes with this by adding the sexist and patronising comment 'Well done that girl, well done' and laughing (line 17). The Prime Minister's response is also formulaic 'My Honourable Friend is quite right', accompanied by laughter and a single audible complaint from an opposition MP that the question has been 'given enough time'.

This transcript underlines two important points about participation in the HoC chamber. First, that illegal utterances, both the jeering, laughing and cheering of collective utterances and those that can be attributed to an individual speaker, can affect the legal turns of the main speaker in ways that the canonical debate form does not allow. Although it is not possible to directly assess the effect of the collective laughter, muttering and cheering on Jane Griffiths' turn, ethnographic interviews with new Labour women MPs show that they view this hostile environment 'as very scary, the chamber is designed that way. It is supposed to intimidate you' (Shaw 2002: Interview A). This intimidating atmosphere of public rebuke and ridicule is likely to have affected Griffiths' performance to some degree and may have been mostly responsible for her hesitancy and her failure to reformulate the question correctly in lines 9–11. The transcript also shows how an individual, illegal and supportive intervention (line 13) has a more direct and beneficial effect on Jane Griffiths' legal contribution as it is only after this prompt that she formulates the question correctly.

Secondly, the transcript shows that to achieve a close analysis of the debate floor, it is necessary to account for and distinguish legal from illegal turns in debates. This can be done by referring to D1 (legal) and D2 (illegal) turn-taking systems because they operate under different rules (Shaw 2000). The numbered lines in Transcript 3.1 are the only parts of the interaction that are recognised officially as being part of the debate, and the only part of the inter-action recorded in the official Hansard report (as mentioned in Section 2.3). Illegal D2 turns have various forms ranging from a number of MPs shout-ing, to a single MP directly supporting or challenging a D1 turn. This dis-tinction between the D1 and D2 turns also provides the basis upon which it may be possible to differentiate between an intervention that is characteris-tic of non-disruptive utterance made in the D2 system and a D2 interruption that directly impinges upon and violates the turn-taking mechanism of the D1 system. Typically, two-part D2 interventions occur when the MP legally holding the floor is interrupted, often by a one-word utterance such as 'rub-bish' or 'hear hear', and is shown in Transcript 3.1 above on line 18 when an MP shouts 'given enough time!' after Griffiths asks her question correctly and the prime Minister starts to respond. Although disruptive, this type of intervention does not elicit a response from the legal speaker and so does not directly impinge on the D1 floor, beyond the possible distraction the interjec-tion may incur. However, a three-part D2 intervention is one in which the legal speaker responds to the illegal intervention and thus the D2 interjec-tion directly affects the progress of the D1 floor. This can be viewed as the strongest marker of powerful and dominant behaviour in debate interaction where 'power is accomplished in discourse both on a structural level – through the turn and type of space speakers are given or can get access to – and on an interactional level through what they can effectively accomplish in that space' (Thornborrow 2002: 8). Example 3.2 shows how a combination of D1 legal and D2 illegal interventions can impinge upon the rights of the D1 legal speaker (Shaw 2006).

Example 3.2 Legal and illegal interventions that disrupt the debate discourse (01/03/99, Transcript)

> CMP = 'current' or 'legal' MP, IMP = intervening or 'illegal' MP, f = female, m = male, (C) = Conservative, (L) = Labour

1	CMP f (C)	: it is very significant that this has not taken place (.)
2		there is an element in my view of deceit in the way in which
3		this legislation (.) has been protect er presented in this house
4	IMP m (L)	: would the right honourable lady give way
5	CMP f (C)	: I will
6	IMP m (L)	: (Give way) has the Hon. Lady been asleep for the last two years

7		the European Court of Human Rights have ordered us to
8		change our laws (.) we have to we have to change the law
9	IMP m (C)	: rubbish (1)
10	IMPm (L)	: (Give way cont'd.) the honourable gentleman from his lazing position
11		says rubbish (.) unfortunately life is life (.) and life says we've got to
12		change the law and we're doing it (.) it's not there is no hidden agenda
13		there
14	IMP m (C)	: of course there is
15	IMPm (L)	: (Give way cont'd) oh rubbish Winterton (.)you really are
16		a silly man (1)
17	MPs	: (laughter)
18	CMP f (C)	: gentlemen (.)
19	IMP m (C)	: no more silly than you
20	CMP f (C)	: I'm really I'm as aware as he is that there's been a debate on
21		the issue from that perspective and that the honourable gentleman
22		opposite has made his (.) contribution to some extent but that does
23		not alter the fact that we are still here debating (.) what is going in
24		this case to be domestic legislation (turn continues)

The woman Conservative MP first allows a D1 legal give way intervention[2] (lines 6–8) on her speech by the men Labour MP. However, this intervention itself is disrupted by a men Conservative MP in two three-part illegal interventions (lines 8–10 and 12–16) that are responded to by the legally intervening men MP (lines 10 and 15). The second of these interventions and its response, accompanied by laughter from other MPs in the chamber, is followed by an appeal for the floor from the woman Conservative MP ('gentlemen' line 18) which is ignored by the intervening MPs and a further two-part illegal intervention is made (with the first part on lines 15–16 and the second part on line 19) before the woman MP finally reclaims her turn (line 20). This extract therefore shows the collapse of the D1 legal floor as the woman MP has given up her turn to a legal intervention on the understanding that the legal floor will be preserved, yet the interactional space is instead occupied by a D2 interaction between the two men. In this way, the egalitarian ideals of the canonical form of the debate (to permit the fair and equal sharing of the debate floor) are hijacked by illegal interventions that remove the speaking rights from the legal speaker.

To assess the participation of men and women MPs in the HoC on the legal floor, turns were counted and classified in a corpus of 60 hours of videos of debate proceedings between 1998 and 2001 (see Appendix A.1.1 for a full list of the events included in the corpus). To undertake this assessment of the participation of the two different groups (women and men), the differential proportions of the two groups must be considered. Table 3.1 above shows that in the 1997–2001 parliamentary term, women accounted for 18 per cent of the politicians in the House of Commons, and men 82 per cent.

Table 3.1 *Table showing the number and percentage of women and men MPs in the 1997–2001 parliament*

Number of women MPs	Number of men MPs	Total number of MPs
120	526	646

% of women MPs	% of men MPs	
18%	82%	100%

Table 3.2 *Table showing the number and percentage of (legal) turns taken by men and women MPs in the whole corpus*

Type of speech event	Number of events	Duration of all events	Total turns	Male turns	Female turns
All debates and question times	59	59 Hours	1926	1609	317
Percentage of total number of turns				83%	17%

When the legal turns were counted and classified, overall women took 17 per cent of all the turns in the whole 60-hour corpus, and men 83 per cent (as shown in Table 3.2 above) and this is close to their 18/82 per cent proportion as groups in the House of Commons at this time.

To assess participation with respect to legal and illegal interventions, a smaller sub-corpus of detailed transcriptions of five debates from the 1998–2001 corpus was examined. These debates were sampled from the 60-hour corpus to give a range of debates on different topics and with different participants. The analysis of this sub-corpus of five debates shows that women made 21 per cent of 'give way' interventions across the five debates, above their 18 per cent representation overall. In contrast, for the illegal D2 turns that were attributable to an MP, men used proportionally more illegal interventions than women (90 per cent overall in comparison to their 80 per cent representation in the parliament). Although the number of attributable D2 turns in the sub-corpus was small, this suggests that women MPs were not using the D2 turns to occupy the debate floor as much as (some) men. Furthermore, of the 41 illegal turns taken in the smaller 1998–2001 sub-corpus, 41% (17) were of the most disruptive three-part D2 turns that impinged upon the debate floor. However, of the four interventions made by women in these debates only one was a three-part intervention that gained a response from the D1 floor (one was a supportive intervention, one a correction of a reference, and one a response to being directly addressed by the MP giving the speech). This means that men were responsible for all but one (98 per cent) of the most disruptive type of intervention in the 1998–2001 sub-corpus of debates.[3]

Apart from the identifiable interruptions described above, there are many instances of 'barracking' (another word for 'heckling'), or comments in the form of short one or two-word utterances such as 'rubbish' (see Example 3.2, line 9). The functions of barracking can be seen as either an attempt to attack the substantive comments made by a speaking MP, or as a tactic to intimidate a speaker in order to make a speech less effective. This second function can consist of extremely personal comments. Although there were no examples of more personal attacks in the corpus of five debates, comments such as 'you nasty little squirt' and 'you pathetic wimp' were given as examples of barracking by an interviewee (Shaw 2002: Interview B). Anecdotally, 'sledging', or saying insults quietly to an MP to undermine them while they are speaking in the Chamber is common, both in the 1998–2001 data and in more recent times: 'It is sort of playground stuff so if they see any weakness, whether it is about your relationship, the way you look, something that has happened to you in the past, you'll hear it and it is little snide comments just designed to get in under the radar an put someone off their game – it's not nice' (Sarah Champion MP, Inside the Commons 2015). As barracking is almost always a type of illegal intervention this data would suggest that women MPs are less likely to barrack than men MPs. Interview data also indicates that this may be the case: 'If I was saying anything it would be "answer the question", so women don't really barrack and if they do it certainly isn't personal' (Shaw 2002: Interview A).

There is also some evidence to show that barracking is used *against* women in an explicitly sexist way. For example, one of the women MPs interviewed (Shaw 2002: Interview A) recounts an incident in which Dawn Primarolo (a Minister) was barracked by a group of MPs shouting at her to 'show us your leg'. The same Minister was also barracked when she answered a question by repeating the answer she had given to the last question. She did this to show the MP asking the question that he could not deliberately misinterpret a question in order to gain a supplementary question on another topic. In response to Primarolo's answer a Conservative MP shouted 'stupid woman' at her, thinking that she had misunderstood the question. On this occasion, the Speaker intervened and the MP who barracked was forced to withdraw his comment. More recently, in 2018, both John Bercow (Speaker of the House of Commons) and Jeremy Corbyn (Leader of the Opposition) have both been accused of using the phrase 'stupid woman' against senior women MPs (Cowburn 2018; Elgot and Walker 2018). Interview data suggests it is common for women to be appraised in terms of their intellectual capabilities in this way: 'Any young attractive woman in the House of Commons is kind of you know an air-head. Which bearing in mind what you have to go through to get into the House of Commons it's a bit you know, but that is the absolute standard' (Shaw 2002: Interview D). This negative stereotyping of women by men according to whether they are intelligent is extremely polarised:

There can be another definition which is super-clever. So you're either a Blair's babe meaning you're just sub-standard or you're a brainy babe (…) You are most likely to just be a Blair's babe but if you can punch your way out of that one you punch your way up to the brainy babes. There's nowhere in-between. (…) It is about women not being able to have the normal range of characteristics. Men can be super-clever, medium clever you know medium thick or thick whereas women have more stereotyped labels. (Shaw 2002: Interview D)

Examples of barracking involving this kind of sexist stereotyping are anecdotally common, and there are examples in the 60-hour corpus of data gathered for this study. An extension of the stereotype that women MPs are 'stupid' is that they are 'clones' and 'Stepford wives' who cannot think for themselves (Shaw 2002: Interview A). In a debate on Manufacturing and Industrial Relations a Conservative MP shouted at Margaret Beckett that she is 'like Dolly',[4] a cloned sheep. This type of sexist barracking is pertinent to the consideration of turn-taking because it may well affect women's success in maintaining a speaking turn. As mentioned above, barracking is a tactic that functions to intimidate a speaker by incorporating personal remarks to make another MP's speech less effective: shouting sexist comments at an MP is likely to have these effects. However, as Example 3.1 shows, barracking is not the only way in which women MPs can be intimidated. Jane Griffiths' question to the Prime Minister shows the hesitancy and confusion brought about by her error, and the laughter of MPs and the patronising remarks of the Speaker add to her inability to make the required intervention. Non-verbal sexist gestures made against women, such as the 'melon weighing' breast gesture have also been reported by MPs (Shaw 2002: Interview A). All these tactics, like the 'hisses, boos, heckles and slow hand claps' made by boys in classroom interaction (Baxter 1999: 219), show that men MPs not only make these illegal interventions more than women, but that women are subject to more obstacles than men in maintaining a speaking turn. This sexist treatment is discussed in detail in Section 5.3 and is a contemporary feature of parliamentary interaction. Cornelia Ilie (2018) finds that women in the HoC are objectified, patronised and stigmatised by a range of such comments. This is also a recurrent finding across parliaments where women speakers have been found to be subjected to more rowdiness and jeers than their male colleagues in different parliamentary contexts. For example, Maria Stopfner (2018) analyses examples of 'heckling' in

Canadian, French and Austrian parliaments and identifies this practice as one that is used to silence women politicians.

The Speaker or moderator is another important role that is integral to the regulatory mechanism of the debate floor. The Speaker's interventions are an important component of the turn-taking system and an analysis of their frequency shows not only which MPs experience interventions and under what circumstances, but also allows a classification of rule-breaking according to which rule-breaking activities are commonly tolerated by the Speaker, and which are not. A detailed analysis of the sub-corpus of the 1998–2001 debates shows that of the 13 interventions made by the Speaker(s) during the five debates, only two were to instruct an interrupting MP not to speak out of turn. This means that most illegal interventions (in this corpus 39 out of 41 illegal turns) are not censured by the speaker and therefore this type of turn is to some degree an accepted part of the debate proceedings. The tolerance of the Speakers towards rule-breaking may partially be explained by the fact that they do not hear everything that is said in the debating chamber and therefore do not always hear illegal interventions. Another reason may be that the Speakers can use gestures and gaze signals to warn MPs that they have noticed their illegal behaviour, and therefore, do not always need to stop the debate in order to reprimand an MP and to curtail 'out of order' speaking turns. However, these considerations do not account for the degree to which the breaking of rules concerning illegal interventions are tolerated by the Speaker. The finding that illegal interventions are largely tolerated by the Speaker is significant because it shows how informal practices, in being permitted, become part of the accepted norms of the institution. Further, if illegal interventions advantage MPs in debates, and men MPs make more illegal interventions than women MPs, then the behaviour of the Speaker can effectively disadvantage women MPs in debates.

Although the amount of data used for this analysis is relatively small, it allows for the identification of possible gendered interactional practices. A further corpus of House of Commons data was analysed in 2009–11 for comparative purposes with the 'new' devolved parliamentary institutions of the UK, discussed in Chapter 4. This comparative data also confirmed the finding that women participated in the legal debate floor in the House of Commons in proportion to their numbers overall. However, like the 1998–2001 corpus, the analysis of the 2010 data found that men were responsible for 97 per cent of all illegal D2 turns. These findings are also borne out by previous research by Carole Edelsky and Karen Adams (1990) and Lyn Kathlene (1994, 1995) who found that men politicians violated turn-taking rules more than women politicians in US televised debates and US state committee hearings, respectively. Similarly, Dionne's (2010) quantitative analysis of HoC committee participation found that women were significantly less likely to interrupt than men, and conversely, men committee members were significantly more likely to interrupt than female members. She also notes that 'No woman, not even the Chair, ever tried to interrupt another woman (…) no woman aside from the Chair interrupted successfully' (Dionne 2010: 63). However, in contrast to Kathlene's (1994) finding that women spoke less and took fewer turns than men, Dionne found that gender did not seem to play a role in chairs' or members' speaking behaviour (number of turns, length of turns and words spoken) apart from in relation to interruptions.

As shown in the examples in this chapter, illegal interventions serve to interfere with the turn-taking mechanism of the D1, and can be used to criticise or challenge a CMP in a debate. Given that 'power' in this context can be defined as control over the limited resource of the floor, this means that men MPs have more control over the interaction – through illegal interventions – and therefore more power in debates than women MPs. In interviews, women MPs identified illegal interventions and cheering as a male activity in which they did not engage, which further suggests that norms of interaction are different for men and women MPs. This indicates that while men and women belong to the same CoP, they are on different terms of participation according to gender. The norms of men MPs' discourse styles are often pervasive in debates – as their gendered behaviour of contributing illegally to debates is often not censured by the Speaker and therefore has to some degree been accepted as a norm of interaction. The finding that masculine discourse styles are treated as the interactional norm in debates relates to the fact that traditionally women have not been represented in this institution and continue to be under-represented. The fact that this pattern is found in the 1998–2001 corpus, and the 2009–11 data, and continues to be observed in analyses today (see further discussions in Chapters 6 and 8 and Ilie 2018) suggests that these norms are possibly resistant to change over time.

3.3   Adversarial Language

3.3.1   Introduction

The HoC is commonly referred to as an adversarial forum and Prime Minister's Question Time (PMQs) is seen as the most extreme display of adversarial politics at Westminster. For this reason, these speech events provide the most fruitful data when trying to establish the linguistic features that contribute to an adversarial style in House of Commons discourse. Once identified in PMQs, adversarial features can be recorded in other speech events, such as Departmental Question Times (DQs). This allows both an assessment of the extent of adversarial speech in the event itself, and also of the individual contributions of MPs.

The reasons for the adversarial nature of PMQs rest on their ritualized role (Lovenduski 2014b) as 'a high-profile party-competition and a well-known accountability instrument' (2014b: 134) where the opposition parties are afforded the opportunity of holding the Prime Minister (PM) to account with a degree of spontaneity not possible in other parliamentary speech events. Lovenduski's insightful description of PMQs as a highly symbolic, ritualised display that is 'emblematic of the Westminster model of politics' views parliamentary ritual as behaviour that is carried out normatively without MPs themselves being aware of its relation to the symbolic and the traditional but instead regarding it straight-forwardly as 'the way things are done' (Lovenduski 2014b: 133). Other characteristics of PMQs include the fact that the media coverage of the event tends to focus on the most adversarial exchanges and this visibility extends to live streaming on the BBC website, live tweets, and headline-grabbing summaries of the main forays between the PM and the Leader of the Opposition (LO). Finally, it is one of the few speech events in which the chamber is full, and the audience of MPs without an official speaking role constantly 'heckle, harrumph or yah boo and emit "hear hears" during and after each exchange' (Lovenduski 2014b: 138), often completely drowning out the speakers, as evidenced in the detailed transcription of Jane Griffiths' question earlier in Example 3.1.

It is often assumed that adversarial norms are masculine, and that women are unlikely, or less likely than their male colleagues to engage in them:

The standard repertoires of adversarial politics are characteristic of behaviour that is more acceptable from men than women. The declamatory, adversarial style of chamber debate favours rhetoric, speechifying, posturing and arcane practice in the House of Commons, rather than co-operation, consensus seeking and real discussion of alternatives. Political practices involving demagoguery, ruthlessness and aggression require qualities that have long been culturally accepted in men but not women. (Lovenduski 2014b: 147–8)

As discussed in Chapter 1 and more fully in Section 5.1, gendered stereotypes about 'competitive' masculine and 'cooperative' feminine speech styles are pervasive in attitudes towards the speech styles of politicians and concur with an overarching discourse of gender differentiation (more fully discussed in Cameron and Shaw (2016) and in Chapter 5). As a male Liberal Democrat MP stated in 2004:

Women…by nature are more consensorial. You know they're not…they don't like conflict…and you know the male role has been one of adversarialists. If you look at the House of Commons, unlike most other parliaments, it's still sort of sixteenth/seventeenth-century adversarials…we even have facilities to carry swords…everything in the House is about swords…everything tells you that this is male…this is aggressive. And I think…women cannot work like that…in their normal lives, so much to do with, if you like, raising a family and carrying out the job depends very much on developing different skills which men don't by and large have to develop, and certainly not male politicians'. (Dionne 2010: 86–7)

Women MPs also attest to a gendered, consensual style that is characterised by 'less aggression and more co-operation, teamwork, inclusiveness, consultation and willingness to listen' (Childs 2000: 68). Childs' analysis 'points to notions of acceptable and unacceptable, legitimate and illegitimate forms of language style appropriate to politics. In these oppositions, the former are associated with male language, modes of interaction and men MPs, and the latter with women's language, modes of interaction and women MPs' (2000: 69). It is unsurprising however, given the overarching nature of stereotypical beliefs about gendered speech styles, that interview data with politicians reinforces these dominant gender ideologies about the competitive/cooperative dichotomy relating to gendered male and female communicative speech styles. As discussed in Chapter 1, and in more detail in Chapter 5, there is no empirical evidence for monolithic gendered speech styles.

This section seeks to address the lack of empirical evidence for the claim that women MPs do not engage in adversarial exchanges by first identifying adversarial features in PMQs. Secondly, I systematically score 200 questions and responses from a corpus of Departmental Questions Times (DQs) and PMQs in the 1998–2001 House of Commons corpus in order to identify adversarial and non-adversarial exchanges. Finally, the frequency with which men and women MPs (of different parties and levels of seniority) perform adversarial questions and responses are assessed. As well as contributing to the growing body of research into male and female talk in public contexts, an analysis of adversarial linguistic practices in debates can contribute to the description of the HoC itself as a setting for speech. Although the HoC is frequently referred to as an adversarial forum, this section aims to identify with more precision the linguistic features that make exchanges adversarial. The main questions explored in this section therefore are: What are the adversarial linguistic features in the questions and responses of MPs, and is there variation in the use of adversarial features by men and women MPs of different political parties and seniority?

3.3.2   Identifying Adversarial Features in PMQs

Research in politics has sought to give accounts of parliamentary questions (Franklin and Norton 1993) and uses PMQs as a measure of legislator's activities and interests (Martin 2014). Analyses of the topics raised in PMQs are also used as a measurement of the substantive representation of MPs with visible minority status (Saalfeld 2011), and in relation to gender (Bird 2005). Lovenduski's (2014b) investigation into the attitudes of MPs and members of the public to PMQs finds that women MPs were significantly more negative than men about PMQs, that deliberate sexism is common, and that expectations of parliamentary performance disadvantage women MPs because they feel excluded by the prevalent masculine norms. Somewhat surprisingly, women members of the public who were surveyed showed more positive attitudes towards PMQs than men, which leads to the conclusion that 'the attitudes of the audience do not coincide with those of the performers' (Lovenduski 2014b: 157). This finding is partly explained by the expectations of the public being in accord with the public masculinity displayed in PMQs, which 'is a barrier to women MPs and would-be politicians because it underpins an expectation that politics is an activity best performed by men' (ibid: 158). Most significantly for this investigation, Lovenduski concludes that PMQs is a ritual that: 'sustains the traditional masculine culture by continually repeating performances of adversarial confrontation' (ibid: 158).

Previous linguistic research into the adversarial nature of parliamentary questions typically focus on PMQs as an unusual speech event in which im/politeness is central to the interaction (Ayala 2001; Bull 2013; Bull and Wells 2012; Culpeper 1996; Harris 2001; Murphy 2014) and is 'not only sanctioned but rewarded' (Harris 2001). The studies point to the discourse of PMQs being composed of face-threatening acts which can be analysed on both propositional and interactive levels (Harris 2001: 465). Harris finds that while many utterances in PMQs 'can only be interpreted as intentionally and negatively confrontational (…) such utterances do not contravene Members' expectation of politeness strategies' (2001: 468). In this way, the Leader of the Opposition (LO) is expected to engage in threatening the PM's positive face and: 'It is these expectations which enable Members of the House as a community of practice to interpret intentional face-threatening acts as an important component of an adversarial and confrontational political process in such a way that they do not lead to either a breakdown in communication or in interpersonal relationships, as would inevitably be the place in ordinary conversation' (Harris 2001: 469). The studies therefore point to the unique characteristics of PMQs and this distinctiveness also lies with the form of exchanges between the Leader of the Opposition (LO) and the PM where the LO has up to six supplementary questions after the original questioning turn. This gives opportunities within exchanges for Sinclair and Coulthards' (1975) concept of 'follow-ups' (Bull 2013; Fetzer et al. 2015; Ilie 2015) and different forms of sustained argumentation, including turning the criticism back on the critic or 'turnabout' (Mohammed 2018). PMQs has also been found to consist of particular formulaic responses showing that ritualistic 'templates' of interaction tend towards being self-referential (Sealey and Bates 2016).

Linguistic investigations into PMQs also provide some evidence to show that the adversarial characteristics of the event remain over time, although there is some variation between certain PM and LO pairings. Bates et al.

(2014) use a Hansard corpus to investigate 30 years of PMQs (from Thatcher to Cameron) and find that PMQs becomes more 'rowdy' over time with more interruptions and interventions by the Speaker. They also find an increased tendency towards PMQs being dominated by LOs, and towards more 'unanswerable' questions being posed. Waddle et al. (2019) also agree with this analysis, finding that Cameron used more personal attacks than previous PMs, and also that PMs tend to use more personal attacks over the course of their premiership. However, with the arrival of Jeremy Corbyn as LO in 2015 this trend was found to reverse. The Corbyn–Cameron exchanges showed the lowest proportion of personal attacks, and not just on the part of the LO himself, who had pledged to take a new, consensual approach to PMQs (see Fetzer and Weizman 2018; Bull and Waddle 2019; and Section 6.2.2). There was a threefold reduction in attacks by Cameron towards Corbyn compared with those he directed at Ed Miliband when he was LO (Waddle et al. 2019: 80). This is discussed further in the analysis of Theresa May and Jeremy Corbyn PMQs in Chapter 6.

In the corpus of HoC speech events taken from the 1997 to 2001 parliamentary term, the PMQ exchanges between William Hague, LO, and Tony Blair, PM, exemplify a number of extremely adversarial characteristics. The spontaneity of these longer exchanges present particular problems for the PM, as Blair himself states in his memoir: 'For those thirty minutes … the prime minister is essentially on the "at risk" register. It is the unpredictability that is so frightening' (Blair 2011). The analyses of these exchanges between Hague and Blair concur with previous descriptions of PMQs (Wilson 1990; Harris 2001; Bull and Wells 2012) which identify the predominant form of questioning turns as having a polar interrogative (yes/no) frame and a series of propositions, pre-suppositions and assertions which seek to gain information or action. These assertions and presuppositions present problems for the PM, as (Wilson 1990) observes: 'If politicians attend to the propositions contained in these pre/post statements they may be seen as trying to avoid the question. On the other hand, if politicians fail to attend to such propositions they may be seen as accepting certain controversial claims as matters of fact' (Wilson 1990: 137). To identify adversarial features of PMQs, the PMQ sessions in the 1997–2001 data corpus were transcribed and the questioning turns were identified as a feature likely to contribute to the adversarial style of the speech event. An example of this is given in Example 3.3 below.

Example 3.3 Exchange between William Hague and Tony Blair (PMQs 03/03/99, Transcript)

Key: WH = William Hague PM = Prime Minister MPs = noises made

1	WH	(…) will the Prime Minister confirm that people <u>waiting</u> in this way of
2		whom there are many <u>more</u> in the last two years (.) do not ap<u>pear</u> on the
3		waiting list figures that were published yester<u>day</u> (1)

4	PM	Madam Speaker the <u>waiting</u> list figures (.) are published and calculated
5		in pre<u>cise</u>ly the same way under <u>this</u> government as under the <u>previous</u>
6		government (.) and we are <u>part</u>ly as a result of money over and above what the
7	MPS	[hear hear]
8		Conservatives <u>promi</u>sed for the National Health Service (.) bringing waiting
9		lists <u>down</u> (1)
10	MPs	[hear hear]
11	WH	Madam Speaker they <u>are</u> calculated in the same way and they show that waiting
12		lists are <u>high</u>er under this government after two <u>years</u> (.) and they show that the
13		<u>real</u> scandal is the number of people waiting to be <u>on</u> waiting lists (.) [<u>like</u> Mr]
14	MPs	[hear hear]
15		Nelson (.) which is <u>double</u> what it was two years ago (.) and <u>isn't</u> the truth this
16		that there are now nearly <u>half</u> a <u>million</u> people <u>waiting</u> for hospital
17		appointments (.) as a <u>direct</u> re<u>sult</u> of managing the National Health Service for
18		the sake of ap<u>pear</u>ances instead of for the sake of <u>patients</u> (.) and <u>aren't</u> the
19	MPs	[hear hear]
20		government now just <u>spinning</u> the figures and <u>playing</u> with <u>politics</u> instead of
21		<u>serv</u>ing the <u>patients</u> (1)
22	MPs	[hear hear]
23	PM	<u>no</u> Madam Speaker (.) first of all I'm <u>grateful</u> for his confirmation that we
24		are in<u>deed</u> calculating the figures in pre<u>cise</u>ly the same way as the last
25		<u>government</u> (.) since his <u>shadow</u> health spokesman has been saying the
26	MPs	[laughter]
27		<u>opp</u>osite for month upon <u>month</u> (.) <u>sec</u>ondly we have <u>brought</u> down health
28		service waiting <u>lists</u> after <u>years</u> of rising lists (.) and <u>as</u> for the number of <u>out</u>-
29		patients (.) I can actually <u>give</u> him the latest <u>figures</u> (.) that during the <u>third</u>
30		quarter of nineteen eighty-eight nineteen ninety <u>eight</u> ninety <u>nine</u> (.) there
31		were sixty-eight thousand <u>more</u> treated than in the previous <u>quarter</u> (1)
32	MPs	[hear hear]
33	WH	well I'<u>ll</u> give him the figures <u>too</u> Madam Speaker (.) <u>four</u> hundred and sixty
34		eight <u>thous</u>and people (.) <u>waiting</u> for hospital appointments compared to two
35		hundred and forty-eight thousand only two years <u>ago</u> (.) they <u>calculate</u> the
36		<u>figures</u> in the same way but they have <u>moved</u> people who <u>would</u> have been on
37		waiting lists to <u>waiting</u> to be <u>on</u> the waiting list (.) and the chair the chairman of
38	MPs	[hear hear]
39		the BMA con<u>sult</u>ants committee has said it <u>himself</u> he says if <u>all</u> you are
40		doing (.) is <u>shortening</u> your waiting list for oper<u>ations</u> and waiting lists to see a
41		consultant are going <u>up</u> (.) then your <u>proper</u> waiting list is getting <u>longer</u> (.) so
42		shouldn't he <u>stop</u> spending a hundred and fifty million pounds dra<u>goon</u>ing
43		GPs into new bu<u>reauc</u>racies (.) and concentrate it on <u>this</u> in<u>stead</u> (.) and reduce
44	MPs	[hear hear]
45		the <u>real</u> waiting lists in our <u>health</u> service (2)
46	MPs	[hear hear]
47	PM	<u>no</u> Madam speaker because he is actually wrong on both <u>counts</u> (.) not merely
48		are we <u>treating</u> more out-patients than before (.) we are also <u>treating</u> several
49		<u>hund</u>red thousand more <u>patients</u> (.) so for both <u>in</u>-patient <u>and</u> out-patient lists
50		we are treating more <u>people</u> (.) <u>in</u> addition from the <u>first</u> of April (.) <u>this</u>
51		government is going to introduce <u>twenty-one</u> billion <u>pounds</u> extra spending in
52		the National Health Service (.) having sorted out the <u>mess</u> left behind us (.) by
53		the <u>Tories</u> (.) that twenty-one billion <u>pounds</u> (.) is op<u>posed</u> by <u>his</u> party (.)
54	MPs	[hear hear]
55		described as reckless and irre<u>spons</u>ible (.) and that is why this <u>country</u> will
56		trust <u>us</u> not <u>him</u> with the <u>health</u> service

Table 3.3 *Question forms used by Hague in PMQs (3 March 1999)*

1) Line 1–3: *Will the Prime Minister confirm that people waiting (...) do not appear in the figures.*
2) Line 15–21: *Isn't the truth this that there are half a million people waiting for hospital appointments as a direct result of managing the National Health Service for the sake of appearances instead of for the sake of patients.*
3) (In the same turn) *Aren't the government now just spinning the figures and playing with politics instead of serving the patients.*
4) Line 42–5: *Shouldn't he stop spending a hundred and fifty million pounds dragooning GPs into new bureaucracies (...) and reduce the real waiting lists in our health service.*

The forms used in the four questions from Example 3.3 are:
(1) Interrogative request (with *will*) and an embedded clause which is a completed proposition.
(2), (3) and (4): Declarative with a negative interrogative frame.

The types of question used in this extract are features of an adversarial exchange, as are the direct refutations that are given as responses. Some types of question are more constraining than others in terms of how easy it is to respond to them or in other words whether they are conducive to a particular response (Harris 1984; Wilson 1990). Table 3.3, shows the question forms that are used by Hague.

The questions in Table 3.3 require a yes/no response and are therefore conducive. Additionally, contracted negatives in the initial position of a yes/no question (in questions 2, 3, 4) are 'used to suggest that the proposition under question is one which is taken to be true (taken for granted)' (Wilson 1990: 141). Wilson suggests that these discourse items can account for the 'leading', nature of questions (1990: 141). Evidence for this is also present in Example 3.3 above as four out of six questions contained negative contractions as part of a negative interrogative frame with declaratives, a structure that Harris (1984) also found to be highly conducive. Another particle evident in question 1 in Table 3.3 is the modal verb 'will'. This was a feature used frequently in Wilson's (1990: 146) corpus of questions from PMQ sessions. He claims the use of 'will' makes a refusal difficult for the respondent because *will* is more polite than other modal verbs such as 'can'.

In this way both the linguistic items used within questions and the form of the questions themselves contribute to an adversarial style in PMQs. MPs cannot ignore very negative assertions made about them or their party, but they must also reply to the final question in a questioning turn. Table 3.4 summarises how Blair responds to one of Hague's turns.

The PM responds to the yes/no question first but gives a 'no' response to a question that is conducive to answering 'yes'. He continues the turn by

Table 3.4 *The assertions, question and responses to one of Hague's turns (Example 3.3 lines 11–31)*

Hague: Assertion 1 – there is no change to the way figures are calculated.
    Assertion 2 – waiting lists are higher under this government.
    Assertion 3 – people are waiting to be on waiting lists.
    Assertion 4 – half a million people are waiting because of poor management.
    Question – Aren't the government spinning the figures instead of serving the patients.

Blair: *No Madam Speaker.* Responds to the final question.
    Responds to assertion 1 – agrees with Hague that there is no change.
    Responds to assertion 2 – waiting lists are lower.
    Responds to assertion 4 – quotes latest out-patient figures to show they are low.

---

responding to three of Hague's assertions, separating the points from each other by explicitly calling the first two 'first' and 'second'. It is noticeable that the PM does not respond to Hague's third assertion (that people are waiting to get onto the waiting lists), and Hague picks up on this and targets the subject a second time in his next turn (Example 3.3, line 37). Blair's initial 'no' response is a very direct, unmitigated response to the question which conforms to none of the politeness or face-saving conventions that would be appropriate in less adversarial contexts. This strategy has the effect of strongly negating the proposition in Hague's question. Blair uses this strategy in three of the six questions in the two transcripts and in each case, there is no hesitation or mitigation of the negative response.

In this way, both Hague and Blair use what can be described as adversarial linguistic features in their questions and responses, respectively. Hague uses polar interrogatives and other conducive forms which have limited options for a response. This puts maximum interactional pressure on Blair to grant assent to the presuppositions and assertions with which Hague prefaces his question, whilst negotiating the yes/no response to the question itself and attempting to introduce the topics that show the government in a favourable light. Blair's direct unmitigated responses (expressed indirectly through the Speaker) that do not respect the face needs of his opponent while directly refuting Hague's claims. However, while the form of questions in PMQ sessions reflects the adversarial nature of the speech event, the form does not determine whether a contribution is adversarial. The questions are constructed in predictable, formulaic, ritualised patterns that can be used for confrontational or supportive questions alike. In this way a conducive question form using 'will' as in 'Will my Right Honourable friend take this opportunity to join me in congratulating the workforce?' can be supportive of the Prime Minister or Minister giving the response. For each of the 200 questions in the PMQ and DQ sessions the

Table 3.5 *Table showing the number of questions asked by men and women MPs showing their parliamentary status and political party in a corpus of PMQs and DQ sessions 1998–2001*

Men/women	Men					Women				
Party	Status					Status				
	Low	Mid	High	Total	%	Low	Mid	High	Total	%
Labour	23	33	2	58	29	13	16	1	30	15
Conservative	28	27	22	77	39	1	4	1	6	3
LibDem	0	0	20	20	10	0	0	0	0	0
other	4	1	4	9	4	0	0	0	0	0
Total	55	61	48	164		14	20	2	36	
% of all Qs	28	30	24		82	7	10	1		18

form of the question was noted, and it was found that 160 of the questions (80 per cent) took a conducive form and 40 (20 per cent) a non-conducive form. This concurs with previous findings that the predominant form of PMQs are yes/no questions (Bull and Wells 2012; Fenton-Smith 2008; Harris 2001; Wilson 1990). This means that conducive forms are used for both adversarial and non-adversarial questions (as half the questions were adversarial and half non-adversarial see Table 3.7 and Figure 3.2) and although they contribute to the adversarial nature of question times, the form of the question itself is not a marker of an adversarial question.

The number of questions asked by men and women MPs in PMQ and DQ sessions overall is a marker of the extent to which both groups of MPs participate in the most adversarial speech event in the HoC. Table 3.5 above shows the number of questions in this small data corpus asked in PMQ and DQ sessions by men and women MPs according to their parliamentary status and political party. The parliamentary status of MPs was divided into low status MPs who were backbenchers with no other parliamentary responsibilities; mid status MPs who had some particular responsibilities (for example a select committee member, or a parliamentary secretary to a Minister); and high status MPs who were party leaders, Ministers, Shadow Ministers or opposition spokespersons.

Table 3.5 shows that 82% (164) of questions in the eleven DQT and PMQT sessions were asked by men MPs and 18% (36) of questions were asked by women MPs. In this sample the number of questions asked is exactly in proportion to the representation of men and women MPs in parliament (82 per cent and 18 per cent respectively).

In order to establish how many of these questions were adversarial and having discounted the form of the question as a characteristic that determines the adversarial nature of a question, the detailed examination of the PMQ sessions identified a predominance of the use of contrasts in the classical rhetorical schema of 'antithesis' which occur both between and within Blair's and Hague's speeches. Antithesis can be linked to a combative political style where 'two contrasting positions are juxtaposed: typically, one position is represented as legitimate while the other is illegitimate' (Charteris-Black 2014: 44). As Adams (1999) observation of televised US political debates, the two speakers construct their opposition to one another by alternating between 'pro' and 'con' attitudes towards a particular topic, which have also been described as 'unbridgeable dichotomies' (Martin 2014: 76). This is evident in Example 3.3 above where the 'up' and 'down' of waiting list numbers is the central claim of each speaker respectively, while another example from a later exchange in the same PMQ session was the 'up' and 'down' of tax rates. The antonyms that orientate the listener towards these contrasts often contain particular word stress. Hague stresses that the waiting list are high on the words 'more' (line 2), 'higher' (line 12), 'double' (line 15), 'up' (line 41), 'longer' (line 41). The PM stresses that they are low on the words 'down' (line 9) and 'more' (line 31). This is one of the standard 'models of argument' that Cockcroft et al. (2014: 66) identify as the 'oppositional model' which functions on the basis of contrasts and has many subvarieties, such as 'contraries' (e.g. good/bad); contradictions (e.g. good/not good); privatives (e.g. blind/sighted) and relatives (e.g. parent/child). For example, in Example 3.3 (lines 17–21), Hague contrasts the government's management of the NHS as being 'for the sake of appearances instead of for the sake of patients' and 'playing with politics instead of serving the patients'.

There are a number of examples in the PMQ sample of these types of contrasts including contrasts between what the government promised to do and what they are actually doing (PMQs 03/09/99), and many contrasts between what 'this government' is doing and what the 'Tory' or 'previous' government did. Typically, a speaking turn ends with a contrast of this kind, for example the PM's final turn in Example 3.3 ends 'that is why this country will trust us and not him with the health service' (lines 55–56); and another final turn ends 'it is this side that is developing (…) the new deal delivering jobs where the Tories delivered despair' (PMQs 03/09/99). Similarly, in the same session, Hague's final turn ends 'before we debate next week's budget isn't it time he started to tell the truth about the last one'. These contrasts are strengthened by the use of pronouns to establish group identities and allegiances in order to emphasise the differences between 'us' and 'them', a category identified by van Dijk (2008) as being particularly relevant to the critical analysis of parliamentary debates. For example, the PM says 'they think it doesn't matter that these families are getting more money' contrasting what 'they' (the opposition) think with what 'we' (the government) think (PMQs 03/03/99).

Another set of features that characterise these exchanges as adversarial is the way in which the speakers describe their opponents and the personal attacks or ad hominem arguments they use to undermine each other. Walton (2009) categorises different types of ad hominem arguments which, regardless of the logical fallacy inherent within them, he claims have a place in political discourse alongside rational deliberation, according to Aristotle's notion of 'ethos'. Ethotic arguments rest on the idea that the best person to give advice on how to proceed in rational deliberation is a 'practically wise person of good character' (Walton 2009: 197). This means that ad hominem arguments pointing out different types of ethotic flaws have an important role to play in political discourse. Politicians must display an ethos that is not elusive otherwise 'there appears to be no consistent set of values she or he stands for a long-term basis' (Walton 2009: 198), but once this ethos is established the politician becomes open to attack. Christopher Reid (2014: 52) analyses the personal accounts of the ways in which Tony Blair (2011) and his advisor Alasdair Campbell (2011) attempted to counter Hague's supremacy in PMQs, showing that their preoccupation lay with providing a 'plausible critique of his character'. Reid cites the rhetorical technique of 'paradistole' to 'describe a trait of character in either a positive or negative sense: courage could be renamed negatively as rashness or rashness could be renamed positively as courage' (Reid 2014: 52).

Similarly, Margaret Thatcher's neutral trait of being 'determined' could be described eulogistically as 'resolute' and dystologistically as 'intransigent'. Reid notes that once Campbell and Blair had identified that Hague 'was a debater and not a leader' (Campbell 2011: 235, cited in Reid 2014: 53) and that this could be used to sum up his leadership as someone who had 'good jokes, lousy judgement', then Blair was able to constrain Hague's performances 'since he could not be seen to occupy the rhetorical space in which his adversaries were trying to trap him' (Reid 2014: 54). Reid describes other ways in which ad hominem arguments have been used in PMQs, with David Cameron (PM) alluding to Ed Milliband's (LO) weakness as a leader and as a person without character. In reply, Milliband displayed Cameron's self-confidence as complacency and remoteness, his forthrightness as belligerence (Reid 2014: 55). Features of ad hominem or personal attack arguments are therefore an important element of the adversarial nature of PMQs with personalization functioning to: highlight cognitive differences; equivocate (avoiding an answer by attacking an opponent) and to attempt 'to disarm or deconstruct their opponent via a concentrated attack on aspects of their character' (Waddle et al. 2019: 80).

The two most common forms of ad hominem argument in PMQs are what Walton (2009) classifies as different types of 'direct ethotic argument', one from moral accountability and the other from veracity. Morally accountable arguments can be seen in Example 3.3 above when Blair describes the Conservative government as 'reckless and irresponsible' (line 55). Hague describes 'the real scandal' (line 13) of waiting lists and later in the same PMQ session says Blair 'failed to answer' a question and says that the government have raised taxes 'by stealth' implying morally unacceptable forms of deceit. Claims from veracity are also common. Hague describes Blair as 'spinning the figures' (line 20) which implies some form of deceit in relation to the 'real' figures. Speakers often claim 'the truth' of their positions and in doing so imply the falsity of their opponent's positions, as in Example 3.3, line 15, Hague claims 'isn't the truth this …'. Other claims to veracity on the same PMQ session (03/03/99) include Hague referring to 'the actual truth of what the CBI say', and asking 'who is telling the truth him or the CBI?' One of the rules of the HoC is that MPs are not allowed to say that other MPs are lying, but this is one of the most common implications made about opponents. In the PMQ session (03/03/99) Hague says that the PM 'told the House business tax had come down and it is an indisputable fact that it has gone up by billions of pounds', and he says that it is time that Blair 'started to tell the truth'.

For the purposes of describing the features of adversarial language, in addition to these two direct ethotic arguments from moral accountability and veracity, it was noted that there are often generic personal attacks that do not necessarily fall into either of these categories such as one speaker saying the other's claim is 'complete and utter rubbish' (PMQs 03/03/99). These types of generic attacks that cannot be straightforwardly attributed to morality or truthfulness were therefore viewed as a third feature of the adversarial nature of the personal attack argument particularly common in PMQs.[5] In addition to this, the final adversarial feature noted in the PMQ exchanges is the rhetorical strategy of hyperbole where opponents or their actions are described in a deliberately aggravated, exaggerated way. This is a feature that 'dramatically raises the stakes in political debates' (Martin 2014: 81). In Example 3.3, Hague says that Blair should stop 'dragooning GPs into new bureaucracies' (lines 42–3), and Blair refers to 'the mess' (line 52) left behind by the Conservative government. Later in the same PMQ session Blair says that 'the Tories delivered despair' (PMQs 03/03/99).

Categories of adversarial language were therefore identified inductively by close examination of the PMQs data in the corpus. This method of determining categories is necessarily flawed and instrumental in arriving at an applicable model of adversarial features that can be used across different speech events to establish the adversarial nature of exchanges. One problem is that the categories are not mutually exclusive and in some cases an utterance belongs to more than one category (for example, an utterance can use contrasts and hyperbole and make an argument from veracity at the same time). In other cases, the classification of, for example, a morally accountable action relies on contextual information which may have a range of possible interpretations. In cases where the categories overlapped, each adversarial characteristic was counted separately. The categorisation was carried out as consistently as possible, accounting for the context of the utterance to interpret the meaning to ensure that within this corpus of data, utterances were classified consistently.

To identify whether the questions asked by MPs in this data set were adversarial or not, the use of the adversarial features described here were noted for each question and response. Seven adversarial categories were used, these were: opposing stances between MPs (such as the 'up and down' or 'pro and con' stances); positive and negative contrasts (typically between the actions of the speaker's party and the opposing party); the use of personal pronouns to strengthen these contrasts (such as *we, they, them* and *us*). Secondly, hyperbolic, aggravated descriptions; generic *ad hominem* arguments or personal attacks, and direct ethotic *ad hominem* arguments from morality and veracity. The presence or absence of these features allowed a question or response to be classified as adversarial or non-adversarial. An example of the way in which I recorded the data is shown in Table 3.6.

As Table 3.6 shows, the men Conservative MP uses three different types of adversarial features in his question. One '+' in the grid represents one or two instances of the particular feature, a second '+' was given if there were more than two instances of a feature. If a question contained one or more of the features in any of the seven different categories it was counted as being adversarial. This method of accounting for adversarial features also meant that it was possible to give each question and response an adversarial score out of fourteen (the maximum number of adversarial points possible).

Out of the 200 questions in the corpus of PMQ and DQ sessions, 101 were adversarial (containing one or more of the seven adversarial features described above) and 99 non-adversarial (containing none of the seven adversarial features). Because this particular sample is very balanced, the numbers in each category in Table 3.7 also represent approximate percentages of the total number of adversarial questions asked. The figures show that 92 adversarial questions were asked by men and 9 by women. This means that only one adversarial question out of every eleven was asked by a woman MP and 10 out of eleven by men which is disproportionate to the one fifth of seats occupied by women and four fifths occupied by men. Most of the adversarial questions (56) were asked by Conservative MPs, 32 by Labour MPs and 12 by Liberal Democrat MPs. Out of the adversarial Conservative questions only 2 were asked by women MPs (although they made up 8 per cent of the party), whereas women Labour MPs asked 7 of the Labour adversarial questions which is just under the one to four ratio of women to men in the Labour party as a whole. However, this still means that out of the 30 questions asked by women Labour MPs only seven (23 per cent)

Table 3.6 *The way in which adversarial features were classified*

MP	Question function	Question form	Contrasts			Hyperbole	Description		
							Generic	Direct ethotic	
			p/c	+/−	pp	Aggravated	Personal	Morals	Veracity
Swayne Con. male *S.C. Member*	Criticises government	*will the PM take time out of his…day to…*				++	+	+	+
PM response	Defends policies/attacks *Con.*			+	+		+		

Table 3.7 *Table showing the number of adversarial questions asked by men and women MPs according to their political party and status*

Men/women	Men				Women			
Party	Status				Status			
	Low	Mid	High	Total (%)	Low	Mid	High	Total (%)
Labour	9	15	1	25	3	3	1	7
Conservative	18	18	18	54	0	1	1	2
LibDem	0	0	12	12	0	0	0	0
Other	1	0	0	1	0	0	0	0
Total (%)	28	33	31	92	3	4	2	9

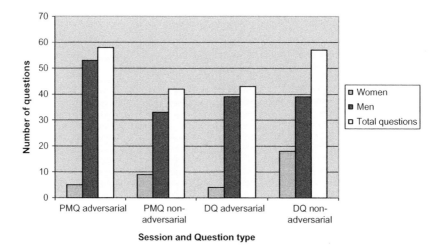

Figure 3.2 Graph showing the number of adversarial and non-adversarial questions asked by men and women MPs in PMQT and DQT sessions.

were adversarial whereas out of the 58 questions asked by Labour men, 25 (43 per cent) were adversarial. This is a substantial difference which cannot be accounted for simply by differences in status groups between men and women Labour MPs.

The number of adversarial and non-adversarial questions asked by MPs differed in PMQs and DQT sessions. Figure 3.2 shows the numbers of adversarial and non-adversarial questions asked by male and female MPs in the different sessions. It shows that out of the 200 questions asked in PMQs and

DQ sessions, PMQs contained more adversarial questions (58) and fewer non-adversarial questions (42), whilst the DQs contained more non-adversarial questions (57) and fewer adversarial questions (43). This shows that out of the two types of session and as predicted, PMQs were more adversarial than DQs. In PMQs, men MPs asked more adversarial questions (53) and fewer non-adversarial questions (33), whereas in DQs men MPs asked the same number of adversarial and non-adversarial questions (39). Out of the questions asked by women MPs in PMQs, 36 per cent were adversarial and 64 per cent non-adversarial (five adversarial and nine non-adversarial), and out of the questions women MPs asked in DQT sessions, only 18 per cent were adversarial and 82 per cent were non-adversarial (four adversarial and 18 non-adversarial questions).

As shown in Table 3.6, each question was given an adversarial score out of a possible maximum of fourteen points according to the use of different adversarial features. Out of the adversarial questions asked by men MPs, most of the questions contained one or two adversarial points. Conservative men asked the most adversarial questions with eight questions containing four or five adversarial points. A few exceptionally adversarial questions (of between seven and fourteen points) were all asked by William Hague in PMQs, so this suggests that this number of adversarial features are not typically used in adversarial questions but are contingent on Hague's style and probably his LO role.

The data also suggests that higher status MPs ask questions that are more adversarial than those asked by low status MPs. This is particularly evident in the questions asked by Conservative men, as those who were low status asked questions with between one and four points. Whereas the mid status conservative men asked questions with between one to six adversarial points. This is also evident in the questions asked by Labour men, with the low status MPs asking questions with one to three points and the mid status MPs asking questions with one to four points (although mid status MPs asked nearly twice as many questions as low status MPs). In the Liberal Democrat party adversarial questions were only asked by high status MPs and most of these were asked by the leader of the party. Out of the nine adversarial questions asked by women MPs, six of them were questions with only one adversarial point. One low status women Labour MP asked a question with four points, and one Conservative woman Minister asked a question with eight adversarial points. The number of questions asked is so small that it is difficult to interpret these results further than to say that there is evidence that at least two women MPs ask very adversarial questions.

The responses that the PM and Government Ministers give to questions in PMQs and DQs provide more evidence about the ways in which MPs use adversarial features. In PMQs, the PM gave 62 adversarial responses to 100

Table 3.8 *Table showing adversarial and non-adversarial responses by senior and junior MPs in DQ sessions*

Men/women	Men			Women		
Adversarial/ Non-adv.	Adversarial	Non-adversarial	Total (%)	Adversarial	Non-adversarial	Total (%)
Status: Senior	26	26	52	6	15	21
Status: Junior	6	15	21	1	5	6
Total	32	41	73	7	20	27

questions. As 58 adversarial questions were asked in PMQ sessions, the PM's responses included four responses that were not prompted by an adversarial question. These four responses were replying to Labour MPs who had asked questions that praised their own government, to which the PM agreed, and then went on to criticise Conservative policies. With the exception of these replies to supportive questions, the number of adversarial features in the PM's responses corresponded to the number of adversarial features in the questions. For example, in the exchanges between Hague and Blair, the PM responded to Hague's questions with an equal or greater number of adversarial features than were contained in the question. Additionally, the direct, unmitigated response of 'no' identified above only occurred in these highly adversarial exchanges between the PM and the LO.

The responses in DQs were much more variable than those in PMQs as different Ministers and junior Ministers are responsible for responding to questions within particular DQs. Table 3.8 shows the numbers of adversarial and non-adversarial responses by different men and women Ministers according to their positions as senior or junior Ministers. The table shows that 52 per cent of responses were given by senior Ministers who were men and 21 per cent by junior men. Senior women Ministers also gave 21 per cent of responses and junior women Ministers only 6 per cent of responses.

The same number of junior men and senior women Ministers' responses were adversarial (6), and only one out of the six responses given by junior women Ministers was adversarial. These figures show that senior men MPs give the most adversarial responses and junior women MPs the least adversarial responses as a proportion of the total number of responses that each group gave. This suggests that it is possible that variation in the number of adversarial responses does relate to the gender of the Ministers with men MPs giving a higher proportion of adversarial responses and women Ministers giving a higher proportion of non-adversarial responses. Additionally, the fact that there was a difference in the number of adversarial responses given by junior men and women Ministers compared to senior men and women Ministers (as a proportion of the total number of responses each group gave) suggests that the variation of adversarial features is related to the seniority of MPs.

The two main questions addressed in this section asked whether linguistic features that comprise an adversarial style can be identified in parliamentary Question Time Sessions; and whether the use of these features varies between men and women MPs from different parties and from different status groups. It was shown that there are identifiable linguistic features that make question time exchanges adversarial. These features include the use of contrasts within and between MPs' turns, and the way in which MPs describe their opponents, particularly using ad hominem arguments. The systematic analysis of 200 questions from PMQ and DQ sessions show that while men and women MPs asked the same number of questions as a proportion of the representation of these groups in the HoC, men asked more adversarial questions than women MPs. This finding was also evident in the responses given by Ministers in DQ sessions as women Ministers gave fewer adversarial responses than men. The use of adversarial features also varied according to the party membership and the status of MPs within the parliamentary hierarchy. Most of the adversarial questions were asked by Conservative MPs, reflecting their party's position as the main opposition to the government. Labour MPs asked fewer adversarial questions, yet they had different choices in terms of the function of their questions as many Labour MPs chose to ask questions that contained no adversarial features and that praised the government (their own party). Although these questions do not contain the adversarial characteristics identified above, these types of questions contribute to the 'deep structure or rhetorical situation of PMQs itself' (Reid 2014: 45) as they overtly support one party in relation to another. As the Labour party had the highest proportion of women MPs and it was Labour MPs, not Conservatives (with a low proportion of women MPs) who praised their party in this way, this may partially explain why women MPs asked fewer adversarial questions overall. This could be investigated further by examining the frequency of adversarial questions asked when the Labour party is in opposition as possibly the number of adversarial questions asked by women Labour MPs (or any party with proportionally higher numbers of women than the Conservative party) would increase with their oppositional role. However, this factor does not account for the lower number of adversarial responses given by women Ministers compared with their male counterparts because the results for women MPs' adversarial questions and women Ministers' adversarial responses are both lower than those for men, and this suggests that gender is a factor affecting MPs' use of adversarial features. All of these points are suggestive rather than indicative of findings, as the numbers used for this study were small, and only used as a guide for qualitative interpretations of the ethnographic enquiry.

The suggestion that most women MPs who asked questions did not adopt an adversarial linguistic style in question times bears out claims made by earlier language and gender researchers (such as Coates 1994; Holmes 1992, 1995; Tannen 1984), and from leadership studies (Eagly and Steffen 1986) that women avoid using a 'typically competitive, argumentative and verbally aggressive style' (Holmes 1992: 131). However, as mentioned in Chapter 1, women's discursive styles in public contexts can be viewed as a way of managing 'socially ascribed expectations that pull in opposite directions' (Walsh 2001: 274) when acting agentively or authoritatively in public contexts. In this way, Judith Baxter suggests that girls find it hard 'to speak effectively in public contexts because of the powerless ways they are positioned in the classroom (and the world) by the discourse of gender differentiation' (1999: 232). The expectation not only that women will speak consensually, avoiding adversarial language, but that women will 'civilise' traditionally male-dominated professions is an assumption contingent on the belief in gendered linguistic styles and can be viewed as one of the obstacles that women face when entering politics. As explained by Dahlerup (1988), women are caught between at least two conflicting expectations: firstly, they must prove that they are similar to and just as capable as men politicians, and secondly, they must prove it makes a difference when women are elected (1988: 279). The 'civilising difference' expectation and the possible consequences for women of behaving in counter-stereotypic, adversarial ways are explored in Section 5.1 and in the case studies in Chapters 6 and 7.

Apart from these social expectations that are thought to constrain women's behaviour, the data also points away from the generalisation that 'women do not use adversarial language'. This is because *some* women use adversarial language in their questions and responses and one Conservative women MP scored eight adversarial points for a single question, which was the highest adversarial score of any question other than in the Hague/Blair PMQ exchanges. This suggests that there are differences between women MPs' use of adversarial features. Margaret Thatcher and Theresa May's performances at PMQs, and those of Harriet Harman, Angela Eagle and Emily Thornberry (standing in for different Prime Ministers and LOs on different occasions) attest to the fact that women proficiently fulfil this role, and do so using the extreme adversarial norms of the event. Harriet Harman states that when she took part in PMQs, she acted confrontationally in accordance with the expectations of her party, saying 'I had to do it that way' (Lovenduski 2014b: 151). Theresa May's adversarial language in PMQs is explored in more detail in Chapter 6 and the extremely adversarial repertoire of Hillary Clinton and Julia Gillard are discussed in Chapter 7. These studies of women leaders, along with the analysis conducted here suggest there is no *straightforward* relationship between gender and adversarial language: there are no clear-cut differences with respect to gender and there is variation in the use of adversarial features within the groups of men and women MPs. Some men use non-adversarial language and some women use extremely adversarial language. The complexity of the use of adversarial language may also be impacted by other intervening factors, such as seniority and party affiliation, with an MPs' position as a senior or junior politician and as a member of the governing or opposition party being an important factor in whether they perform confrontational rhetoric as part of their parliamentary role.

3.4 Changing the 'Key' of Debates

3.4.1 Introduction

One of the most striking characteristics of the House of Commons is that although it is an extremely formal, regulated forum in which serious debate takes place, there are many examples of humorous exchanges, banter and ironic gestures. These non-serious exchanges can be viewed as having particular functions, and as a departure from the official norms of serious debate in which a humorous or ironic 'key' (Hymes 1972a, 1974) replaces the usual gravitas of debate proceedings. The ability of MPs to manipulate and change the 'key' of a speech event from its serious norm to a marked humorous or ironic tone is likely to construct them as powerful participants in the debating chamber. This section focuses on the functions of humour and the extent to which it is gendered in this CoP: do men and women engage in humorous exchanges, and are they equally positioned as targets of humour? Additionally, I identify the practice of 'filibustering' as a fundamentally ironic rule-breaking practice that exploits the serious 'key' of debates in order to gain political advantage. The full 60-hour data corpus of video recordings from the 1998 to 2001 corpus is used for this analysis, which comprises not only the debates and Question Times used in the previous sections, but all the different types of speech event which occur in the debating chamber, including Private Member's Debates, Private Notice Questions, Statements by Government Ministers and Opposition Debates.[6]

3.4.2   Humour in House of Commons Debates

Within the 60-hour 1998–2001 data corpus described above there are many instances of humorous exchanges. The frequency with which humorous talk occurs is in some ways surprising, as it has been suggested that whilst humour is pervasive in casual conversation, it is typically less frequent in formal contexts (Adelswärd 1989; Mulkay 1988; Holmes and Marra 2002). This suggests that humour has particular functions within the context of HoC debating chamber. Additionally, humorous talk in this sample of parliamentary discourse is mostly produced by men rather than women MPs. This section aims to identify humorous talk, thereby adding to the ethnographic description of the systems of shared understandings of the CoP. I also discuss the gendered nature of the construction of humour in the HoC, which I analyse in greater detail when considering homosocial bonding in Chapters 5 and 6.

Assuming laughter can be linked to humour, many of the instances of laughter in the HoC are produced within adversarial exchanges. For example, when Tony Blair attacks the LO, William Hague, in PMQs, it is common for members of his party to laugh and cheer at every point scored by Blair against his opponent. These personal attacks and political jibes are regarded as examples of 'humorous talk' for the purposes of this analysis, and this humour is seen as an integral part of the adversarial attack. The laughter of MPs in these exchanges is part of the verbal assault upon an opponent, rather than a spontaneous response to a humorous utterance. Example 3.4 shows that although Ian McCartney's comment about his own accent and Michael Fabricant's hair (on line 5) is clearly intended to be humorous, it does have an adversarial function as well. The humour is offered as a response to a serious question, so it serves to change the 'key' of the debate, evade the question and also to belittle the content of the question and the questioner. What is unusual about this type of humour (compared to the other types of adversarial personal attacks studied in the previous section) is that the topic (Fabricant's hair) is ridiculous, and that it is accompanied by a self-deprecating remark by Ian McCartney about his own accent.

Example 3.4 Trade and Industry Questions (1) (02/04/98, Transcript)

  MF = Michael Fabricant (Conservative), IM = Ian McCartney (Labour Minister)

1	MF:	what does the chairman of the low <u>pay</u> commission say about what the
2		minimum wage should be in Northern <u>Ire</u>land say (.) compared to
3		south east United <u>King</u>dom (1)
	MPs:	[hear hear]
4	IM:	I'll I'll deal with the Honourable Gentleman (.) if he doesn't mention
5		my <u>accent</u> I won't mention his <u>hair</u> (6)
	MPs:	[laughter]
6	1MP:	It's <u>not</u> his hair (4)
	MPs	[laughter]

7	IM:	m my Honourable (1) my Honourable friend er from a sedentary
8		position er (.) mentioned it is not his hair (.) I would not be so so cruel
9		as to suggest such a thing (2)
	MPs	[laughter]
10	IM:	er er c c could I say to the Honourable gentleman (.) he is trying hard
11		to to defend the indefensible (.) the truth of the matter is (.) that the
12		British people want the National Minimum Wage to meet the needs (turn
13		continues)

In this example, the self-deprecating reference may be a strategy which allows him to ridicule an opponent whilst making the humour seem more acceptable because he is also directing it at himself. It could also be that the use of humour in these examples actually indicates a degree of cross-party solidarity. The nature of McCartney's humour diffuses any real hostility and emphasises that both he and his opponent are on the same level. In this way, the use of humour may signal a shared membership (over-riding party political differences) in which adversarial norms are understood to be an accepted superficial enactment of the differences between MPs. This solidarity between men MPs may also be one of the ways in which the fraternal networks (Walsh 2001) and the culture of the 'gentleman's club' is perpetrated. Other possible functions of this type of exchange may be as a 'time buying' strategy where the humorous talk allows the responding MP time to construct a reply. McCartney also appears to be inviting the audience of other MPs to respond to his humour as he leaves time, for laughter at the end of his turn. Within this time the humour can also be developed by other MPs. This is shown clearly in Example 3.4 where an MP intervenes illegally to collaborate with the humour (line 6) which is then responded to by McCartney (line, 7–9).

Humorous talk may also function to keep the attention of the MPs in the chamber. Just as collective illegal interventions (such as cheering and shouting) serve to involve the audience in what is being said, so humour and the response of laughter serves to direct MPs' attention towards the content of speeches. An example of how humour arrests the attention of MPs occurs in the same Question Time session when McCartney returns once more to the humour originated in Example 3.4. This is shown in Example 3.5.

Example 3.5 Trade and Industry Questions (2) (02/04/98, Transcript)

IM = Ian McCartney (Labour Minister)

1	IM:	I put a question to the Honourable Gentleman (.) do you know of any
2		country in the world (.) who have introduced a National (.) a National
3		minimum wage for hairdressing that has stopped those in that country
4		from having a haircut (.) it is absolute nonsense to suggest that people
5	MPs	[laughter]

```
6              people (.) will lose will lose out by the introduction of a National
7              Minimum Wage (3)
8    MPs                      [laughter]
```

Here, some twenty minutes after the extract represented in Example 3.4, McCartney alludes to hairdressing and 'having a haircut' (line 4), but it is not until line 7 when he completes the turn that the other MPs in the chamber fully comprehend the allusion. The humour is not as overt as that in Example 3.4, but as it does serve to gain the attention of the MPs at a point in the day when there is a lot of talking and movement in the chamber because PMQs is about to start.

The fact that instances of humorous talk most commonly begin in the first utterances made by a new speaker also suggests that it may have a time-gaining or attention-gaining function. Humour can be seen as a way of allowing a new speaker to set up a speaking turn – both to organise what they are going to say and to make sure that the audience is listening. Example 3.6 shows an example of this 'setting up' function.

Example 3.6 Amendments to Crime and Disorder Bill (22/06/98, Transcript)

VC= Vernon Coaker (Labour backbencher)

```
1    VC:    can I first of all Mr Deputy Speaker apologise er to the House for the
2           fact that er that er I too missed er much of the er contributions from the
3           respective front benches (.) er and could I ask the Home Secretary
4           whether it is possible to have such an anti-social behaviour order on
5           some of our train companies (laughs) so so that we can actually arrive
6           on time and er when we plan to and when we plan to do (.) er on a on a
7           serious point can I just very much agree (turn continues).
```

Another common feature is that these types of interactions often stretch over several turns and are constructed between different MPs. Often a Question Time session will have an intertextual running topic which is exploited for humorous purposes, as with the joke about Fabricant's hair in Examples 3.4 and 3.5. Another example of this occurred in PMQs when the Prime Minister began by listing his engagements for the day which included an appointment to be interviewed on the 'World Wide Web'. This is alluded to throughout the session. Firstly, Dennis Skinner MP starts his question to the Prime Minister 'When I was surfing the internet today ...' which creates much laughter from MPs. The Prime Minister responds to this by saying that he had come across a website called 'meet your heroes live' which included Dennis Skinner 'Madonna, the Wombles and the Spice Girls' which is also responded to with laughter from MPs. Finally, Hague uses the running joke in an adversarial way when he says that he's not surprised the Prime Minister needs two weeks to prepare questions for the internet sessions as he certainly cannot answer them live. The intertextual and homosocial functions of these running jokes are discussed further in the contemporary analyses of HoC PMQs in Chapters 5, 6 and 8.

The functions of humour within debates therefore fall into two broad categories. First, humour has an organisational function whereby it helps to start an MP's speech, or it keeps the attention of the listeners. Secondly, the use of humour has a range of functions related to the nature of the humorous mode itself. According to Mulkay (1988) 'humorous' and 'serious' can be thought of as distinct modes where 'humorous' is the subordinate mode. Mary Crawford claims that:

The key to understanding how people accomplish serious interactional goals through this subordinate mode of discourse is the recognition that people can use humour to convey messages that they can then deny, or develop further, depending upon how the message is received by the hearer. Because it is indirect and allusive, the humour mode protects the joker from the consequences that his or her statement would have conveyed directly in the serious mode. (1995: 134)

This idea of the humour – allowing the speaker to 'get away with' more than is possible in the serious mode or 'speak "off the record"' (Eggins and Slade 1997: 156) – is particularly pertinent in debates where the whole speech event is a competitive arena. Opponents can score more points by using humour than they can by using the serious mode alone. Whilst humour can be used to score points against opponents it can also function to minimise the threat to the 'positive face' (Brown and Levinson 1987) of participants. This means that whilst using humour to score points against a participant, their membership within the social group is not necessarily threatened and may even be strengthened. In addition to minimising a participant's accountability for their actions, humour can also allow taboo topics to be included in conversations: 'When the taboo topic is framed as a joke it does not become part of the "real" discourse' (Crawford 1995: 134). There is evidence to suggest that humour is used in debates to allude to taboo topics. Sexual activity and sexist jokes are frequently referred to in HoC debates, as discussed further in Section 5.3.

Having outlined some of the possible functions of humorous talk in debates and Question Times it is now possible to consider the frequency of the use of humour by MPs as shown in this study's collected data. For some MPs humour forms part of their personal rhetorical style. Most of the occurrences of humorous talk by men MPs were by Dennis Skinner, Donald Dewar and Ian McCartney. These three MPs all had high status within the parliament as Dewar and McCartney were Ministers at the time the debates took place, and

Skinner was a long-standing MP with a reputation for speaking forcefully in parliament. It is clear that the use of humour varies greatly between speakers, and it may be that an MP's position within the parliamentary hierarchy in terms of rank and prestige is a factor in the frequency with which they produce humour. Although this is difficult to ascertain because Ministers and high-status MPs get more speaking turns in debates and Question Times than back-bench MPs, evidence from other settings also provides support for a link between humour and status. Ruth Laub Coser (1960) and Franca Pizzini (1991) undertook research into humorous talk in mixed-sex hierarchical settings (a psychiatric work group and a maternity ward). Coser found that humour followed the staff hierarchy of rank and prestige, with those at the top using more humour and often directing it downward. Pizzini also found that the initiators and targets of humour mirror the hospital hierarchy. Additionally, Ruth Coser found that whilst women staff members demonstrated a capacity for humour they deferred to men who produced 99 out of 103 witticisms at staff meetings. As Crawford notes 'Men made more jokes; women laughed harder' (1995: 144). Pizzini noticed that nurses who joked amongst themselves failed to do so in the presence of doctors. Also, when humorous remarks were initiated by someone low in the hierarchy, the intended recipients 'let them fall into silence without laughing', preventing the humour from disrupting the status quo (1991: 481). Similarly, in data corpus of debates very few instances of humorous talk were produced by women MPs. Apart from a few humorous adversarial exchanges produced by women Ministers in Question Times, there was only one example of a joke made by a woman back-bench MP. This is shown in Example 3.7 below.

Example 3.7 Prime Minister's Question Time (01/07/98, Transcript)

MM = Margaret Moran (Labour backbencher)

1	MM:	will my right Honourable Friend join me in congratulating all of those
2		who signed a deal this week er an iniv innovative leasing deal (.)which
3		will bring one hundred and seventy million pounds worth of private
4		investment and four and half thousand jobs to Luton airport (.) a deal
5		which will retain that airport in public ownership despite all of the
6		efforts of the previous government (.) will he look to ways of
7		extending this public private partnership arrangement to other areas of
8		the public sector (.) and when he is next asked whether he has wafted
9		in from paradise (.) as I'm sure he often is (.) will he be able to
10		honestly answer (.) no Luton airport

Here, the woman MP uses humour at the end of her speech by alluding to a 1970s television commercial which mentioned Luton airport (lines 9–10). While she is speaking there is a lot of noise in the chamber, so it may be that she is using humour here to attract the attention of other MPs. As in Pizzini's research; however, the response to her joke is minimal – only a few MPs respond to her joke with laughter.

In attempting to explain the differential use of humour by men and women, previous research has found that women's humour in conversations is more often context bound and 'jointly created out of the ongoing talk' (Jenkins 1985: 138) and less often performance-related than male conversational humour. In another study of what makes people laugh in conversations, Ervin-Trip and Lampert (1992) observe that women's comments were judged to increase camaraderie and empathy. In the same mixed-sex study, men were found to be more likely to initiate a humorous key than women, whilst women were more likely to collaborate and build upon someone else's humorous remarks than men (Ervin-Trip and Lampert 1992). In their study of self-deprecating humour, Ervin-Trip and Lampert found that the self-deprecations of the men were often exaggerated, unreal or false – 'a kind of Walter Mitty fantasy' (1992: 115) – and that men's remarks often took the form of 'flip wisecracks' rather than the personal, true anecdotes more often produced by women.

Whilst the research outlined above was carried out on informal conversations rather than more public arenas, the performance element of men's humour seems particularly relevant to the HoC and public speaking in general. Also, if women's humour tends to be supportive and collaboratively produced it runs against the adversarial norms of the HoC, making it questionable whether the HoC is a place where this type of humour is feasible. However, given the evidence that professional men and women use a range of linguistic styles that are coded masculine and feminine, it may not be that women somehow *cannot* produce this type of humour, but instead women may be deterred from doing so because of the way it is received by the audience. As Ervin-Tripp and Lambert point out 'laughter is a spontaneous index of affect which is rewarding enough to get people to make jokes and other humorous moves in order to evoke laughter' (1992: 108). Recall that Pizzini found that humour made by low status participants was not responded to and thus, the status quo was maintained. Perhaps, the male-dominated HoC recognises the value of male humour and offers this 'reward' of laughter to men. Women's humour may not be valued or recognised as belonging to the dominant discourse, so the reward of laughter is not forthcoming. Thus, there would be little incentive for women to contribute humour. A Labour woman MP refers to the difficulty of creating humour when she says 'you have to feel very much at your ease when you are making a joke otherwise you are taking a risk' (Shaw 2002: Interview D). She also says that 'It's all very well for the men to be cracking jokes as they're amongst their own but women are in a much more hostile territory'.

The identification of women being in 'hostile territory' links to the description of women in public institutions having an 'interloper' status (Eckert 1998). As mentioned earlier, men MPs' humour may signal cross-party solidarity which may further marginalise women MPs. Although superficially this humour consists of adversarial exchanges of 'one up-manship', these exchanges depend upon a background assumption of cooperation. As Deborah Cameron observes: 'even if the speakers, or some of them, compete, they are basically engaged in a collaborative and solidary enterprise (reinforcing the bonds within the group by denigrating the people outside it)' (1997a: 58). Alternatively, men MPs may be using the collaborative enterprise of humour to engage in a type of verbal duelling where points are scored (Cameron 1997a). Either way, this co-operative competition appears to be between men and not between women in the HoC. The same senior Labour woman MP is explicit about the gendered nature of humour:

I think that when you are making a joke you are asserting the way that you are as at home as anyone else and it kind of just doesn't work. It just looks phoney because everybody knows that women are not as at home, unless they are Margaret Thatcher. If you are Prime Minister you've got so much else in terms of your command of the situation so she would make jokes and put people down in a humorous way. But you don't have the underdogs cracking a joke basically and women are the underdogs'. (Shaw 2002: Interview D)

Whether 'underdogs' in terms of status or gender this analysis of humour suggests that MPs' use of humorous talk differs according to both these factors. The use of humour in general can therefore be viewed as a gendered linguistic practice in debates as women MPs seldom used humour in their speeches, and they did not engage in sexist humour. Sexist humour denigrates women outside the (male) group and reinforces the dominant male culture in debates. This practice is discussed in detail in Chapter 5.

3.4.3   Irony and Rule Breaking – Filibustering

'Filibustering' is the process by which a group of MPs from one party attempt to speak for so long in a debate that there is no time left for the debate to be resolved, or no time left for the following debate to be started. It is a tactic which plays with and challenges the debating rules for political gain. As mentioned in 3.4.1, it is also a process which adopts an ironic or covertly humorous key. The occurrence of filibustering is infrequent – there are only three instances of this process in the sixty-hour 1998–2001 data corpus. The overwhelming majority of MPs participating in the filibusters are men, so this is another gendered linguistic practice that was not typically undertaken by women MPs.

This analysis of filibustering is closely related to the analysis of floor apportionment undertaken in Section 3.1 of this chapter. Example 3.8 below shows an example of filibustering taken from a Private Member's Bill debate. In this case, the Conservative men who engineer the filibuster do not oppose the amendments to the Fireworks Bill that have been proposed. Their aim is simply to ensure that there will be no parliamentary time left for discussion of the Private Member's Bill next on the agenda. The amendments under discussion are extremely minor changes to the wording of the Fireworks Bill. Usually, these amendments would be passed swiftly. The Speaker reads out the amendment number, and asks 'Ayes to the right' (the government bench) who would respond 'aye' (indicating their agreement to the amendments), and then call out 'Noes to the left' (to the opposition bench) to which opposition members would remain silent if they agreed with the amendments, or shout 'no' if they disagreed. If the response is 'no' from the opposition, then the amendment must be debated. There is nothing to stop the opposition bench from shouting 'no' to the amendment (simply to waste parliamentary time) even though they agree with the amendments.

In the same way at the end of the debate, the Speaker asks the same question to both sides of the House. If the opposition shout 'no' again, the MPs have a 'division,' requiring a formal vote. In this Fireworks Bill, the opposition shouted 'no' at the end of the debate on each amendment which forced a division on each one and therefore wasted more time. When the votes were counted it was found that 50 MPs voted for the amendments and none voted against. Therefore, the opposition had forced a vote to take place even though they did not want to vote against the bill. This practice plays with the rules that are in place to ensure the democratic process is fair. For example, any MP can shout 'no' to an amendment and then change their mind and vote for it in the division. This rule is exploited because opposition members know they are going to vote *for* the amendment when they shout 'no'. Example 3.8 below shows an example of this filibuster in process.

Example 3.8 Private Member's Bill: Fireworks Bill (03/07/98)

    DM = David Maclean (Conservative backbencher) SP = Deputy Speaker

1	DM:	now one accepts that when you draft something like the explosives act
2		er er drafted er or passed into law in eighteen seventy five (.)
3		pyrotechnics and explosives change from time to time (.) new ones get
4		invented and (.) relatively harmless materials wh wh and regulations
5	SP:	order order (.) I'm listening with patience to the Right Honourable
6		Member (.) but I must remind him that the scope of the amendment
7		to which he is speaking (.) is whether or not (.) regulations made under
8		clauses one two or fourteen three (.) should be subject to the affirmative
9		resolution procedure (.) that point (.) and that point only (.) Mr Maclean

10   DM: thank you Mr Deputy Speaker I I shall er er concentrate purely on that(.) I was
11   trying to make a point and I'm sorry I didn't make it precisely enough or or clearly
12   enough (.) that regulations (.) may be a sensible way to deal with the changes in
13   (.) f er explosives or fireworks technology which take place one wouldn't expect
14   to bring in a new act of parliament (.) any time er [or an affirmative]
15   SP: [there's no point] in the Right
16   Honourable Member repeating his error (.) Mr Maclean (.)
17   DM: Mr Deputy Speaker (.) the question before us the was whether the
18   Minister (.) if he uses his powers to amend the explosives act or the fireworks act
19   (.) should be subject to the affirmative or the negative er procedure (.) the
20   Lordships have said that the affirmative procedure er would be better in this case
21   (.) er I take the view (turn continues)

In this speech David Maclean is in flagrant disregard of the debate rules. He is discussing general matters about procedure in an attempt to prolong the debate rather than discussing the amendment (whether the Secretary of State should be able to use an affirmative or negative resolution procedure if emergency changes need to be made to the implementation of the Bill). The Deputy Speaker intervenes to attempt to stop the filibuster (on lines 5–9 and 15–16) but fails to stop the MP from prolonging his speech. David Maclean shows very little respect for the Speaker's authority as is shown when the Speaker intervenes (lines 5–9) saying that he is 'losing patience' with the MP for talking about matters outside the amendments under consideration. Maclean replies by apologising for not making what he was saying 'clear enough', implying that it is not he who is at fault, but rather the Speaker for misunderstanding what he was saying. The Speaker asserts his authority by intervening again to ask that the MP 'does not repeat his error' (line 16).

The ability to resist and challenge the Speaker's authority can be viewed as the strongest expression of an MP's dominant behaviour in debates. It is clear that the process of filibustering is undertaken by MPs who regard themselves as being powerful enough to disregard the Speaker's interventions. Furthermore, the tone of these filibustering speeches is highly ironic. This irony exploits the fact that everyone in the chamber is aware that the MP is breaking the rules, but nothing can be done to stop him. An example of this ironic tone is the repeated emphasis on the 'importance' of what everyone present knows is an utterly unimportant amendment. Maclean exaggerates the usefulness of the amendment by saying that the Lords have 'done a service to the people of this country' by recommending the changes. This type of ironic statement is treated as humorous by the other MPs taking part in this filibuster. During Maclean's speech, the video recording clearly shows another MP, Eric Forth, laughing and sniggering when Maclean makes an obvious deviation from the topic of the amendment and when he defies the Speaker's interventions. Forth attempts to cover his laughter by hiding behind the 'order papers' and putting his hands in front of his mouth, but his amusement at the situation is clear. This covert humour is a highly collaborative enterprise in which the amusement is shared by the MPs taking part in the filibuster.

The second example of a filibuster takes place in the third reading of the Finance Bill in July 1998. As in the Fireworks debate, this Bill would normally be passed very quickly but on this occasion the government are responsible for the filibuster. This is extremely unusual because filibustering is normally thought of as a weapon of the opposition used to oppose government legislation. In this case the government were filibustering their own proposed legislation in order to decrease the amount of time available to be spent on the next-scheduled debate: the Lords' amendments to the Teaching and Higher Education Bill which proposed the introduction of student loans. This was a highly unpopular policy and many Labour and opposition MPs (and the House of Lords) disagreed with its introduction. It is possible to identify that a filibuster is taking place because of the extreme length of the speeches; the number of Speaker's interventions instructing the speakers to stop discussing irrelevant matters; and references to the filibuster made by other MPs who do not agree with it. This is shown in Example 3.9 when Alex Salmond explains his reasons for not giving way to a government MP.

Example 3.9 The third reading of the Finance Bill (1) (01/07/98, Transcript)

    AS = Alex Salmond (SNP Party Leader)

1   AS: I'm not giving way to the Honourable Member and I'll tell him exactly
2   why (.) there is more than a suspicion (.) on this side of the House (.)
3   that Government Members are extremely anxious not to move onto
4   the next debate (.) on student loans (.) now I don't make any comment
5   about House of Commons tactics (.) I've used them myself (.) but the
6   Honourable member will forgive me (.) if I don't assist them in
7   delaying an embarrassing debate (.) on student finance which many
8   members in the Labour Party don't want to see (turn continues)

Here the filibuster process and the reasons behind it are explicitly mentioned to expose the government's tactics. Interestingly, Salmond admits to deploying 'the tactic' himself, showing how embedded these rule-breaking practices are in the institutional culture. He expects and receives no censure for this admission, and his statement shows how informal practices such as overt rule-breaking can become part of the accepted 'way things are done' in the institution. The Conservative MP Nicholas Soames also tries to draw attention to the filibuster in a 'point of order'. This is shown in Example 3.10.

Example 3.10 The Third Reading of the Finance Bill (2) (1/07/98)

NS = Nicholas Soames (Conservative backbencher); DS = Deputy Speaker

1	NS:	Mr Deputy Speaker (.) would you not <u>agree</u> that we are witnessing a
2		sus<u>tain</u>ed and con<u>cert</u>ed (.) <u>fili</u>buster on on this Bill (.) and and and is it
3		<u>not</u> the case (.) Mr Deputy Speaker that such practice is to be de<u>plor</u>ed
4		<u>by</u> the Chair
5	DS:	<u>order</u> (.) the Chair is <u>only</u> aware of speeches which are <u>in</u> order or <u>not</u>
6		in order (.) and er er speeches that I've been hearing <u>have</u> been in order
7		(.) except where I have chosen to er cor<u>rect</u> them (.) er it <u>has</u> been
8		known for debates on the Third Reading of the Fi<u>nance</u> Bill to go on
9		for <u>several</u> hours

In this example Soames attempts to draw attention to the filibuster – itself a somewhat ironic move as he is known for taking part in them himself. His attempt to appeal to the Speaker exemplifies the circular argument with which most points of order are turned down (if something was said in a speech then in must be 'in order' or the Speaker would have ruled it out of order at the time). Despite attempts like these to stop the filibuster the government prolonged the debate for two hours and forty minutes. The main participants in the filibuster are men back-bench MPs, in particular Christopher Leslie MP and Derek Twigg MP. However, unlike the Fireworks Bill filibuster some women MPs participate. Example 3.11 below shows an intervention made upon Christopher Leslie's speech by Helen Southworth, a Labour back-bench MP.

Example 3.11 The third reading of the Finance Bill (3) (01/07/98)

HS = Helen Southworth CL = Christopher Leslie (Labour backbencher)

1	CL:	speaking for my<u>self</u> I am often con<u>fused</u> by my <u>own</u> tax af<u>fairs</u> (.) and now I can
2		pick up a <u>tele</u>phone (.) and speak to a <u>friendly</u> voice on the other end (.) a friendly
3		<u>tax</u> officer on the other end of the line (.) er er ex<u>plain</u> er my pre<u>dic</u>ament and (.)
4		<u>hope</u>fully get a very simple and er common-<u>sense</u> solution to my si<u>tu</u>ation (.) and
5		<u>this</u> will be available very sh<u>ort</u>ly to the the <u>wider</u> part of the popu<u>lation</u> (.) er a
6		<u>pil</u>ot study is being under<u>taken</u> in terms of er <u>tele</u>phone claims for the Inland
7		<u>Rev</u>enue (.) and this is I understand a Bill making provision to start this off in
8		<u>Scot</u>land (.)
9	HS:	will my <u>Hon</u>ourable Friend give <u>way</u>
10	CL:	yes I will (.)
11	HS:	does my honourable friend ag<u>ree</u> that this is one of the <u>many</u> measures that this
12		government is con<u>sider</u>ing and beginning to <u>imp</u>lement (.) that is reducing the
13		<u>bur</u>den on industry and on <u>bus</u>iness (.) and that re<u>duc</u>ing that burden is <u>very</u>
14		im<u>port</u>ant to <u>bus</u>iness (.) and <u>once</u> again that we are <u>listening</u> and taking <u>action</u> (1)
15	CL:	well that's <u>right</u> (.) one of things that <u>bus</u>inesses complain to <u>me</u> about in <u>my</u>
16		constituency (.) is the endless <u>form</u>-filling (turn continues)

This transcript shows Christopher Leslie's filibustering turn, which is intervened upon by the Helen Southworth (line 9). Although the intervention is not very long it serves to give Christopher Leslie another topic with which to prolong the debate. Southworth is therefore participating in the filibuster by being part of the group of MPs who are sustaining each other's speaking turns. However, Southworth does not give a speech so her participation in the filibuster is limited. One other woman Labour MP, Louise Eilman, takes part in this filibuster by making a speech. However, her speech is extremely short in comparison to those made by her male colleagues: hers is seven minutes long whilst Christopher Leslie's speech is fifty-one minutes long. Women MPs therefore participate in a supporting role and men MPs lead this filibuster. This debate on the Finance Bill was proposed by two women Ministers, Helen Liddell and Dawn Primarolo. Although Helen Liddell was the Minister responsible for introducing and summing up the debate, neither she nor her Ministerial colleague (Dawn Primarolo) took part in the filibuster. Their speeches were concise, and they did not intervene upon filibustering Labour colleagues to prolong the debate. Indeed, in all three examples of filibustering in the data corpus, front-bench politicians from all parties did not participate. Back-bench MPs presumably took responsibility for the filibuster because front-bench MPs cannot be seen to be participating in the dubious pursuit of time-wasting.

Based on these examples of filibustering it is possible to claim that filibustering is a linguistic practice which is mainly undertaken by men. Interview data also suggests that filibustering is viewed by some women MPs as a male practice. One woman MP suggests some reasons for this:

Because women have been the pressure for making the House of Commons more rational, sort of making the debate more coherent and more transparent, having an argument where there is one but not having an argument where there isn't one. Because women have been in the forefront of the hours changing and because for women time is a commodity which it is not for men then filibustering is a bit of a contradiction in terms for women. (Shaw 2002: Interview D)

Participants in a filibuster disregard the Speaker's authority, the debate rules and the legislative process. The participants themselves often show evident amusement and active enjoyment in the process. These linguistic practices are highly collaborative examples of the way in which the 'key' of a speech event may be changed to a non-serious tone for a particular political advantage.

3.5   Discussion – Gender and Rule-Breaking in the 1998–2001 House of Commons Corpus

The question posed at the beginning of this Chapter was: How do women in politics participate in debate forums, particularly in those that are historically male-dominated, and in which women are still vastly under-represented and men over-represented? What are the constraints and obstacles that they face in institutions such as the UK HoC, and how can this be illuminated by detailed linguistic analyses of the debate floor? The analysis of floor apportionment showed that the official or legal contributions of women MPs (both allocated speaking turns and 'give way' interventions) are proportional to their representation in the institution, and both women and men are in theory subject to the same official rules. There is therefore nominal equality between men and women MPs in terms of participation, and women MPs are not disadvantaged as speakers in a straightforward way in this CoP. This finding was not predicted by previous research on gender and participation in public speech events. For example, Lyn Kathlene's (1994, 1995) research on floor apportionment in US state legislatures found that men took more turns than women in committee hearings, and Edelsky's (1981) research on male and female participation in university faculty meetings similarly found that men took more turns than women. Apart from this equality of participation in the legal floor of the HoC at this time, there are some substantial differences between the linguistic practices of the two gender groups and it is possible to argue that these differences disadvantage women MPs. Men dominate the illegal floor by making illegal interventions that can also encroach upon the legal floor. This means that men make more interventions than women MPs overall, and this practice constructs men MPs as more powerful participants as they assume their entitlement to break the rules. Additionally, women MPs appear reluctant to adopt the most adversarial forms of parliamentary discourse, and as adversarial language is highly valued in this context this may disadvantage them. It is possible that women MPs in their reluctance to use adversarial language are missing the opportunity to be seen as effective speakers by their superiors, and this may disadvantage their political advancement. Finally, women seem to be excluded from or marginalised by certain practices that involve the manipulation of tone – like joking and filibustering. These practices seem to reinforce 'fraternal networks' (Walsh 2001) through cross-party solidarity between men. These practices also assert a high level of competence and confidence with arcane parliamentary procedures. As with rule-breaking practices, the fact that these practices are used mainly by men constructs women as peripheral members of the CoP.

Therefore, the differences in the linguistic practices of men and women MPs show that gender was a salient factor affecting their terms of participation within the HoC CoP in the 1997–2001 term. These gendered linguistic practices appear to construct women as peripheral members because rule-breaking activities, adversarial language, and humour are practices mainly or wholly undertaken by men. One possible explanation for these differences could be that women consciously choose to behave differently by rejecting the male, elitist, old-fashioned traditions of the Commons. An alternative explanation is that the different behaviour of men and women MPs is a result of coercive forces within the CoP which mean that women are made to feel like 'interlopers' (Eckert 1998) in the community – subject to negative sanctions such as sexist barracking and negative stereotyping. Penelope Eckert (1998) suggests some explanations for women's adherence to norms and rules. She reports the findings of her research on phonological variation in two CoPs of US high school adolescents ('Jocks' and 'Burnouts'). This study showed that it was girls (rather than boys) in the two CoPs who were responsible for using the most standard variants in the CoP which valued standard language, and the most non-standard variants in the CoP which valued non-standard language. She concluded that: 'the constraints on girls to conform to an exaggerated social category type are clearly related to their diminished possibilities for claiming membership or category status' (1998: 73).

This conformity may be realised by other forms of linguistic behaviour (including turn-taking) and related to different types of CoPs. Eckert argues that women moving into prestigious occupations and especially elite institutions 'are generally seen as interlopers and are at greater pains to prove that they belong' (1998: 67). With this 'interloper' status, women are more subject than men to negative judgements about superficial aspects of their behaviour (such as dress, or style of speech). The observation that women are interlopers who are subject to the negative effects of gender stereotyping can be related to Kanter's (1977) idea of tokenism, and Yoder's (1991: 183) observation that studies of tokenism in gender inappropriate occupations have found that women 'experience performance pressures, isolation, and role encapsulation, but men do not'. Eckert suggests that the way in which women can 'prove their worthiness' is 'meticulous attention to symbolic capital' (1998: 67). She notes that: 'While men develop a sense of themselves and find a place in the world on the basis of their actions and abilities, women have to focus on the production of selves – to develop authority through continual proof of worthiness' (1998: 73). Women MPs' avoidance of rule-breaking (or meticulous adherence to the rules) can therefore be viewed as one of ways in which women MPs make sure they are 'beyond reproach' in a CoP which views them as 'outsiders'. It is likely that both these explanations play a part in explaining men and women MPs' differential linguistic practices. In an analysis of the marginal position of women priests in the Church of England, Clare Walsh finds that their position is partly the effect of their own belief in women's 'civilizing difference', and partly the effect of sexist reactions to them by male priests and by the media. Walsh finds that 'what *is* clear is that their language and behaviour is more likely than those of male colleagues to be fractured by competing, and often contradictory, norms and expectations' (Walsh 2001: 201).

In interviews, women MPs identified practices such as barracking and cheering as male activities in which they consciously did not participate. They also expressed the belief that women MPs behave differently from men: 'we're doing things differently and we know we're doing things differently' (Shaw 2002: Interview A). However, some of the interviewees expressed contradictory attitudes in this respect. Having identified 'male' practices and stating women did not engage in them, this interviewee also claimed that they had to 'ape the men's behaviour because that's the only way you're going to get anywhere'. There is also evidence to suggest that there are differences between individual women MPs, as some of them embrace the masculine norms of the HoC and adopt these 'male' linguistic practices: for example, one extremely adversarial question is asked by a senior woman Conservative MP. The fact that women MPs do not have consistent reactions to the avoidance of these 'male' linguistic practices suggests that women MPs' *choice* of non-participation in these practices cannot fully explain the differences found.

Some women MPs overtly recognise their status as that of 'interloper': 'my strategy is to try and be an insider. When quite clearly I was never going to be an insider in the House of Commons my strategy was to build up my strength outside' (Shaw 2002: Interview D). Women MPs are constructed as outsiders by sexist barracking, which is common (see the more detailed discussion in Chapter 5), and their exclusion from cross-party exchanges expressing solidarity. This may serve to strengthen the 'fraternal networks' (Walsh 2001: 301) against women MPs. Negative sanctions outside the chamber are also pertinent, as the media characterisation of the women MPs who were elected in 2007 as 'Stepford wives', 'clones' and 'Blair's babes' clearly had an effect on the women themselves, and the theme was taken up and used against them through barracking within the chamber. The imposition of these negative sanctions upon women MPs may mean that they can only pay 'meticulous attention to symbolic capital' rather than attention to their actions and abilities to prove their worthiness (Eckert 1998: 67–73). This has also been viewed as the double bind between being professional and being feminine: 'When a woman is placed in a position in which being assertive and forceful is necessary, she is faced with a paradox; she can be a good woman but a bad professional, or vice versa. To do both is impossible' (Lakoff 1990: 206). These coercive forces may therefore result in women MPs avoiding rule-breaking or norm-challenging practices to satisfy the requirements of their 'interloper' status by being 'beyond reproach' with respect to the formal CoP rules. Whether for personal advantage or for strategic political gain such as the self-consciously political rule-breaking behaviour of the NIWC (Walsh 2001: 117), an understanding of the way in which language, gender and power are constructed in these public contexts can give women a clearer basis from which to consider undertaking the 'critical acts' that promote institutional change. In Chapter 4 I broaden this analysis to scrutinise participation in much newer CoPs – the devolved institutions of the U.K.

4   Women's Linguistic Participation in the New Devolved Assemblies of the UK

4.1   The Devolved Political Assemblies as Communities of Practice

4.1.1   Introduction

The starting point for this chapter is that women's participation in the traditional, national parliament of the House of Commons (HoC) at a time of change in 1998–2001 was restricted, and that women were positioned as interlopers in the highly masculinised forum. At that time, after the first Tony Blair government in 1997, the UK's devolution process involved granting selective legislative and other political powers to the Scottish Parliament (SP), the National Assembly for Wales (NAW) and the Northern Ireland Assembly (NIA). The creation of these new political institutions allows the opportunity to investigate gender and participation in political institutions that differ from Westminster in several key respects. First, women are founder members of these institutions and therefore do not have to contend with the traditional patterns of historical male domination found at Westminster (Mackay et al. 2003). Second, these devolved institutions were devised with egalitarian ideals and inclusive objectives to the fore, including considerations of the inclusion and increased representation of women (Chaney 2004; Mitchell 2010). Finally, contingent on these considerations, the institutional practices, standing orders and – in the SP and the NAW – the physical layout of the institutions are intended to promote equal participation of the members. It was hoped that the new devolved institutions, which all had their first terms in 1999, would represent a new type of politics and 'a move away from the old "command and control" model to more fluid models which would promote wider participation and inclusion' (Brown 2005: 3). Together, these factors have been claimed to offer women increased opportunities for representation and participation. The aim of this chapter is to account for gender and linguistic participation in these institutions in their third parliamentary terms (2007–11)[1] to establish whether this is actually the case. In doing so it seeks to address the second set of questions set out in Chapter 1: How successful have the 'new' devolved institutions of the UK been in encouraging equal participation of all members?

What are the particular interactional procedures that can be thought of as making a forum more egalitarian?

The devolved institutions have the authority to legislate on 'transferred matters', but not on matters that are not explicitly 'reserved' or 'excepted' by Westminster. All Bills passing through the assembly still have to receive royal assent to become law, even though the UK monarch has no formal role within the institutions. While these three institutions have in common their timing in the UK devolution programme, there are also substantial differences between them. The main differences between the SP the NIA and the NAW are their size (the NAW has 60 members, the NIA 118 and the SP 129), and that of their physical locations, with the SP and the NAW having new, purpose-built parliament buildings and the NIA occupying an existing set of parliament buildings at Stormont, Belfast. Political scientists have pointed to the complex relationships contributing to the 'new', both in terms of new political actors and new political institutions. This has led to questioning 'why the introduction of new formal rules does not always result in the outcomes intended and desired by institutional designers in different contexts' (Chappell and Waylen 2013: 600). It is certainly the case that although two out of the three institutions were born into new physical spaces, much of the interactional infrastructure was copied across from HoC speech events, including the adoption of a version of 'Prime Minister's Question Time' (PMQs – see detailed discussions in Chapters 3 and 6) in all three institutions. Some have suggested that the 'new' politics associated with the devolution programme has unclear aims and is 'based on an ill-defined notion of an ideal norm and a flawed existing institution' (Mitchell 2010: 100).

Nevertheless, most feminist scholars in politics concur that the creation of the new devolved institutions in the UK offers researchers of political institutions opportunities to ask: 'In what ways can "new" institutions incorporate gender equality and gender justice from the outset in their institutional design and in their daily enactment by actors, including new actors? What is the promise and limit of institutional change from a gendered perspective?, (Mackay and Waylen 2014: 490). The ethnographic descriptions and discourse analytic data presented in this chapter help to address these questions by focusing on linguistic participation in these three institutions. The data was collected and analysed as part of a research project[2] which ran between 2009 and 2011 (i.e. within the 2007–11 third parliamentary term of the institutions) and aimed to further an understanding of the factors affecting the political representation of women in these new political institutions ten years after they were established. As described in Chapter 2, and demonstrated in the HoC analysis in Chapter 3, a mixed method approach was used to assess the linguistic participation of politicians by classifying different types of speaking turns and quantifying them in relation to gender, political party and the seniority of politicians in these CoPs. Ethnographic observations and interview data and the detailed analysis of the debate floors aimed to identify the linguistic and cultural norms and practices in debates and establish the extent to which they may be gendered. This chapter therefore starts with a description of the most salient features of the NIA, the SP and the NAW, based on archival, historical and ethnographic data (observations and 45 interviews with politicians) in Section 4.1. The archival and historical information presented here is taken from parliamentary documents – such as, the 'Standing orders' and the websites of each institution.[3] A list of all the dates, duration and type of speech events in this 2009–11 corpus of data, and a list of interviewees and their political parties are given in Appendix B. In line with the ethical considerations of the research project, interviewees' comments included in these descriptions are not attributed to individuals, but only the gender and party of the interviewees are given (where relevant) and where it does not compromise their anonymity. Following the general description of these CoPs, the quantitative assessment of speaking turns in each institution is presented (Section 4.2), and a detailed analysis of the debate floors undertaken (Section 4.3), including ethnographic observations about the debate floors and their formal and informal routines and practices. Then, based on these findings, the characteristics of these institutions that are thought to affect equal participation are described in Section 4.4. Finally, an assessment of the progress of women politicians in the new institutions (including more recent developments such as the all-woman leadership in the SP since 2015), and the continuing barriers to their equal representation and participation are discussed in Section 4.5.

4.1.2   Description of the Northern Ireland Assembly (NIA)

The NIA was established in December 1999 after a pre-devolution or 'shadow' period. It has been suspended on five occasions since then – the longest of these suspensions were between October 2002 and May 2007 and from January 2017 to January 2020. The Assembly is in the Stormont Parliament Buildings in the Stormont Estate in the east of Belfast. The parliament building was originally home to the Parliament of Northern Ireland which governed the region between 1921 and 1972. The chamber was designed as a replica of the debating chamber of the HoC, with the Speaker's Chair at the head and two opposing rows of seats facing each other. However, the chamber is more of a horseshoe shape than the HoC as some seats face the Speaker at the opposite end of the chamber. The public viewing gallery is situated above these seats. The Assembly is open to the public and there is a small shop and café near the main entrance. The main entrance leads directly into the 'Great Hall' through which the elected politicians, called 'Members of the Legislative Authority' (or 'MLAs') can enter the debating chamber. MLAs' offices are distributed through the upper floors of the Parliament buildings (Figures 4.1 and 4.2).

Figure 4.1 Image of the Northern Ireland Assembly building, Stormont, Belfast. (Source: Tim Graham/Contributor/Getty Images.)

Figure 4.2 Image of the debating chamber of the Northern Ireland Assembly, facing the Speaker's chair. (Source: 'Assembly Chamber' by Northern Ireland Assembly is licensed under CCBY-ND 2.0. www.flickr.com/photos/niassembly/7440311610/in/album-72157630281414678/.)

MLAs are elected to the Assembly under the principle of power-sharing and the d'Hondt method, a party-list proportional representation system. Power-sharing is the arrangement by which the two biggest political communities in Northern Ireland (Unionist and Nationalist) are guaranteed a share of power. Power-sharing has several mechanisms in order to ensure that roles and decision-making powers are shared between Unionist and Nationalist parties. Firstly, each MLA must designate themselves either 'unionist', 'nationalist' or 'other' to account for their political position in relation to power-sharing. Unionists are traditionally protestant and supportive of the 'union' of Northern Ireland with England, Scotland and Wales. The unionist political parties in the 2007–11 term were the Democratic Unionist Party (DUP) and the Ulster Unionist Party (UUP). The nationalist politicians are traditionally catholic and supportive of the idea that Northern Ireland should break from the UK and form a 'united Ireland' with the Republic of Ireland. The nationalist parties in the 2007–11 term were Sinn Féin (SF) and the Social Democratic and Labour Party (SDLP). Other parties in the assembly include the Alliance Party (a non-sectarian party) and the Green Party. Certain resolutions must receive support from MLAs representing the full-spectrum of the different communities mentioned above. This 'cross community support' is necessary to make changes to the standing orders, to elect the Speaker (the moderator) and for some other financial legislation. The d'Hondt method is used to appoint Ministers to the executive, and this ensures that ministerial representation is in proportion to the number of seats a party has in the assembly.

In the elections in May 2007, 108 new MLAs were elected with the Democratic Unionist Party (DUP) and Sinn Féin (SF) as the two biggest parties. These two parties then put forward the First Minister and Deputy First Minister, respectively. Table 4.1 shows the number of men and women MLAs in the third term of the assembly in each political party.

Politicians in the NIA who were interviewed for the project agreed that the NIA is a traditional forum. However, the politicians evaluated the traditional characteristics of the Assembly in different ways. On the one hand, some MLAs found the Assembly 'stuffy' and 'over Westminsterised' – mentioning the dress code (men must wear a jacket and tie) – and formal debate rules were described as restrictive and 'old-fashioned' practices. On the other, some MLAs felt that the traditional nature of the parliament 'served a purpose' to give the proceedings sufficient formality and gravitas. Observational and interview data both suggest that the assembly remains sharply divided along Nationalist and Unionist lines, described by one Alliance Party MLA as 'red and green issues: tribal politics'. MLAs talk of individuals who will not stand next to their colleagues from opposing parties to have their photograph taken, or share the Stormont lift with them, and who refuse to speak to one another socially in the corridor. One MLA describes the animosity she feels

Table 4.1 *Table showing MLAs in the Northern Ireland Assembly (third term 2007–11)*

	Women	Men	Total
Democratic Unionist	2	34	36
Sinn Féin	8	20	28
Ulster Unionist	0	18	18
SDLP	3	13	16
Alliance	1	6	7
Green	0	1	1
Independent	1	0	1
Speaker	0	1	1
Total	15* (14%)	93 (86%)	108

*17 per cent is used for the period in which the data was collected as Hanna Carmel (SDLP), Naomi Long (Alliance), and Iris Robinson (DUP) left the Assembly over the duration of the project (October 2009–April 2011).

coming from the party opposing her in the chamber by saying 'they hate their eyes for looking at you'. This animosity is expressed in the chamber itself through barracking and by Members 'laughing, smirking and talking amongst themselves' when a political opponent is speaking (see Examples 4.4a and 4.4b). The chamber is also viewed by interviewees as a context that is 'unforgiving if you get something wrong'. However, several MLAs from across the parties in this third term of the assembly agreed that some elements of this animosity had 'mellowed with time' and although it was still evident that 'they are going to be a while getting over the history' there was some sense that 'we're getting there'. MLAs also suggested that the debating chamber seemed to be the place where animosity was expressed, whereas in other speech events, such as committees, there tended to be 'less grandstanding' and that 'adversaries in the chamber work comfortably together in committee'. It is also worth noting that the wider working environment of the assembly does not reflect the animosity in the chamber and has a friendly, helpful and non-hierarchical atmosphere.

The Irish language is used in the Assembly by a number of MLAs. Some MLAs use Irish for the opening and closing of their speeches, and others use it for more substantial parts of their speeches. The Standing Orders (official rules) state that languages other than English can be spoken, but that the content of the speaking turn must be spoken in English immediately afterwards. The use of Irish and Ulster Scots is seen by many MLAs as an important right. At the time of conducting the research, Ulster Scots was rarely used in the assembly but there was a strong campaign for its use,[4] which has increased over time but was not discussed by interviewees. Irish-speaking MLAs said they would prefer bilingual signage and simultaneous translation in the chamber. The use of Irish in the chamber was viewed by many MLAs as politically motivated. One Sin Féin MLA said that 'someone once said that every word of the Irish is equivalent to every bullet in the struggle', and there are differing opinions about the use of Irish in the chamber. One DUP MLA said that the use of Irish was 'irksome at times' because some MLAs 'just use it as a weapon' when they are not very proficient at speaking the language and they 'can't speak it and they can't read it – they read it very badly'. However, another SDLP MLA who described Irish as his first language said that he sometimes genuinely forgets to say 'question number one' to the Speaker in English but says it in Irish by mistake. He said that he's 'not ramming it down anyone's throat', but that he still gets 'pulled up for that' by the Speaker. Irish language speakers report some quite aggressive comments used against them when they speak in Irish, with opposing MLAs calling it 'leprechaun language' and 'gibberish' and subjecting them to 'constant sneering, tittering and talking' when Irish is spoken in the chamber. Interestingly, opposing perceptions are also evident in MLAs' appraisal of the advantages and disadvantages of using Irish in the chamber. Irish speakers view their use of Irish as a disadvantage because it reduces their speaking time – because it takes twice as much time to speak Irish first and then give the translation in English – and non-Irish speakers claim that Irish speakers are at an advantage because they get 'twice the time' to speak.

4.1.3   Description of the Scottish Parliament (SP)

The Scotland Act, passed in Westminster in 1998, allowed for the establishment of the SP on 1 July 1999. Between 1999 and 2004 the Parliament was temporarily located in the General Assembly Hall of the Church of Scotland on the Royal Mile in Edinburgh. The new Scottish Parliament building was opened in October 2004 and is in Holyrood, Edinburgh. The building was designed by Enric Mirales and incorporates complex leaf-shaped buildings and a semi-circular debating chamber (see Figure 4.3). The buildings also contain offices for the Members of the Scottish Parliament (MSPs) and committee rooms. The public can access the foyer and public café within the building and book tickets in advance to view the proceedings or a guided tour of the parliament (Figure 4.4).

The Scottish Parliament was granted the right to take responsibility for 'devolved matters' under the 1998 Scotland Act. In the election of May 2007, the Scottish Nationalist Party (SNP) emerged as the largest party, with one more seat than Scottish Labour. Consequently, no single party gained an

Figure 4.3 Image of the Scottish Parliament, Holyrood, Edinburgh. (Source: Jeff J. Mitchell/Staff/Getty Images.)

overall majority. The SNP were not able to arrange a coalition deal with any of the other parties and therefore governed as a minority government with the support of the two Green Party members. Alex Salmond, the leader of the SNP was voted First Minister of the Scottish parliament on 16 May 2007. As in the NAW, there are two types of MSPs in the Scottish Parliament, with 73 of the 129 seats designated for 'constituency MSPs'. Voters have two votes – one for their constituency MP and a second vote for a political party. This second vote is used for the 'additional members system' in which 56 'List MSPs' are elected (seven from each of eight electoral regions). The d'Hondt method is used to allocate seats to parties proportionally according to the number of list votes for each party and the number of seats won by the party in the region. The moderator of the SP is referred to as the 'Presiding Officer'. Table 4.2 shows the numbers of men and women MSPs in each party in the third term of the Scottish Parliament.

Most Members of the Scottish Parliament (MSPs) who were interviewed liked the horseshoe 'spread out' nature of the debating chamber, describing it as 'non-confrontational' and 'less intimidating'. However, some MSPs felt that the layout of the chamber was not conducive to 'good debate' as members are so far away from each other. There were comments that this 'lowered the temperature' in debates, making them less interesting. Further, some stated that the chamber was 'not an interactive or spontaneous place'. The placement of the microphones was an issue for some MSPs who felt that having a

Figure 4.4 Image of the chamber of the Scottish Parliament, Holyrood, Edinburgh with the Presiding Officer's (moderator's) Chair on the left. (Source: Christopher Furlong/Staff/Getty Images.)

microphone on one side meant that you could not turn to address people. It was also noted that an additional microphone was added to the First Minister's lectern to combat this problem in First Minister's Question Time. The layout of the chamber also means that background conversations occur frequently – either from a sedentary position or by members standing and talking at the back of the chamber. Some members felt this occurred partly because of the design of the spacious chamber, and partly because the microphones do not pick up these conversations. When observing from the gallery, it is striking how many different conversations are carried out in the chamber, especially when the chamber is full. It is also noticeable that MSPs bang their desks or applaud to show agreement with the person giving the speech.

Table 4.2 *Table of MSPs in the Scottish Parliament (third term 2007–11)*

	Women	Men	Total
SNP	12	35	47
Labour	23	23	46
Conservatives	5	12	17
Liberal Democrats	2	14	16
Others	1	2	3
Total	43 (33.3%)	86 (66.6%)	129

4.1.4   Description of the National Assembly for Wales (NAW)

The National Assembly for Wales (NAW), which is to be re-named the 'Welsh Parliament' from 2021, was created by the Government of Wales Act in 1998 following a referendum on devolution in 1997. Initially in 1999 the Assembly had no powers to pass primary legislation. The Government of Wales Act 2006 meant that the Assembly gained limited primary legislative powers following the 2007 election. These laws are known as Assembly Measures and can be enacted in specific fields and matters within the legislative competency of the Assembly. It was only at the end of this third term of the assembly that a 'Yes' vote in a referendum on 3 March 2011 gave the Assembly the power to legislate on the 20 devolved areas independently of UK parliament. The new NAW building (Senedd) is in Cardiff Bay, Cardiff. The red-brick 'Tŷ Hywel' building, which is now used for Assembly Members' (AMs) offices is connected to the Senedd by a walkway, and initially housed the debating chamber from July 1999 to March 2006. The Senedd contains the debating chamber and committee rooms, and it was constructed using traditional Welsh materials. As shown in Figure 4.5, the building's exterior walls are mainly made of glass and this transparency is intended to symbolise the openness of Welsh democracy. The public gallery or 'oriel' is a public seating and exhibition area in the Senedd, and the glass floor allows members of the public to look down into the Siambr and committee rooms below. The Siambr itself is a circular chamber under a wooden cowl, surrounded by a circular viewing gallery. The 60 AMs sit at wooden desks in the circular chamber which was designed in this way to promote a less confrontational style of debate and is shown in Figure 4.6.

After the 2007 election no party held a majority of seats so a Welsh Labour-led 'red-green' coalition between the Welsh Labour party and Plaid Cymru (the Welsh nationalist party) was agreed. The 60 AMs are elected to the Assembly for a term of four years under an 'Additional Members System', where 40 members are elected through their constituencies in a 'first past the

Figure 4.5 Image of the National Assembly for Wales, Cardiff Bay. (Source: Matthew Horwood/Contributor/Getty Images.)

Figure 4.6 Image of the debating chamber of the National Assembly for Wales, facing the Presiding Officer. (Source: Loop Images/Contributor/Getty Images.)

Table 4.3 *Table showing AMs in the National Assembly for Wales (third term 2007–11)*

	Woman	Men	Total
Labour	16	10	26
PC	7	8	15
Conservatives	1	11	12
Liberal Democrats	3	3	6
Others	1	0	1
Total	28 (47%)	32 (53%)	60

post' system, and the remaining 20 members are elected using the d'Hondt method of proportional representation from five electoral regions. The moderator of the NAW is referred to as the Presiding Officer'. Table 4.3 above shows the AMs in each political party in the 2007–11 term.

In interviews, Assembly Members (AMs) generally agreed that the small, circular chamber had a relaxed atmosphere which led to a consensual, non-threatening environment for speakers. As the numbers of AMs are small it was thought that the relationships between them were generally good, and they had a chance to address issues with each other outside the chamber. One member said that AMs can be 'horribly rude' to each other in the chamber but friendly outside in the Members' rooms. Some AMs thought that the atmosphere was sometimes too friendly, and that some informal practices (such as calling each other by first names, rather than by more formal address terms) were detrimental to the formal nature of proceedings in the chamber. The debating chamber (Siambr) and the parliamentary building (Senedd) were universally liked by Assembly Members who said that the Senedd is always busy and well used by members of the public and the café and shop are easy to access. However, some noted that the lack of a common area shared between Assembly Members and members of the public was a drawback. The public enter the building from the front of the Senedd (bay) entrance, whereas AMs enter the chamber directly from their office building (Ty Hywel) behind the chamber so therefore do not meet unless they have a specific arrangement to do so.

The use of both Welsh and English languages in the Assembly was supported by all members who were interviewed. The translation services in the chamber were thought to work well and include headphones with live audio-translation for all AMs and officials in the chamber and members of the public in the viewing gallery. Three quarters of those interviewed spoke Welsh to some extent and half spoke Welsh in the chamber. All spoke English. AMs observed that barracking and interventions tended to be in

English, rather than Welsh. One Welsh-speaking member said that Welsh-speaking AMs do not intervene on an English-speaking AM in Welsh in order 'to be fair', and another said that she prefers to intervene in English rather than Welsh so it doesn't 'break the flow' of the debate. This AM said she used English when she wanted to speak in a more adversarial way with or about another politician 'When I want a bit of banter a bit of exposing whoever I'm trying to talk about, I would come to that bit in English', suggesting that these types of exchanges possibly work best when they are given in English as it is the language common to all members. A Welsh-speaking woman AM discussed the interactional consequences of speaking Welsh: 'there is an issue as well when I do speak Welsh in the Chamber I'm very conscious I get less interventions because obviously they've got translation and maybe they've missed, you know, I've moved on to the next point', and she saw this as a drawback because she would like to respond to the interventions. Several Welsh-speaking AMs conversely said that they used Welsh as a tactic so that they did not receive unwanted interventions. One woman AM said: 'if I know I'm in for a difficult time I will absolutely speak in Welsh so I have the excuse not to receive interventions'. The same AM claimed that this 'advantage' to speaking Welsh was recompense for the fact that Welsh speakers 'have less time to say things' because speaking Welsh 'takes longer' than speaking English. While there were no negative comments about the bilingual provision in the Assembly, two AMs who did not speak Welsh expressed concerns over the cost of maintaining the translation services. It was also claimed that although some members of the Conservative Party speak Welsh, they 'choose not to in the chamber'. Some AMs thought that speaking English in the chamber 'had more of an impact' because what they said was more likely to be taken up by the media. Interestingly, the interviewees who were Welsh speakers thought that Welsh was spoken in the chamber between a third and three-quarters of the time and one AM thought she spoke in Welsh 95 per cent of the time. However, Welsh was spoken as some part of a speaking turn (from one word to an entire turn) for only 11 per cent of the time in the sample of 13 days of proceedings used for this study.

4.2   The Analysis of the Debate Floor

4.2.1   The Quantitative Analysis of Debate Turns
Across the Four UK Parliaments

To find out whether men and women participate in proportion to their representation in the institutions overall, a sample of different types of speech events (question times, statements and plenary sessions) was collected for

each of the three devolved institutions and also from the HoC for comparative purposes. The period of the sample was between October 2009 and May
2010. During this period between 12 and 13 days of proceedings in each
assembly were analysed. Each turn in each speech event was noted and classified according to its type – for example response, question, Speakers' intervention, give way intervention – and according to the speaker (male, female
and party affiliation). This represents 65–70 hours of proceedings and
between 3,500 and 4,000 speaking turns in each institution (see Appendix
A.2.1 for details of the dates and amount of data collected in each site). The
Official Report (OR) in each assembly was used to quantify and classify
the speaking turns. The reports were used because their full coverage of
all the speech events allowed the quantification of a large number of speaking turns in given period of time. In the only bilingual chamber, the NAW,
the reports are produced in both English and Welsh, so the English version
was used to account for the speaking turns. As already observed (see Chapter
2 and Shaw 2018) ORs do not cover all 'out of order' utterances accurately
and illegal interventions are often excluded. Usually an 'out of order' or illegal intervention only appears in the OR if the person giving the speech (the
'legal' speaker) responds to what is said by the illegal or 'out of order' speaker
(or is a D2 three-part exchange – see Section 3.2). This means that often, the
D2, two-part illegal interventions that do not elicit a response from the person giving the speech are not included and there is only a partial representation of illegal utterances in the ORs. For this reason, not every speaking
turn in the official report is attributed to a named speaker, and therefore it
is not always possible to attribute a turn to a man or woman. A category 'U'
was used to show when the speaking turn was not attributable to a particular
politician.

In order to establish the participation of men and women politicians in
each assembly, the number of speaking turns was compared to their overall representation in each institution. Figure 4.7 shows that women's representation in the NIA was the lowest at 17 per cent (and the closest to the
20 per cent representation of women in the HoC); 35 per cent of seats in
the SP were occupied by women; and the NAW neared parity with 47 per
cent women Assembly Members. Figure 4.8 shows the overall percentage
of speaking turns taken in the sample of debates across the four institutions. It shows that in the NIA, SP and the HoC men and women's speaking
turns came within 2 per cent of their representation overall. However, in the
NAW, women took proportionally fewer turns and men took more than their
representation in the assembly as a whole (women took 32 per cent of the
speaking turns and their representation was 47 per cent). This is surprising
as the NAW had the highest proportion of women that had ever been elected
to a UK political institution at this point, nearing parity with men and the

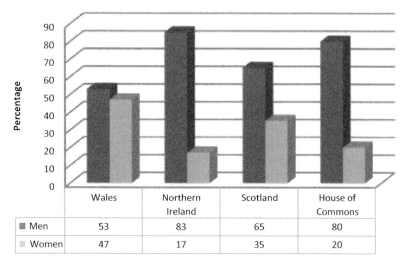

	Wales	Northern Ireland	Scotland	House of Commons
Men	53	83	65	80
Women	47	17	35	20

Figure 4.7 Graph showing the percentage of men and women politicians in each institution in 2007–11.

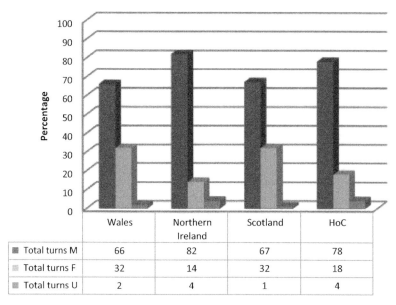

	Wales	Northern Ireland	Scotland	HoC
Total turns M	66	82	67	78
Total turns F	32	14	32	18
Total turns U	2	4	1	4

Figure 4.8 Graph showing the percentage of speaking turns taken by women and men in the sample for each institution.

50:50 democratic ideal. This also appears to contradict the expectation of the 'Critical Mass Theory' (Dahlerup 1988), which, as mentioned in Chapter 1, suggests that the greater the proportion of a minority in an institution, the greater their participation and influence is likely to be. In order to explore these issues more thoroughly, I made distinctions between speaking turns according to the degree of agency and control that the politicians had over them. In this way, participation could be analysed according to the institutional arrangements for allocating speaking turns (according to political party and role) as distinct from the speaking turns that were spontaneously acquired by politicians on the debate floor.

In this way, the speaking turns were classified into:

1. Turns taken by the moderators (Speakers, Deputy Speakers, Presiding officers and Deputy Presiding Officers);
2. Speeches, questions and responses ('allocated turns');
3. Give way requests, give way turns, give way refusals, points of order, out of order utterances, responses to out of order utterances ('spontaneous turns').

The turns taken by the moderators in each parliament are designated by their official interactional and symbolic role in regulating and enforcing conduct and debate rules. They differ across institutions according to individual rules of each – in the NAW and the SP the moderators need to enforce rules about the length of speeches, for example. The assessment of the moderators' speaking turns showed that in the HoC 6 per cent of all the turns were made by the Speakers and in the NIA sample of debates 14 per cent. In these two institutions all the Speakers' interventions were made by men, none by women. In Scotland 10 per cent of all the turns were Presiding Officers' interventions and of these 23 per cent were taken by women and 77 per cent by men. In Wales, just under 10 per cent of all the speaking turns were taken by the Presiding Officers – and of these 12 per cent were taken by women and 88 per cent by men. This means that the lack of women taking Presiding Officers' turns accounts for the slight under-representation of women's speaking turns overall in Scotland. However, the much bigger discrepancy between men and women's speaking turns (15 per cent overall) in the NAW is not accounted for by the difference between men and women in Presiding Officers' speaking turns alone.

The other speaking turns were classified as 'allocated turns' or turns that are assigned to speakers according to fixed institutional rules and mechanisms closely related to a politician's role, party affiliation, and whether they are in a government or opposition party. Allocated turns, apart from those of the Speakers, as discussed above, were categorised as 'speeches', 'questions' and 'responses'. Overall, these three types of allocated turns accounted for

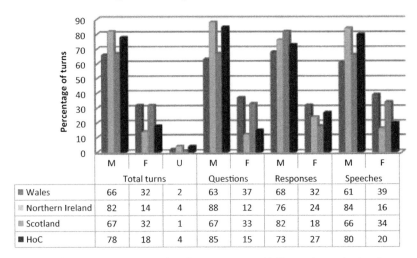

	M	F	U	M	F	M	F	M	F
	Total turns			Questions		Responses		Speeches	
▨ Wales	66	32	2	63	37	68	32	61	39
▨ Northern Ireland	82	14	4	88	12	76	24	84	16
▨ Scotland	67	32	1	67	33	82	18	66	34
▪ HoC	78	18	4	85	15	73	27	80	20

Figure 4.9 Graph showing the percentage of 'allocated turns' taken by men and women politicians in a sample of proceedings from each institution.

60–70 per cent of the turns taken in the institutions. The percentage of these turns in each institution taken by men and women is shown in Figure 4.9.

The main category of 'speeches' is related to the formal allocation of turns according to the seniority, role and political party of politicians. These turns are allocated by party, with senior ministers and shadow ministers taking responsibility for the proposal and opposition of the motion and the final summing up or closing speeches. While politicians of any seniority can make a speech in a debate, the speeches are regulated by party affiliation with each of the main parties speaking in turn. Figure 4.9 shows that the number of speeches in all the institutions apart from the NAW were made in proportion to the numbers of men and women in the institution overall. The number of speeches made by women in the NAW was 5 per cent under their representation in the assembly.

The allocated turns classified as 'questions' occurred in the Prime Minister's or First Minister's Question Times and departmental question times. The percentage of politicians asking questions in the Scottish Parliament was within 2 per cent of the men and women representation in the parliament. In the other institutions the men asked proportionally more questions than the women in relation to their representation overall. The allocation of speaking turns also relates to the seniority of politicians, as the party leaders in Prime Minister's and First Minister's questions times are allocated questioning turns and sometimes supplementary questions. Similarly, in question times for a particular Minister, politicians with particular roles in relation to a topic

(Shadow Minister, chair of a committee) are allocated turns first. The proportion of men and women asking questions therefore also reflects the number of men and women in these senior positions in each institution. Similarly, the proportion of men and women politicians giving responses in each assembly is also determined by the number of men and women in senior and Ministerial roles. In this category women in the HoC and in the Northern Ireland Assembly gave more responses than men in relation to their representation overall. In Wales and Scotland men gave proportionally more responses than women. This therefore reflects the proportion of men and women in Ministerial roles in this particular sample of Question Times.

The final set of questioning turns is described as 'spontaneous turns' because politicians have more control over their contributions. In these categories a politician can choose to make a 'give way' request by asking if they can intervene on another's speech. If they are giving a speech, they can choose whether to 'give way' to another speaker in a debate. Similarly, a politician can elect to make a 'point of order' or an illegal intervention or respond to an illegal intervention. Spontaneous turns, unlike allocated turns are therefore not directly linked to seniority, party political affiliation or particular parliamentary roles, although these factors may still have a bearing on them.

Spontaneous turns together accounted for 10–20 per cent of all turns taken across the assemblies, so they represent a far smaller proportion of the overall turns than allocated turns. Figure 4.10 shows that the numbers of women making 'give way' requests were proportionally very high in Scotland (21 per cent higher than their representation in the parliament) and very low in the National Assembly for Wales (34 per cent lower than their representation in the parliament). Give way requests made by women were also proportionally lower in the Northern Ireland Assembly and the HoC (2 per cent and 9 per cent, respectively). Similarly, the proportion of women making give way interventions in the National Assembly for Wales was extremely low (28 per cent lower than their representation in parliament), and therefore the proportion of men making give way interventions was high. The proportion of women making give way interventions in Scotland was 12 per cent higher than their representation in parliament, men lower. In interviews MSPs agreed that taking a 'give way' intervention in a speech can be detrimental and intimidating, either because it represents a challenge to the speech, or because it takes up too much of the time allocated for the speech, which is strictly controlled in the SP and the NAW. Some long-standing MSPs claimed they had the experience to know 'who to let intervene and who to ignore'. Members claimed that some MSPs avoid taking interventions altogether, and this was taken as a sign of weakness. Some MSPs added that members who don't take interventions 'should be intervened upon' to show that the chamber

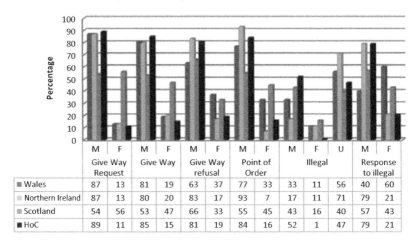

	M	F	M	F	M	F	M	F	M	F	U	M	F
	Give Way Request		Give Way		Give Way refusal		Point of Order		Illegal			Response to illegal	
■ Wales	87	13	81	19	63	37	77	33	33	11	56	40	60
▨ Northern Ireland	87	13	80	20	83	17	93	7	17	11	71	79	21
▨ Scotland	54	56	53	47	66	33	55	45	43	16	40	57	43
■ HoC	89	11	85	15	81	19	84	16	52	1	47	79	21

Figure 4.10 Graph showing the percentage of 'spontaneous turns' taken by men and women politicians in a sample of proceedings from each institution.

'should be an interactive place'. Women made slightly more give way interventions in the Northern Ireland Assembly (5 per cent) and slightly less than their representation in the HoC (5 per cent). The proportion of women and men refusing to give way showed a different pattern. In the National Assembly for Wales women made up 37 per cent of the refusals (10 per cent under their representation in the assembly). This means that in the NAW women AMs refused to give way more than they requested to intervene or made give way interventions. In the Scottish Parliament, the Northern Ireland Assembly and the HoC, men and women refused to give way in proportion to their representation in the institutions overall. Give way interventions are closely linked to the mechanisms regulating the debate floor, and in particular the timed nature of debate turns. When politicians' speeches are limited to a specific amount of time they may be less inclined to take an intervention. Similarly, when politicians feel that they are unable to secure a speaking turn in a debate, they may be more likely to attempt to intervene in order to ensure they can make a contribution.

Points of Order can be raised by any politician on the debate floor and are the mechanism by which politicians can make an appeal to the Speaker that a debate rule has been broken. Points of order should be directly linked to the 'Standing Orders' of the institution, and it should be made clear which rule a particular point of order relates to. However, like give way interventions, points of order are often used in unorthodox ways by speakers to gain the debate floor and allow their contribution to be heard and recorded in the

OR. These bogus points of order are raised when a politician wishes to contribute but does not get permission to do so. In these cases, bogus points of order do not relate to complaining about rule-breaking at all but are instead used to raise substantive points. In this sample of debates, men raised more points of order (in proportion to their representation in the institutions) than women in the NIA, the NAW and the HoC. Women raised more points of order in the SP than their representation in the parliament overall might imply (45 per cent of points of order were raised by women MSPs, and their representation was 35 per cent). In interviews, both men and women MSPs claimed to use bogus points of order to get their points across and recorded in the OR. One MSP also suggested that these bogus points of order can be used by Ministers to 'neutralise on-the-record damage' by correcting a factual error that they have made in a way that will be officially recorded in the report.

As covered in the analysis of HoC discourse in Chapter 3, illegal interventions are only partially represented in the ORs. Commonly, illegal interventions are represented as 'interruption' in OR transcripts with no further information relating to the content of the intervention except an interrupted speaker's response to the illegal intervention. Alternatively, where a politician has not been identified (but the illegal speaking turn is represented in the OR) the turn is labelled as being spoken by 'a Member'. As Figure 4.10 shows, most illegal turns were not attributed to a named individual. The majority of illegal turns remained anonymous in the Northern Ireland Assembly (71 per cent) and the National Assembly for Wales (56 per cent). Anonymous turns also accounted for a large proportion of illegal interventions in the HoC (47 per cent) and the Scottish Parliament (47 per cent). Of the illegal interventions that can be attributed to speakers, the HoC only had 1 per cent of interventions given by women (52 per cent could be attributed to men MPs). Although this is only a rough measure of illegal interventions (because so many of them cannot be attributed to men or women), this appears to bear out the finding in Chapter 3 that women do not tend to participate by breaking the rules in this way in this institution (Shaw 2000). This result also shows this pattern persisted over the 10 years between the two sets of 1998–2001 and 2009–11 HoC data.

In the type of turn classified as 'response to illegal intervention' – or those defined in Chapter 3 as 'attributable illegal interventions' – where a speaker replies to an illegal intervention, there are some surprising results. In the National Assembly for Wales, 60 per cent of this type of intervention was made by women, and in all the other institutions women proportionally undertook more of this type of intervention than men. This needs further investigation as although this category of turn only represented 1–2 per cent of the total number of turns in each institution, the fact that these responses appear to be gendered may add to the overall account of interactional rule-breaking practices in the institutions. In interviews, politicians identified responding to an illegal intervention as a way of 'naming and shaming' a politician who has intervened illegally because the act of responding ensures the illegal intervention appears in the Official Report of the proceedings. This could indicate that women politicians disproportionately use this tactic as a defence against unparliamentary behaviour and as a way of controlling an unruly debate floor. This is also borne out by MSPs who said that they had been targets of barracking when they were new members, but that they have tended to receive fewer such interventions as their experience has grown and they have developed strategies for dealing with it. For example, a woman MSP said that when she used part of her speaking turn to respond to an MSP who was barracking her, this was described by her colleagues as 'her finest hour'. Alternatively, responding to an illegal intervention is less about taking control of the floor and more about feeling obliged to respond to the substance of the illegal challenge. This could mean that women politicians are disproportionately intimidated by illegal challenges and are less able to ignore them, or that they feel that the most effective way to deal with an illegal intervention is to respond to the issues that they raise. But, responding to illegal intervention may disadvantage women politicians because it allows the infringement of the interrupting MP into their speaking turn.

The significance of the findings of the quantitative analysis of the debate floor rests on the indication that overall, apart from in the NAW, women and men politicians participate in proceedings in relation to their proportions in the institutions. Although the unequal gendered pattern of representation in the NAW is partly explained by the high number of turns taken by men, rather than women, Presiding Officers, this does not fully account for the disproportionately low participation of women AMs across all speaking turns. Possible reasons are likely to rest on the distribution of speaking turns and gendered representation across the institution (see Section 4.4). The second significant finding is that in all the devolved institutions women and men take part in illegal interventions in proportion to their representation overall, which is a very different pattern from that found in the HoC. This could indicate that women are not positioned as 'interlopers' in the devolved institutions in the same way that the analysis of the HoC in Chapter 3 suggested. Recalling that the quantitative assessment of debate turns has particular limitations because of its reliance on the ORs, the quantitative analysis was complemented by more detailed analysis of 'out of order' discourse to establish exactly how politicians occupy the debate floors – and to further the ethnographic description of the institutions.

4.3 The Close Analysis of the Debate Floors in the Scottish Parliament, the Northern Ireland Assembly and the National Assembly for Wales

In this section I present further analyses of each of the debate floors of the SP, NIA and the NAW. In some cases, the examples are drawn from ORs of events that were observed in situ from the galleries, but for which no video recording was available (these are labelled 'Official Report'); in other cases, the events were observed and then transcribed from video recordings (according to the conventions on p. viii) and are labelled 'Transcript' in order to differentiate between the two types of transcription.

4.3.1 The Debate Floor of the Scottish Parliament

The quantitative analysis of debate turns showed that in the SP women and men participate in the full range of the different types of speaking turns, including illegal interventions. This was also found in an earlier study of the SP (Shaw 2002) when the new parliament was under construction and the parliament convened in the General Assembly Hall of Church of Scotland in the Royal Mile in Edinburgh between 1999 and 2004. In both studies the women and men MSPs made full use of the spontaneous turns and give way requests, give way interventions and illegal interventions. The ethnographic interviews and observations, together with the close analysis of out-of-order discourse suggests that out of order utterances are frequently good natured in style and tend towards jocular humour between members who appear to know each other well. This banter most frequently occurs between women and men. A typical example of this humour can be seen in Example 4.1.

Example 4.1 Humour in the SP (11/11/09) Plenary: Scotland's Historic Environment (Official Report)

> Participants: MR = Michael Russell (SNP); CP = Cathy Peattie (Scottish Labour Party); DPO = Deputy Presiding Officer (Alasdair Morgan)

1	MR:	Finally, I add that my visit to the museum allowed me to drive a steam
2		engine so I am eternally grateful to the member's constituency because
3		I achieved one of my ambitions.
4	DPO:	You have made me very jealous Mr Russell.
5	CP:	I recognise the minister's interest and the positive response that he had
6		from the people whom he met. He will be aware of my passion for steam trains.
7	MR:	On a point of order Presiding Officer I should have noted that the member
8		was on the footplate of the steam engine with me
9	DPO:	Perhaps we had better get back to the built environment.
10	CP:	Mr Russell people are going to start talking more can be done to give
		support (turn continues)

Here the Deputy Presiding Officer makes a jocular remark which transgresses the debate rules because he is not making an intervention that relates to his role as moderator (line 4). Cathie Peattie responds positively to Michael Russell's initial comment about driving a steam train (lines 5–6), adding in that she has a 'passion' for steam trains. Michael Russell manipulates the serious tone (or 'key') of the debate (initiated by the Deputy Presiding Officer) to make a mock point of order for comic effect (lines 7–8). The Deputy Presiding Officer then attempts to bring the topic back 'to the built environment' (line 9), collaborating with the humour. Cathy Peattie initiates another joke by saying 'people are going to start talking' (line 10). This is an informal, light-hearted exchange with sexual (normative, heterosexual) humour resting ironically on the 'passion', of being 'on the footplate' with someone that could make people 'start talking'. Unlike some instances of parliamentary illegal interventions, this does not appear to be carried out for tactical advantage or political gain, and it is an example of sexually allusive humour co-constructed between men and women. This contrasts with other types of sexual humour, particularly in the House of Commons, which is normally constructed by men and is one of the ways in which homosocial ties and fraternal bonds are reinforced (see further discussion and examples in Section 5.4). While it is likely these all-male exchanges also exist in the SP, no examples were found in this sample of data. Example 4.2 shows a more adversarial exchange that nevertheless is light-hearted in tone.

Example 4.2 Illegal exchanges (12/11/09) Plenary: Central Scotland Green Network (Transcript)

Participants: GF = George Foulkes MSP (Lab/Co-Op), CH = Christopher Harvie MSP (SNP), RC = Roseanna Cunningham MSP (SNP); DPO = Deputy Presiding Officer, Trisha Godman

1	GF:	we had that er er rather gauche candidate er for the SNP in er Glasgow North East (.)
2		blurt out that they are going to spend nine <u>mill</u>ion pounds on the referendum (.)
3		un<u>law</u>ful legislation no purpose of this er to this body at all (.) er and that is a a <u>total</u>
4		waste of money nine <u>mill</u>ion pounds which could be used for this for this
5		[particular]
6	CH:	[It could be] used for Michael Martin's [pension]
7	GF:	[I am sure] that the professor will have

8		an opportunity later on to blurble on from[a a a a a from a fr (.) from] from a a
9	RC:	[He is taking [lessons from you]
10	CH:	[I yield to the master]

11	GF:	from a [standing position] [from] a standing position rather than a
12	DPO:	[not from a] sedentary position [please]
13	GF:	sedentary position (.) so that nine million pounds would be better spent on this
14		programme and I would support that (.) so that's my main concern (turn continues)

In this more adversarial exchange both women and men MSPs break the debate rules to illegally intervene upon the main speaker's speech. In the first instance, Christopher Harvie speaks out of turn in (line 6) in response to George Foulkes' criticism (lines 1–5). George Foulkes continues to describe Harvie negatively as the 'professor' who is going to 'burble on' (lines 7–8), at which point both Roseanna Cunningham and Harvie respond to this criticism by intervening illegally (lines 9 and 10, respectively). When this happens Foulkes' turn is disrupted and he hesitates (line 8) before defensively drawing the Deputy Presiding Officer's attention to the transgression of the rules 'from a standing position' (line 11). The Deputy Presiding Officer then intervenes to restore order (line 12). This example shows the rights of the main speaker (George Foulkes) are infringed upon by a woman and a man who both manipulate the key of the debate to create a jocular/adversarial objection to Foulkes' rather personal criticisms (the 'gauche' candidate in line 1, and the 'professor' who will 'burble on' in lines 7–8). Example 4.3 shows a much more adversarial question posed by a women MSP in First Minister's Question Time.

Example 4.3 Illegal interventions and adversarial questions (04/04/10) First Minister's Question Time (Transcript)

KW: Karen Whitefield MSP (Labour); PO = Presiding Officer, Alex Fergusson; FM = First Minister, Alex Salmond

1	KW:	Thank you Presiding Officer (.) First Minister (.) last week you urged the RMT and
2		ScotRail to descr to resolve what you described as an unnecessary dispute (.) I have a
3		letter here (.) which states that the decision to run driver-only trains on the new
4		Airdrie to Bathgate rail link (.) is one for Trans Transport Scotland (.) that means that
5		it is ultimately a decision for ministers (.) First Minister I am sure that you did (.) not
6		wish to give a misleading (.) impression to Parliament (.) can you confirm that it is
7		ultimately a decision for Transport Scotland (.) and can you tell the Parliament (.)
8		what action your Government will take (.) to resolve this dispute (.)
9	PO:	First Minister
10	FM:	(.) er c can I say t to the member that why last week er er I said that the
11		Government were very concerned (.) er about the safety arguments that were put
12		forward by RMT er therefore as a result of the meeting we did two things (.) we
13		asked Transport Scotland to check with three (.) er safety bodies in terms of the
14		operation o of driver and ticket-examiner er trains (.) the replies that came back
15		indicated that they didn't have safety concerns (.) that shouldn't have been a
16		surprise to Karen Whitefield (.) because of course (.) I pointed out last week to her
17		[that some sixty per cent of services] that run in
18	KW:	[that's not what I was asking about]

19	FM:	Scotland run on that basis (.) and of course the past administration (.) operated and
20		[launched services] (.) [on that] basis
21	KW:	[what I was asking]
22	PO:	Miss [Whitefield]

23	FM:	the Government is taking extremely seriously the points that the RMT made there is
24		to be a further (turn continues)

This example shows a woman MSP (Karen Whitefield) asking the First Minister an adversarial question because it contains an inference that the First Minster has misled the parliament (lines 1–8). The MSP illegally intervenes upon the First Minister twice to insist that he answers her question (lines 18 and 22). The Presiding Officer then calls Whitefield to order by naming her (line 23). This example is significant because it shows a woman MSP challenging the authority of the two most senior members of the SP: the Presiding Officer and the First Minister.

In interviews, women and men MSPs admitted to barracking and speaking out of turn. Often MSPs had contradictory attitudes towards this, saying they did not approve of the practice but nevertheless took part in barracking. Some MSPs felt that barracking was justified when a Minister was failing to respond to a question or not giving a 'straight answer', but not when making personal attacks on other members, which was thought to be a rare occurrence. Some MSPs felt that the Presiding Officers should control barracking more because certain 'repeat offenders' are responsible for most of these interventions and they should be stopped. One or two MSPs admitted using barracking in an adversarial way 'to go in for the kill', although this was uncommon. It was also noted that it is easier to barrack from the back of the chamber, and that young or inexperienced MSPs tend to be barracked the most 'because they haven't got a clue'. Some MSPs described this behaviour as 'bullying' because it was aimed at inexperienced MSPs and intended to put them off. This can take different forms, including the 'constant muttering of back-chat' and saying 'rubbish' when an individual is making a speech as a tactic to 'undermine their confidence and put them off their stride'. A woman MSP also noticed that a common tactic is to turn away from the speaker and theatrically ignore them by talking to a colleague next to them in order to 'put someone off'. Other tactics reported by MSPs included one MSP saying that she speaks quietly in the chamber so that members must listen to her more carefully and are more attentive to her speech. Another member said that he delays taking an intervention so that he has passed the relevant point in his speech by the time the intervention is finally made. This effectively reduces the impact of an adversarial or critical intervention. Another MSP said that she has learned to signal the end of the speech to get more time and consciously uses phrases like 'in conclusion' before the conclusion of her speech in order to make the Presiding Officer think that she is just about to finish. She says 'you see them physically sit back and I know I've got another thirty seconds'.

These reflections from MSPs about interactional strategies on the debate floor show that speaking time is of some concern, and the timed aspects of the speeches increase this sense of competition, both in terms of trying to prolong speaking time, but also in terms of giving and taking interventions.

The analysis of the debate floor in this section also shows that the SP at this point in 2009–11 was characterised by a mixture of jocular and sometimes sexual banter between women and men, and that women and men seemed to engage in all types of adversarial exchanges, including challenging the authority of the Presiding Officer and the First Minister. The fact that, by 2015, this parliament had developed into one in which all the leaders of the main parties were women, led by Nicola Sturgeon as First Minister, also indicates that egalitarian conditions were such that women were enabled to reach the top of the institutional and political party hierarchies.

4.3.2   The Debate Floor of the Northern Ireland Assembly

The quantitative analysis of debate turns showed that men and women in the Northern Ireland Assembly participated in all of the different types of speaking turns (there were no categories in which they did not participate). The Assembly had the most illegal interventions of all the parliaments, and the 17 per cent of women in the parliament took part in at least 11 per cent of these illegal interventions, whereas men took part in at least 17 per cent (71 per cent were not attributable to an individual speaker). Women were slightly underrepresented overall (taking 14 per cent of the turns), but this includes the turns taken by the all-male roles of Speaker and the Deputy Speakers which represented 14 per cent of all the speaking turns in the institution. If these turns are excluded, then women spoke for 16 per cent of the time, which is close to their representation in the Assembly as a whole.

Illegal 'out of order' utterances are frequent and confrontational in the NIA. They occurred in both plenary and question time sessions and both men and women MLAs take part in these interventions. Examples 4.4a and 4.4b show a woman MLA, Dolores Kelly of the SDLP party, repeatedly disrupting the debate floor.

Example 4.4a 09/02/10 at 4pm. Joint Statement by the First Minister and Deputy First Minister on the Hillsborough Castle Agreement on the devolution of Police and Justice (Transcript)

Participants: DK = Dolores Kelly (SDLP) MLA = Members of the Legislative Authority; SP = Speaker (Willie Hay) DFM = Deputy First Minister, Martin McGuinness (Sinn Féin) NC = Ní Chuilín (Sinn Féin)

1	DK:	Mister (.) Mister Speaker er could could the Minister (.) also confirm that the
2		parades working group which is a set-up er is is a set up and indeed that that that
3		that the Ashdown proposals are the only ones on the table (.)
4	SP:	First Minister
5	DFM:	well I I can certainly confirm that if er Sinn Féin had of accepted the SDLP position in
6		relation to er how we deal with this issue that for the remaining term of this

7		Assembly the powers over policing and the courts and justice would reside in the
8		hands of British Government
9		direct rule [Ministers (.)]
10	DK:	[No nationalist] need [apply]
11	DFM:	[that's] the reality so the contention that has
12		been made is absolutely without any foundation [whatsoever (.)]
13	DK:	[*unclear*]
14	SP:	<u>O</u>rder
15	DFM:	That is the reality (.) the contention that has been made is absolutely without any
16		foundation [whatsoever (.)]
17	DK:	[*unclear*]
18	SP:	Order
19	DFM:	the confusion that is clearly evident in the SDLP's [mind in relation (.)]
20	DK:	[there is no] confusion
21	DFM:	well (.) er (.) we certainly had confusion when the
22		former leader of the [SDLP said that he]
23	DK:	[there's no confusion]
24		wanted to see d'Hondt being run again (.) which would have meant the collapsing of
25		a Department and absolute certainty that the Department of Justice and its
26		responsibilities over that would have been taken by a unionist Minister (turn
27		continues)

Example 4.4b Joint Statement by the First Minister and Deputy First Minister on the Hillsborough Castle Agreement, continued (09/02/10) (Transcript)

1	NC:	Thank you, a Cheann Comhairle I thank the First Minister and deputy First Minister
2		for their statement here in the House today I suppose my question has been partly
3		answered but it is in relation to the er current Parades Commission if there's any
4		details of the roles of this current Parades Commission working group er and er and
5		the new or improved processes rolled out and just to say that I am convinced, now
6		more than ever, that er the er stoops [sorry the SDLP] is quite happy
7	DK:	[no stoop unclear]
8	SP:	Order order I really now must insist on Dolores Kelly Mrs Kelly I really have to say
9		[you are coming] very close to challenging the authority of the Chair (.)
10	MLAs:	[loud muttering]
11	SP:	coming very close coming very close to it (2)
12	FM:	approaching the working group issue (turn continues)

In Example 4.4a, Dolores Kelly asks the Deputy First Minister a question (lines 1–3) but then repeatedly interrupts him when he responds (on lines 10, 13, 17, 20 and 23). She resists the authority of the Speaker by replying directly to Martin McGuiness, as in lines 20 and 23 when she responds that there's 'no confusion'. She disregards the Speaker and flouts the strict turn-taking rules of the debate. In 4.4b, another woman MLA, Carál Ní Chulín also takes confrontational stance against Kelly by calling her party the 'stoops' (referring to a nickname of the SDLP as the 'stoop down low party') in line 6. This example shows that women MLAs participate in some of the most adversarial exchanges with the most powerful moves (such as resisting the authority of the Speaker), and in the most important speech events.

Women MLAs are over-represented in Ministerial responses to questions (they took 24 per cent of responses), which reflects the fact that three out of thirteen positions on the Executive committee of Ministers are taken by women (women represent 23 per cent of the executive). There was some evidence to show that some women Ministers were subject to a high level of barracking and interventions. Catriona Ruane, the Sinn Féin Minister for Education at the time the sample was taken, was reported by interviewees as being the focus for Unionist aggression and disruption in the NIA (Shaw 2013). Most of the MLAs saw barracking as a characteristic part of proceedings in the chamber. Some MLAs said that they enjoy the 'banter' associated with out of order utterances in the chamber, and it is expected that people 'get a bit of a roasting in there' because 'that's the confine of politics' and 'you should be able to withstand those criticisms'. One man described this banter by using a sporting metaphor saying it is 'no different from a game of rugby' in that you can 'go at it "ding dong"' with another Member 'and then joke about it afterwards'. A woman MLA admitted to enjoying 'winding Martin up' (referring to Martin McGuinness, Deputy First Minister), saying that she waited to see him turning red in the face in order to 'know that you've hit home'. MLAs agreed that 'we all heckle, but sometimes it is personal' and that there was a difference between general shouts of 'rubbish' and more personal attacks on individuals. A woman MLA said that she deals with barracking by trying not to take attacks personally, and by trying to see them as a function of her public role as an elected representative. Two other MLAs said they tried to deflect personal attacks by using humour. A senior men MLA observed that politicians have different styles in the chamber, and that some MLAs 'encourage banter', whereas others do not. He said that when the Speaker can perceive that a MLA is deliberately trying to disrupt another MLA's turn 'deliberately, knowing they are easily put-off', the Speaker tends to 'step in', whereas he leaves other MLAs who are quite good at 'taking the comments'.

4.3.3   The Debate Floor of the National Assembly of Wales

The NAW debate floor is distinctive in that spontaneous turns are less common than in the other institutions and account for only 10 per cent of the overall turns. The Presiding Officer's interventions are proportionally much more frequent than the other institutions and represent 12 per cent of all the speaking turns. The Presiding Officer's interventions are most commonly used to regulate the timing restrictions imposed on speaking turns. Illegal interventions only account for 1 per cent of speaking turns in the Assembly, but when they occur they are usually made in Question Time sessions. Example 4.6 in the next section of the chapter shows Ann Jones, a Welsh Labour AM, illegally intervening and ignoring the admonition of the Presiding officer in a debate on the Queen's Speech (16/06/10). AMs noted that barracking was characteristic of the Assembly, although it tended not to be personal in tone, and most commonly occurred as muttering or single word interjections such as 'rubbish' or 'shameful'. One AM pointed out that the small size of the Assembly meant that 'you can't detach yourself from the person you are attacking' and the more 'human scale' of the assembly meant that there would be interpersonal consequences if someone was verbally attacked in the chamber. AMs identified a range of tactical behaviours related to barracking these included 'flouncing out' of the Assembly to express opposition, or making comments in a 'stage whisper' to a neighbour in order to 'put someone off'.

AMs differed in their opinions about barracking as some AMs felt that it was an integral part of the debate discourse that showed people were engaged with a contribution. One man AM said they'd rather their speech was greeted with barracking than with silence, and another said that they took barracking to be a normal part of plenary sessions that stopped the proceedings being too 'dull'. Another said that they looked forward to the 'insults' and that he took them as a 'badge of honour'. While both men and women AMs said they took part in barracking, none of the women AMs embraced it quite such an enthusiastic way. One woman AM said she'd only barrack men AMs but not other women, and that barracking was sometimes used to put off 'weaker members'. Several women AMs said that they disliked barracking and that they found it an intimidating, masculine practice. Two women AMs said they had privately complained to the Presiding Officer about getting barracked in the chamber, and that they had received less barracking after they had done so.

4.4   What Makes a Political Institution More Egalitarian?

As described in Section 4.1, it was hoped that the new devolved institutions would allow increased descriptive representation of women in the institutions, as well as a substantive cultural change promoted by 'an open, simple and modern style of operating' (Brown 2000: 545) and 'family friendly' hours. The numerical representation of women at 32 per cent in the SP and particularly the 47 per cent representation of women in the NAW is a great improvement on the 18–20 per cent in both the HoC and the NIA in this third term in 2007–11. The analysis of gender and participation and particularly the classification of different types of speaking turns in this chapter allows the identification of some of the ways in which women's numerical representation affects their overall involvement in debates. Additionally, the detailed analysis of the debate floors and the ethnographic interview data points to characteristics of these new institutions that contribute to a more egalitarian ethos in these CoPs.

First, the classification of speaking turns into those that are allocated and those that are spontaneous allows an additional lens through which the description of the institutional debate floors can be viewed. Participation within allocated turns (speeches, questions and responses) are contingent on seniority and party affiliation, while spontaneous turns can be made by any politician at any point in a speech event. The relationship between the interactional characteristics of different speech events, and the opportunities and restrictions for participation that they offer participants is a possible area for further research. Variation in the proportion of speeches and question times in institutions may affect participation overall and offer an additional comparative dimension when considering factors affecting inclusion. For example, Figures 4.11 and 4.12 show the proportions of different speech events in the SP and the NAW.

Figure 4.12 shows that the sample of speech events from the NAW had 51 per cent of the most restricted type of turn (questions and responses), and 26 per cent of speeches. The SP shows a different pattern, with 36 per cent of questions and responses and 32 per cent of speeches. While this was not the focus of the research project and a larger sample of speech events would be needed to investigate these interactional patterns more fully, it is possible that there is a relationship between the proportion of different types of speech events in an institution and the participation and involvement of its members. Alongside questions about the degree to which different speech events promote or exclude contributors according to party, seniority and institutional roles, it may also be possible to suggest an ideal combination of speech events that would ensure the greatest opportunities for the participation of all members. Examining these interactional patterns also offers some possible explanations for the finding that women in the NAW only took 32 per cent of the speaking turns despite their representation of 47 per cent or near parity overall. One possible explanation for the finding may be found in the combination of two factors: first, the high proportion of the most restricted type of allocated turns in the NAW (and the lowest proportion of spontaneous turns across the institutions); and second, the uneven proportion of women in political parties across the assembly, with the Conservative Party with only one woman MLA. An analysis of the speaking turns in the NAW corpus according to political party is shown in Figure 4.13.

Figure 4.13 shows that although the 13 Welsh Conservative Party AMs occupy 21 per cent of the seats in the Assembly, they take up 28 per cent of the speaking turns. As only one of the Conservative AMs was a woman, and if this debate sample is representative of speech events in the assembly, then this accounts for women's under-representation in relation to speaking turns in the NAW. Given the high proportion of allocated turns and the mechanism

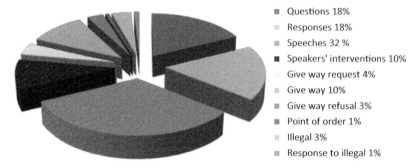

■ Questions 18%
▨ Responses 18%
▨ Speeches 32 %
■ Speakers' interventions 10%
  Give way request 4%
▨ Give way 10%
■ Give way refusal 3%
■ Point of order 1%
▨ Illegal 3%
■ Response to illegal 1%

Figure 4.11 Chart showing the percentages of different types of turns taken by MSPs in the Scottish Parliament.

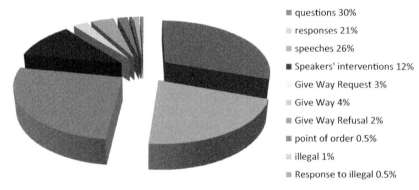

■ questions 30%
▨ responses 21%
■ speeches 26%
■ Speakers' interventions 12%
  Give Way Request 3%
▨ Give Way 4%
■ Give Way Refusal 2%
■ point of order 0.5%
▨ illegal 1%
■ Response to illegal 0.5%

Figure 4.12 Chart showing the percentages of different types of turns taken by AMs in the National Assembly for Wales.

of allocation between the four main parties, this could effectively mean that women have very little chance of taking a turn allocated to the Welsh Conservative party and they are therefore almost excluded from a quarter of the allocated speaking turns. This explanation is also borne out by observational data, as when watching the proceedings in the Siambr from the viewers' gallery it was striking that when looking towards the Conservative seats the Assembly appeared to be a men-only chamber rather than an institution with almost 50:50 men and women representation. Furthermore, this explanation would also suggest that the numbers of women in an institution as a factor on its own are not enough to ensure equal participation. It would rather support the idea that there needs to be a 'critical distribution' between political parties and institutional roles if equal participation is to be achieved when turns are allocated in this way.

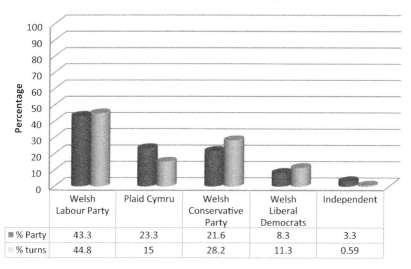

	Welsh Labour Party	Plaid Cymru	Welsh Conservative Party	Welsh Liberal Democrats	Independent
% Party	43.3	23.3	21.6	8.3	3.3
% turns	44.8	15	28.2	11.3	0.59

Figure 4.13 Graph showing the representation of political parties in the National Assembly for Wales and the total speaking turns by party in the sample of proceedings (not including the Presiding Officers' interventions).

The discourse analytic, interview and observational data also identify particular linguistic characteristics of the devolved institutions that set them apart from the more traditional HoC. These are most usefully characterised by *informality* and *flexibility*, both in the adherence and rigidity of the imposition of formal rules, and in the accepted linguistic conventions of the institutions. As Rosa Malley notes in her ethnographic comparison of Westminster and the Scottish Parliament that the 'informality of the Scottish parliament was striking from the outset' (Malley 2012: 714). The example in Chapter 3 (Example 3.1) of the new woman MP, Jane Griffiths, struggling to correctly formulate a question to the Prime Minister in the HoC, strongly contrasts with similar transgressions across the devolved institutions. Example 4.5 below shows the same transgression of the debate rules by a woman MSP at the beginning of the SP in 2000.

Example 4.5 First Minister's Question Time (07/12/00) (Transcript)

MM = Margo MacDonald (SNP), PO = Presiding Officer (Donald Dewar), FM = First Minister (Henry MacLeish)

1   MM: thank you Presiding Officer (1) if we could return to earth and leave
2   Mars behind (.) I wonder if the First Minister recalls with me that
3   following the winter crisis (.) [in the NHS]

4	PO:	[no I'm sorry] you haven't asked (.) <u>o</u>rder
5	MM:	oh I know (.) he <u>knows</u> what my first question <u>was</u> though I think
6	PO:	no no order you <u>must</u> read out your first question
7	MM:	oh (.) <u>right</u> we'll go through the <u>form</u> [(laughs)] to <u>ask</u> the First Minister
8	MSPs:	[laughter]
9		how he plans to (1) recruit the required number of nurses for <u>hospitals</u>
10		to cope with seasonal ad<u>missions</u> this winter (1)
11	FM:	er Margo (.) I'm really sorry that the procedures of the House <u>force</u> me
12		to answer your <u>first</u> question and then we can get onto the <u>real</u>
13		business after that (turn continues)

(Shaw 2006)

This example illustrates several points in relation to the differences between the HoC and the SP (Shaw 2006). Not only is it an example of a woman MSP making a joke (which is rare in the HoC), but it also shows a woman MSP challenging the fundamental procedures of the chamber. Margo MacDonald is right in saying the First Minister knows her question already, he does. Her attempt to by-pass reading out the question means she is challenging the accepted and official norms. The fact that the First Minister apologises twice (on lines 4 and 11) for having to enforce the rules suggests that the woman MSP's position is given some sympathy within the chamber. The data from the HoC suggests that this type of challenge is unlikely to be undertaken by a woman MP and it is rare that the Speaker's authority is challenged in this way, although as noted in Chapter 3, some men challenge debate rules when filibustering. Furthermore, this exchange also shows the lack of formality in the SP when compared with the HoC as first names rather than formal forms of address are used.

It has been suggested that parliamentary address forms are particularly sensitive to in-group membership, out-group positioning and parliamentary status (Ilie 2010). Ilie finds that in the HoC there is a high degree of compliance with the use of formal address terms – such as 'My Right Honourable Friend', 'the Honourable Lady/Gentleman' – and the use of the third person singular pronoun 's/he', rather than the more direct second person singular pronoun 'you' – which concurs with the rule that MPs must not address each other directly, but only through the Speaker. Ilie notes there are non-reciprocal uses of address forms, for example when the Speaker addresses members using 'you', but the MPs cannot use this form. Similarly, MPs making interventions from a sitting position frequently use the direct second person form, but responses to illegal interventions adhere to the rules and use the third person form or a more formal title. In the devolved institutions, the Standing Orders make no specific requirements for address forms, beyond that politicians should address each other through the Speaker. In the SP MSPs confirmed that pronouns ('you', 'she') and first names were often used in the chamber rather than the more formal formula of full first name and surname or an address title (Mr, Mrs, Sir etc.)

and surname. Members thought that it was important to enforce the rule that all speeches are addressed through the Presiding Officer to make the interaction less personal and aggressive. However, it was noted that this rule is frequently flouted, and that some MSPs do not appear to understand the rule or correct themselves when instructed to do so. It was also suggested by an interviewee that the rules governing forms of address have become more formal over time, and that at the beginning of the parliament it was permissible to use a member's first name. According to MSPs, the Presiding Officers increasingly tend to correct this informal use and insist on the more formal forms of address.

In the NIA there were also differing opinions evident in MLA's comments about address forms, where some politicians preferred the traditional '*Westminstery*' titles such as 'right honourable gentleman/lady' and others preferred address terms to be as informal as possible, and to use first names only. This variation in opinion is also mirrored in the use of address terms in debates: In the exchange partially represented in Examples 4.4a and 4.4b Dolores Kelly is referred to by her official title 'the Member for Upper Bann' also the more informal 'Dolores Kelly' and 'Mrs Kelly' (Line 8 of Example 4.4b above). In the NAW, AMs either use the term 'Assembly Member', or more frequently first names only, particularly in committees. Some AMs, particularly Conservatives (Feld 2000) thought that the atmosphere was sometimes too friendly, and that some informal practices such as calling each other by first names, rather than by more formal address terms were detrimental to the formal nature of proceedings in the chamber. The difference in the use of address forms between the more formal HoC and the NAW was particularly evident when Cheryl Gillan led the Queen's speech debate in her then-new role as Secretary of State for Wales in June 2010. Example 4.6 shows an AM's reaction to Cheryl Gillan's incorrect use of the NAW address forms.

Example 4.6 Sustained Illegal Interventions: The National Assembly for Wales 16 June 2010 (Transcript)

Participants: CG = Cheryl Gillan; AJ = Anne Jones (Labour); DPO = Deputy Presiding Officer; AMs = An Assembly Member

1	CG:	I think that the single new back-to-work programme will provide <u>nume</u>rous new
2		opportunities for national and local partners (.) to con<u>tri</u>bute to the coalition
3		Government's programme (.) to tackle er unemployment (.)
4	AJ	well you haven't convinced me
5	CG	Um(.) well I may not have convinced the Honourable Lady as she says from a

6		sedentary position (.) [but I am] (.)
7	AJ	[I am not] an honourable lady I am an [Assembly Member]
8	DPO	[um ex<u>cuse</u> me]

9	CG	um well the the honourable Assembly Member (.)
10	AJ	no I am an Assembly Member
11	CG	an Assembly Member (.) an Assembly Member um and I'm sorry I'm I'm not trying to
12		convince her (.) I'm trying to reassure the people that she may have frightened

13	CG	out<u>side</u> this Cham[ber]
14	AJ	[no] I am not the one who is frightening [them]
15	CG	[that] we [<u>are</u> looking]
16	(.)	
17	DPO	[Ann Jones](.)

18		please
19	CG	that we are looking at this area and we

20		[will approach it with compassion] (.)
21	AJ	[unclear----------------------------]

22	CG	in <u>clos</u>ing (.) Madam [Presiding Officer Deputy] Presiding Officer I
23	AM	[hear hear]
24	AJ	[unclear---------------------]

25	CG	reiterate how impressed I have been in my first few weeks as Secretary of State at
26		the <u>new</u> relationship that we are trying to forge and we are forging between
27		Westminster and Cardiff (.) I say in all sincerity I want this relationship to be based
28		on mutual respect and cooperation because I believe *(turn continues)*

(Shaw 2011)

As described in Shaw (2011), this extract shows a woman AM initially interrupting the Secretary of State to contest the remark she has made about the back-to-work programme, saying 'you haven't convinced me' (line 4). Gillan responds to this illegal intervention and refers to the interrupting AM as 'the Honourable Lady' (line 5), highlighting the AMs, illegal intervention from a 'sedentary position'. The AM makes another illegal intervention to correct Gillan by saying 'I am not an Honourable Lady I am an Assembly Member' (lines 7–8). Line 9 shows an example of other initiated self-repair (Sacks et al. 1974) when Gillan says 'The Honourable Assembly Member'. The AM interrupts once more to correct her by saying 'No, I am an Assembly Member', to which Gillan says 'An Assembly member, an Assembly member' (line 11) in a further example of other initiated self-repair. This is like Chilton's (Chilton 2004: 107) example of repair in parliamentary question times in that when Gillan eventually corrects herself she does so with 'what intuitively sounds like weary condescension' (Chilton 2004: 107) in order to preserve her face. Gillan then accuses the interrupting AM of 'frightening people' outside the chamber, which gives rise to another illegal intervention (line 12–13). The deputy Presiding

Officer intervenes, but the AM continues to disrupt the debate floor (lines 21 and 24). Finally, Gillan attempts to control the floor by a change in footing (Goffman 1981) in which she clearly signals the final part of her speech by saying 'in closing' (line 22). This change in footing is recognised by a Conservative AM supporter who shouts 'hear hear', although the interrupting woman AM illegally intervenes once more while Gillan introduces her closing remarks.

The example transcripts from the devolved assemblies therefore show a less authoritarian enforcement of the rules in comparison to the HoC, and the interview accounts point to a more inclusive atmosphere. Formality has been observed to annihilate 'popular competence' in speaking (Bourdieu 1991: 71) and it is claimed that 'the more formal a situation is, the more able it is to impose by itself alone the recognition of the legitimacy of the dominant mode of expression' (Bourdieu 1991: 70). These legitimate modes appear to be more informal and therefore accessible to speakers in the devolved institutions. Informality therefore contributes to the claim that women feel more 'at home' in the new institutions: 'Scottish and Welsh women politicians feel a strong sense of entitlement and belonging; in turn, their presence is regarded as normal and unremarkable' (Mackay and McAllister 2012: 730). To this extent, the devolved institutions of the NAW and the SP appear to have succeeded in creating a more egalitarian culture in debates. Furthermore, the research has shown that in all the devolved institutions women politicians take part in rule-breaking and so do not appear to be positioned as interlopers in the ways that women in the HoC were shown to be in Chapter 3. This section has attempted to identify the factors that contribute to this egalitarian culture. The next section aims to assess women's progress in the devolved institutions and identifies remaining barriers to their equal representation and participation.

4.5 Women's Progress in the New Institutions

Having described the interactional details of the institutional debate floors and the possible gendered effects of different interactional patterns and norms, this section starts with a general description of interviewee accounts of women's progress in the different CoPs. Unlike the NAW and the SP, in the NIA there was agreement among men and women MLAs that the institution was 'male-dominated', reflecting women's low numerical representation. It was also acknowledged that the number of women in the wider parliamentary administration was inadequate. One man MLA did not know the proportion of women in the assembly, and another thought that 17 per cent representation was 'quite good'. A woman MLA described the NIA as 'male, pale and stale' and another added 'grey' to this list to emphasise the lack of diversity in the chamber, not only in relation to gender but also race and age. A woman MLA said 'it's just the sheer number of men in grey suits with grey hair sitting there, not a lot of younger faces, of women, of ethnic minorities'. A woman MLA said that she had been surprised by the masculine 'performance' aspect of the chamber which involved 'back-slapping and insincere comments passed across the chamber for political gain'. Women MLAs also agreed that barracking was characteristic of proceedings, one woman MLA saying that 'it is important to shout out' and join in because 'you have to find your voice in these male-dominated assemblies'. Some women MLAs thought that there seemed a degree of cross-party support between women, but that this was limited because of the small numbers of women. A woman MLA reported being supported by women in private but said she wanted them to 'stand up and be counted' and support her when she was being barracked in the chamber. This hostile environment for women is thought to because of cultural factors (Whiting and Braniff 2016) and because of a lack of commitment to positive measures to increase women's candidacy and representation overall. This does not appear to have changed despite Arlene Foster becoming Northern Ireland's first woman leader (as leader of the Democratic Unionist Party [DUP] in 2016) followed by Michelle O'Neill becoming leader of Sinn Féin in 2017.

In the NAW, women AMs' views about the gendered nature of the assembly also differed. Women AMs who had been in the Assembly since the first term in 1999 tended to view the role of women in the assembly more positively than newer members. Longer-serving women AMs felt that there was cross-party support for women if they were attacked in the chamber: 'if any man did behave badly then he'd be dealt with, we'd send the girls around'. This contrasted strongly with younger members' views who claimed that there was 'no sisterhood, especially from older women'. Younger women AMs felt that being young and being a woman made speaking in the chamber 'more nerve-wracking' and that women members 'might get more stick'. Another newer woman AM claimed that longer serving men AMs were sometimes patronising towards her, telling her that her interventions in the chamber were not relevant to the topic. However, AMs thought that women and men participated equally in debates and that the assembly chamber did not feel overly masculine. AMs had very different views about whether women were disadvantaged in the assembly. Several men AMs said that gender made no difference at all in the assembly and people were judged on their merits. Most of the women AMs felt that positive discrimination was important to maintain the level of women's in the Assembly. There is some history of women's leadership in the NAW, with Kirsty Williams as the leader of the

Welsh Liberal Democratic party 2008–16; and Leanne Wood the leader of Plaid Cymru from 2012 to 2018.

In the SP, MSPs reported that women and men seemed to participate equally in the chamber. MSPs agreed that the chamber itself did not feel 'masculine' but seemed to be a place where women and men could contribute equally to all different types of speaking turns, including adversarial ones and those that challenge the authority of the most senior members. Many of the comments about women's participation were positive, stating that there were many positive role models in the parliament for women politicians and that women participated across all topics, not just on the 'soft' topics that are stereotypically associated with women. There was also some support for the view that the high numbers of women MSPs in the first term of the parliament helped women's participation. One MSP said 'possibly because it is new, and possibly because there were so many women in the first session and we've always had one woman at least as Presiding Officer so it doesn't feel difficult because of that'. This suggests that the involvement of women from the start of a new parliament with strong representation in all roles can contribute to encouraging women's participation. This was subsequently borne out by the success of women leaders in the SP, with the election of Ruth Davidson as leader of the Scottish Conservative Party in 2011; Nicola Sturgeon to leader of the Scottish Nationalist Party and First Minister in 2014; and Kezia Dugdale to the leader of the Labour party in 2015–17. This means that for a two-year period in 2015–17 the three leaders of the main parties were all women. In our analysis of women leaders in the 2015 UK General election campaign (Cameron and Shaw 2016), an extract from First Minister's Question time in the Scottish Parliament was used to examine gender and adversarial communicative norms in politics. In the extract of an exchange between Nicola Sturgeon and Kezia Dugdale we observed that the adversarial norms of this event had been preserved in a context where women's leadership has become normalised (Cameron and Shaw 2016: 117–18).

The emergence of the women leaders in the SP has been argued to be 'a result of collective action over time' rather than the individual agency of individual leaders (Robinson and Kerr 2018: 643). While the hierarchical concept of leadership was not a central concern of devolution campaigns (Robinson and Kerr 2018: 643), the SP shows how the 'newness' of institutions can offer opportunities for 'gender concerns to be incorporated more easily and fundamentally at the outset of an institution's life than it is to "add them at a later stage"' (Waylen 2008: 273). However, there is no single, straightforward pattern of progress and feminist institutionalist scholars (see Chapter 1) have explored 'why gender reforms have been so vulnerable to regress, even in new institutional contexts' (Mackay 2014: 550), as the numerical description of women in institutions has varied with time. Putting forward the key concept of 'nested newness' in which 'the new is embedded in time, sequence and its institutional environment' it is suggested that new institutions are 'better understood as bounded innovation within an existing system' (Mackay 2014: 552). According to Mackay, this concept of nested newness must be considered as a gendered concept in which 'institutions are not gender neutral but are actively constructing and reproducing gender relations and ideologies' (Mackay 2014: 553). This is certainly the case for the devolved assemblies that have an intrinsic, inescapable relationship with the HoC at Westminster, as evidenced by the preservation of the norms of different devolved versions of PMQs. So much so that 'any effort to compare the new devolved institutions with the Westminster model runs the risk of seeing differences that only exist in one or other imaginings of the Westminster model' (Mitchell 2010: 99). This paradox also appears to inflect on decisions about institutional design and implementation, as Mitchell observes in relation to the SP, the decision to adopt the term 'parliament' rather than 'assembly', the adoption of a mace in the chamber and the establishment of First Minister's Question Time. He claims: 'The parliament needed to conform to public and elite conceptions of what a real Parliament looked like and that meant it had to have the familiar hallmarks of Westminster, the parliament familiar to both the public and the elite' (2010: 108). Consequently, although there is some evidence of 'new regendered paths and outcomes' in new institutions, nevertheless 'the institutions and norms of the Westminster model exert a considerable drag' (Mackay 2014: 560–1). This process is also able to be traced through linguistic conventions and norms, as observed with the reported increasing formality of forms of address over time in the SP towards those used in the HoC that were noted in the previous section. Mackay also observes that new institutions tend to 'fall back on the old' to 'fill in the gaps' and that opportunities for alternative mechanisms regarding executive accountability, other than the PMQs format were missed: 'Thus a new formal rule was displaced by the introduction of an old formal (Westminster) rule; and in doing so, new informal norms, which assigned value to typically feminised attributes of collaboration rather than competition, were undermined by the reassertion of old and masculine coded norms of adversarial parliamentary performance' (Mackay 2014: 563). This 'falling back' on the old is thought to reduce opportunities for reform and symbolically the reaffirmation of traditional norms and rules 'also reaffirms the gender status quo' (Mackay 2014: 243).

The linking of adversarial performances with masculine norms is critically examined in Chapter 5 as although this model is thought to disadvantage women politicians (Mackay 2014; Goetz 2003) it also contributes to the 'gendered discourse of differentiation' (Sunderland 2004) relating to gendered political styles. This belief in gendered styles of communication is particularly evident in the interviews with politicians across the UK political institutions. In the SP accounts of gender differences between men and women MSPs were common and often contradictory. A men MSP claimed that women did not bring a consensual style to the parliament and that the idea that they would was 'nonsense' that had not been borne out by experience, because women seemed to participate equally. However, many MSPs believed there were gendered differences between MSPs with men more likely to be aggressive in the chamber than women, even though women can 'hold their own'. Although women and men MSPs take part in barracking, some MSPs viewed this as a male practice. One woman MSP described it as 'unladylike behaviour' and claimed that she judged women who barracked more harshly than men. When asked if female voices were characteristic of barracking in the chamber, one MSP answered that women's voices can be heard, but judged this negatively, saying these tended to be the more 'strident voices'. Women were also thought to go into topics 'in more depth' than men and be less likely to produce superficial sound bites. The ways in which women are described imply that underlying stereotypes about gendered behaviour are still salient. One men MSP described women as being 'no shrinking violets when it comes to holding their own in debates', another described forceful women MSPs as 'honorary men'. A woman MSP recounted an incident in the chamber where a men MSP told a forceful woman MSP 'I wouldn't like to take short pay home to you', at once reinserting the authoritative woman politician into a domestic and relatively powerless role. Although often presented in a jocular or ostensibly flattering manner, as suggested in the previous section, these types of comments show the persistence of traditional stereotypes in relation to women and men. A male MSP claimed that it was harder for women politicians: 'women in politics can be accused either of being a kind of monster if they develop the thick skin and the toughness that men are used to having but men don't get accused of being monsters and if they don't (get accused of being a monster) they get accused of being of having a kind of weakness that men often don't get accused of having'. These kinds of contradictions and competing pressures on women seem to be present, although the parliament clearly offers women a more supportive and egalitarian environment than older and more traditional parliaments.

In the NIA there was also a common perception amongst MLAs that women and men had different communicative styles, and that women tended to 'posture less' and 'not to repeat themselves for the sake of being seen to say something'. Women were also attributed with being more empathetic than men and aiming for long-term rather than short-term strategies to 'get the job done'. Women were characterised as 'being able to give as good as they get' in the chamber and are 'not easily intimidated because they have come through a political career'. A woman MLA reportedly responded to barracking by saying 'Ay my husband shouts at me as well and I don't take any notice of him either', at once normalising and resisting male dominance.

In the NAW, the discourse of the 'strong woman' was also evident with women AMs described by a men AM as having 'plenty of steel' and being 'more capable of taking anybody on at any time'. However, the same AMs also thought that men were 'more boisterous' than women and that women had a less adversarial style that 'had less of a pantomime element' than men. As in the SP, the way in which women are described implies that underlying stereotypes about gendered behaviour are still salient. One of the men AMs claimed that 'some of the ladies are being more aggressive than they need to be', and most AMs thought that women and men had different 'styles' and that this related to gender. This view was also shared by several women AMs, who said that women tended to barrack less than men and that women 'do not want to put their message across in that way'. However, some of these women also admitted to taking part in barracking themselves. One woman AM said that she thought that women were 'not taught' to be aggressive, and that they would prefer not to take part in this kind of behaviour.

The belief in gendered linguistic styles presents multiple problems for women politicians and there is no empirical evidence to support the claim that men use authoritative language and women consensual language (see Chapters 1 and 5–8). As discussed in Chapter 1, it has been claimed that 'new' women members in political institutions, and those involved in new institutions from the start are burdened by the expectation that they will bring a 'civilizing difference' to those institutions. This expectation means that women's public rhetoric is likely to be fractured by competing, often contradictory norms and expectations (Walsh 2001). These beliefs can also contribute to the negative assessment of women when they take part in adversarial or stereotypically masculine linguistic practices (Shaw 2013). This can lead to women in leadership positions facing the double bind between professionalism and femininity: 'If she talks like a manager she is transgressing the boundaries of femininity: if she talks like a woman she no longer represents herself as a manager'(Holmes 2006). In this way, stereotypical views about male and female styles of speech affect women's evaluation in public contexts and are closely linked to the more overt and essentialising opinions about gender roles expressed sexism in these institutions.

Politicians across the institutions reported sexist behaviour towards women, particularly in the NIA. Interviewees asserted that this male-dominated space can be intimidating for women and that 'people here think it is their divine right to shout at a woman' and that women were particularly targeted because 'they think we'll just give her a hard time and she'll fall in and collapse'.

Most MLAs agreed that in the first term of the Assembly, women politicians in the Northern Ireland Women's Coalition (NIWC) were the subject of much abuse, and that the Assembly has a 'history of attacking women'. These first MLAs were 'moo-ed' at in the chamber and were told by one man MLA that 'they should be at home doing the dishes'. One woman MLA reported that 'Many of the men feel that the woman's place was in the home and certainly not in the debating chamber and one that makes decisions even, horror of horrors!' In the SP, some women MSPs claimed that there was a degree of informal cross-party support amongst women and that this deterred overly sexist behaviour towards them. An MSP said that men supported women because 'they know that they will be challenged by a strong group of women if they don't'. In the NAW a woman AM claimed that she was subject to sexist abuse in the chamber by a Conservative man MP who:

Used to sledge all the way through my speeches [He said] 'God this woman is useless, oh my God I can't believe she just said that, this woman is completely insane I've never heard such crap in all my life' and I'd have him by the side of me 'cause the small the Chamber was quite small so it's like we were we were literally seated cheek by jowl and he would be next to me giving it all that.

In addition to sexist behaviour in the chambers the sexist, negative representation of women politicians by the media was one of the most recurrent themes in the interview data from women across all the devolved assemblies, and this is investigated further in the next chapter.

The evidence from the interview data therefore suggests that regardless of the gains for women in terms of numerical representation and more equal participation in the devolved institutions presented in Sections 4.1–4.3, some significant barriers to women's political participation and representation remain. The most significant of these are the three interlinked concerns identified in this section: stereotypical beliefs in gendered linguistic styles of communication; sexism in political institutions; and the representation of women politicians in the media. The next three chapters of the book examine these aspects by first discussing these barriers to women's representation and political performances in more detail in Chapter 5 and then undertaking detailed case studies of the ways in which women leaders perform linguistically in adversarial contexts; how they resist sexist comments; and their strategies for performing agentic, authoritative leadership in political contexts.

5   Barriers to Women's Participation in Politics

5.1   Stereotypical Views of Women's Professional Behaviour

The analysis of the 1998–2001 HoC in Chapter 3 and the 2010 devolved data in Chapter 4 showed that political institutions differ in the extent to which women participate and feel that they belong. However, ethnographic data also shows that the main barrier to women's participation in politics – and in public life more generally – is that the 'public voice of authority' is associated with men, and political institutions tend to instantiate stereotypically 'male' discursive norms (Baxter 2010, 2018; Cameron and Shaw 2016; Holmes 2006; Lovenduski 2014a; Shaw 2000, 2006; Walsh 2001). As already suggested, women in politics are considered 'out of place' because of cultural expectations and stereotypes about gender and communication. Feminine discursive norms are not considered to be part of the language of public and professional life. Leadership research shows that traits that are perceived to be typical of women are thought to be at odds with traits that are 'required' of successful leaders, leading to a 'lack of fit' between gender and leadership (Heilman 1983). This can give rise to social and economic penalties (also known as 'backlash') in response to women behaving agentively and in counter-stereotypic ways (Rudman et al. 2012). In this chapter, I review how these cultural norms and expectations – particularly in relation to language – can hinder women's political progress, before going on to examine how women politicians in leadership positions have negotiated them in Chapters 6 and 7.

I first consider the general stereotypical claims made about women's and men's linguistic behaviour in the workplace by focusing on gendered speech styles: the evidence for their existence and the way in which a belief in such styles can hinder women's progress in politics. Then I examine a particular linguistic ideology that is particularly relevant to politics: the 'different voice' ideology. This ideology states that women speak with a 'different voice' from men, and that this different voice is less adversarial and more consensual than the typical masculine speech style. In Section 5.3, I examine the mobilisation of these gendered stereotypical beliefs as sexist language, attitudes and behaviours and consider examples of sexist language in the HoC. Section 5.4

examines the fraternal networks that appear to present obstacles to women's participation in political life. Finally, in Section 5.5, I consider women's negative and stereotypic representation in the media as one of the main barriers to women's participation in politics.

Women in politics must perform in contexts that are routinely and stereotypically associated with men. To succeed they must do so carefully and without incurring negative evaluations for 'not being feminine enough.' Thus these women encounter the double bind of women in public life. The strictures placed on women and men to conform to stereotypical notions of masculine and feminine linguistic behaviour can be viewed as part of the 'rigid regulatory frame' (Butler 1990: 33) of beliefs and expectations about appropriate gendered communicative norms between individuals. It has been shown that 'people's beliefs about what men and women *should* be like further cause them to evaluate women who behave contrary to feminine stereotypes as unlikable, undeserving of organizational rewards, and even subject to social and economic penalties' (Brescoll 2016: 416). As indicated in Chapter 1, these stereotypical views about normative gendered behaviour are rooted in deeply held beliefs about gender order and 'gender differences discourse', with '*difference* being for most people what gender is all about' Sunderland (2004: 52). Such essentialist beliefs in gendered dichotomies cut across all aspects of behaviour but those specifically related to language have been described as linguistic ideologies that 'are representations which *idealize* their object, rendering the actual complexity of linguistic practice more intelligible through simplification, generalization and stereotyping' (Cameron and Shaw 2016: 5).

These types of generalisations are summarised by Holmes (2006) and are illustrated as a list of the dichotomies of essential differences that have been widely cited in relation to male and female differences in communicative or interactional styles. Although the list takes no account of other aspects of social and stylistic variation or contextual factors (Holmes and Stubbe 2003), it is nevertheless useful in pinpointing the most common gendered stereotypes relating to speech, or at least, those 'strongly associated with middle-class white men and women in the construction of their normative and unmarked gender identity' (Holmes 2006: 6). The differences are arranged in dichotomous pairs, shown here with the 'feminine' features first and the 'masculine' features second:

Indirect vs direct
Conciliatory vs confrontational
Facilitative vs competitive
Collaborative vs autonomous
Minor contribution (in public) vs dominates (public) talking time
Supportive feedback vs aggressive interruptions

Person/process orientated vs task outcome orientated
Affectively oriented vs referentially oriented
(adapted from Holmes 2006: 6)

As described in Chapter 1, and as the constitutive and indexical conception of the relationship between language and gender would suggest, men and women have been shown to draw upon a range of linguistic features and speech styles that are coded 'masculine' and 'feminine'. For example, in our study of the televised 2015 UK General Election televised debates (Cameron and Shaw 2016), we found that the most successful politicians were able to appear as both 'articulate' and 'authentic' (Winters and Carvalho 2015) by using a range of affective, combative, personal and humorous strategies (see further discussion in Section 5.2). Similarly, Wodak's (2003) study of women parliamentarians in the EU found that they use a range of strategies to successfully promote themselves and their political interests which she classified into three different 'gender role constructions'. These roles first drew on associations that could be stereotypically coded as masculine, including 'assertive activist' and 'expert'. The final role had a more complex relationship to gender – the 'positive difference (special bird)' – where a woman politician had 'managed to come to terms with all her differences, which have served to marginalise her, and to emphasise them. She "turns the tables" and strategically redefines the traditionally negative connotations into positive attributes' (Wodak 2003: 689). Across workplace contexts outside politics, studies have also found that men and women draw upon a range of linguistic styles (for example Baxter 2010; Holmes 2006; Mullany 2007) and that 'in contexts where they need to assert authority and bolster perceptions of themselves as effective leaders, both women and men make use of more direct ways of speaking, adopting features which typically index masculinity (…) equally however, both women and men make use of more facilitative and negotiative strategies when these are deemed to be more effective means of accomplishing their workplace objectives' (Holmes 2006: 439).

It appears that the normative feminine speech styles are increasingly prized as part of a successful workplace repertoire. Stereotypical feminine, facilitative styles are viewed as 'better' than masculine ones, particularly in customer-service oriented workplaces (Cameron 2000). In business studies there is also a suggestion that 'transformational, collaborative and relationship oriented' leadership skills are increasingly desirable (Kram and Hampton 2003). Men can therefore benefit from adopting normative feminine styles, yet women continue to be evaluated negatively for behaving in counter-stereotypic ways. Findings show that displays of 'masculine' authority by women lead others to judge them more negatively in relation to measures of femininity and likeability (Rudman and Fairchild 2004). Overt expressions of dominant behaviour by women (such as direct demands) negatively affect their likeability, whereas implicit dominant behaviour (such as eye-contact) do not (Williams and Tiedens 2016). This suggests that the tightrope of impression management that accompanies women behaving with authority is complex and risks negative evaluations unless achieved in subtle ways. Similarly, both linguistic research and leadership studies show that self-promotion in the workplace poses particular problems for women. Wagner and Wodak show how the women in their study promoted themselves in non-normative ways using cooperative and non-antagonistic success stories, suggesting that they needed to 're-write the conditions for success' (2006: 406). Leadership studies have shown that unless mitigated in these ways, women who self-promote at work are viewed as being overly dominant and are less likely to be selected for promotion than women who do not self-promote at all (Rudman et al. 2012).

Women's behaviour is also fractured by competing demands related to the gender-emotion stereotype – where women are seen as being more emotional than men (Brescoll 2016). Women's greater emotionality has even been referred to as the 'master stereotype' (Brescoll 2016), not just because of its strength and pervasiveness, but also because 'it serves as an overarching organising principle for other related beliefs' (Shields 2002: 3, cited in Brescoll 2016: 416). This stereotype can be related to language and communication in many ways; as forceful, passionate speech (and indeed volubility) can easily be interpreted as 'over-emotional' when delivered by a woman – she may be regarded as 'lacking emotional control'. Emotional control is viewed as essential for making rational decisions and so this stereotype means that women leaders incur negative assessments of their capabilities, although this shows some variety when related to racial stereotypes as well as gender (Brescoll 2016: 424–5). Brescoll identifies 'two complex minefields' relating to the gender-emotion stereotype: the amount and the type of emotion to be displayed. She finds that even minor emotional displays can incur negative penalties, especially when conveying dominance (anger, pride), but that failing to display enough emotion can also be detrimental 'because unemotional women are seen as failing to fulfil their warm, communal role as women' (2016: 415).

Although women and men in the workplace have been shown to draw on a range of speech styles coded 'masculine' and 'feminine', there is a recurrent gendered speech pattern that is found in many public arenas. Men speak more than women (speak for longer and take more speaking turns) in a range of formal public settings. For example, it has been found that in small-group deliberation women spoke less than men, regardless of the whether men or women made up a larger or smaller proportion of the group. Further, research has shown that men spoke more than women even when they were in a minority of one in a group of five (Karpowitz and Mendelberg 2014). In another study in the US Senate it was found that for men 'power' increased their volubility, but there was no such effect for women (Brescoll 2011). In other words, women's speaking time did not increase even when they were in powerful and senior positions. Explanations for this recurrent finding of male dominance in public talking time are likely to hinge upon the gendered norm of speaking with authority, which is associated with men (Karpowitz and Mendelberg 2014). The strength of this correlation of authority with masculinity is thought to marginalise women in the public sphere and undermine women's confidence to perform with authority. It has also been suggested that women are concerned that increased volubility will result in negative consequences (Brescoll 2011) as agentive women leaders can be viewed as extremely dominant, controlling and arrogant in what has been called the 'dominance penalty' (Rudman et al. 2012: 166). There is also some evidence to suggest that these backlash penalties mean that even powerful women conform to gendered stereotypes about language, with one study showing that women leaders opted not to take the floor in meetings because they did not want to be disliked or appear too 'pushy' (Brescoll 2011).

5.2   Adversarial Politics, the 'Different Voice' Ideology and the Burden of the Civilising Difference

One of the most significant ways in which stereotypical beliefs in gendered communication styles affect women in politics is that they can be expected to carry the burden of the 'civilising difference' (Walsh 2001). As discussed in the analysis of adversarial language in the HoC in Chapter 3, this means that the widely held belief in women having consensual speech styles positions women in male-dominated institutions as pioneers of less combative and more cooperative styles. Alongside the heightened visibility and other obstacles that women face in politics, an additional burden upon them is therefore that they are somehow expected to 'civilise' hitherto male-only spaces. However, the belief that women can civilise these institutional spaces 'often fails to take account of the many mechanisms by which they continue to be marginalised and segregated within these institutions' (Walsh 2001: 207). Walsh explains that: 'Appeals made by others, and sometimes the women themselves, to their putative qualities as good listeners, good communicators and "fixers" have been used to rationalize their concentration in a narrow range of, usually subordinate, institutional and organizational roles' (Walsh 2001: 207). A central thesis of Walsh's research – which includes case studies of women politicians in the HoC and women priests in the Church of England – is that when women enter such professions, the traditional gendered division between private and public spheres becomes 'replicated *within* civil and public sphere institutions and organisations' (Walsh 2001: 207) with women occupying a disproportionate number of subordinate roles. This claim is substantiated by work in political science that shows several gendered power asymmetries operate in political institutions. There is a gendered hierarchy of prestige attached to certain roles and concerns, and these 'privilege' male-defined interests and priorities (Franceschet 2011). The dominance of men in some committees such as finance, foreign affairs and industry reinforces the fact that these are the 'power committees' (Franceschet 2011; Kathlene 1995). On the other hand, 'soft' policy issues and committees are deemed to be 'women's issues' which, within the gendered hierarchy 'are considered to be of less national or strategic importance' (Franceschet 2011: 56).

This shows that there is a link between gendered communication styles and gendered topics and positions within political institutions, and that both of these are linked to asymmetrical power relations. As the interview data in Chapters 3 and 4 shows, women politicians attest to being agents of institutional change and feeling an expectation for 'making the debate more coherent and more transparent, having an argument where there is one but not having an argument where there isn't one' (Shaw 2002: Interview D). There are a number of assumptions underlying this belief that will be discussed in this section. First, that women – by some essential and fundamental characteristic – naturally adhere to consensual rather than more adversarial speech styles. Second, that women are willing and able to transform or 'feminise' these traditionally male-dominated spaces. Third, that male spaces are 'too' adversarial and confrontational and need to be civilised, which concurs with the view that normative feminine (facilitative and cooperative) speech styles are increasingly prized over masculine (competitive and adversarial) ones.

The belief that women have more facilitative styles than men has already been mentioned as one of the core stereotypical features of normative feminine speech. This is also referred to as the 'cooperative/competitive dichotomy' in language and gender research as it relates to earlier work in the field that tended to identify formal features of conversations as markers of these differing styles (Cameron 1997a). For example, Coates (1989) identifies linguistic features that are typical of cooperative talk among women friends that are thought to minimise conflict such as the use of epistemic modal forms and hedging. The women in Coates' study are also thought to produce supportive speech by the latching of turns and the use of minimal responses which results in the joint negotiation of turn-taking and distribution of the floor through the progressive and collaborative development of topics as 'participants build on each other's contributions and jointly arrive at consensus' (Coates 1989: 119). On the other side of the dichotomy, some research has shown that in a single-sex group, men prefer a 'one-at-a-time', more individualistic conversational floor, and earlier studies find that men dominate women in mixed-sex interaction (by interrupting them, occupying the conversational floor, or by ignoring them), for example Zimmerman and West (1975); De Fransisco (1991).

However, analysts such as Cameron (1997a) and Hewitt (1997) point to the complexity and multi-faceted nature of competition and cooperation. They show that cooperation can be constructed in many ways and that the two attributes are not mutually exclusive in conversations. This means that 'there will usually be some degree of competition among speakers, if not for the floor itself then for the attention or approval of others' (Cameron 1997a: 58). The competition in women's friendship groups can be expressed as support for others while at the same time attending to an individual's own position in the group: 'The "egalitarian" norms of female friendship groups are, like all norms, to some degree coercive: the rewards and punishments precisely concern one's status within the group (among women, however, this status is called "popularity" rather than "dominance")' (Cameron 1997a: 59).

In politics, the competitive/cooperative dichotomy has roots in earlier work that has been referred to as the 'different voice' ideology (Cameron and Shaw 2016). Taking its name from the influential work *In a Different Voice* by Carole Gilligan (1982), this ideology is based on the notion that women in politics have distinct behaviours that set them apart from their male colleagues. Gilligan's main thesis is that women and men have different processes of ethical reasoning, with women relying more on a sense of morality when making political decisions, having an ethic of care and responsibility as an alternative moral perspective rather than the more traditional (and normatively masculine) ethic of justice. While this work is based on observations from psychology, the notion of a 'different voice' also extends to and has influenced work on gender and language and in particular the 'two cultures' model evidenced in the popular work of Tannen (1990) and Grey (1992). This model holds that childhood socialisation in single-sex peer groups leads to 'miscommunication' between men and women because there is a lack of understanding of the other 'culture'. The 'two cultures' model has been criticised for its apolitical stance and for its methodological approach (as it relies on interview data rather than direct observations) (Troemel-Ploetz 1991; Cameron 2007; Goodwin 2006; Uchida 1992). As mentioned in Chapter 3, empirical studies have cast doubt on the existence of such clear-cut distinctions between the communication styles of boys and girls (Baxter 1999; Goodwin 2006). Similarly, Asterhan (2018) conducted experimental social psychological research into gender and the use of four different argument types (deliberative argumentation, disputative argumentation, quick consensus seeking and private deliberation) by students in an educational setting. Her research showed that there was no difference in the frequency with which the women and men in her study used 'disputative argumentation' or 'quick consensus seeking' strategies.

In political contexts, empirical work has also refuted the existence of such a clear-cut distinction between the communication styles of women and men. The investigation of gender and adversarial questions in the HoC in Chapter 3 found that while overall women asked fewer adversarial questions than men, some women asked the most adversarial questions, and this was linked to factors other than gender such as seniority (the more senior, the more adversarial) and incumbency (opposition MPs ask more adversarial questions than those in government). Cornelia Ilie (2013) finds that both men and women MPs in the HoC use 'master suppression techniques' including ignoring someone, ridiculing them and blaming and shaming them. These empirical findings suggest that, regardless of the high expectations on women to civilise male spaces, many political roles nevertheless demand a full range of direct, confrontational approaches on the one hand, and compassionate, cooperative qualities on the other. For example, a political leader who is wholly facilitative would be deemed weak, but a purely confrontational and authoritarian leader would be viewed as lacking compassion and not having the required empathy to relate to the everyday experiences of voters.

Nowhere is this more evident than in the genre of the televised political debate, as politicians must manage interaction and the floor by seizing opportunities to speak, but must also appear 'authentic', compassionate and in-tune with the concerns of the electorate. In our study of the televised 2015 General Election televised debates in the UK (Cameron and Shaw 2016) we found that the successful leaders, regardless of gender, were able to accomplish the adversarial styles demanded by the TV debate genre. The most successful leaders could fulfil the adversarial, confrontational demands of the genre fluently but also appear compassionate and sensitive to the needs of others. Nicola Sturgeon (Leader of the Scottish National Party [SNP]) was one of the leaders who managed these expectations most successfully by combining 'ways of speaking that signal authority, confidence and combativeness with ways of speaking that steer the audience away from the potentially negative interpretations of those qualities so that viewers will not perceive, say, authority as bossiness, confidence as arrogance, and combativeness as aggression' (Cameron and Shaw 2016: 127). Humour, in the form of quick quips and asides helped her to manage these opposing demands by mitigating her more adversarial contributions and tempering her authority with a 'warmness' of manner. The case studies in Chapters 6 and 7 give further examples of how Theresa May, Julia Gillard and Hillary Clinton managed their authority to attempt to avoid the negative evaluations. These impressions have been shown to disproportionately affect women, rather than men, when acting in positions of authority (Rudman and Fairchild 2004; Williams and Tiedens 2016).

In professions such as politics and law – and some academic disciplines such as philosophy – which are said to have adversarial models at their core, it follows that a belief in the 'different voice' ideology will view women in these areas as being both disadvantaged and marginalised by adversarial discursive norms. Interestingly, in the Scottish Parliament, (as noted in Chapter 4) women have played a prominent part since the beginning, and all-female leaders enact combative, adversarial roles in question-time sessions (Cameron and Shaw 2016). This leads to the suggestion that the First Minister, Nicola Sturgeon: 'with the advantages of incumbency and long experience, is in a particularly strong position to change the rules of engagement and set a different tone at FMQs [First Minister's Question Time], but she evidently prefers the combative style' (Cameron and Shaw 2016: 119). The criticisms and challenges associated with contexts like adversarial parliamentary exchanges can be viewed as a defining feature of argumentative discourse (Asterhan 2018: 67), and the theory of agonism (Mouffe 2013) sees the potential benefits of the 'radical negativity' of some types of political conflict.

Parallels can be drawn between politics and philosophy, where feminist critiques of the adversarial tradition in philosophy tend to split into two camps when considering the possible effects of adversarial discourse on women. In the first view, it is thought that 'conditions of hostility' do not generate the most productive forms of philosophical reasoning, they cause other types of argumentation to be overlooked and this is seen as disadvantaging or marginalising women because they are thought to be less comfortable with adversarial argumentation (Moulton 1983). However, other philosophers have acknowledged the difficulties in assuming a homogenous female perspective and have emphasised instead 'widely divergent experiences, including the experience of conflict and contradiction' (Grimshaw 1987: 20). There is also potential confusion in conflating the questions of *women's* suitability to conflictual styles and the more general question of whether adversarial practice 'leads to bad reasoning' (Rooney 2010: 205). More considered proponents of adversarial argument see advantages within it for critical thinking and political merit (Govier 1999).

As noted in the discussion of adversarial language in the HoC in Chapter 3, adversarial speech events such as 'question times' have the important democratic function of scrutiny and are one of the only ways that governments can be publicly held to account. With this function to the fore, conflictual, confrontational styles would seem appropriate to pursue and scrutinise weaknesses and flaws in the government's policies or conduct. However, for others, the rituals of adversarial combat – such as the verbal jousting seen in PMQs – form part of the practices that privilege some (white, male) members over others. They contribute to 'practices, discourses and images' which make the HoC 'an unmistakably masculine gender regime' (Lovenduski 2014b). One way of resolving these opposing perspectives is to conceive of adversarial language as having two different manifestations in parliamentary discourse, one that is productive (and seeks rational scrutiny through opposition); and one that is related to unnecessary point-scoring and seems to embody schoolboy humour and personal attacks. The role of gender in adversarial political language will be considered in the case studies in Chapters 6 and 7 leading to a discussion of these alternative perspectives in the concluding discussion in Chapter 8.

5.3   Sexist Language towards Women Politicians

5.3.1   Forms of Sexist Language

In this section I consider the forms sexism takes in politics to elucidate the ways in which it marginalises, excludes and deters women from participating. Sexism can be thought of as 'an index of ongoing conflict between men and women, particularly in the public sphere' (Cameron 2006; Mills 2008: 2) and the operation of sexist language is often predicated upon stereotypical associations relating to masculinity and femininity. The conflict reflected in sexist comments and jokes form part of the repertoire of discursive practices that are constantly shaping and (re)constructing masculinity and 'femininity' in different contexts. In this way sexist comments work by exploiting and exacerbating women's inferior position in society by alluding to their perceived 'natural' (and subordinate) characteristics. Sexism can thus take as many forms as there are essentialising beliefs about women in society and is part of the apparatus of hegemonic masculinity (see further discussion in Section 5.4). These beliefs range from the objectification of women as sexual beings for the service of male desire, to the casting of women in domestic rather than professional roles and also include the portrayal of women as intellectually inferior to men. While many of these sexist assumptions about femininity take on seemingly benign manifestations in popular discourse, the assertions that women are, for example, manipulative, nagging and cannot drive (Sunderland 2007; Mills 2008) are all potentially damaging and more or less exclusionary, depending on the context.

Sara Mills (2008) recounts the experiences of two women bus drivers who resigned from their jobs, citing constant sexist comments and jokes about women's ineptitude and inability to drive as the reason. She explains that 'both these women are extremely competent drivers, but they stated that the repeated jokes about and reference to such problems in driving ended by undermining their confidence' (Mills 2008: 40). She goes on to explain how they were continually undermined by comments such as 'Oh you're on with her, watch yourself' by co-workers implying that she might crash the bus. An important point here is that these types of comments can be thought of as not overtly sexist, but 'it was the repetitive and tedious nature of these comments, both by workmates and the general public, which contributed to their decision to leave' (Mills 2008: 40). This example raises some key points in relation to sexist language, not least that multiple sexist comments, even those thought to be relatively innocuous, can have profound consequences on women's participation in historically male-dominated workplaces of different types, including politics. This is recognised in many professional contexts in their policies about sexual harassment – which recognise that it is the interpretation of 'unwanted' comments, rather than any intent with which they are delivered, that is the determinant of whether behaviour is deemed to be considered harassment.

The example also raises the point that sexism can be categorised into 'overt' and 'indirect' forms (Mills 2008). However, as there is no consensus on what constitutes 'overt' sexism (Mills 2008), and as its meaning is context dependent, many have viewed sexist language on a continuum of directness/indirectness. The overt or direct end of the continuum would include gender systems in language (Pauwels 1998: 36), and this is particularly evident in political institutions where masculine forms are often adopted as the institutional norm. For example, in the Italian parliament, both gender groups still tend to mostly use masculine unmarked terms when addressing women politicians (Formato 2014). In the Polish parliament, the masculine grammatical gender is used by all politicians when referring to positions and titles, and masculine proper nouns and pronouns are perceived as 'gender neutral' (Galea and Gaweda 2018). In English, where there are no such grammatical possibilities, the gender system is expressed in less pronounced ways, such as the use of the generic 'he' pronoun, and gendered word endings like '-ess' or '-ette'. On the other end of the scale, indirect, covert or 'subtle' sexism exists through 'deep-seated, naturalized, androcentric assumptions' (Lazar 2005: 20). This 'benign' sexism has been found to be prevalent in the Polish parliament where women are routinely addressed as 'dear Ladies' and 'lovely (or beautiful) women' which reinforces their subordinate role (Galea and Gaweda 2018: 279).

However, the direct/indirect continuum only reflects one dimension of complexity regarding sexism and language which is 'better conceptualised as a multi-faceted phenomenon occurring in a number of quite complex systems of representation, all with their place in historical traditions' (Cameron 1990: 14). Irony and humour can further complicate the classification and interpretation of sexism as it can be cast 'knowingly' and often in a historical frame. Williamsons's (2003) notion of 'retrosexism' refers to ways in which sexism is cited ironically as an old-fashioned trope. She describes it in the following way: 'Retro-sexism is sexism with an alibi: it appears at once past and present, "innocent" and knowing, a conscious reference to another era, rather than an unconsciously driven part of our own' (Williamson 2003). This type of sexism operates in the same way as non-ironic, straightforward sexism but positions people who oppose it as failing to see the irony and the intended humour. In the mid-1990s the word 'sexism' was also cast as 'old fashioned' in ways that the words 'racism' and 'homophobia' were not (Gill 2011: 61). This led for calls to revitalise the term to reflect its 'agile, dynamic, changing and diverse set of malleable representations and practices of power' (Gill 2011: 62). It is also necessary to see sexism as operating 'as part of a larger field of sexual politics that is constituted by whatever contending forces that are active around gender relations in a given time and place' (Cameron 2006: 3). These contending forces are not just around feminist political movements aimed at improving women's position, but also 'institutions and movements that function as vehicles for the expression of gender conservatism, anti-feminism, or male supremacism' (Cameron 2006: 3).

In this way, political institutions – particularly traditional ones such as the HoC (and also the Italian and Polish parliaments) – can be thought of as vehicles of sexism and are an extreme illustration of this complexity because of their highly ritualised traditions, hierarchical masculinist structures and exclusionary practices. Cheryl Collier and Tracey Raney's comparative study of sexism in 'Westminster style' national parliaments (in Australia, UK and Canada) identify three characteristics that work together 'to reinforce sexism and sexual harassment in legislative spaces' (2018: 437). These aspects are first, the 'myth' of neutrality of MPs, which 'serves to further entrench the norms of hegemonic masculinity that dominate legislative spaces' (2018: 438); second, adversarial styles of politics, thought to reinforce 'macho' cultures in which sexism thrives; and finally, the 'parliamentary privilege' designed to protect MPs' freedom of speech but also allows them to avoid sanctions for sexist behaviour (Collier and Raney 2018: 439). Many of the examples of sexist verbal behaviour in this context and explained in detail in the following section also count as verbal harassment. Verbal harassment is a form of unlawful discrimination under the Equalities Act 2010 (Parliament UK 2010). Verbal or physical conduct of a sexual nature counts as harassment when the behaviour is either meant to – or has the effect of – violating someone's dignity or creating an intimidating, hostile, degrading, humiliating or offensive environment. It is also significant in the identification of harassment that if someone submits to (or rejects) the behaviour, this may explicitly or implicitly be linked to a condition of their employment or employment decisions affecting the person who has been subjected to the harassment. This means that institutions with unclear systems of line management and the deployment and promotion of staff are much more likely to foster conditions in which sexual harassment can flourish.

For sexist language to 'count' as verbal sexual harassment it must be excessive or repetitive. So, one isolated comment may not count as verbal sexual harassment, but if it was excessive (for example, an explicit sexual proposition) then it would be considered harassment. Similarly, continual exposure to 'low-grade' comments (such as one person demeaning another by referring to them without using their correct professional title or by calling them 'love' or 'dearie') could also be considered verbal sexual harassment. Therefore, there is no clear line between verbal sexual harassment and seemingly more innocuous sexist comments. The distinction between 'overt' and 'indirect' sexist comments is not relevant here as the identification of harassment depends on the context – on the amount and tone of the harassment and the extent to which the victim considers the comments unwelcome. This difficulty of pinpointing precise definitions of sexism and verbal harassment can itself be a deterrent to reporting these events as 'they often occur behind closed doors and can turn in to a "he said, she said" battle that they [victims] feared they would lose' (Taylor et al. 2018: 49).

As already noted in this section (and discussed in more detail in Chapter 3), the HoC is an example of the dominance of a culture of traditional masculinity. Sexism in the HoC tends to exist in both subtle and direct ways but also notably occurs in extreme forms that would not be found in most professional workplaces. The sexist behaviour of (some of) the MPs can illustrate both how linguistic sexism operates and how the progress of feminist, anti-sexist ideologies are slowed, resisted and stalled. For this reason, the HoC is used here to map out the characteristics and functions of sexism in political institutions. However, this does not suggest that sexism mainly or only occurs in this institution and further examples of sexism from different political institutions and contexts are drawn upon in the Chapters 6 and 7 case studies.

5.3.2   Sexist Language and Sexual Harassment in the UK House of Commons

As discussed in Section 5.3.1, the HoC is a workplace in which sexism can be extreme, and in which sexual harassment is reported to be commonplace. It is a context in which sexism has been 'normalised' or made ordinary through its regular occurrence. This workplace can be thought of as a 'chilly climate' for women (Hall and Sandler 1982), a controversial phrase which is nonetheless useful in highlighting 'the way in which seemingly inconsequential practices can become cumulative, failing to recognise women's contribution, devaluing their contribution, resulting in loss of confidence and marginalisation' (Savigny 2014: 797). There are many anecdotal accounts of sexism and sexual harassment in the parliamentary estate, alongside sexist comments and behaviour in the chamber. Occasionally sexist comments are given a high degree of scrutiny, as when David Cameron told a senior Opposition MP, Angela Eagle, to 'Calm down dear' in April 2011; or when John Bercow, the Speaker, allegedly called a senior woman MP a 'stupid woman' and 'fucking useless' in an aside in the chamber in April 2018[1]; and when Jeremy Corbyn, party leader and LO was accused of calling Theresa May a 'stupid woman' under his breath in December 2018 (Elgot and Walker 2018). These examples have been commented upon frequently (Collier and Raney 2018; Ilie 2018), but care must be taken not to simply 'cherry pick' examples of sexism according to the political attention they gain in the media. Given that parliamentary discourse and sexism are intertextual (developing over time and across events) and pervasive (occurring as a normalised part of debate interaction) more systematic accounts of the occurrence of sexist language are necessary. For this reason, all the sexist comments in the 60-hour 1998–2001 HoC corpus were identified, and examples of the different types are presented below.

Anecdotal accounts of different types of sexist comments and sexual harassment are common in the HoC interview data and more widely in biographies of parliamentary life by women MPs over the last twenty-five years (for example Gorman 1993; Harman 2017; McDougall 1998; Nicholson 1996; Phillips 2017). It is also clear that this type of behaviour is not confined to previous decades. As mentioned in Chapter 1, it has continued as part of the contemporary culture of parliament with allegations of sexism, sexual harassment and sexual assault in 2017 leading to the resignation of two government Ministers, Michael Fallon and Damian Green.[2] All the allegations of this time were made against male perpetrators, and although both men and women alleged that they had been the victims of sexual misconduct or harassment, most of the victims were women. These allegations led to the setting up of a Cross-Party Working Group on an Independent Complaints and Grievance Policy which found that 19 per cent of 1,377 staff responses to a survey reported experience of sexual harassment, with twice as many women reporting than men (Parliamentary Report 2018). This is a high proportion and, like women's responses to sexist language already described, represents a threat to women's progress and participation in parliament. Apart from forcing women to resign from their job (as in the example of the bus drivers), sexual harassment has been shown to have a number of effects across different workplace contexts ranging from 'anger, depression, and low self-confidence' (Mellgren et al. 2018: 265) to behavioural adjustments such as changing body language or type of clothing (Mellgren et al. 2018: 272) to limiting movement and avoiding particular places (Graham et al. 2017).

It has been argued that sexual harassment in Westminster should be understood as 'a systemic, cultural problem, rather than a question of problematic individuals' (Krook 2018: 65). Indeed, for most modern professional workplaces, examples of sexism and sexual harassment such as those described here simply do not occur and would be instantly castigated with very negative reputational consequences for the perpetrator. However, for the different types of workers (from clerks to security staff) in the HoC as well as the 650 Members of Parliament, sexism and sexual harassment appears to be normalised and many participants do not feel that that they can act to report or deter these behaviours. Harriet Harman describes this:

My friends would talk about their bitter disappointment that Labour MPs would use their position of authority to be sexual predators. And yet, it still didn't occur to them, or to me, that such things could be reported. To whom? It was an abuse of power in a working environment and deeply resented, but there was no sense, at that time, that we could do anything about it. (Harman 2017: 12)

Harman sees this predatory sexist culture following on from a traditionally male-dominated institution where 'young women are trying to break into a field dominated by older men, there are inevitably men who'll seek to abuse their power for sexual purposes' (Harman 2017: 11). Gender theorists agree with this position claiming that sexual harassment 'is often at high levels when women enter what are traditionally men's domains and occupations' (Hearn 1992: 175). From my own ethnographic interviews, observations and close analysis of debate discourse it appears that the HoC has several interrelated features that lead to a sexist culture in which sexist comments, verbal sexual harassment and predatory behaviour is common:

1. A numerically male-dominated workplace where masculine or 'fraternal' networks have always been pervasive and in which male dominance is normalised;
2. A workplace culture determined by party allegiances in which staff are expected to prioritise political party over their own wellbeing;
3. A culture in which 'resilience' is seen as an essential quality for employees, even if that resilience means putting up with being a target of sexism and sexual harassment. This is coupled with an assumption that sexual harassment is routinely ignored and tolerated;
4. An institution with strict, arcane workplace hierarchies with political elites at the top. Elites have proportionately more power at the top of this hierarchy than other workplaces because of their political mandate, making them appear immovable. Furthermore, people in the lower levels of this hierarchy often have an attitude of servitude which strengthens and reinforces power differentials and turns a blind eye to the aberrant behaviour of those at the top;
5. Opaque internal systems for reporting harassment and possibly a lack of transparency relating to other systems for re-deploying staff and for staff promotion. This lack of transparency can allow inequities where 'a word in the ear' carries sway but is not part of a process that is open to scrutiny;
6. Irregular working hours during which socialising, late night attendance and drinking in the various bars of the institution is the norm.

Some of the worst examples of verbal sexual harassment happen in the debating chamber itself and in the division lobbies, particularly when an MP is voting against her own party. Theresa Gorman (a Conservative MP) recounts the following experience when she was voting against John Major's Conservative government when they were trying to ratify the Maastricht treaty (1991–3). On this occasion, when it was clear that Gorman would vote against the government, two men MPs from her own party sat either side of her in the debate and engaged in what she describes as 'banter' across her:

One said something like, 'You know she's talking about voting against the government?' The other one said, 'I always said we shouldn't let women in here in the first place. They're a thundering nuisance.'
I realised they were trying to provoke me, but it was a bait I wasn't going to rise to.
The first said, 'A woman's place is in the home.'

'Yes, flat on her back.'

I felt trapped. I didn't want to get up and leave. Why should I? On the other hand, I didn't want to just sit there as if I didn't mind (…)

One of them said, 'Do you think Teresa would be any good on her back? I wonder what kind of knickers she wears.' What he went on to say, I cannot bring myself to repeat here, but I could no longer put up with it. I exploded

'Why don't you go somewhere else and find someone else to talk dirty to if you feel like that?'

'I thought you'd be enjoying it. I thought that was what you liked about this place – plenty of men' (Gorman 1993: 131–2).

In this case, if the anecdotally reported exchange can be taken as accurate, the extract begins with Gorman being referred to by her colleagues as if she is not present. This is a bullying tactic that allows the perpetrators the heavily ironic conceit of pretending that the target of the comments is not privy to the conversation and this allows them to make direct, personal and explicit comments as if they were in private. The extract starts with the more legitimate objection of the MPs (that Gorman is voting against the government) but this comment is swiftly gendered by the responding MP falling back on the stock questioning of women's eligibility and right to be MPs as they are a 'nuisance'. This moves to the placing of all women, and therefore Gorman as well, into the domestic sphere with the cliched 'a woman's place is in the home', but this is escalated further by women's domestic role then being cast as their availability purely for the sexual gratification of men. Gorman is physically trapped by her position in between the two men and reports feeling unable find an adequate response so she is constrained both physically and rhetorically. The final section of this reported exchange becomes more offensive and personal as the men speculate about 'Teresa's' sexual performance and her underwear. Although Gorman reportedly responds at this point, the final comment about 'enjoying' the abuse further demeans her by eradicating her professional motivation and replacing it with a purely sexual rationale, at once reducing her status and defining her through the lens of male fantasy and desire.

This episode is shocking because of the personal and sexual nature of the attack but also because it contravenes accepted professional standards in the workplace. The means to resist the infringements of those standards are limited both because of the hierarchies and structures listed above, and because these behaviours are hidden from public view. Other reports of hidden physical violence against women in parliament are also shocking, and although women are often reluctant to be identified, some make anonymous claims of being subjected to physical violence: 'A government minister came up to me and literally pinned me by my neck up against the wall in the lobby and screamed at me and said: "You've done it now, you've done it now"' (Ashley 2004). Emma

Nicholson MP also reports physical violence when, like Gorman, she voted against her own party: 'Physical assault by a member of one's own party is not an everyday hazard of voting in the House of Commons. So I was the more taken aback when, having for the first time voted against the Government in a division, I felt someone push roughly past me as I stood in the crowd near the Serjeant at Arms and hit me, hard in the stomach' (Nicholson 1996: 9). The private nature of these hidden physical attacks together with victims' lack of recourse to formal reporting mechanisms are particularly chilling. When Nicholson complained to party Whips[3] about this abuse she was 'taken to task for voting against the government' (1996: 9) and did not receive a reply to her official written complaint about the incident.

Such examples of physical and sexual harassment undertaken clandestinely are certainly on the extreme end of the scales of directness and severity of sexism (and indeed the latter examples could be classified as criminal assault). Another form of pernicious, hidden verbal behaviour is that of 'sledging' or delivering aggressive and personal critical comments to someone sotto voce so they cannot be heard by the Speaker or picked up by the microphones in the chamber. As suggested in the analysis of the 1998–2001 HoC corpus in Chapter 3, these (often sexist) comments are designed to put someone off, break their concentration or to rile them so that their performance is affected. The comments are similar to barracking and share the ability to put a speaker off course, the former by a quiet insult in the ear and the latter by a loud, public shout. Both have inherent humiliations and are equally off-putting. As described in Chapter 3, these comments are likely to focus on 'any weakness' (Sarah Champion MP, BBC 2015). For women this includes supposedly complimentary comments about their physical attributes, intellectual capabilities, appearance and age – such as, 'isn't she a pretty girl', 'Isn't she a feisty young thing' and 'Hasn't she got nice legs' (McDougall 1998: 180). As also noted in Chapter 3, physical gesture is used in a sexist way and is designed to intimidate women. There have been reports of male MPs making 'melon-weighing' gestures (intended to represent a woman's breasts) across the chamber at women MPs. Other anecdotal reports include Conservative front-bench men MPs sitting in a row and swinging their heads and bodies to one side all at once when a woman opposite crosses her legs (to show that they are all collectively looking up her skirt). Although these reports are now some years old, there are current MPs who were victims and perpetrators of this harassment. This behaviour objectifies women and subjects them to the male gaze, undermining and intimidating the victims by eradicating their professional status, skills and standing and replacing this with a single sexual characteristic.

Many of the seemingly more innocuous forms of sexism such as jokes, quips and nicknames are made in plain sight and as part of the 'legal' debate discourse. The normalising of these 'trivial' behaviours can be viewed as part of the same culture as the extreme behaviours illustrated above with sexist verbal 'play' acting as an index of the cultural and institutional menace of the more extreme and serious forms. Sexist comments and jokes are delivered – for the most part without censure or critical note – in the most public forum possible: the debating chamber. These joking and light-hearted comments are often couched in terms of 'just a bit of fun', 'only a joke' or simply 'unintended'. In this way, if a victim of the sexism does complain then they are subtly positioned as being at fault: for not having a sense of humour; failing to understand a joke; being too sensitive; or misinterpreting a remark.

Sexist comments and jokes in politics are, with some notable exceptions, made by men and for men. They reinforce the homosocial bonds and fraternal networks that underpin traditional institutions such as the HoC and which are discussed in some detail in Section 5.4. Examples of sexist and sexual humour are common in the 1998–2001 HoC corpus and are made exclusively by men. Sexual humour and the assumptions underlying sexual jokes about male-female relationships 'may function both to express male dominance and to support and strengthen it' (Crawford 1995: 145). Mulkay (1988) has examined the representation of women in men's sexual humour and found there to be four basic principles. These principles are: the primacy of intercourse (all men want is sex); the availability of women (all women are sexually available even if they pretend not to be); the objectification of women (women exist to meet men's needs and are passive); and the subordination of women's discourse (women should be silent) (Legman 2006; Mulkay 1988: 134–51).

There are examples of men MPs' jokes about sex in the 1998–2001 HoC corpus which are based on these principles. In Example 5.1 below Nick Palmer jokes about how often men think about sex:

Example 5.1 House of Commons debate (Third Reading of the Finance Bill 01/07/98; Transcript)

NP = Nick Palmer (Labour Backbencher) 1MP = An unidentified male MP

1	NP:	we often criticise <u>Mini</u>sters for Departmental-itis (.) and for focussing
2		ex<u>clu</u>sively on their <u>area</u> (.) and I think that <u>we</u> in the Cha<u>mb</u>er are
3		also somewhat also guilty of <u>that</u> (.) but er (.) as typical de<u>bates</u> like
4		this one (.) you get <u>speci</u>alists in their particular area coming in (.) and
5		so to<u>day</u> we have er more fi<u>nance</u> ne<u>rds</u> (.) er than you'll see in a
6		month of <u>Sun</u>days anywhere <u>else</u> (.) um and er the (.) it is <u>said</u> that the
7		average <u>man</u> thinks about <u>sex</u> every twenty minutes of the <u>day</u> (.) and I think the
8		population at large would be al<u>arm</u>ed to know that in our
9		little <u>sub</u>-population there are people who think <u>more</u> often than that
10		about the public sector <u>borr</u>owing requi<u>rem</u>ent (2) (laughs)

11	1MP:	not all of us
12	MPs:	[laughter]
13	NP:	[laughs] I'll
14		exempt the Honourable Member (1) (laughs) now the I'd like to look at
15		three aspects of how the finance Bill affects different (turn continues)

This joke fulfils the principle identified above that men's jokes about sex assume the primacy of intercourse. It is men who think about sex every twenty minutes rather than women. Although the joke is that the MPs present in the debate think more often than every twenty minutes about financial matters, the joke is extended by another men MP who collaboratively affirms that he thinks more often about sex than finance. It is noteworthy that this debate is proposed by two women Ministers[4] who are excluded from this joke as it is made from a heteronormative male point of view, but perhaps more significantly, it objectifies them.

Another sexual joke about a Ministerial woman MP is when Margaret Hodge is described by a man MP as being 'seduced':

Example 5.2 House of Commons debate (Further Education 06/07/98; Transcript)

PW: Phil Willis (Liberal Democrat spokesperson) SP = Speaker

1	PW:	the Select Committee has recognised the problems of FE funding (.)
2		and the new resources it proposes are exceedingly welcome (.) but (.)
3		I believe that the treasury has seduced the select committee (.) and
4		its expectations as er not obviously the Honourable member for
5		Barking Mr Deputy Speaker (.) I would never accuse anyone of
6		seducing er seducing her (.) but um (.) sh she is far no she (1)
7	MPs:	[laughter]
8		I think at this point I will move on but um (1)
9	MPs:	[laughter]
10	SP:	order (.) perhaps it would be helpful if the Honourable Gentleman
11		found another simile (.) Mister Willis (1)
12	MPs:	[laughter]
13	PW:	I do believe I do believe that the hand of the Treasury has been
14		on Labour members in the select committee (.) and er
15	1MP:	that's worse
16	PW:	no it isn't (.) um and that in fact what the Honourable Member for
17		Barking was in fact er honest enough to say that she did not feel that
18		they'd gone far enough (turn continues)

In this example the joke fulfils the second and third of the principles identified above. Applying the word 'seduced' to Margaret Hodge at once makes her seem sexually available and causes her to be objectified. The intervention by the male Deputy Speaker recognises that the joke infringes the rights of the MP to whom it is applied, but the intervention itself is made in a humorous way and the Deputy Speaker also collaborates in the construction of humour. As well as jokes about sex, humour in debates can also be directed towards topics about women in degrading or derogatory ways. Example 5.3 shows Frank Dobson making a joke in response to a serious question about the treatment of women prisoners:

Example 5.3 House of Commons question time (Health Department Questions 02/06/98, Transcript)

PS = Phyllis Starkey (Labour Backbencher) FD = Frank Dobson (Health Minister)

1	PS:	can I ask my Right Honourable <u>Fri</u>end (.) in making app<u>oi</u>ntments to <u>H</u>ospital Trust
2		Boards (.) whether he has ever <u>know</u>ingly app<u>oi</u>nted anyone who <u>adv</u>ocates chaining
3		women prisoners to their <u>beds</u> as an aid to <u>chil</u>dbirth (1)
4	FD:	well er er well er er (.) (smiles) no no Madam <u>Sp</u>eaker (.) but I I work on the pre-
5		supposition that <u>nob</u>ody's <u>perf</u>ect (laughs) (turn continues)

In this example Phyllis Starkey's question criticises the actions of the Health Secretary, Frank Dobson. This is presumably why his response contains a humorous retaliation. However, the fact that Dobson reacts to a serious question from a woman about women in this way seems to indicate that he places little value on the concerns of both Phyllis Starkey and on the women in question.

Example 5.4 House of Commons question time (Defence Questions (06/04/98; Transcript)

CR = Christine Russell (Labour Backbencher) JR = John Reid (Defence Minister)

1	CR:	Does the Minister agree with <u>me</u> (.) that we should re-ex<u>am</u>ine the role
2		of the T.<u>A</u>. (.) and as I have a very <u>lar</u>ge T.A. presence in my
3		const<u>it</u>uency (.) I would like the Minister to at least cons<u>id</u>er giving the
4		T.A. perhaps a more <u>heavy</u>weight role (.) than what they have at the
5		m<u>om</u>ent (1)
6	1MP:	heavyweight
7	7MPs:	(laughter)
8	JR:	can I er <u>than</u>k my honourable Friend for that <u>help</u>ful (2)
9	MPs:	(laughter)
10	JR:	intervention er I think she is absolutely right we <u>should</u> consider giving the Territorial
11		Army a more <u>us</u>able more <u>rel</u>evant (.) and as <u>she</u> said more <u>heavy</u>weight <u>ro</u>le (1)
12	MPs:	(laughter)
13	JR:	in that di<u>rect</u>ion (.) I <u>also</u> ag<u>ree</u> with her that (turn continues)

In this example when Christine Russell refers to the Territorial Army being given a more heavyweight role men MPs in the Conservative opposition laugh and repeat the word 'heavyweight' (line 6). The humour here is created because the repeated word 'heavyweight' is used to refer to the physical appearance of Christine Russell. The Defence Minister John Reid supports Russell by thanking her for her question (line 8) and repeating the word 'heavyweight' with its originally intended meaning. In doing this Reid shows that he is opposed to the joke created by the opposition MPs. In this example men MPs ridicule both the serious question made by a woman MP and her physical appearance.

These types of jokes about sex and sexist jokes about women's appearance or attributes may discourage women from participating in humour:

When someone sends the message 'I consider women to be less than full human beings' framed as humour, it is difficult for others to reject or even directly address the message. After all sexist intention can easily be denied 'I was only joking' 'can't you take a joke?' 'lighten up' 'just kidding'. One simple reason that women as a group may appear less humorous is that they are unwilling to participate in their own denigration. (Crawford 1995: 135)

It seems apparent that there is little that women can do to combat these types of jokes and comments. A senior woman Labour MP describes an occasion in a Question Time session when men Conservative MPs started to make squeaking noises when a woman MP asked a question because she had a high-pitched voice. She says: 'It is totally sexist and designed to knock her off course before they'd even heard what her question was. It was a perfectly ordinary question which any man could have asked but she paid a price because she was a young woman and had a high-pitched voice and nothing more' (Shaw 2002: Interview D). This MP refers to the same incident later in the interview when she says that the young woman MP could not take any action against this treatment: 'Saying I've been the subject of sexism would be as likely to make her a victim of more of it (...) that can work both ways you can either have people supporting you or you can have people criticising you as a whinger' (Shaw 2002: Interview D). This comment elucidates the sexist culture in which sexism is tolerated, but complaining about it is not. However, there is some evidence that more recently, in the Theresa May government formed in 2017, the Speaker (John Bercow), has attempted to identify sexist practices in the HoC debating chamber. This is shown in example 5.5 below from 27 March 2018 (Debate on the Commonwealth). Boris Johnson answers a sycophantic question from an MP from his own party about supporting the Commonwealth, 'Will my Right Honourable Friend confirm that the upcoming Commonwealth summit is an opportune moment for us to demonstrate the strength and diversity?'.

Example 5.5 House of Commons debate (Commonwealth 27/03/2018; Transcript)

```
1    BJ:     I passionately agree with you (.) cos it's the most astonishing (.) it is the it is the most
2            a say no (.) says the says the Labour er Front Benches (.) that's their attitude (.)
3            that's [their attitude (.) isn't that]
     MPs:           [     shouting      ]
4    BJ:     [extraordinary isn't that isn't that isn't that extraordinary] er this is this is an
     MPs:    [                          shouting          ]
5            institution (.) say no says the Noble and Learned Lady the Baroness (.)
6    MP:                                                              disgusting
7    BJ:     whatever it is I can't remember what it is (.)
8    MP:                                   Nugee
```

9	BJ:	Nugee (.) er the I mean what an extraordinary thing (.) this is an an institution er that
10		er encompasses 2.4 billion people (.) some of the fastest growing economies
11		some of the fastest growing economies in the world (turn continues)

Here, Johnson (the Foreign Secretary) refers to Emily Thornberry as 'Lady Nugee', however, this is not the correct title for her as this is a title gained by marriage to her husband, Sir Christopher Nugee. She should be referred to using the formal address system set out in the parliamentary rules or 'Standing Orders' – as the 'Right Honourable Member for Islington South and Finsbury'. Johnson appears to struggle to remember Thornberry's name, 'the noble Lady Baroness whatever it is' at which point he is prompted collaboratively by a fellow Conservative MP to call her 'Lady Nugee'. The Speaker intervenes, as shown in Example 5.6 below:

Example 5.6 House of Commons debate (Commonwealth 27/03/2018; Transcript)

1	SP:	O order (.) I didn't want to be unkind (.) or discourteous to the Foreign Secretary (.)
2		but I say on (.) advice as the Clerks swivel round to me (.) two things (.) first of all we
3		don't name-call in this Chamber (.) and secondly (.)
4	MPs:	hear hear
5		secondly (.) I am dealing with the matter (.) and the right honourable Gentleman will
6		listen and benefit from listening (.) secondly we do not address people (.) by the
7		titles of their spouses (.) [the Shadow] Foreign Secretary has a name (.) and it's not
	MPs	[hear hear]
8		Lady something (.) we know what her name is (.) and it is inappropriate and frankly
9		sexist (.) [to speak in those terms (.) and]
	MPs	[hear hear shouting]
10	SP:	I am not having it in this Chamber (.) that is the [end of the matter no matter how
	MPs	[clapping clapping
11	SP:	senior a Member (.) that parlance is not legitimate it will not be allowed] and it
	MPs:	clapping clapping clapping]
12	SP:	will be called out and I require no chuntering from a sedentary position (.) from any
13		occupant of the Treasury Bench (.) [I've said]
	MPs	[hear hear]
14		what the position is (.) and believe me that is the end of the matter (.)
15	MP:	well said
16	SP:	I hope I have made the position extremely clear to people who are not well
17		informed about such matters

Here the Speaker admonishes Johnson for using the incorrect title. Notably, there is a good deal of mitigation in the Speaker's admonition, revealing the difficulty the Speaker has in negotiating his own authority with the high status of Johnson as Foreign Secretary. The Speaker mitigates the chastisement by starting with a negative frame to his purpose 'I don't want to be.' followed by two adjectives that seem at odds with the purpose of the admonition – 'unkind' and 'discourteous'. In saying that he wants to show Johnson 'kindness' the Speaker is at once establishing his authority (it is within his remit to bestow kindness), but also showing face-saving deference (he needs to say he does not wish to 'upset' or be impolite to Johnson). Agency for the admonition is also mitigated, with the Speaker claiming that he is only doing so 'on advice' as 'the Clerks swivel round to me', rather than by his own volition (line 2). However, these mitigating features contrast with the rest of the Speaker's turn, as subsequently his criticism becomes very forthright and direct, instructing MPs not to name-call (although it is not possible to identify from the video or Hansard data exactly which MP this is addressed to). Then he instructs an MP (probably Johnson) to listen to him, repeatedly using the 'will' verb form with the function of giving orders that is usually reserved for parent/child interaction ('the honourable Gentleman will listen and will benefit from listening' on line 6). The second part of his admonition to Johnson is to reprimand him for using the wrong address term for Emily Thornberry, who the Speaker refers to as 'the Shadow Foreign Secretary'. The Speaker uses the institutional and inclusive 'we' in this instruction 'we do not address people by the title of their spouses', but he gets more forceful as he continues the turn – presumably because of the resistance or 'chuntering' from the 'Treasury bench'. There is a good deal of support for the Speaker's intervention with cheering and, much more unusually, clapping when he calls the behaviour 'sexist' (line 9).

Johnson replies to the Speaker by making an apology to both him and Emily Thornberry:

Example 5.7 House of Commons debate (Commonwealth 27/03/2018) Part 3

1	BJ:	Mr Speaker (.) can I crave your indulgence just to (.) prostrate myself before you and
2		(.) and to and to and to apologise for any inad inadvertent (.) er sexism or or er
3		discourtesy (.) [er that er you you] may have deemed me to be er er to have been
4	MP:	[shouting]
5		guilty of and I and I and I heartily er tender my apologies to the er er right
6		honourable Lady opposite if if if she was offended by what I said and I meant (.) I
7		meant no harm (.) I meant no harm Mr Speaker and I and I and I apologise
8		unreservedly to to if I've if I've offended the feelings of the of the Right Honourable
9		Lady (turn continues)
10	SP:	I thank the Foreign Secretary for his gracious apology as far as I am concerned if I
11		can use the expression again (.) that is the end of the matter

The hyperbolic language 'crave your indulgence' and 'prostrate myself' gives the impression Johnson is in a royal court, begging forgiveness from the ruler. It is heavily ironic and insincere, even to the extent that it does not accept any wrongdoing, stating the apology is for 'any inadvertent sexism of discourtesy that you may have deemed me to be guilty of'. This way the apology is deflected towards the perception of guilt by the Speaker, rather than the guilty deed undertaken by Johnson (as in its straightforward form it would be: 'I am sorry I did something wrong'). The apology directed to Thornberry is equally insincere as it takes a conditional form 'if she was offended', shifting responsibility from the sender of the message (Johnson) to the receiver of the message (Thornberry), subtly positioning Thornberry as at fault for her emotional interpretation of his words 'offending her feelings'. The Speaker then replies to Johnson, ostensibly to accept the irony-laden 'gracious apology', but clearly to have the last word in relation to Johnson's inauthentic response.

The interest of this exchange lies in the sexism inherent in the use of Thornberry's husband's title by Johnson, in the Speaker's reaction to it, in Johnson's reaction to that reprimand, and in the way this was represented in the media (see the further analysis of this example in Section 5.5 below). It also exemplifies the way in which parliamentary exchanges of this type need to be scrutinised across chains of linked or connected events (Agha 2003; Wortham and Reyes 2015) as this was not the first time Thornberry had been referred to as 'Lady Nugee'. David Cameron used this title to refer to her in April 2016, Theresa May used it in February 2017 (discussed in detail in Chapter 6); and in October 2017, five months before this event, Johnson referred to Thornberry as 'Lady Nugee'. As explained in the detailed analysis in Chapter 8, these chained events offer further contextual information which, in this case, might lead to a possible interpretation that Johnson is knowingly taunting Thornberry by referring to her in this way. Although this is not possible to speculate about the intentions of the speaker, it is at least possible to identify that the use of gendered forms of address such 'Lady Nugee' have connotations of domesticity and servitude that are non-reciprocal between men and women and therefore can be used to subtly undermine and wield power over opponents. Efforts to challenge sexism in political institutions are often met with 'fierce personalized, sexualized, and gendered backlash' (Galea and Gaweda 2018: 278), and this is explored further in the case studies in Chapter 6.

5.4   Hegemonic Masculinity, Homosocial Bonding, Fraternal Networks and the 'Boys' Club'

As Chapters 3 and 4 show, political institutions vary according to their gender composition, interactional practices, linguistic norms and participation and the degree to which women feel that they are 'interlopers'. To understand these inequities, it is necessary to do more than examine the relations between women and men, as 'the nature of gender relations is such that asymmetries exist between men and women and among men and women' (Bird 1996: 120; Connell 1987). Connell's theoretical concept of hegemonic masculinity shapes the overall framework of gender relations by identifying 'the maintenance of practices that institutionalize men's dominance over women' and is 'constructed in relation to women and to subordinate masculinities' (Connell 1987: 185–6). Multiple masculinities exist in society but it is hegemonic masculinity that is 'the culturally dominant ideal of masculinity toward which men are encouraged to strive' (Bjarnegård 2013: 18). When considering the barriers that exclude women from public life generally and from politics in particular, it is necessary to consider the how the workings of hegemonic masculinity are manifested through exclusionary practices. The barriers to women's participation and representation in politics discussed in this chapter (gendered stereotyping, sexism and sexual harassment, and the representation of women politicians in the media) can be linked to the workings of hegemonic masculinity. Women interviewed for the 1998–2001 HoC project and the NIA in the 2009–11 devolved parliaments project attested to the existence of the 'old boys' club'. As one Labour woman MP states: 'I'm not a man and I never went to a public school and I suppose if I were both those things I'd be very comfortable here. You get used to it but I'll never be at home in that kind of environment' (Shaw 2002: Interview C). Similarly, Jess Phillips refers to the preponderance of men and of a certain *type* of men employed in parliament: 'It's great if you don't know someone's name here, you can just guess at Will, Tom or Ben and you have ninety per cent chance of being right' (Phillips 2017: 55).

The metaphor of the boys' club has been used to refer to the discourses and practices shared between men that constitute and institutionalise men's dominance over women (Bird 1996; Fisher and Kinsey 2014). This is achieved through 'homosocial bonding': 'in any male-dominated society, there is a special relationship between male homosocial (*including* homosexual) desire and the structures for maintaining and transmitting patriarchal power, a relationship founded on an inherent and potentially active structural congruence' (Sedgwick 1985: 25). Sedgwick's theoretical approach to language and gender is that there is a complex relationship between homosociality, homosexuality and homophobia in which men have a disrupted relation of male homosocial and homosexual bonds, whereas women have a much more continuous relationship between homosocial and homosexual bonds (Haywood et al. 2018: 57). Homosociality is one of the mechanisms of hegemonic masculinity and in political institutions 'taken-for granted practices and gendered discourses embed a "masculine blueprint"' that 'legitimizes men's place as parliamentarians and privileges men' (Galea and Gaweda 2018: 276–7).

Taken-for-granted homosociality can take many overt forms, as noted by Fisher and Kinsey in their study of the boys' club in academia it is at times highly visible 'this can be at the pub during and after work, via corridor conversations, 'matey' greetings, pats on the back or handshakes at the start of committee meetings' (Fisher and Kinsey 2014: 52). They also note the existence of much less visible forms of homosociality, such as male-only networks based on sports and drinking. In political institutions where women feel like the 'outsider within', linguistic practices, as shown in Chapter 3, are an important mechanism for masculine displays and the exclusion of women. Barracking, and other linguistic practices that are perceived as 'masculine' by women MPs serve to underline their peripheral membership of the CoP. As a woman Labour MP states:

I clapped in the Hunting Bill when we won the vote on that I think it is a much more natural way to respond I hate those 'hear hears' and I hate the banging on the table tops and I hate the 'hear hear' because it is a boyish noise and that is why I don't do it I mean the public understand it as a normal thing to do but the 'hear hear' is a really animal thing to do and that's really men's behaviour or waving order papers as well I mean I've never done that. (Shaw 2002: Interview C)

Men MPs also identified the different homosocial groups and their functions, with a Labour MP positioning himself outside these networks:

There are a number of old boys' networks that exist in this place (.) I put it in the plural because I think they tend to divide along the party lines although they will have a lot in common you know there may be a Labour old boys' network and a Tory old boys' network. But what they have in common is that they are defending the traditions in this place. (Shaw 2002: Interview F)

The idea here that men are 'defending' traditions through their informal networks implies an encroachment, imposition or threat to the status quo. Historically, the biggest change in the gender balance occurred in 1997 as the numbers of women MPs rose from 58 in 1992 to 117 in 1997. This would also concur with the claim that an increased number of women in institutions that have hitherto been male-dominated can actually lead to a 'thickening or defensive strengthening fraternal networks' (Walsh 2001: 19). Similarly, Kanter (1977) and Bjarnegård (2013) note that conditions of uncertainty mean that people fall back on 'social bases for trust' (Kanter 1977: 49) because 'the greater the uncertainty, the greater the pressures for those who have to trust each other to form a homogeneous group' (Kanter 1977: 49). The accumulation of what Bjarnegård describes as 'homosocial capital' can be 'interpreted as an investment in predictability' and it is needed most when institutions are at points of change and uncertainty (2013: 25). Therefore, while the increase in women in male-dominated professions has 'at least called into question the unproblematized status of the implicitly masculinist belief systems that predominate in these domains' (Walsh 2001: 204), it is possible that in response to this change, fraternal networks and homosocial bonds were reinforced.

Women can also play a role in the reinforcement of masculine hegemony and gender inequality. For example, Walsh (2001: 20) describes Margaret Thatcher as a 'male-identified woman' who failed to promote women and even discriminated against them. Women in most professional workplaces are dependent on male networks for access to resources and so must attend to heterosexual relations in order to succeed. Existing power structures mean that 'women benefit more from heterosocial behaviour than from homosocial behaviour, whereas the opposite is true for men' (Bjarnegård 2013). Women's dependency on men in male-dominated institutions is the reason for and contributes to the difficulty of establishing women's networks, as described by a Labour woman MP in the 1998–2001 HoC corpus:

I think it would be good if we could get women of all parties together but I don't think it will happen I think Labour women work together but I think Tory women MPs most of them don't think there's a problem but some of us do talk to each other between ourselves but I suspect that once you're here people would resent belonging to it because it would get out. It wouldn't be a secret and the men would use it 'Oh look there's a group of women MPs they must be weak to need that' you just can't afford to draw attention to the fact that you're a woman. (Shaw 2002: Interview B)

This woman MP accepts the supremacy and judgement of 'the men', in this revealing statement in which she attests to feeling compelled to hide 'the fact' of being a woman. As identified in Chapter 4 this is not a common sentiment expressed by woman politicians across all the UK institutions, with a woman AM in the NAW showing a confident and robust belief in all-women networks. When discussing sexist, misogynist behaviour in the HoC, one woman AM in the NAW was clear about differentiating the newer devolved Assembly saying: 'It's a gender balanced institution fairly full of women-identified women and if any man did behave like that he'd be dealt with I mean we'd send the girls round'. The existence of women's networks in the newer political institutions of the SP and the NAW indicate these institutions are more gender-balanced numerically and that women are less dependent on men, with homosocial bonds being expressed by both groups of women and men. However, the pervasive nature of fraternal networks means that they are nevertheless thought to operate across institutions other than parliaments, such as the media. This can lead to women's under-representation in terms of the amount of coverage they gain, and to their representation in the media being aligned to sexist stereotypes, and this will be examined in Section 5.5.

5.5   The Representation of Women Politicians in the Media

5.5.1   The Under-representation and Framing of Women Politicians in the Media

This section considers the relationship between women politicians and the media as a major barrier to women's participation in politics. First, I consider women's attested under-representation in the media overall before identifying some of the mechanisms or frames by which they are represented, and some examples of the ways these frames operate in different media, with a particular focus on the representation of women's language. Then, by returning to media representations of the 'Lady Nugee' example discussed in Examples 5.5–5.7, I illustrate how linguistic analyses of media texts can illuminate and reveal how masculinist power structures are reinforced and maintained. Finally, I consider how these depictions may affect and deter women from entering and participating in political life. Although it is necessary to consider 'media' in all its forms (newspapers [online and print], radio, television and different social media platforms) in order to establish how women are represented, this will necessarily be a selective account of some of the most notable patterns of gendered representation across different media. These patterns are further examined in relation to the media representation of individual leaders in more detail in the case studies in Chapters 6 and 7.

One of the most significant aspects of the media representation of women politicians is that they have consistently been shown to be under-represented in comparison with their male counterparts – even when allowing for the fact that they are a small minority of politicians overall – and this is exacerbated when gender and race intersect (Gershon 2012). Women are under-represented as sources of expertise and in news stories (De Swert and Hooghe 2010; Harmer 2017) and this could be a consequence of women's placement in the private, rather than the public sphere. It could also be because of the 'cross institutional fraternal networks' (Walsh 2001: 62) that support this divide – meaning that women are unlikely to be called upon and therefore their ideas and perspectives are omitted or marginalised. Women are also under-represented as media producers, and research has shown that – in spite of some improvements over time – women's journalistic roles are still limited. This role limitation may also be 'a potential explanation for more global gender disparities in news media coverage' (Cotter 2011: 2519). Finally, women are under-represented as media actors, or subjects (Adcock 2010; Harmer 2017; Ross and Carter 2011; Ross and Comrie 2012; Sensales and Areni 2017; Shor et al. 2014). In their longitudinal study of UK and Irish political news reporting from 1995, Ross and Carter found that although there had been a positive improvement in the representation of women in the media over time, this appeared to have plateaued with women consistently taking up only one third of news stories (Ross and Carter 2011). Studies of gender and media coverage in election campaigns have provided useful data on this topic, as the candidates usually stand for comparable political positions and the campaigns occur over a specified time period. Emily Harmer shows how, in the UK General election of 2017, women only accounted for 36 per cent of all individuals featured in the news coverage, even though the most prominent politician in the study (appearing in 37 per cent of all newspaper items) was the incumbent Prime Minister, and a woman, Theresa May (Harmer 2017: 64). This study also supports the claim that women are under-represented across all media roles – 29 per cent of media sources and 20 per cent of blogs referred to were authored by women, and women were excluded from being referred to as sources for more specialist political reporting as 'every individual pollster or other kind of expert who received any mention or reference in the news was male' (Harmer 2017: 64).

There is an intrinsic relationship between sex-based stereotypes and gendered mediation, as women have been shown to be trivialised and objectified by their representation in the media: 'Whether the women in question are mothers or motorists, prostitutes or politicians, in all cases they are first framed by their biological sex, then by their behaviour, and only then (and only if it is absolutely necessary to the story) by their professional occupation' (Ross 2017: 58). This marking of sex, or 'gender marking' is frequent in coverage of women who aspire to top leadership positions as 'first woman Prime Minister' or more simply 'woman politician' (Falk 2010; Trimble 2017). This underscores their novelty and promotes the idea that a woman's gender is significant to the way she conducts her professional duties *differently* from men (Falk 2010). Women in politics are also 'circumscribed by a gendered frameworld' which has particular nuances (Ross 2017: 58). In this way, gendered discourses of 'outsiders winning against the odds' and 'breaking the mould' alongside being represented as 'agents of change' position women in particularly precarious ways (Norris 1997; Ross 2017). As noted by Ross, these characterisations are not stable as the first two are ephemeral (they can only occur once), and the final one, by emphasising change in the same way as the 'different voice' ideology, can 'set up women to fail as they prove unable to fulfil our realistically high expectations of them' (Ross 2017: 58).

The ways in which women politicians are objectified and trivialised by their gendered mediation have been researched extensively and documented in detail (for example, Cameron and Shaw 2016, 2020; Mavin et al. 2010; Ross 2017; Sreberny-Mohammedi and Ross 1996; Trimble 2017). Women's appearances are routinely referred to before their policies, as with Theresa May's leopard skin shoes, Hillary Clinton's 'pantsuits', or Nicola Sturgeon's haircut 'like a Tunnock's tea-cake'. In the US research literature this tendency is commonly referred to as 'Hemlines, Husbands, Hairstyles' (Mavin et al. 2010: 559), and in the UK the Fawcett Society launched a 'Views not Shoes' campaign[5] in 2015, which aimed to 'call out' sexist media representations of women politicians: 'The most powerful politicians in the UK are women. It's about time the press stopped giving shoe commentaries and started focusing on their views and policies' (Fawcett Society 2015). Men politicians can also be the focus of comments on personal appearance and fashion choices, but 'a preoccupation with women's appearance and sexual attractiveness reinforces a pre-existing gender inequality (the tendency to judge women more by their looks than by their words) in a way that the same preoccupation, applied to men, does not' (Cameron and Shaw 2016: 92). As observed by Trimble et al. (2013: 476) 'by highlighting politicians' bodies or family lives, news reports perform gender work', and this will be further explored in the case studies of women political leaders in Chapters 6 and 7.

A focus by the media on women politicians' relationships and family can be seen as part of a process of personalisation (Trimble et al. 2013; Ross 2017) and 'intimization' of politics (Trimble 2017). But, configurations of 'the private' have different meanings for women and for men: 'While men are understood as seamlessly cohabiting in the public and domestic realms, women's lives are more typically defined by their roles, and duties, as wives and mothers' (Trimble 2017: 91). Women are positioned awkwardly in relation to divorce, their partners or spouses, and having or not having children. Among the Canadian, New Zealand and Australian women prime ministers of Linda Trimble's study, she found that news writers were confounded by the presence or absence of a 'first man' and often 'resorted to evaluating men's compliance with norms of hegemonic masculinity and familial patriarchy' (2017: 95). She also found that childlessness was problematic for women prime ministers: 'For Shipley, the presence of children was normalized, while for Campbell, Clark and Gillard, their absence was highlighted, assessed as culturally anomalous, and linked to the woman leader's personal character and her capacity to make decisions in the interests of families' (2017: 95). There is no straightforwardly advantageous position for women leaders to adopt in relation to their domestic and private lives however, as even though Shipley gained an advantage through her 'normative' family life shielding her from the 'intense and invasive sexualisation' experienced by the other women leaders, the '"wife of" motif prevailed' (Trimble 2017: 217) and the separation of her family and political life were questioned. In contrast it has been suggested that men politicians are able to capitalise on their normative family situations and discussing their families can be used as a strategy to boost their popularity (Trimble 2017; van Zoonen 2006).

Such strategies can also be viewed as part of a necessary endeavour on the part of politicians to establish *authenticity*. Politicians need to appear sincere, truthful and 'real' for the electorate and as they communicate this through different types of media outlets (television, newspapers, social media etc), this is best conceived of as a 'mediated authenticity' (Enli 2015). The construction of mediated authenticity relies on 'trustworthiness, originality and spontaneity' (Enli 2015: 3), and spontaneity has been identified as a particular characteristic of political 'authentic talk' in which 'traces of scriptedness or rehearsal for performance are avoided or effaced' (Montgomery 2001: 460). Given that there is dissonance between the role 'politician' and other 'out of place' bodies according to class, race and gender (Puwar 2004a), it follows that the construction of mediated authenticity will be more challenging for women, as they are already positioned as unique, unusual and 'other'.

Analysts have observed that the framing of women in professional life by the media often resorts to basic and generalised archetypes. Rosabeth Moss Kanter's (1977) notion of four stereotypes of professional women has been particularly useful to encapsulate the reductive, sexist and generalised ways that women politicians are presented in the media. These roles express the ways in which men in professional life can make sense of and interpolate women into the world of work. Kanter describes these stereotypes as 'role traps' in which token women in organisations are at once 'snared' but that also function to legitimate them by placing them 'in a category that men could respond to and understand' (1977: 233). The different roles are:

1. Mother (nurturing, maternal, emotional, non-sexual)
2. Seductress/ sexual object (sexually desirable, available and/or predatory)
3. Pet (treated with humour and 'a cheerleader for shows of prowess')
4. Iron maiden (competent, powerful, lacking support and perceived as 'tougher' and 'more masculine' than they actually are) (Kanter 1977: 233–6).

The stereotypes have been used to investigate the media coverage of different women politicians such as Sarah Palin, Hillary Clinton, Kamala Harris, Theresa May, Nicola Sturgeon and US news anchor Megyn Kelly (for example in, Baxter 2010, 2018; Cameron and Shaw 2016; Carlin and Winfrey 2009; Dolan et al. 2017; Gordon et al. 2017). The media coverage of contemporary modern women politicians often fits the characterisations of these role descriptions – or draws on one or more of them. This is discussed in more detail in the case studies in Chapters 6 and 7. It has also been claimed that black women politicians are framed even more narrowly than their white female colleagues, as 'mammies, jezebels, or sapphires' (West 2012). These roles are comparable to Kanter's stereotypes, with the 'mammie' corresponding to 'the mother'; the 'jezebel' as the seductress/sex object, and the sapphire most closely aligned to the 'iron maiden' with the addition of a 'black angry woman' element (Dolan et al. 2017: 123). Although there is little scholarship to establish the impact of these frames on black women's candidacies 'they are undoubtably damaging and insulting to black women across the board' (Dolan et al. 2017: 123).

Women politicians may, of course, tap into and exploit these patterns of gendered mediation for their own advantage. They are not necessarily simply victims of stereotyped media representation, and they may be instrumental in creating their own representation in the media. For example, Sarah

Palin emphasised her 'mother' role – coining the phrase 'mamma grizzly' (Trimble 2017) – and therefore possibly drawing on two of Kanter's stereotypes (the mother and the 'iron maiden'). By doing this she managed to 'foreground her alignment to the patriarchal family form, while at the same time highlighting strength and determination' (Loke et al. 2011: 213 cited in Trimble 2017: 9).

5.5.2   Gender and Mediated Representations of Speech and Voice

The voices of women are often represented in stereotypic and negative ways in the media. The critical assessment of the sound of women's voices contributes to the overall difficulties women have in negotiating the competing gendered norms and expectations of political office: 'political women are censured for speaking too softly, too diplomatically, too much, too pointedly, too passionately, or in a manner critical of patriarchy and other hegemonic power structures' (Trimble 2017: 188). Tanya Romaniuk investigated the gendered representation of Hillary Clinton's voice as a 'witch's cackle' (2016), and this is discussed in more detail as part of the case study in Chapter 7. In our 2015 study of UK General Election TV debates, we found that the voices of the women leaders (Leanne Wood, Nicola Sturgeon, and Natalie Bennett) were characterised in the media by disparaging quotatives such as 'squeak', 'bark', 'scowl', and 'snap' which index an affective stance or evoke aspects of voice quality (Cameron and Shaw 2016: 106). Judith Baxter (2010) finds that a range of negative adjectives are used to describe women leaders, and many of these similarly allude to aspects of the voice: '*hard, difficult, scary, tough, mean, bullying, assertive, aggressive, volatile, overpowering, shrill, hysterical, emotional, moody and irrational*' (Baxter 2010: 157 – italics in original). Linda Trimble finds that Canadian Prime Minister Kim Campbell's voice was described as 'unduly loud, shrill, childish, and whiny' (Trimble 2017: 185). As shown in the 1998–2001 HoC interview data in Section 5.3 on sexism, women politicians in the chamber are vilified for having 'squeaky' voices, and this is probably one of the most common negative characterisations of the voices of women politicians. Describing someone as having a 'squeaky' voice, like many of the adjectives used, connotes a voice that is overtaken by emotion and is out of control, tapping into the core stereotype of emotional women leaders described by Brescoll (2016) and discussed in Section 5.1. Another connotation of a 'squeaky' voices is with a mouse or small animal (Cameron and Shaw 2016: 106), and has the attendant connotations of ineffectual, powerless and bothersome. The 'squeaky' characterisation of women's voices is often accompanied by the description 'shrill' and 'whine', that also evoke animal sounds – in these cases of birds and dogs. A 'shrill' voice is one that, like a 'squeaky' one, has become over-emotional to the point of incomprehensibility. It is not pleasant to listen to a shrill and squeaky voice, nor does it carry a coherent message, let alone an authoritative one. As Mary Beard (2017) notes, women are often described as 'strident' and their contributions are likened to 'whinging' and 'whining'. In response to a description by an internet troll of her as 'whining' she writes: 'Do these words matter? Of course they do, because they under-pin an idiom that acts to remove authority, the force, even the humour from what women have to say. It is effectively an idiom that repositions women back in the domestic sphere (people "whinge" over things like the washing up)' (Beard 2017: 30). In this way, negative descriptions of women's voices reinforce masculine gender norms and firmly position women outside the public sphere. Many of these descriptions of women's voices allude to the relative higher pitch of a woman's voice in comparison to men's. Although the average frequency of pitch is 125 Hz for men and 210 Hz for women there is significant overlap of average pitch ranges between women and men – in other words there is a good deal of flexibility in the average ranges and pitch level is not an exclusive feature associated with women or men (Graddol and Swan 1989; Swann 1992). However, the pitch of an individual's voice is part of the gender order, the social learning and behaviour that index masculinity and femininity and as such has great ideological and cultural significance. This means that, on the whole, men do not exploit pitch variability to sound like women, and vice versa (unless, as noted in transgender research, they do so as part of the process of male-female or female-male transition (Knight 1992)). The ubiquitous example of pitch change in relation to gender and politics relates to Margaret Thatcher, who – according to the accounts of her biographers – was advised to lower the pitch of her voice by her 'spin doctor', Gordon Reece (Wilson and Irwin 2015). Reece thought the broadcasting of PMQs for the first time put Thatcher at a disadvantage because 'she had to be at her shrillest to be heard over the din' and that 'holding a steady and equable tone … would eventually drive through, not over or under, the noise' (Wapshott and Brock 1983: 169, cited in Atkinson 1984: 115). The details of this seemingly unverifiable process vary – in some accounts she was helped by Lawrence Olivier, in others a speech coach at the National Theatre, and advised by the advertising guru Lord Bell at Saatchi and Saatchi [Atkinson 1984; Gardner 2014; Sawer 2012]. But over time, Thatcher's voice did change in pitch (it became lower) and in speed (it became slower). As her biog-rapher, Charles Moore, reportedly wrote: 'Soon the hectoring tones of the housewife gave way to softer notes and a smoothness that seldom cracked except under extreme provocation on the floor of the House of Commons' (cited in Gardner 2014). Thatcher therefore successfully adopted a lower pitch of voice that was more in-line with the normative, masculine political voice of authority. She did not escape her critics for doing so, however, and while many found the change gave her authority and gravitas, her 'opponents regarded her new voice as both nannying and condescending' (Sawer 2012). The salience of the popular narrative of Thatcher 'changing the pitch of her voice to become more like a man' is culturally and ideologically interesting as it expresses a common acceptance, or rationale for her success: yes, she was the first woman PM, but she had to assume the qualities of a man to achieve it. The popularity and cultural resonance of this story is perhaps part the struggle to come to terms with the fact of having had a woman Prime Minister.

There is evidence to show that Thatcher was given good advice to lower the pitch of her voice, however, as different studies have shown that the electorate prefer lower pitched rather than high pitch politicians. Klofstad et al. (2012) recorded men and women saying 'I urge for you to vote for me this November', then they manipulated each recording to produce both a higher and a lower pitch recording of the original. When participants were asked to vote for either the higher or the lower pitch versions of each voice, *both* men and women selected the lower-pitched versions more than the high-pitched ones. This finding was also borne out by Tigue et al.'s (2012) experiment which found that participants selected lower-pitched candidates 67–69 per cent of the time. Further research elucidated that for both men and women, lower pitch was evaluated more positively than higher pitch, although men and women received different types of evaluations. For men, lower pitched voices were associated with dominance, attractiveness and physical strength, whereas for women lower pitched voices were associated with dominance but a higher pitch signalled attractiveness (Klofstad et al. 2016). This of course encapsulates the problem facing women in political life – they can either enact professional roles well, or 'femininity', but unlike men and masculinity, it appears they cannot easily do both at the same time.

5.5.3   Linguistic Analyses of Gendered Representations in Media Texts

As described in Chapter 2, Critical Discourse Analysis (CDA) is used as a central discourse analytic method for the analysis of both parliamentary discourse, and for the identification of gendered discourses in media texts. In this section I return to the 'Lady Nugee' example, not only because it relates to the gendered mediation of political actors, but also to the other core interlinked themes identified in this chapter: gender stereotyping, sexism and the operation of fraternal networks in politics and across public institutions. Table 5.1 below shows ten newspaper headlines (both print and online) reporting on the naming of Emily Thornberry as 'Lady Nugee' by Boris Johnson in March 2018, and the subsequent reprimand he received from the Speaker, John Bercow, as was discussed in Section 5.2.

Using Fairclough's (1995) three-dimensional model for CDA it is possible to identify salient textual features relevant to the identification of overarching gendered and political ideologies. First, it is possible to identify the presence or absence of the three actors in this example: Boris Johnson is referred to in all the headlines, Emily Thornberry in eight out of ten of the headlines, and John Bercow (the Speaker) in five out of ten of the headlines. The naming of these three participants is also significant with all three of them being referred to by their first names and last names, or by their surnames alone in the different headlines. The differences lie in that Johnson is the only participant who is referred to by a nickname 'BOJO' (Table 5.1d) and by his first name 'Boris'. The other two politicians are referred to by their official title or role and their name (Table 5.1c) and Thornberry is the only participant anonymised by being referred to as 'female MP' (Table 5.1i) and whose political allegiance is specifically highlighted (in this case as a negative trait) by modifying her name with 'Corbyn ally'.

Johnson is clearly the central and most newsworthy actor in this 'story' (and the nickname and first name are markers of friendly allegiance), but he is represented in diverse ways politically. Bercow appears in fewer headlines through the use of the agentless passive construction (in Table 5.1d, e, i, and j) where Johnson is the subject of the sentence and appears first in the headlines. Johnson is 'accused', 'forced', 'admonished' and 'rebuked', but Bercow, the 'accuser', is not included. This serves to draw the readers' attention away from the 'accuser' by making the reprimand appear as an impersonal function of institutional discourse, and puts more emphasis on the 'accused' (Boris Johnson) and the 'crime' (sexism). Conversely, in Table 5.1a–c, John Bercow is the subject of the active sentence in which he directly reprimands Boris Johnson. Here, the act of reprimanding Boris Johnson is emphasised, rather than the 'crime' itself. The hyperbolic way in which John Bercow's admonition is described also indicates where the newspapers' political interests lie – Bercow is represented as being out of control emotionally, conducting an 'epic rant', 'furious rant' 'rages' 'ballistic telling-off'. It is not surprising that at this point, newspapers are either supporting Boris Johnson or John Bercow. Johnson is viewed as far-right, pro-Brexit politician and Bercow is viewed by some as a liberal, progressive and modernising Speaker. This means that the political alignment of newspapers support or oppose each politician accordingly.[7]

Alongside these political orientations, gendered ideologies are also evident. Firstly, the portrayal of the sexist event itself is significant as the word 'sexist' or 'sexism' appears in inverted commas or scare quotes in every example. As has been claimed, 'the effect of scare quotes is to turn an expression meaning "X" *into* an expression meaning "so-called 'X'" (Haack 2003: 18), signifying that the judgement of 'sexism' is not straightforward and definitive, but a

Table 5.1 *Newspaper headlines about the naming of Emily Thornberry as 'Lady Nugee' in the UK House of Commons on the 27 March 2018*[6]

a. **John Bercow reprimands Boris Johnson for 'sexist' Emily Thornberry taunt** (*The Telegraph*)
b. **John Bercow's epic rant at "sexist" Boris Johnson calling Emily Thornberry "Lady Nugee"** (*New Statesman*)
c. **Speaker Bercow rages at 'sexist' Boris Johnson in the Commons after he calls shadow foreign secretary Emily Thornberry 'Lady something'** (*Mail Online*)
d. **BOJO SEXISM STORM: Boris Johnson is accused of sexism in the Commons after he calls Corbyn ally Emily Thornberry by her husband's name** (*The Sun*)
e. **Boris Johnson forced to make grovelling apology for 'sexist' remarks after BALLISTIC telling-off** (*Mirror online*)
f. **Boris FORCED to apologise for 'sexist' comment to Thornberry after Bercow's FURIOUS rant** (*The Express*)
g. **Boris Johnson told off by Speaker for 'sexism'** (*BBC News website*)
h. **Johnson apologises for 'sexist' reference to Emily Thornberry** (*The Guardian*)
i. **Boris Johnson admonished for 'sexism' after calling female MP by husband's name** (*the Independent*)
j. **Boris Johnson Rebuked For 'Sexist' Behaviour Towards Emily Thornberry** (*Huffington Post*)

subjective matter implying uncertainty. Of course, there is an element of subjective interpretation to the identification of sexism (see Section 5.2) but the newspapers' distancing use of the word 'sexism' at least shows how carefully these publications need to position themselves in relation to these accusations. The media coverage itself is also noteworthy as when Emily Thornberry raised her objection to the Prime Minister, Theresa May, for referring to her as 'Lady Nugee' on 6 February 2017, the media coverage of this event was minimal (see also Section 6.2). This suggests that an event involving exactly the same naming practices, but one in which Thornberry was a much more active participant with a woman Prime Minister as an opponent, was not deemed as newsworthy as this later event between the two men politicians, Johnson and Bercow. This example also relates to points above about the under-representation of women in political reporting, with eight of the articles in Table 5.1 written by male political correspondents, one by a woman (Table 5.1f) and one anonymously authored by *The Spectator*'s 'Media Mole', who nonetheless appears as a male 'mole' journalist in the cartoon representation. In this way, it is possible this is an example of cross-institutional fraternal networks that deem news about and by and for men as more significant than that about, for and by women.

Further scrutiny of media depictions of this event can also lead to more detailed interpretations of the event itself, as both *The Spectator* and *The Telegraph* allude to the naming of Emily Thornberry as 'Lady Nugee' as intentional. *The Telegraph* article refers to this as a 'taunt' (Table 5.1a), and the *New Statesman* article (Table 5.1b) goes on to describe this as 'a tiresome Tory joke about the shadow foreign secretary Emily Thornberry being married to Sir Christopher Nugee'. The 'inadvertent' stumbling over Thornberry's name by Johnson seems less plausible in the light of these interpretations by political correspondents. Similarly, the descriptions of Emily Thornberry in some newspaper reports after she stood in for Jeremy Corbyn as Leader of the Opposition in PMQs (See Chapter 3 for a detailed description of PMQs) on 12 July 2017 are revealing. In an article entitled 'The real reason Tories call Emily Thornberry "Lady Nugee"... and it isn't sexist' by Michel Deacon of *The Telegraph* he explains:

Tories don't call Ms Thornberry 'Lady Nugee' because they expect her to take her husband's name. They call her Lady Nugee because it suits her (....)
Lady Nugee. It captures her manner, her tone, her bearing – her grandeur. 'Ms' simply doesn't do her justice. It has to be 'Lady'. See her as she sails into the Commons, resplendent, majestic, a royal yacht made flesh. Watch as she rises to face the House, posture erect, smile imperious. Marvel at the insouciance with which she squashes her opposite number, dismissing him as though he were an impertinent footman. At any moment I half expect her to snap her fingers, address the Speaker as 'my good man', and bid him fetch her a gin and tonic. (Deacon 2017)

This depiction is clearly tapping into a negative stereotype of a woman performing in the most high-profile speech event in the UK parliament. Not only is the article sexist on this level (just because it does not accept female authority), but there are traces of classic misogynistic gendered discourses that underlie the 'because it suits her' statement.[8] This feels like victim-blaming of the 'because she deserves it' variety and orients to a 'queenly' imperious stereotype of a person who nonchalantly occupies an undeserved and imagined position at the top of a social hierarchy. The stereotype further implies a lack of self-awareness and a smug complacency. This works best as a criticism of a left-wing woman because it positions her as a hypocrite, at odds with socialist and working-class values, further denigrating her authority. The fact that this article was written some time before the Boris Johnson/John Bercow extract supports the idea that this is an interdiscursive, chained event unfolding and strengthening over time. This is discussed further in the case study of Theresa May in Chapter 6 and in the concluding Chapter 8.

5.5.4   Why Does It Matter? How Does Gendered Mediation Affect Political Representation and Participation?

While the negative characterisations of women politicians in the press are no longer surprising to us – Theresa May's shoes, Hillary Clinton's witch's cackle, Emily Thornberry sailing into the House of Commons like a 'royal yacht made flesh' – they are nonetheless pervasive and damaging to women's participation and representation in politics. Five patterns of sexist reporting that dissuade women from entering politics have been identified as:

1. Under-representation in the media compared with men;
2. A focus on irrelevant factors such as family and appearance;
3. Women are trivialised and scrutinised in terms of their competence;
4. Women's political positions on women's issues will be in focus;
5. Political influence and/or competence if they win is questioned.
   (Wasburn and Wasburn 2011)

More explicit effects of gendered mediation on women who have already entered the world of politics have also been noted. Amanda Haraldsson and Lena Wängnerud (2019) investigate how media sexism can affect women's willingness to stand for political office by using data from the Global Media Monitoring Project to establish the relationship between sexist media coverage and women's representation in different parliaments across the world. They found a significant relationship between the level of sexist coverage and the share of women candidates in different parliaments. They hypothesise that 'indirect exposure to sexism through media would have a bystander effect on women's political ambition' (2018: 4). This idea relies on a notion of 'ambient sexism' which holds that witnessing sexism decreases the self-esteem and then reduces the career aspirations of those observing it (Bradley-Geist et al. 2015: 29). This is related to another concept in the research literature on leadership – that of 'stereotype threat'. This holds that knowing one is being evaluated negatively 'through the lens of a negative stereotype' can undermine achievement, in particular by decreasing motivation and engagement leading to underperformance (Hoyt and Murphy 2016: 388). In an experimental setting, research has suggested that women and men become less fluent and 'use more tentative language' when exposed to different gendered stereotype threats relating to 'leadership' and 'relationship maintaining abilities' (McGlone and Pfiester 2015: 126).

Women politicians are certainly positioned in yet another series of double binds relating to their representation in the media: 'appear too feminine and the media you will not take you seriously. Appear too masculine or too neutral and your appearance will be picked over and ridiculed and you will be described as too dowdy to be considered fit for power' (Mavin et al. 2010: 558). Negative representations of women politicians by the media was one of the most recurrent themes in the 2010 devolved parliament interview data from women across all the devolved assemblies. One woman AM in the NAW says:

When I first got here there was a lot of like media attention about what I wore what I looked like pundits used to refer to me as Assembly Spice (...) so I used to get reported for what I wore used have my picture in the paper just because it was my picture so at that stage it was very much struggling to actually get yourself reported for something that you'd actually said or contributed'. (Woman assembly member, NAW)

All women interviewed in the NAW agreed that newer women AMs had been the subject of extreme criticism in the press, and that this was not acceptable. Most politicians in the SP reported that women were the subject of ferocious criticism by the media in the first session of the parliament in 1999, particularly in relation to the way they dressed and some MSPs' 'west coast accent', and that this kind of gendered criticism is likely to deter women from entering politics. Similarly, in the NIA a woman Minister, discussing her sexist treatment in the debating chamber and in the media, says: 'The number of young women that said to me I wouldn't do your job for love nor money it's and I get huge support out on the ground and they just go it's horrible what they're doing.' In the 1998–2001 HoC interview data a number of women MPs related the influx of new MPs in 1997 as being the subject of particularly negative and sexist media representations. As mentioned in Chapter 3, these tended to centre on their 'lack of intelligence' and the fact that they were depicted as unthinking 'clones' or 'Stepford Wives':

I think it's a conscious thing of the press who are continually continually niggling. So the barracking is not just in the chamber the nasty stuff the real nasty stuff is the press and what the press say about us. The fact that we can't think for ourselves – we've had the biggest variety of single-minded women in this place ever – and yet they have to think of some way to bring us down to undermine us. I've got quite a feminist argument coming out – I wouldn't go so far as to say it's a male plot – but because we won't behave like the men therefore it is not a valid way of behaving therefore it must be because we're stooges or whatever. That's where it is very important – and it is very difficult not to get caught up in it all because the easy way is to behave like they are – but to say no there's a different way of doing it equally robust equally enjoyable equally with the banter but not about being nasty or vicious or trying to put people off. Yes I want to try and floor them in their arguments but I don't want to undermine them as an individual. It's about challenging their ideas not challenging the person. (Shaw 2002: Interview A)

This is an interesting opinion as it includes many of the issues covered in this chapter – the woman MP sees the depiction of women as unthinking 'stooges' by the press as a consequence of refusing to take up a combative style in the parliamentary chamber. She attests to trying to 'do things differently' and pioneer a more consensual style that does not rely on personal attacks on individuals. In this way the MP is articulating the 'civilising difference' role of women by adhering to the 'different voice' ideology – a position that has been identified in this chapter as an additional burden upon women and one that is not borne out in women's actual performance in political arenas. This emphasises the ideological significance of gendered beliefs about communication and highlights the complexities of disentangling *beliefs* about linguistic behaviour (whether by the media, academic researchers, or the politicians themselves) from their actual *performance* in political contexts. The next two chapters will consider how the barriers to women's participation identified in this chapter have been managed and negotiated by three women leaders: Theresa May (Chapter 6) and Julia Gillard and Hillary Clinton (Chapter 7).

6   Case Study: Theresa May

6.1   Introduction: Rationale for the Selection and Inclusion of Case Studies

So far in this book, empirical investigations of gender and language use in UK parliaments have been analysed and presented in order to investigate women's participation in politics. As outlined in Chapter 2, different ethnographic and discourse analytic methods have been used to measure and evaluate the factors that affect women's linguistic participation. The analysis of officially recorded parliamentary discourse; transcriptions of video recordings of proceedings; and interviews with the participants themselves led to the identification of barriers to women's progress in politics, discussed in detail in Chapter 5. The next two chapters aim to focus on *how* successful women leaders negotiate the barriers discussed at length in the preceding chapter: the stereotyping of women, and in particular their speech and communication styles; sexism and sexist language directed at women politicians; hegemonic masculinity, fraternal networks and the 'old boys' club'; and the representation of women politicians in the media. These overlapping categories affect women in multiple and differing ways that can only be understood through the lens of the particular context within which they are performing. For this reason, I have chosen to undertake *case studies* of three women leaders in relation to the particular obstacles and barriers that are the most relevant to their political contexts. I therefore seek to answer the question posed in Chapter 1: What are the effects of sexism, fraternal networks, high visibility and gendered discourses of linguistic performance upon women politicians, and how do successful politicians like Theresa May, Julia Gillard and Hillary Clinton attempt to resist and counter these effects?

The case study approach aligns to calls for research that seeks to understand leadership in ways that are qualitative, and that focus on discourse and how leadership is enacted (Baxter 2010; Ilie and Schnurr 2017). As Judith Baxter notes, early work into leadership assumed that leaders 'were born rather than made' (2010: 11) before the focus turned to theories which centred on the behaviour of 'effective' leaders. The analysis of language use, and of leaders performing leadership in a range of settings and contexts can show how leaders enact, reproduce or resist institutional relationships by using a variety of coercive and collaborative strategies (Holmes and Stubbe 2003). Therefore, in Chapters 6 and 7, I undertake case studies of Theresa May, UK Prime Minister 2016–19; Julia Gillard, Australia's first woman Prime Minister 2010–13; and Hillary Clinton, first woman Democratic Party presidential nominee for the 2016 US presidential election. In each case I first analyse aspects of their political performances in 'critical gendered moments' where gendered discourses are explicitly discussed or contested, and then I consider aspects of their gendered representation in the media. The case study of Theresa May is the most detailed of the three because I am able to draw upon the detailed ethnographic descriptions and analyses of HoC parliamentary interaction undertaken in the first half of the book (Chapters 3 and 4). I chose to focus on Julia Gillard as she is known for facing and challenging sexist abuse in the Australian House of Representatives (HoR), and also for her gendered representation in the Australian media. As the HoR is a 'Westminster style' parliament, I am also able to undertake analyses of parliamentary interaction, particularly occurring between Gillard and her main adversary and LO, Tony Abbott. Finally, I focus on Hillary Clinton and particularly her 2015–16 presidential bid. Clinton is perhaps the most high-profile women politician of recent times and faced particular obstacles (not least in having Donald Trump as a political opponent) relating to her position as the first woman candidate for the US presidency.

All these leaders are can be seen as *exceptional*, because they have reached the highest levels of their profession in an era when it is still rare for women to do so. Although there are now more women political leaders than ever before, in 2019 there are still only 10 heads of government in the world who are women, and most do not serve in the role for more than four years (Trimble 2017: 5). These leaders have therefore found ways to negotiate the representation of female authority as unnatural and emasculating, and the various double binds affecting women in politics described throughout this book. There are further similarities and differences between the three women leaders: Gillard and Clinton are both political 'firsts', as the first Australian woman prime minister and the first US presidential candidate respectively, and were from political parties on the left of the political spectrum. Theresa May was the second woman prime minister of the UK, and belongs to the right-wing Conservative Party. She possibly escaped some of the excessive media scrutiny and high visibility thought to be attached to the novelty accorded to women 'firsts', and the possible ways in which her traditional conservatism intersects with her gender are discussed in this chapter.

6.2   Theresa May

6.2.1   Introduction

Theresa May became UK Prime Minister on 13 July 2016. As the second woman Prime Minister after Margaret Thatcher, comparisons between the two were as sexist as they were inevitable. May could possibly have sought to capitalise on the comparison with Thatcher to find favour within her own party. For example, and as discussed in more detail in Section 6.3, in her first session (PMQs) with Jeremy Corbyn, the leader of the Labour party and LO, she finished her final response to him by describing the characteristics of a 'bad boss' before leaning across the dispatch box and theatrically saying 'remind him of anyone?'. Media commentators claimed that 'Theresa May turned into Thatcher before our very eyes' (Meyjes 2016), and that she was 'channelling Thatcher' in this performance. Yet, over the course of her premiership from 2016 to 2019 this early performance style of May and her use of devastating Thatcher-like responses was not borne out. Instead, she became known for her repetitive, rehearsed phrases such as the 'strong and stable' mantra of the 2017 General Election Campaign, or the tautological 'Brexit means Brexit' when explaining her adherence to the outcome of the June 2016 referendum in which the UK voted to leave the EU. This led to perhaps the most devastating characterisation of May, that of the 'Maybot',[1] an automaton that can only produce a fixed set of answers, regardless of the relevance to the question posed.

The sexist representations of May being 'like Thatcher' not only reflect the paucity of women in authoritative roles and more specifically in holding the office of Prime Minister, but also ignore significant differences between the two women. May was much more experienced in the highest levels of government than Thatcher when she took office, having been Home Secretary between 2010 and 2016. May also claims to be a feminist and supports increasing women's role in parliament. She appointed a woman Home Secretary when she became Prime Minister and co-founded the 'Women2Win' campaign to elect more women to the Conservative party.[2] This is unlike Thatcher who refused to acknowledge that women faced discrimination, and her staff were 'organised in a perfectly gendered division of labour with women doing typing, cleaning and looking after her wardrobe' (Webster 1990: 66). Traditional roles and conservativism tend to go hand-in-hand, however, as May showed when she was interviewed with her husband, Phillip, in a rare and what one must presume calculated personal domestic revelation just before the General Election in 2017 that there are 'boy jobs and girl jobs' in the home.[3] There are also other signs of her complex relationship to femininity – on the one hand being a self-confessed shoe-lover and playing up to the leopard-print kitten-heel image, but on the other, claiming that 'this is not something that defines me either as a woman or a politician, but it comes to define me in the eyes of the newspapers'

(May 2009). Similarly, in relation to feminism, despite her claim that she wants 'to see more women in politics and in government because greater women representation makes a difference to everyone's lives' (May 2018a), her voting record on women's issues does not support a feminist agenda. She has supported more restrictive abortion laws, cuts to child tax credits, public sector jobs and social care and: 'In this respect she follows Thatcher in failing to support other women through her social policy decisions' (Thompson and Yates 2017: 131).

As shown in the timeline of events in Table 6.1, May's term as Prime Minister was exceptionally turbulent and politically fraught. She showed extreme resilience and staying-power to survive such a disastrously and tactically ill-advised General Election in 2017. Other problems for her arose when she failed to respond quickly or genuinely to the victims of the Grenfell fire tragedy immediately after the General Election in 2017. In September 2017 she lost her voice in her speech to the Conservative party conference and was approached by a prankster as she apologised for the dismal election result at the same time as the letters of the slogan behind her 'building a country that works for everyone' gradually fell off the wall (Figure 6.1). This speech was dubbed 'the worst ever' and 'a car crash' (*The Sun*, 4 October 2017) but she managed to survive the calls for her resignation that arose in the aftermath of the speech and sought to make light of the situation by saying she 'needed a stiff drink afterwards'.[4] Other difficulties later in this period included facing opposition from within her own party to a plan for leaving the EU reached with her cabinet in July 2018 (dubbed the 'Chequers plan'), culminating in the resignation of the 'Brexit secretary' David Davis and the Foreign Secretary, Boris Johnson a few days later. Later in 2018 and early 2019 May survived two 'no-confidence' motions, one from her own party and one proposed by the LO, Jeremy Corbyn in the HoC. She faced continual problems negotiating a Brexit deal for withdrawing from the EU, with her own fraught negotiations with the EU leading to a deal which was only to be rejected by MPs in the HoC in January and February 2019. Her failure to secure a parliamentary consensus for her Brexit deal ultimately led to her resignation in June 2019, and she was replaced by a new Prime Minister, Boris Johnson, on 23 July 2019.

These setbacks and obstacles make May's premiership seem more precarious than most incumbencies and seem to fit descriptions of the 'glass cliff' position which is claimed to be associated with women leaders. This 'glass cliff' is an observed tendency in which women are more likely to be appointed to leadership positions that are risky or precarious (Ryan et al. 2016). Originally this phenomenon was identified in response to claims that women leaders 'wreaked havoc on companies' performance' (Ryan et al. 2016: 447). To investigate this, researchers set out to explore the relationship between a company's success and the appointment of women leaders (Ryan and Haslam 2005). They found

Table 6.1 *Timeline of Theresa May's premiership and significant events, 2016–19*

Date	Event
23 June 2016	Brexit referendum: Britain votes to leave the EU
24 June 2016	David Cameron, Prime Minister, resigns
11 July 2016	Theresa May becomes leader of the Conservative Party
13 July 2016	Theresa May becomes Prime Minister
20 July 2016	Theresa May's first Prime Minister's Question Time (PMQs) with Jeremy Corbyn as leader of the opposition
18 April 2017	Theresa May announces a General Election for 8 June 2017
8 June 2017	Theresa May is re-elected as Prime Minister in the General Election but fails to maintain a majority and is forced to make a minority government with the Democratic Unionist Party (DUP) of Northern Ireland
4 October 2017	Theresa May gives 'disastrous' conference speech at the Conservative Party conference
July 2018	May agrees 'Chequers Plan' (a plan for a deal with the EU over Brexit) with her cabinet
July 2018	Boris Johnson (Foreign Secretary) and David Davis (Minister in charge of Brexit negotiations) resign over May's 'Chequers Plan'
September 2018	EU negotiations over Brexit stall in Salzburg (20 September)
25 November 2018	Theresa May's revised Brexit Deal Accepted by EU Leaders
4–10 December 2018	House of Commons Brexit Debate: May postpones vote on EU deal
12 December 2018	Theresa May Wins No-Confidence Vote called by her own Conservative Party MPs
15 January 2019	MPs vote to reject Theresa May's EU Brexit deal in the HoC by a record-breaking 230 votes, the largest ever government defeat
16 January 2019	Theresa May wins no-confidence vote proposed in the HoC
14 February 2019	MPs vote to reject Theresa May's EU Brexit deal in the HoC (2nd time)
24 May 2019	May announces her resignation outside 10 Downing Street
7 June 2019	May stands down as leader of the Conservative Party; but continues to be Prime Minister until the election of a new Leader and Prime Minister
23 July 2019	Result of Conservative Leadership contest, May stands down and Boris Johnson appointed in her place.

Figure 6.1 Image of Theresa May giving her speech at the Conservative Party conference in September 2017. (Source: Carl Court/Staff/Getty Images.)

that rather than causing businesses to fail, women leaders were more likely to be appointed at particularly precarious points of crisis, and thus coined the term 'glass cliff'. However, they also noted that the set of circumstances leading to this position are often framed as 'women's problems' when in fact the phenomenon is more accurately described in part as being driven 'by the fact that men are given preferential access to cushy leadership positions' (Ryan et al. 2016: 453). As outlined in Chapter 1, these leadership metaphors need to be treated critically to avoid androcentrism and to ensure that the metaphor itself does not encourage the treatment of women leaders as a homogenous group – ignoring individual contexts and characteristics. It is with the precise contexts in mind that this case study will now focus on aspects of Theresa May's parliamentary linguistic performances and how they relate to the obstacles of gender stereotyping in relation to adversarial language, the operation of fraternal networks in formal institutions and gendered media representations.

6.2.2   Theresa May: Adversarial Language in Prime Minister's Question Time

The Prime Minister's Question Time (PMQs) exchanges between Theresa May and Jeremy Corbyn (the leader of the Labour Party and therefore the 'Leader of the Opposition' [LO]) provide an opportunity to examine gender and language use in one of the most adversarial of political events. As discussed in Chapter 3, PMQs are characterised by ritual insults and ruthless hyperbolic descriptions of opponents and their political errors and embarrassments. The mocking, ironic tone of the delivery of PMQs and the accompanying jeering, barracking and braying from the floor of the chamber create a weekly spectacle that gains more media coverage than any other political event. PMQs exchanges between May and Corbyn are particularly interesting for the analysis of gender and political language because Jeremy Corbyn's stated aim in PMQs was to challenge adversarial norms of the event by enacting them in a 'different way' – one that is more consensual. On the other hand, Theresa May's performances, as the only woman in the position of receiving questions at PMQs since Margaret Thatcher, gives an opportunity to examine how a woman leader performs in this extremely adversarial speech event. Therefore, both May and Corbyn are not *typical* performers in this context – May because she is a woman Prime Minister and Corbyn because he is a male Leader of the Opposition who overtly eschews the 'masculinised' interactional norms of the event and attempts to make them more consensual.

Stereotypical notions of gender and communication discussed in Chapter 5 hold that women are less disposed to perform in these sorts of contexts and men are more at ease because the adversarial norms concur with stereotypical ideas about masculinity and communication. In this section I first give an assessment of the overall adversarial performances of May–Corbyn, using the adversarial 'score' (described in Section 3.3) in a sample of their PMQs exchanges. Then I identify the characteristics and strategies of each of the speakers in order to identify how they face the interactional and adversarial challenges of PMQs and suggest ways in which gender may play a part in these performances.

To investigate May and Corbyn's use of adversarial language across a period of PMQs, 24 PMQs sessions were sampled between July 2016 and July 2018. These were sampled evenly across the 59 PMQs occurring in this two-year time-period (see Appendix C for a list of events in the sample), and were scored according to the adversarial features set out in 3.3.3: opposing stances between MPs; positive and negative contrasts; the use of personal pronouns to strengthen these contrasts; hyperbolic, aggravated descriptions; generic ad hominem arguments or personal attacks, and direct ethotic ad hominem arguments from morality and veracity. Over the 24 sessions (each session comprised of sequences of six questions and answers between the Prime Minister and the LO), the average adversarial 'score' across all the sessions of PMQs sampled was '17'. The number of adversarial points ranged from 6 in the least adversarial PMQs to 29 at the most adversarial. The most and least adversarial PMQs had clear circumstances that dictated their tone and style. The most adversarial exchange was on 26 April 2017. This was the last PMQs before the 2017 General Election, so it was essential for each leader to display their strength and undermine their political opponent at this point. Thus the circumstances seem to account for the exceptionally high use of adversarial language (Waddle et al. 2019: 77 also note this tendency of 'playing to the crowd' in PMQs near general elections). The least adversarial display took place on the 28 June 2017 and, as the first PMQs after the General Election (in which Theresa May lost her majority), this would usually be a highly adversarial event. However, this was also the first PMQs after the fire disaster in the Grenfell Tower block of flats.[5] The tone of PMQs can therefore be affected by external occurrences and contexts. Overall, the adversarial 'score' of these PMQs sessions show that May–Corbyn exchanges are much less adversarial than the Hague–Blair exchanges discussed in Chapter 3, which ranged between 36 and 47 adversarial points per six-part PM–LO exchange.[6]

May used slightly more adversarial linguistic features than Corbyn overall, but the scores were similar (May's score was 217 and Corbyn's 197 across the 24 sessions). May used more adversarial features than Corbyn in 13 sessions and he used more than her in 10 sessions (in one session they used the same amount). Over time, the sessions did not become more adversarial, although 7 of the occasions in which Corbyn used more adversarial features than May occurred in the last year of the sample, which suggests he became more adversarial over time (see Appendix C for details). Figure 6.2 shows how much May and Corbyn used each of the seven categories of adversarial language identified in Chapter 3. The first category representing the 'pro/con' contrasts (such as the 'up' and 'down' of crime figures) were used the same amount by both May and Corbyn, showing that a 'pro' stance was routinely countered by a 'con' stance – or vice versa – in the course of a PMQ exchange. Similarly, the generic personal attacks – for example, saying that an opponent is 'incompetent', 'wrong', or 'muddled' – were undertaken equally by May and Corbyn, also perhaps showing a 'tit for tat' pattern in trading these kinds of ethotic slights. The second 'positive/negative' category refers to the reinforcement of contrasts with the positive or negative actions of Labour/Conservative governments and political parties. This feature was used far more by May than Corbyn as she tended to stress the positive actions of the current (Conservative) government with the negative actions or policies of Corbyn's Labour opposition party, but he did not respond using this adversarial feature. May also uses the next category (personal pronouns such as 'we', 'them' and 'us') to further strengthen these contrasts, but Corbyn does not, which also puts less focus on the collective identity of the Labour party in comparison to May's 'we, the government'. However, Corbyn used three adversarial categories more than May: hyperbolic or aggravated descriptions, attacks based on morality and those based on veracity. May used hyperbolic descriptions sparingly and alluded to morality very little and veracity not at all. This pattern of adversarial language

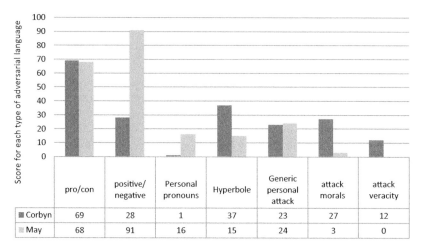

	pro/con	positive/ negative	Personal pronouns	Hyperbole	Generic personal attack	attack morals	attack veracity
■ Corbyn	69	28	1	37	23	27	12
▦ May	68	91	16	15	24	3	0

Figure 6.2 Graph showing how much May and Corbyn used each of seven adversarial features in a sample of PMQs.

perhaps reflects May's reticence to tackle Corbyn's integrity when that is his purported strength as a leader. Corbyn, however, frequently alludes to May's government being underhand about their treatment of the National Health Service, for example, or the cuts in education and social security funding.

One possible explanation for the relatively low level of adversarial features in May–Corbyn PMQs overall is the fact that Jeremy Corbyn made a conscious effort to 'do PMQS differently' and in a more consensual way. Given that there appears to be a reciprocal 'tit for tat' pattern to some of the PMQs adversarial features, this more consensual approach could account for the relative lack of adversarial features in the PMQ exchanges overall, and this has been shown to be the case in earlier PMQs exchanges between Cameron and Corbyn (Bull and Waddle 2019). Jeremy Corbyn's innovative way of conducting PMQs began in his first session on 16 September 2015, where he questioned David Cameron, the incumbent Prime Minister. Corbyn set out his intent to conduct PMQs in his role as Leader of the Opposition (LO) in a different way. As part of his first question to David Cameron he said:

Example 6.1 Jeremy Corbyn's first PMQs question to David Cameron (16/09/2015; Official Report)

> I have taken part in many events around the country and had conversations with many people about what they thought of this place, our Parliament, our democracy and our conduct within this place. Many told me that they thought Prime Minister's question time was too theatrical, that Parliament was out of touch and too theatrical, and that they wanted things done differently, but above all they

wanted their voice to be heard in Parliament. So I thought, in my first Prime Minister's Question Time, I would do it in a slightly different way (…) So I sent out an email to thousands of people and asked them what questions they would like to put to the Prime Minister and I received 40,000 replies.

Two-and-a-half thousand people emailed me about the housing crisis in this country. I ask one from a woman called Marie, who says, 'What does the government intend to do about the chronic lack of affordable housing and the extortionate rents charged by some private sector landlords in this country?' (Hansard: 16/09/2015, Volume 599, Column 1037)

This first question, from 'Marie', started a pattern of questioning in this manner (sometimes referred to as 'crowdsourced questions' [Hazarika and Hamilton 2018]; or 'public questions' [Bull and Waddle 2019]), ostensibly non-adversarial, non-theatrical and letting the 'voice of the electorate' into the parliamentary discourse. In the question cited above, the 'wh-form' or information-seeking question is very different from the conducive and confrontational question-forms (such as 'Isn't it the truth that..?') identified in Chapter 3 as being highly adversarial and characteristic of the much earlier Hague–Blair exchanges.

By the time May became Prime Minister in July 2016, Corbyn had already established this form of questioning, also referred to as 'brought-in-ordinariness' through the quoting of 'ordinary' people in an elite event (Fetzer and Weizman 2018). One of the advantages of Corbyn's 'questions from the electorate' lay in the fact that his opponents were unable to criticise or attack the question directly without appearing to criticise, attack or condescend to a member of the electorate. This restricted the Prime Minister's options for an adversarial response. In this way, a 'consensual' move by Corbyn actually had a strategic effect on his opponent by constraining her responses. Another aspect to Corbyn's questioning turns is that often his questions are rhetorically hard to answer and adversarial, but the fact that they are 'from the electorate' acts as a smoke-screen for these combative effects. Example 6.2 below shows a later PMQs question from Corbyn directed at Theresa May:

Example 6.2   Question from Corbyn to May in PMQs (26 April 2017; Official Report)

Laura, a young primary school teacher, wrote to me this week to say, 'I'm seeing a decrease each year in available cash to provide a quality education to the children in my class and an increase in reliance upon our parent teachers association.' Is the Prime Minister still denying the fact that funding for each pupil is still being cut? (Hansard: 26 April 2017, Volume 624, Column 1102)

This question gives a statement of 'fact' by quoting an observation made by a teacher 'Laura' but then goes on to add a much more conventional PMQs question form, a polar interrogative that, as discussed in Chapter 3, constrains the respondent because is it a conducive form that nevertheless must be opposed. Here the Prime Minister needs to deny that funding is being cut, but rhetorically that response positions her as the leader who is 'still denying' something. This falls into the category of what has been described as an 'unanswerable question' or one that is 'designed deliberately to provoke discomfort and/or evasion' (Bates et al. 2014: 256), and it is an adversarial interactional move.

In the sample of 24 PMQs between Corbyn and May between July 2016 and September 2018, Corbyn used this technique of posing questions from the electorate in almost half of the sessions throughout the time-period.[7] One of the distinctive features of these questions is that Corbyn often does not take full advantage of the sequence of six questioning turns to build on one particular topic but asks six entirely unrelated questions. In this way, he covers a greater number of questions from the electorate but in doing so eschews possibly the greatest tactical advantage that PMQs offers – to mount a spontaneous and sustained series of questions in order to scrutinise the government's actions or plans. However, the 'crowdsourced' questions serve to personalise and de-institutionalise the context of PMQs in that they represent the everyday concerns of 'real' people, even though, as mentioned above, they can serve as 'cover' for combative questions and also constrain the responses of the Prime Minister. Theresa May has a number of strategies for dealing with these questions. The first is to adopt the personal tone of the question in her response:

Example 6.3 Theresa May's responses to Corbyn's 'questions from the electorate' (Official Report)

(a) 'Let me first say to Jenny that I fully understand and appreciate the concerns individuals have..' (Hansard: 7 September 2016, Volume 614, Column 325)
(b) 'May I first of all say to Colin that I think all of us in this House recognise the difficulties people have…' (Hansard: 19 October 2016, Volume 615, Column 797)
(c) 'I have recognised since I came into this role that there are people in this country, like Christine, who are finding life difficult.' (Hansard: 18 October 2017, Volume 629, Column 833)

The examples of Theresa May's responses show that she refers to the questioner by their first name, mirroring Corbyn's use of address form in the question. This allows her to personalise her own response and to suggest that she is interested in the individual concerns of members of the public. A second strategy that May developed a year or so after becoming PM and facing Corbyn's 'questions from the electorate' was simply to request that the question should be sent to her. For example, on 11 October 2017, in response to Corbyn's question 'from Georgina' about the implementation of the controversial 'universal credit' scheme, she says: 'First, may I say to the right hon. Gentleman that I would be happy to look at the case of Georgina if he would like to send me those details?' (Hansard: 11 October 2017, Volume 629,

Column 323). This move enabled May to use this request a month later in response to another of Corbyn's questions from the electorate, where she replied: 'The right hon. Gentleman might like to send the letter through. In an earlier Prime Minister's questions, he raised a specific case of an individual who had written to him about her experience on universal credit – I think it was Georgina. As far as I am aware, he has so far not sent that letter to me, despite the fact that I asked for it (Hansard: 15 November 2017, Volume 631, Column 357)' This response enabled May to reveal Corbyn's questions as disingenuous. If he was so concerned about the welfare of people like 'Georgina', why would he not send her the details so she could act upon them? The answer is, of course, that Corbyn's questions are a tactic aimed to reveal May and the Conservative Party as uncaring, out of touch and unconcerned about people's needs. Reportedly, May's 'team' were 'delighted by Corbyn's team's negligence and the political opportunity it left for her' (Hazarika and Hamilton 2018: 125).

A final way in which May dealt with Corbyn's 'electorate' questions, and also more generally with his 'information seeking' questions was to avoid answering them by reiterating the details of the government's plans, policies and proposals in detail. Two examples of this are shown in Example 6.4 below.

Example 6.4   Theresa May's 'providing information' responses (Official Report)

(a)   In response to a question from Corbyn about a pay rise for NHS staff:

CORBYN: …..Well, this is right now, and the Prime Minister is here right now. How about an answer right now?

MAY: As I have explained to the right hon. Gentleman and the House in the past, the way in which we approach the whole question of public sector pay is through the work of the pay review bodies (…)
   Perhaps I could just explain something else to the right hon. Gentleman, because I fear that for all his years in Parliament there is one thing that he has failed to recognise – Government has no money of its own…. It collects money in taxes from businesses and people to spend on the NHS (Hansard: 18 October 2017, Volume 629, Column 835)

(b)   In response to a question from Corbyn on starter homes for first-time buyers:

MAY: The right hon. Gentleman started his question by making reference to the issue of starter homes and the upper limit in London of £450,000. I have sat on these Benches and heard him raise that with my right hon. Friend the Member for Witney (Mr Cameron) on a number of occasions when he was Prime Minister. Can I just explain this to the Leader of the Opposition? If he looks at house prices across the country, he will see that they vary. In Liverpool, the average house price is just over £116,000. In London, the average house price is just over £676,000. That is why we have a higher limit for starter homes in London. If he objects to that, he needs to tell his constituents why he is against their having opportunities to get on the housing ladder. (Hansard: 16 July 2016, Volume 613, Column 816)

Corbyn's questions elicit condescending responses from May that emphasise 'explanations' of what are commonly known facts. The first response in the Example 6.4a contains one adversarial feature (the generic personal attack that Corbyn has 'failed' to do something). The response is evasive in that it does not answer the question about NHS cuts and disregards the critical aspects of the question (that the question has not been answered before). In the second example shown in Example 6.4b, May uses the phrase 'Can I just explain...' again and patronises Corbyn by stating the obvious – that house process vary across the country. May uses this as a tactic frequently to reduce Corbyn's questions to simple requests for information and she gives unnecessary, patronising explanations. May's technique of responding to Corbyn in this long-winded, evasive and faux-explanatory style is character-istic of her responses overall. This has also been identified as an evasion that May uses in televised political interviews and has been described as: 'gives non-specific response to a specific question' (Bull 2016). In a more recent study of May's evasion in PMQs with Corbyn, she was found to have a highly distinctive evasive style, producing replies to Corbyn's questions only 11 per cent of the time which makes her more evasive than previous PMs, includ-ing David Cameron (Bull and Strawson 2019). Interestingly, the same study also found that she equivocated as much to Corbyn's 'crowdsourced' questions as she did to his more conventionally constructed questions (Bull and Strawson 2019).

These evasive responses in PMQs, coupled with Corbyn's 'electorate letter' questions have led commentators and journalists to describe the May–Corbyn PMQs as 'boring'. For example, *The Sun* newspaper describes the May–Corbyn exchanges as 'PM-snooze' where 'Theresa May and Jeremy Corbyn bore everyone to tears after another repetitive PMQs' (Cole 2017). However, Theresa May's performances in PMQs are also peppered with more adversarial responses. Often her final response in a PMQs con-tained what appear to be rehearsed 'put downs' of Jeremy Corbyn. Her first PMQs was one such occasion, in which an otherwise sedentary set of exchanges became enlivened in her last response, as shown in the tran-script in Example 6.5.

Example 6.5 Theresa May's final response in her first PMQs with Jeremy Corbyn (20 July 2016, Transcript)

1	TM:	I I'm interested that he refers to er the situation of some <u>work</u>ers who might have
2		er some job insecurity (.) er a and potentially unscrupulous bosses I sus<u>pect</u> that
3		there are many Members on the opposition benches (.) who might be fa<u>mil</u>iar with
4	an	unscrupulous [boss]
5	MPs:	[laughter]
6	TM:	[er] a boss who does not listen to his workers (.)
7	MPs:	(cheering)

8	TM:	er a boss (.) who requires some of his workers to double their workload (1)
9	MPs:	(cheering)
10		a boss (.) and maybe a boss who exploits the rules to further his own career (1)
11	MPs:	(cheering)
12	TM:	remind him of anybody
13	MPs:	more more (shouting)

Here, May uses the classical rhetorical device of the *tricolon* (Cockcroft et al. 2014: 229), to turn Corbyn's question about employment into an attack on his leadership. The three-part structured syntactic parallelism of Corbyn's flaws as 'a boss who …' starts on line 6 (he does not listen) and continues on line 8 (he asks his workers to double their workload) and finally, on line 10 'exploits the rules to further his on career'. Each of the three clauses ends with cheering from the Conservative MPs, which builds in volume until the last line is delivered on line 12. Here May leans forward across the dispatch box towards Corbyn and delivers the lines 'remind him of anybody' with exaggerated emphasis on 'remind'. Clearly, this is supposed to 'remind' Corbyn of his own position as a leader, or 'boss', but, as mentioned at the beginning of the chapter, this was also taken by the UK media as an allusion to May's own performance being reminiscent of Margaret Thatcher. This seems to be a self-conscious and highly planned attack which appears to play to this comparison. In this example we also see one of the paradoxes of May's leadership style: it is often these highly planned, unspontaneous, rhetorically meticulous contributions that gain May positive applause from her own party and positive press coverage. However, it is also in these moments that we witness May at her most awkward, and her enactment of authority seems utterly strained and unconvincing. Example 6.6 below gives another example of this clearly rehearsed approach.

Example 6.6 Prime Minister's Question Time (1 February 2017, Transcript)

1	JC:	President Trump (.) has torn up international agreements on refugees (.) he's threatened
2		to dump international agreements on climate change (.) he has praised the use of
3		torture (.) he has incited hatred against Muslims (.) He has directly attacked women's
4		rights (.) just what more does the President Trump have to do (.) before the Prime
5		Minister will listen (.) to the one point eight million people (.) who have already called (.)
6		for his state visit in (.) invitation to be with[drawn]
7	MPs:	[shouting (3)]
8	SP:	[the Prime Minister]
9	PM:	the right honourable Gentleman's foreign policy (.) is to object to and insult the
10		democratically elected Head of State (.) of our most important ally (.) let's just see what
11		he would have achieved in the last week (.) would he have been able to protect British
12		citizens from the impact of the Executive order (.) [no]
13	MPs:	[no]
14	PM:	would he have been able to lay the foundations of a trade deal (.) [no]
15	MPs:	[no]
16	PM:	would he have got a one hundred percent commitment to NATO [no]
17	MPs:	[no]

18	PM:	<u>that</u> is what Labour has to offer this country (.) <u>less</u> protection for British citizens (.)
19		<u>less</u> prosperous <u>less</u> safe (.) he (1)
20	MPs:	SHOUTIN[G
21	SP:	[OR<u>DER</u>]
22	PM:	<u>he</u> can lead a <u>prot</u>est (.) <u>I'm</u> leading a <u>count</u>ry

In this example, May launches an explicit attack on Corbyn with a set of three rhetorical questions about Corbyn's leadership. Each hypothetical question takes the same form, starting 'Would he have been able to...?', before giving a list of her own achievements (lines 12, 14 and 16), each time prompting her Conservative MPs to roar back the answer 'No' (lines 12/13; 14/15; and 16/17). Finally, as with Example 6.5, May finishes the exchange with a flourish: 'he can lead a protest, I'm leading a country'. May seems to achieve an ad hominem argument against Corbyn that points out ethotic flaws. As mentioned in Chapter 3, when deployed as the rhetorical technique of *paradiastole* (or the presentation of personal virtue as vice), this seems to be a particularly effective in PMQs. May comes close here to representing Corbyn's eulogistic trait of 'consensual politician' as the more dystologistic trait of 'ineffective and weak leader'. Corbyn does not develop a consistent ethotic argument against May in this period.

According to some political commentators, final lines like these were part of a planned strategy in preparing May for PMQs. Her team of advisors reportedly 'Worked on a series of generic "ends of answers" – attacks, lines, jokes, general contrasts of the Labour and Conservative positions – which could be deployed at any time' (Hazarika and Hamilton 2018: 159). However, the results in terms of how effective May is in PMQs appear to be mixed. It is clear that this strategy plays to the media representation of PMQs where often only one video clip is reported on the national news channels and websites. In this case, final, rehearsed lines of contrasts such as those represented in Examples 6.5 and 6.6 are more likely to grab the attention and be 'newsworthy'. It is unlikely that many people watch the entire speech event of PMQs (and even more unlikely that they read it in the Hansard the following day), so these 'sound bites' and flourishes represent the most popular coverage of PMQs. On the other hand, May's awkwardness and wooden delivery of these lines give the impression of a leader who is not at ease, and for whom spontaneity is extremely difficult. This is nowhere more evident than in her clearly rehearsed attempts at humour. For example, at one PMQs, she attempts to ridicule Corbyn by saying: 'The train's left the station, the seats are all empty, the leader is on the floor, even on rolling stock they are a laughing stock'[8] (Hansard: 7 September 2016, Volume 614, Column 325). This led to criticism from commentators and journalists from across the political spectrum with one commenting: 'her pre-scripted anti-Corbyn jibes came over as unprovoked, gratuitous and consequently rather cheap' (Sparrow 2016). Of course, and more seriously for May, these scripted and rehearsed lines contributed to her characterisation as the 'Maybot' (Crace 2016).

Analysis of the May–Corbyn PMQs is therefore complex. There is no straightforward winner in this particular interactive game, indeed, at times it appears that there are two losers. Both May and Corbyn have weaknesses that are painfully evident and perhaps augmented in the public 'theatre' of PMQs. Corbyn does not appear to be strategic in his approach to May in that he often fails to build six questioning turns that really challenge the Prime Minister. He sometimes appears hesitant, taking in-breath pauses in the middle of clauses, and he does not produce humorous or pre-planned final lines. He attempted pre-planned humour on one notable occasion when he referred to May as 'not so much the Iron Lady as the irony Lady',[9] which was subsequently described in the press as 'the worst PMQs joke of all time' (*The Mirror*, 18 January 2017). His use of personalised 'crowdsourced' questions make the proceedings long-winded and dull. They are also predictable – and as mentioned above – and May devised strategies to deal with them.

In relation to language and gender, the analysis of May–Corbyn PMQs shows that both participants produce adversarial questions and responses. May and Corbyn do therefore challenge stereotypic notions of masculine and feminine speech 'styles' as neither of them conform to the 'man as adversarial' and 'women as consensual' stereotype associated with the 'different voice' ideology discussed in Chapter 5. May's highly planned and rigidly delivered lines conform to the adversarial norms of PMQs, but yet her discomfort in performing in these public forums (also made evident by her refusal to take part in the General Election TV debates in 2017) shows that this is not a role she relishes. As only the second woman Prime Minister receiving questions in PMQs, and as a single case study, it is not possible to make generalisations about her linguistic style according to gender. Apart from noting that she confounds gendered stereotypes by using adversarial language, we can also observe that possibly no Prime Minister (man or woman) before her has delivered such planned and obviously rehearsed lines in responding to questions. Her style in PMQs could be described as 'hyper-controlled' and therefore it is possibly related to the coercive forces in the House of Commons CoP identified in Chapter 3, whereby women need to pay 'meticulous attention to symbolic capital' in order to 'prove their worthiness' (Eckert 1988: 67). Given that the analysis in Chapter 3 suggested that traditional parliaments such as the HoC are 'gendered spaces' in which the setting and the communicative tasks together become an index of a gendered style (Freed 1996: 67) it could be that May's 'hyper-controlled' style can be linked to the notion of a 'linguistic habitus' in which 'silence or hyper-controlled language' is imposed on some people (Bourdieu 1991: 82). While these kinds of impositions and constraints seem less applicable to a woman leader like May, who has excelled within this institution to the extent that she has reached the top job of prime minister, it is likely that given the nature of the CoP and the previous findings about gendered linguistic norms, that gender is in relevant to May's performances. This will be further explored in the next section where May's relation to the institutional parliamentary networks and norms, particularly the fraternal networks, will be explored.

6.2.3   Theresa May: Language, Sexism and Fraternal Networks

It has been claimed that hyper-controlled language, such as that used May in PMQs, can be related to women's heightened visibility in male-dominated forums and the fact that 'institutions are organised to define, demonstrate and enforce the legitimacy and authority of linguistic strategies used by one gender – or men of one class or ethnic group – whilst denying the power of others' (Gal 1991: 188). As discussed in the previous chapter, strong fraternal networks and the old boys' club can contribute to the reinforcement of this dominance whilst denying others 'the liberties of a language that is securely established' (Bourdieu 1991: 82). Theresa May presents an interesting case with which to examine the operation of fraternal networks because she is a woman and she occupies the most senior position of all MPs within this male-dominated institution. Her presence at the top of the parliamentary hierarchy allows both for an investigation of how a male-dominated institution adopts and assimilates women in leadership positions, and how she performs linguistically in order integrate with or resist these networks.

One way to try and identify critical gendered moments relating to fraternal networks in parliamentary discourse is to analyse 'gendered discourses' within the interaction that seem to either reinforce or resist hegemonic masculinity. As part of a critical approach, gendered discourses represent 'ways of seeing the world' (Sunderland 2004) and offer the identification of different 'subject positions' of individuals according to the specific context of the discourse. As noted in Chapter 2, gendered discourses are ideological and can be viewed as 'systematic relationships between knowledge and power that affect the way people speak, interact, view and represent the world' (Baxter 2018: 9). Individuals can be positioned differentially in relation to power and subject positions can be revealed as powerless, resisting, coerced or reproducing existing power structures within discourse. Identifying gendered discourses is subjective but should be grounded in linguistic evidence rather than being simply and unproblematically viewed as being 'out there' waiting to be discovered by the discourse analyst (Sunderland 2004: 45). This section investigates May's linguistic performances to explore how she is positioned by and positions herself within gendered discourses relating to fraternal networks. These 'critical gendered moments' are examples in the two-year time-period when May specifically orients to gender categories and/or gender relations in her parliamentary performances. These were selected systematically from the PMQs data presented in the previous section but also more impressionistically from examples that appeared to be culturally significant and gained media publicity and attention in this period.

As mentioned in earlier discussions, May holds that she is a feminist and supports the cause of promoting women in parliament (see Childs and Webb 2011 for a more detailed account). In PMQs on 7 February 2018 she orients explicitly to the cause of the suffragettes on the anniversary of some women obtaining the right to vote.[10] Wearing a replica ribbon of the suffrage movement, she responds to Corbyn's question (which also alludes to the anniversary) as shown in Example 6.7:

Example 6.7   Prime Minister's Question Time (7 February 2018, Official Report)

1	JC:	It is of course the anniversary of women first getting the right to vote in 1918, and I
2		pay tribute to all those who campaigned all over the country to achieve that right. We
3		should understand that our rights come from the activities of ordinary people doing
4		extraordinary things to bring about democracy and justice within our society, and
5		those women who suffered grievously, being force fed in Holloway prison in my
6		constituency, and those who suffered so much need to be remembered for all time.
7		Working-class women as well as many other women fought for that right, and it is
8		one we should all be proud of (turn continues to include a question on policing)
9	TM:	May I first say to the right hon. Gentleman that we should be saluting all those who
10		were involved in that struggle to ensure that women could get the right to vote? I was
11		very pleased yesterday to have the opportunity to meet Helen Pankhurst, the great-
12		granddaughter of Emmeline Pankhurst, and to see that that memory is being kept
13		going. As I said yesterday in my speech, I heard about the suffragettes' fight from my
14		late godmother, whose mother was a suffragette and both of whose parents knew the
15		Pankhursts. (Hansard: 7 February 2018, Volume 635, Column 1484)

Here May exactly repeats Corbyn's tribute 'to all those who campaigned all over the country' (line 2) by saying that 'we should be saluting all those who were involved in that struggle' (lines 9–10). This is perhaps an attempt to redress the focus away from the 'working-class women' mentioned by Corbyn on line 8 towards *all* women, or else it is simply an unintentionally clumsy repetition. May attempts to personalise her relation to the suffrage cause, using a first-person singular pronoun 'I' to allude to the speech she gave on the anniversary. She further personalises this by alluding to her 'late godmother, whose mother was a suffragette and both of whose parents know the Pankhursts' (lines 14–15). May seems keen to emphasise her pro-feminist stance and credentials both in comparison to Corbyn and also beyond her duty of marking the anniversary simply as a function of her role as prime minister, possibly also because the 'co-option of feminism by prominent Conservatives is politically painless, does not require extra spending or taxation, and may win votes – it is thus a relatively straightforward choice for career-minded Parliamentarians' (Swift 2019: 320). Similarly, a month later, also at PMQs and shown in Example 6.8, May responds to Corbyn's recognition of International Women's Day:

Example 6.8 Prime Minister's Question Time (7 March 2018, Official Report)

```
1   JC:   Tomorrow is International Women's Day – a chance both to celebrate how far we
2         have come on equality for women but also to reflect on how far we have to go, not
3         just in this country but around the world (turn continues to ask a question about
4         Saudi      Arabia)
5   TM:   I thank the right hon. Gentleman for telling me that it is International Women's Day
6         tomorrow. I think that is what is called mansplaining. (Hansard: 7 March 2018, Volume 637, Column
            298).
```

In this example, May constructs a gendered discourse that is at once pro-women and anti-Corbyn, the use of the popular term 'mansplaining' meaning 'unnecessary explanation of a topic by a man to a women' (ironically, the 'unnecessary explanation' part of this description seems to fit May's own PMQs responses to Corbyn). May is therefore using a pro-women discourse against Corbyn in an adversarial way to make him appear overbearing, inauthentic and sexist.

These examples show May constructing pro-women discourses that would appear to run against the prevailing male-dominated norms of the institution unlikely to promote women. To a certain degree, May is also required to recognise such anniversaries and events as a function of her official role. However, both these exchanges in fact align to and conform with the wider discursive norms of the institution which prize one-upmanship and competitive displays. These pro-women discourses accrue power for May and that is largely because they are partisan: they are not directed at men within her own party but form part of a wider discourse of bolstering her own position and competitive jousting with the opposition in PMQs.

In addition to these overtly pro-women gendered discourses, there are also examples of May opposing women in non-supportive ways. Example 6.9a below shows Theresa May addressing Emily Thornberry as 'Lady Nugee', and Example 6.9b shows Emily Thornberry subsequently raising a 'point of order', and then the Speaker and Theresa May responding.

Example 6.9 (a) Theresa May calls Emily Thornberry 'Lady Nugee', (b) Thornberry's 'point of order' and the subsequent responses (Informal European Council debate, 6 February 2017, Transcript)

(a) Theresa May calls Emily Thornberry 'Lady Nugee'[11]

```
1   TM:    the (.) er concern has been expressed er at this Council meeting and er not only at
2   this   council meeting but at others about (.) the er the role that er Russia is playing in a
3          number of ways (.) in terms of the er the interference they are taking (.) and the
4          Shadow Foreign Secretary is shouting at me 'by you' (.)
5          er yes Lady Nugee (.) by me   [(5)          ]
6   MPS:                                 [Laughter (5)]
7   TM:    [the er the er but it is a matter of continuing concern] and will remain a subject
8   MPS:   [laughter                                               ]
9   TM:    on which we discuss
```

(b) Emily Thornberry's subsequent 'point of order' at the end of the debate and the response from the Speaker and Theresa May

1	ET:	Mr Speaker (.) <u>is</u> it in order for the Prime Minister to refer to a Member of this <u>House</u>
2		(.) not by her <u>own</u> name but by the name of her <u>hus</u>band (.) and <u>sec</u>ondly for the
3		<u>rec</u>ord (.) Mr Speaker I have <u>nev</u>er been a <u>lady</u> and it will take a great <u>deal</u> th than
4		me being married to a knight of the <u>real</u>m in order to <u>make</u> me [one
5	MPs:	[laughter]
6	1MP:	[apologise]
7	TM:	er Mr Speaker (.) I did not in any att er way intend
8		to be dis<u>ord</u>erly in this House (.)
9	1MP:	yes you <u>did</u>
10	TM:	and I have to (.) and I have to <u>say</u>
11		if <u>if</u> the Honourable Lady is concerned about the reference that I made to her of
12		course I will apologise for that (.) I have to say to her though (.) that for the last
13		<u>thirty-six</u> years I have been referred to by my <u>hus</u>band's <u>name</u> (5)
14	MPs:	Laughter (5)
15	SP:	<u>ORDER</u> er <u>O</u>rder (.) no <u>sed</u>entary <u>shriek</u>ing from the Honourable Gentleman for
16		Rhondda is re<u>quired</u> I have the <u>mat</u>ter (2) in <u>hand</u> (.) <u>two</u> points very simply <u>first</u> of
17		all thank you to the Prime Minister for what she has just said <u>sec</u>ondly in so far as
18		there is any uncertainty on this <u>mat</u>ter let me dispel that un<u>cer</u>tainty and I do so
19		from my <u>own</u> knowledge and on the professional advice of the <u>Clerk</u> (.) we refer in
20		<u>this</u> Chamber to Members by their con<u>stit</u>uencies or if they have a title (.) for
21		example shadow Minister (.) by their <u>title</u> (.) to refer to them by <u>another</u> name is <u>not</u>
22		the right thing to do but the Prime Minister has <u>said</u> what she has <u>said</u> and I <u>thank</u>
23		her for <u>that</u> and we will leave <u>this</u> matter <u>there</u>

This example occurs over a year *before* Example 5.5, where Boris Johnson addresses Emily Thornberry as 'Lady Nugee' and is censured by the Speaker (John Bercow). As discussed in that section, this is not the correct official parliamentary title for Thornberry as this title is one gained through her marriage to Lord Nugee. In Example 6.9a it is evident that Thornberry is challenging May from a seated position as May claims that Thornberry is 'shouting' at her (line 4) (although Thornberry's interjection is not visible or audible in the video recording and so does not appear in the transcribed example). The significance of this example is that May explicitly orients to the 'wrong' address form 'Lady Nugee' (line 5) having already correctly addressed Thornberry as 'the Shadow Foreign Secretary' (line 4). This is a punishing and adversarial 'put down' of Thornberry, who has clearly annoyed or even angered May with her illegal intervention(s): May's hesitant speech in lines 1–4 could have been caused by Thornberry's heckling. The way in which the use of 'Lady Nugee' functions as a denigration of Thornberry has already been discussed in detail in Section 5.3.2, and it rests on her being viewed ironically as a privileged 'lady', which positions her as hypocritically at odds with the socialist ideals of her party.

On one level, it is an exertion of power over an individual to knowingly name them by a title that they have explicitly rejected for themselves, or that does not fit the institutional discursive norms for address terms that are produced routinely and unproblematically. It is not as if Thornberry is diverging from the discursive norms of the parliamentary CoP to insist on her official title – in fact it is May who is uncharacteristically breaking the interactive rules and norms of the institution. Thornberry underlines May's rule-breaking by raising a 'Point of Order'[12] to draw the Speaker's attention to this infringement. As shown in Example 6.9b, Thornberry complains formally to the Speaker about May's use of the address term, no doubt capitalising on May's infringement of the rules by making it more prominent: to the detriment and possibly embarrassment of May. As Example 6.9b shows, Thornberry complains about being addressed by a name associated with her husband and then plays on the polysemous word 'lady'. She says 'I have never been a lady...' (line 12) where lady here means 'genteel and polite woman' rather than meaning simply 'the wife of a Lord'. This is also part of a feminist gendered discourse, not just about refusing to be addressed by a husband's title, but also about not being called a 'lady' because it has negative connotations of marital servitude and submission to men (or at least this is the case for *some* feminists, see Friedman [2013] and Reid Boyd [2012] for further interpretations and uses of the word).

May's response to the Point of Order first denies intending to be 'disorderly', a claim which is responded to by a single female voice (possibly Thornberry) saying 'yes you did' (line 18). May then offers an apology, but like Johnson's apology to the Speaker for the same infringement (Example 5.7) this is a mitigated apology made in a conditional form 'if the Honourable Lady is concerned, of course I will apologise for that' (line 21) which subtly shifts the ownership of the offence away from May (for breaking the rules) and onto Thornberry (for being 'concerned'). To mitigate the apology further, May then adds: 'I have to say to her though' (line 12) where 'though' signifies a contrasting or oppositional stance to the previous one that contained the 'apology'. May then constructs another gendered discourse about naming when she addresses Thornberry directly and says: 'for the last thirty-six years I have been referred to by my husband's name' (line 13). This declarative statement is made without evaluation or explanation, yet this is clearly a correction or opposition to Thornberry's choice about naming. The gendered discourse of May's statement constructs her as a woman 'who is proud to take the name of her husband, despite knowledge of the feminist stance against doing so'. It is also possible that May is implying that Thornberry's stance is 'politically correct', where this term refers to anti-sexist moves that are denigrated or rendered absurd (Mills 2003). May appears to be retaliating after Thornberry has caught her out with a Point of Order and this utterance at once opposes Thornberry's naming choice and reiterates May's conservative or traditionalist stance on gender-relations. Sexism, anti-sexism and political correctness are contested terms, and as set out by Mills (2003: 136), should be viewed as a set of discursive practices that are respectively: 'interpreted by some as discriminatory' (for example, the 'sexist' naming of Thornberry as 'Lady Nugee'); 'a set of metadiscursive practices aimed at combating discrimination' (for example, the 'anti-sexist' Point of Order raised by Thornberry and the Speaker's support for that position); and 'a negative characterisation of that position of critique' (the framing of Thornberry's position on naming as 'politically correct' or 'wrong' by May). May's final assertion about her marital naming choice can also be thought of as an overtly 'pro-men' stance that reinforces masculine hegemony (as defined in Chapter 5) because the convention of a woman taking a husband's name on marriage is seen by some as a naming practice that institutionalises men's dominance over women (Mills 2003). May's response certainly finds male approval with her own party as, according to both the visual and audio recording, it is men who are responsible for the lengthy and sustained laughter after her reply (line 22).

As noted in the previous chapter, fraternal networks function in complex ways to create and reproduce male dominance in institutions through a variety of practices, including sexism and sexist humour. In the examples of sexist humour described in Section 5.3.1, humour and the seemingly more innocuous or trivial forms of sexism are often made 'in plain sight' on the debate floor. It was also observed that sexist comments and humour in the 2000 data corpus were made exclusively by men. Theresa May would therefore seem unlikely to collaborate with comments and exchanges of this type, perhaps particularly because of her lack of success in engaging in humorous exchanges in PMQs as described earlier. However, on one occasion, May, perhaps inadvertently, contributes to one such exchange, shown in Example 6.10. In this example from PMQs, a Conservative MP, Peter Bone, known for his light-hearted and humorous remarks about his wife, Mrs Bone, asks Theresa May a question.

Example 6.10 Transcript of exchange between Theresa May and Peter Bone PMQs 19 October 2016

1	PB:	Mr Speaker (.) as you might know it is my <u>birth</u>day today [(1)]
2	MPs:	[Shouting (1)]
3	PB:	[And er] the Prime Minister
4		has already given me a huge birthday present er by letting everyone know (.) that we
5		will be out of the European Union no <u>later</u> than the thirty-first of March 2019 (.) so
6		could I <u>press</u> her for another present (.) um her excellent policy her excellent policy
7		of closing Victorian prisons (.) and opening them and opening the modern ones the
8		er is a spot-on policy (1)
9	MP:	here here
10	PB:	would she support the reopening of Wellingborough prison er as part of this
11		excellent programme (.) or would she rather just sing happy birthday [(1)]
12	MPs:	[cheering/laughter (1)]
13	SP	Prime Minis[ter]

14	TM:	[can] say to the I am very happy to wish my him a very happy birthday
15		today many happy returns I hope that Mrs Bone is going to treat the occasion in an
16		appropriate manner [and er er (8)
17	MPs:	[Laughter (8)]
18	TM:	Can I can I er [can
19	SP:	[O O O ORDER (.) I want to hear what is [coming next]
20	MPs:	[laughter]
21		calm down Mr Speaker (laughs) on the serious issue about prisons (.) I welcome the
22		fact that my hon. Friend applauds the policy we are following of closing out-of-date
23		prisons and building new ones (turn continues)

Bone starts by telling the House that it is his birthday, and jokingly asks May for a 'present' – to reopen a prison in his constituency – or else 'sing happy birthday' (line 11). The other MPs respond to Bone with laughter from the outset as this speaker has a certain reputation for jocular displays. The question itself is disrespectful, positioning May awkwardly and changing the 'key' of the question from serious to humorous. At the same time Bone rather impertinently gives May an 'option' between granting him his wishes or singing – neither of which are desirable options for her – and so she is disempowered by the question. May needs to manage her answer carefully as Bone clearly has the floor of the chamber behind him, partly because his 'jester' persona has been constructed and contextualised in a series of 'chained events' (see further discussion in Chapter 8). A humorous response is risky for May: as mentioned in the PMQs analysis above, making jokes is not one of her strengths. However, like all disempowering moves that limit the interactional choices of the recipient, she must not look as if she 'can't take a joke' and appear humourless and must collaborate with the collective, shared humour.

May attempts to respond to Bone's humour by alluding to 'Mrs Bone' and saying 'I hope Mrs Bone is going to treat the occasion in an appropriate manner' (lines 15–16). This is taken by the collective audience of MPs as a sexual reference, suggesting Mrs Bone will grant Mr Bone sexual favours on his birthday. This interpretation is only possible because Bone has referred to his wife in this manner and with this type of insinuation on numerous previous occasions (see discussion in Chapter 8). It is not clear whether May intends to make a sexual reference, but it could be that she rather awkwardly tried to enter Bone's jocular frame, then remembered he makes jokes about his wife, and attempted to share in this humour without realising the sexual inference it would draw. It would certainly be odd for a woman prime minister to intentionally make a sexual joke about another MPs wife, and this is precisely why women are usually side-lined from such heterosexual, sexist 'banter' in institutional discourse. It seems more likely from May's facial reaction to the sustained and rather exaggerated laughter from the other MPs that she did not intend to make a sexual joke and has made a blunder. The laughter comes mainly from men Conservative MPs and the sustained waves of laughter appear to be directed as much to May's discomfort as to the 'joke' itself. When May tries to regain the floor but fails to do so amidst the laughter (line 18), the Speaker steps in but also collaborates with the joke. He says 'I want to hear what's coming next' (line 19), meaning that he wants to hear more about the sexual favours. This is also greeted by laughter from the other MPs, before May responds that he should 'calm down Mr Speaker' (referring to the fact that he is sexually 'interested' in Mrs Bone's actions).

This extract conveys many of the complex and interwoven heteronormative, sexist and masculinist assumptions that construct and reinforce fraternal networks in the male-dominated parliament. Women are positioned peripherally in this CoP and May, regardless of her powerful position as Prime Minister, is in a double bind from the outset. Each option – to joke or not to joke – frames her in ways that are unfavourable to her performance. The whole chamber, including the Speaker, routinely sanction sexualised jokes about 'Mrs Bone'. This is a woman who is not present and who is subordinated by being referred to only as the 'butt' of a joke and only in relation to her husband. In extending and collaborating with the joke, May positions herself precariously as the perpetrator of sexist humour against a woman but also partially and by virtue of her sex, as recipient. As Sara Mills explains:

We might want to question whether the process of laughing at a sexist joke directed at oneself is always empowering, however. We may feel that we have to laugh at sexist jokes in order not to lose face in order to appear 'one of the boys'. Admitting that we recognise a joke as sexist can put us in an interactional fix, classifying ourselves as a victim of sexism, which might clash with our professional status. (Mills 2008: 14)

Contesting this humour in the context of PMQs would not be an option for May because 'humour is so universally regarded positively; those who complain are dismissed as killjoys' (Holmes 2006: 214). This is a joke so ostensibly trivial, off-the-cuff, and light-hearted that it would be even more difficult to contest it without negative consequences. Nevertheless, as mentioned in Chapter 5, the tolerance of these seemingly trivial humorous exchanges and the collective acceptance of them can be viewed as an index of much more serious and pervasive sexist behaviour. It is possible that, in playing along with this inadvertent sexist joke, May is resisting the silencing that can occur in public spaces as a result of women's objectification and sexualisation (Crawford 1995; Mills 2008). While these interpretations are necessarily subjective, we can draw from these critical gendered moments that

May negotiates the sexist culture of the HoC, and the fraternal networks that provide the foundation for that culture, in different ways. The 'Lady Nugee' example shows that her conservative brand of feminism allows her to adopt and hold up as an emblem her adherence to traditional normative female roles that support the workings of hegemonic masculinity. Her awkward joking and attempts to join (or at least actively manage) the collective, sexist humour of the debating chamber seem to backfire and position her as the brunt rather than the perpetrator of such humour.

6.2.4   Theresa May: Gendered Media Representations

As suggested in Chapter 5, one of the main ways in which women politicians are disadvantaged by their media representation is that they are simply not included as much as men, and media representation is crucial for politicians – especially for more senior politicians – in uncertain periods such as those surrounding general elections. In the UK, it has been noted that election campaigns are increasingly becoming more 'presidential' in style. This means that elections are increasingly being fought like a 'horse race' between the leaders of the main political parties rather than as a manifesto on policy details or more local concerns. This can be thought of as a 'game frame', which is a device used by journalists to represent a complex political event in simplified terms to make the event more interesting and comprehensible (Trimble 2017). In the 2017 UK General Election, the horse race was between Theresa May and Jeremy Corbyn and this meant that women's media representation was boosted by the fact that one of the frontrunners was a woman. May was the most prominent politician in the news coverage, with one study showing that she appeared in three out of every ten news items in the month before the election (Deacon et al. 2017). However, as discussed in Chapter 5, although May appeared in 37 per cent of all news items about the election, women overall still only accounted for 36 per cent of all the individuals covered (Harmer 2017).

As mentioned in Chapter 5, women politicians are often objectified and trivialised by their gendered mediation and May is no exception to this. Media references to May's shoes date back to 2002 when she was the newly appointed 'chairwoman' of the Conservative Party and made a speech at the Conservative Party conference wearing a pair of leopard-skin kitten-heeled shoes. She has worn similar leopard-print shoes on a number of significant occasions since then, and they have often drawn media attention. In a newspaper interview mentioned in Section 6.2.1, she discussed how references to her shoes can detract from her message. However, she also suggests that this can be a useful 'ice-breaker' in meetings. While in the same interview, she says that she feels unable to wear 'boring' shoes for fear of attracting negative media comment (Walsh 2015). These somewhat contradictory assessments indicate a complex set of interrelated pressures and demands, alongside a certain desire on May's part to express her individual style. Similarly, her 'chunky power necklaces and matching bracelets' along with her 'awe-inspiring red-nailed manicures' (Mower 2016) have been singled out by some in the media as her 'signatures', although it is noticeable that the fashion accoutrements are always peripheral. In a *Daily Mail* article this is described in the following way: 'Jewellery is a permissible way for a leader to express her personality within the rigid template of tailored coats, matching dresses and suits that women at the top of business and politics have deemed appropriate these days' (Mower 2016). Emblematic accessories were also the preserve of Margaret Thatcher who was famous for her handbags, even giving rise to the term 'handbagging' (meaning 'to beat opponents'). For both leaders, these overt and self-conscious displays perhaps allow them to perform femininity within a 'rigid template' of leadership that is routinely and normatively associated with men and masculinity.

In a focussed study of three newspaper texts referring to the same event, Judith Baxter (2018) uses Kanter's archetypes (mother, seductress, pet and iron maiden described in Chapter 5) to analyse the gendered mediation of May. The three newspaper articles all refer to May's first cabinet reshuffle immediately after she took office as Prime Minister in July 2016. Baxter finds that May is constructed in accordance with the stereotype of 'iron maiden' and 'battle-axe', and to a lesser extent as a 'queen bee'. She also finds traces of the seductress archetype within one of the articles using the leopard (from the leopard-print shoes) as 'feline: charming, sexy, yet cruel' (Baxter 2018: 47). Baxter finds that May 'is not necessarily depicted as *unsuitable* for leadership; rather, she is constructed as a *monstrous* version of what a leader is expected to be' (Baxter 2018: 48). In this analysis, the use of violent imagery of war shows the decisive actions of the leader that might have been acceptable in a leader who was a man, are 'unnatural and frightening; when conducted by a woman Prime Minister' (Baxter 2018: 48).

There are also more routine sexist depictions of May using the title 'Mrs May' whereas references to David Cameron (the previous prime minister) are made without a title. This emphasises May's subordinate relation to her husband and further suggest that she is 'primarily a wife and that her actions in the role of PM may be at odds with her normative gender identity' (Baxter 2018: 39). A more explicit example of this occurred in May 2019 in the period just before May's resignation when the cover of the *Metro* newspaper showed a picture of May and her husband, Phillip, with the headline

'Just tell her Phil' and the sub headline 'Top Tories urge husband to persuade May to quit'. Her frequent description in relation not just to her husband, but also to her father, are also sexist. She is frequently described in media accounts as the 'vicar's daughter', for example, as 'the shy, grammar-school-educated vicar's daughter' (Glaze 2018) whose 'naughtiest' childhood act was to 'run through fields of wheat' (May 2017b). These representations subordinate May by both infantilising her and anchoring her to paternalistic structures of authority and tradition. They also position May as from another time, removed from 'everyday' reality, often stoically 'getting the job done' out of sense of duty, rather than representing her as an agentive contemporary leader. The representations of May as 'daughter' also have echoes of Margaret Thatcher's representation as the 'grocer's daughter.' Although the vicar and the grocer have quite different connotations with respect to social class, it seems that neither woman, despite holding her prominent post, can be allowed to exist fully apart from their attachment to authoritarian, patriarchal figures.

Baxter's (2018) analysis does not find traces of the 'mother' archetype but finds that May is characterised in direct opposition to it, with references to 'caring' juxtaposed with the 'steel Lady striking' (Baxter 2018: 47–8). However, it could be that the particular context of the re-shuffle in Baxter's study played into the 'iron-maiden' and 'battle-axe' tropes, as elsewhere the characterisation of May as 'Mummy' has been identified, albeit often with a particular spin as a 'wise mother' or 'Mother Theresa' (Thompson and Yates 2017). Thompson and Yates suggest that: 'Here, the fantasy dimensions of the response to May tap less into a Freudian model of Oedipal desire but instead hint at pre-oedipal anxieties about the maternal body – fears that continue to be expressed culturally when it comes to women holding positions of political power who are seen as usual [sic] and even a bit strange' (Thompson and Yeats 2017: 131). They note that women leaders are often framed by preoccupations with their bodies, and that May is no exception. Mavin et al. include a much-earlier commentary about May when she was Shadow Leader of the House in 2007: *The Daily Mail* described her as wearing 'a bright pink wrap dress' that was disapproved of because 'as if the dress were not eye-catching enough, Mrs May also had a serious amount of cleavage on show' (Mavin et al. 2010: 563). This leads them to conclude that: 'Women political leaders have to do gender "just right". Fetching shoes were appropriately feminine but a show of breast cleavage was going too far and too obvious a reminder of her difference' (Mavin et al. 2010). Another *Daily Mail* front page famously represented Theresa May and Nicola Sturgeon sitting side-by-side, both wearing knee-high skirts with the headline 'Never mind Brexit, who won legs-it!' (Vine 2017). This is a blatant placing of physical attributes before the two powerful women

Figure 6.3 Graffiti image of Theresa May, June 2017. Mortimer St, London W1. (Source: Unknown artist, photo by Sylvia Shaw.)

leaders' political message and policies, and the casting of the article as 'light-hearted' by the (woman) journalist who wrote it, does nothing to mitigate its demeaning message.

Thompson and Yates also see the media's focus on May's fashion choices as part of this preoccupation with and framing of the body: 'her "Prime Ministerial Style", her "low-cut tops" and even her womb when the issue of her child-free status resurfaced in the election' (Thompson and Yates 2017: 131). There is also some evidence of sexualised framings of May, some of which are ironic (as in the graffiti image of May as Marilyn Monro in 'Some Like it Hot' shown in Figure 6.3), but also in-line with the 'battle-axe' archetype as a dominatrix. May's leopard-skin shoes and high heels are often used as sexualised images, and none less than on the front page of *The Sun* on the day she became Prime Minister.[13] The words 'Heel, boys!' depict nearly a full-page image of May's feet and heels (in her leopard-skin and diamante shoes) treading on a set of photographs along the bottom of the page. The photographs show the men she has ousted being trampled by May's shoes, with the directive 'Heel, boys' at once ordering and infantilising them in an overtly dominant and sexual way.

Unlike many women political leaders, May's voice itself does not seem to be represented in the media in overly gendered terms. She is not commonly depicted as 'shrieking', 'squeaking' or having a 'shrill' voice as media depictions of other leaders have been described (Cameron and Shaw 2016). However, the 'Maybot' depiction of her gives rise to succession of descriptions of her manner of speaking, here best described by the Maybot creator, John Crace:

Example 6.11 Descriptions of May by John Crace as the 'Maybot'

(a) 'The London mayor is doing a very good job' she *monotoned*. But what about Donald Trump? "The London Mayor is doing a good job."' (Crace 2018: 165)
(b) 'I believe in Britain she said in her *trademark Maybot tone that suggested she believed in nothing whatsoever*' (Crace 2018: 166)
(c) 'This summit has been a huge personal success, and Britain remains a confident, outward-looking and enthusiastic member of Europe,' said a hollow-eyed, *flatlining* Theresa sounding *diffident* and *introverted*' (Crace 2018: 49)
(d) 'I'm. Whirr. Determined. To be. Clunk. Determined to focus on the. Clang. Things the British people determined.' (Crace 2018: 54)

Here Crace represents May's voice, demeanour and actions as that of a robot, an automaton controlled by others, and this is evaluated as a *gendered* representation in the concluding summary of this case study.

6.2.5   *Summary*

This case study of Theresa May's linguistic style can be summarised as showing that in the debating chamber during PMQs she has a highly unusual style. This alternates between an extremely evasive – yet straightforward – explanatory way of responding to questions and an adversarial – but formulaic – response. The analysis shows that she does not conform to the gendered stereotype of having a consensual style but instead seems to exhibit a rehearsed and practised type of adversarial style. This hyper-controlled style is possibly gendered in that it exhibits a lack of ease (or discomfort) with the surroundings of the CoP, which has been shown to be highly masculinist in its practices and workings. In this way, and despite May's seniority, she could still be positioned peripherally in this highly masculinised CoP. The close analysis of critical gendered moments of parliamentary interaction showed that May, a self-declared feminist, juxtaposes her feminist stance with much more traditional viewpoints (as, for example, reiterating her desire to be called by her husband's name as an adversarial move against Emily Thornberry in Example 6.9b). May is also positioned in complex ways in relation to sexist discourse and the operation of fraternal networks. These networks operate in ironic and humorous ways and May is positioned awkwardly in the 'Mrs Bone' extract (Example 6.10) in that she seemingly stumbles into making a sexual joke about another woman who is not present. The collaborative nature of the response and the collective laughter of MPs (that seems directed at May as much as the joke itself) exposes a paradox of female leadership. How can a woman be fully included within the 'core' practices of a community that is constructed by fraternal networks and sexist practices? May's performances are thus fractured by the competing demands of performing authoritative leadership and mitigating the dissonance of being a woman Prime Minister. The critical moments discussed in detail in this case study illustrate some of the difficulties she faced in the performance of her authority and her femininity in a context that rewards male networks and norms.

May's ability to be agentive in relation to her critics can be seen as a strength. She is resilient enough to take criticisms and misfortunes and turn them to her advantage. Her awkward dancing on a trip to Africa in 2018 was repeated both on the same Africa trip a few days later and at the start of the 2018 Conservative party conference, along with an allusion to the disastrous speech at the same conference a year earlier. She said 'You'll have to excuse me if I cough during this speech; I've been up all night supergluing the back-drop' (May 2018c). She was also resolute and seemingly immovable in the face of criticism from her own party, facing defeats in the HoC and two votes of 'no confidence' (see Table 6.1). Criticism from her own party included the long-standing Conservative MP, Ken Clark, who was caught on camera call-ing Theresa May 'a bloody difficult woman'[14] just before her appointment in July 2016. May responded by appropriating this phrase and using it to describe herself on a number of occasions. On the 3 May 2017 she used it rather aggres-sively to outline her 'tough stance' on Brexit, saying: 'I was described as one of my colleagues as a "bloody difficult woman" and I said at the time that the next person to find that out would be Jean Claude Junker' (May 2017a). She also used the phrase in a television interview in September 2018: 'There's a difference between those who think you can only be bloody difficult in public and those who think, actually, you bide your time, and you're bloody difficult when the time is right – and when it really matters' (May 2018b). In this case it is possible the 'bloody difficult in public' reference is to Boris Johnson, who had just publicly criticised her plans for Brexit. May also used the phrase about herself in a Tweet in order to support the international 'Women's March' on the 4 March 2018. She tweeted 'Here's to all the "bloody difficult women" out today on the #March4Women', accompanied by a screenshot of a google search for 'bloody difficult woman' with Theresa May as the top 'hit', see Figure 6.4. In these examples, May takes charge of the 'bloody difficult woman' discourse to her advantage, changing the paradiastolic casting of 'dif-ficult' as 'intransigent' to the more eulogistic casting of it as 'determined',

Figure 6.4 Screenshot of Theresa May's Tweet about being a 'bloody difficult woman' 4 March 2018. (Source: https://twitter.com/theresa_may.)

'strong' or 'committed'. In the final example she uses it to expose the sexism of the phrase and to tap into a discourse of feminist solidarity with the marchers.

The case study shows May's citing of feminist beliefs on a number of occasions, even though the way she does this would be viewed as problematic by many feminists (as with the Thornberry Example 6.9b). Laurie Penny from *The New Statesman* describes May's 'ascendance' as 'the feminist revolution in the same way that the Charge of the Light Brigade was a military triumph'. Penny adds that 'The fact of being female does not mean a leader will deliver for women', while citing May's political stance on immigration and abortion as running contrary to women's interests (Penny 2016). In research investigating conservative feminism in the US, it is noted that: 'As gender conscious actors, conservative women demonstrate the centrality of women to conservative movement politics. Rarely, however, do the leaders studied here criticise other conservative movement organizations or men for excluding and/or promoting sexist policies (including the lack of denunciation of President Trump's explicitly sexist language and actions)' (Schreiber 2018: 75). Recent studies of conservative feminism find that conservative women's representative claims are often viewed as 'wolves in sheep's clothing' where 'women are claiming to act for women but adjudged, ultimately, to harm women's interests' (Celis and Childs 2018: 6). They suggest that although it is important to recognise the heterogeneity of women's positions and interests, research is needed to 'determine whether conservative women are acting as "good representatives" on the ground' (Celis and Childs 2018: 21) in ways that do not promote anti-feminist outcomes. Certainly, a more rigorous study of the ways in which conservative women, particularly May, act in ways that are beneficial for women would further this debate.

The case study suggests that many of the representations of May in the media fall within the entirely predictable and sexist treatment of women in politics who must manage their femininity carefully because 'they are still othered because the doing of gender well does not fit with the masculine hegemony of UK government' (Mavin et al. 2010: 564). The analyses show that although May behaves authoritatively and agentively as a leader, the media reattaches her to established gender stereotypes (Mavin et al. 2010: 562). This often involves a focus on her appearance and her body, aligning to archetypal roles of the 'iron maiden' and the 'battle axe' (Baxter 2018; Kanter 1977). These characterisations of May are often partially positive and offer her a kind of grudging respect for 'getting the job done'. Yet even these representations are gendered, with May being placed firmly in the domestic sphere with constant references to her 'organisational skills' and 'housework'. In the context of Brexit and the febrile confusion in the Conservative party surrounding the 'exit talks' in this period between 2016 and June 2019, May was often cast as the sensible, somewhat unremarkable and rather tedious domestic worker – dutifully tidying up the mess that other politicians have created.

The more unusual and pervasive characterisation of May as the 'Maybot' is more nuanced in its reattachment of May to gendered stereotypes but nevertheless turns on its alignment to the 'master stereotype' of women's emotionality (Brescoll 2016) mixed with a nod to the 'women's intellectual inferiority' stereotype. On the surface the 'Maybot', robot characterisation does not appear to be gendered, surely a man speaking in such controlled and obviously rehearsed ways would invoke similar characterisations? However, the characterisation rests on May's perceived lack of emotional engagement, which has been shown to be an intolerable position for a woman (but not a man) to occupy (Brescoll 2016). Further, emotionality has been linked to authenticity for political leaders 'understandings of authenticity are tied to *emotional qualities* – an "authentic politician" is one who is able to feel compassion for voters, to be able to deliver the policy changes they need' (Wahl-Jorgensen 2017: 69). Theresa May's failure to exhibit emotion in-line with gendered expectations therefore leads to a perception of lack of authenticity and the characterisation of her as robotic. The other implication of the Maybot image is that of an unthinking being, relying not on its own thoughts but being controlled by others. This robot characterisation links to the

Figure 6.5 Theresa May crying at the end of her resignation speech, 24 May 2019. (Source: Leon Neal/Staff/Getty Images.)

representations of women MPs in the ethnographic interviews in the HoC 1998–2001 corpus described in Chapter 3. The HoC interviewees reported being referred to as 'Stepford Wives' and 'clones' because of their perceived unthinking loyalty to the Blair leadership – always on message, never critical. The Maybot therefore lacks both intelligence and emotionality and as such encapsulates May's counter-stereotypic performances in terms of gendered expectations. It is interesting to note that the entire UK print media chose the image of May shown in Figure 6.5 below for their front pages after her resignation speech on 24 May 2019. This picture depicts the final few seconds of May's resignation speech in which she says that she resigns with 'no ill-will but with enduring gratitude to have had the opportunity to serve the country I love', breaking into tears for the final three words. It seems that May's media story was finished to the satisfaction of all when her emotions finally showed.

7 Case Studies: Julia Gillard and Hillary Clinton

7.1 Julia Gillard

7.1.1 Introduction

Julia Gillard was the first woman prime minister of Australia (in office between 2010 and 2013 see Table 7.1). Before she became PM she was a member of the Australian parliament for the Labor Party from 1998, and then subsequently took up roles in the shadow cabinet when the opposing Liberal party was in power between 1998 and 2007. When Labor won the General Election in 2007 she became Deputy Prime Minister to Kevin Rudd, before replacing him as Prime Minister in 2010 when Rudd resigned and she was elected leader of the Labor party unopposed. Her ascendance to the position of Labor party leader and therefore PM was a result of a leadership challenge to the incumbent PM, Kevin Rudd. Initially, Gillard's 'first woman' status was celebrated, but 'the spectre of Rudd haunted Gillard throughout her tenure' (Trimble 2017: 218) because she had deposed him.

Gillard has been selected for inclusion as a case study not only because she occupied the most senior political position in Australia between 2010 and 2013, but because she is known for facing and fighting extreme sexism in the Australian parliamentary chamber. She is renowned for her 'fighting talk' and fierce criticism of her main adversary and LO, Tony Abbott, and for the sexism she faced throughout her career, but particularly during her time as PM. She is also famous globally for what has come to be termed as her 'sexism and misogyny speech' given in the Australian Parliament in 9 October 2012, and the subsequent negative framing of the speech by the Australian media immediately afterwards.

Gillard was also the first unmarried Australian Prime Minister and had no children. This led to deeply misogynistic claims that 'she was incomplete, and unfit to lead a nation' and 'deliberately barren' (Varney 2017: 28). In an insightful analysis of interviews conducted with Gillard between 2010 and 2012, Jasmin Sorrentino and Martha Augoustinos note in detail how carefully Gillard plays down her own identity as a *woman* politician

Table 7.1 *Timeline of Julia Gillard's premiership and significant events, 1998–2013*

Date	Event
1998–2007	Member of Parliament (Australian House of representative)
2001–7	Member of the Shadow Cabinet
2006–7	Deputy Opposition Leader
2007–10	Deputy Prime Minister
2010–13	Prime Minister (took office 24 June 2010)
27 February 2012	Gillard survives leadership challenge vote
9 October 2012	'Sexism and misogyny speech'
26 June 2013	Gillard defeated by Kevin Rudd in a leadership vote, and resigns as PM

and distances herself from a potentially problematic feminist identity. They also note how Gillard manages constructions of herself as an ambitious politician, which is a risky label for her as she was increasingly perceived as ruthless for the way in which she deposed Rudd to claim the premiership. She cleverly constructs her rise to power as incidental, and as taking an opportunity when it arose rather than allowing herself to be constructed as the ambitious person who had always had her sights on the job. Similarly, when questioned rather intrusively about her 'choice' not to get married or have children, Gillard represents herself in contradictory ways. She oscillates between representing these personal decisions as choices on the one hand and as a result of chance on the other. This is another manifestation of the classic double bind of women in politics: 'By positioning herself as choosing not to marry, Gillard may be perceived as rejecting traditional cultural norms and therefore may have negative consequences in terms of her ability to relate to the public. In stark contrast, for Gillard to attribute her life to chance would render her as someone who does not have control over her life' (Sorrentino and Augoustinos 2016: 401). These observations show that Gillard is good example of a woman political leader who has faced all the barriers to women's progress identified in Chapter 5 and who has directly and publicly resisted the sexism that has been directed towards her. Here I give a brief description of Gillard's adversarial political language in her exchanges with Tony Abbott before discussing the sexism she was subjected to inside and outside the parliamentary chamber. Then I examine her 'sexism and misogyny speech' and review subsequent analyses showing how this speech was framed in the media (Holland and Wright 2017; Sawer 2013; Trimble 2016, 2017; Worth et al. 2016; Wright and Holland 2014). Finally, I show how media representations of her speech and voice reflect many of the difficulties she faced during her time as Prime Minister.

7.1.2   *Julia Gillard: Adversarial Language and Sexism*

The Australian national parliament, based in the national capital of Canberra is a bicameral parliament with two elected chambers, and is often referred to as the 'Commonwealth parliament'. The upper house, or 'Senate' comprises of 76 directly elected members taken equally from across the different states of Australia and is modelled partly on the Westminster House of Lords, and partly on the US Senate.[1] The lower house, the House of Representatives, has 148–150 members and is run under the 'Westminster system' and broadly follows the conventions and procedures of the HoC in the UK with a number of adaptations. This means that in spite of its modern, spacious, semi-circular chamber (completed in 1998), it can be thought of as a traditional, male-dominated parliament and is a suitable comparator to the HoC. The number of women in the parliament has struggled to rise to 29 per cent in 2016. It has been slow to gain parity partly for cultural reasons and sexist beliefs about women in public life; and partly because of the lack of positive measures across the board to ensure more women are elected (Sawer 2013). Australia was the slowest country in the world to take on women politicians, with an astounding 41-year lag between the point that women were able to become members of parliament and the point that a woman was first elected (Sawer 2013). Like the HoC, the HoR is thought to be a highly masculinised space with entrenched 'norms of masculinity that dominate legislative spaces' (Collier and Raney 2018: 438). It has been described as a highly sexist and misogynistic environment (Sawer 2013). In their case study of sexual harassment in the HoR, Cheryl Collier and Tracey Raney find that it is an institution in which: 'We see men closing ranks to protect their own partisan colleagues and to silence women who draw attention to the bullying tactic of sexual harassment' (2018: 440).

When Julia Gillard took office as Prime Minister in 2010 she already had extensive speaking experience in parliament and this undoubtedly would have contributed to the confidence with which she spoke in the chamber, particularly when facing Tony Abbott (the LO) across the dispatch box. The House of Representatives (HoR) have a 'Question Time session' which, like the question times sessions in the HoC, are the focus of public and media interest. However, unlike the HoC, question times or 'Questions without notice' happen daily at 2pm and are taken by all Ministers together as a group with the Minister responsible for the area to which the question is addressed responding to the question (Commonwealth Parliament 2018). In order to assess Julia Gillard's performances in 'Questions without notice' sessions (henceforth 'QTs') a number of QTs were sampled across the period of her premiership. The differences between the parliaments meant that it was not possible to use the adversarial 'score' for the HoR as the practices and norms of the parliaments differed in a number of respects. Apart from the fact that the Prime Minister and Ministers share the responses according to their particular area of responsibility, the LO does not have the opportunity for six questioning turns in a row, as in the HoC. Instead, any questioner is allowed a supplementary or follow-up question (at the discretion of the Speaker) and after the allocation of a question from the opposing side: 'the practice of alternating the call between the right and left of the Chair has the effect that follow-up questions are not immediate' (Browning et al. 2018: Ch 15). A further difference is that the questions and responses are bound by time limits – with 30 seconds for a question and three minutes for an answer.

Apart from these regulatory differences, it became apparent on initial observation of the question times that there are a number of informal practices that mean the speech events in the HoC and the HoR operate in different ways. Although the HoC chamber is extremely rowdy at PMQs, the Speaker does not tend to tolerate single verbal utterances that relate directly to the 'legal' speaking turn. In the HoR, however, this seems to be more tolerated by the Speaker, and unparliamentary language is a common practice in this CoP (Graham 2019). Single, 'illegal' utterances appear to be common in the HoR and are only censured by the Speaker when they are extremely offensive or blatantly contravene a rule. As noted for the HoC in Chapter 3, there seems to be a great deal of slippage between the official rules and the informal practices of the HoR, although there is some acknowledgement of this in the official documentation of the parliament procedures:

Questions must not contain inferences, imputations, insults, ironical expressions or hypothetical matter; nor may they be facetious or frivolous or attribute motive. Speaker Andrew acknowledged that many questions convey an element of imputation; and that his general attitude was not to intervene where the imputation was directed to a difference in philosophy or viewpoint, but to intervene where the attribution of personal motive was such that it could not be ignored. (Browning et al. 2018: ch 15)

So, it is not that the HoR is more disorderly overall than the HoC (the HoC is very loud and collective cheering, jeering and shouting is the norm), but that illegal interventions which affect the legal progression of turns are more routinely tolerated in the HoR than in the HoC. Similarly, it appears that the level of adversarial language in the HoR is higher than in the HoC. Certainly, the May–Corbyn exchanges are much less adversarial than those between Gillard and Abbott (see Examples 7.1–7.6). These examples of Gillard's responses in question time and the adversarial language directed at her therefore give an impression both of her parliamentary style and the parliamentary culture of the HoR – which certainly warrants more extensive and systematic investigations that fall outside of the scope of this case study.

In the absence of a searchable video record of HoR events from the period of Gillard's premiership, the Official Report of the HoR (referred to as the

'Hansard') has been used as a record of parliamentary discourse (although, as discussed in Chapter 2 and in Shaw [2018], this is a selective and partial representation). Example 7.1 shows part of a QT session in which Tony Abbott asks Julia Gillard about the negative effects on property prices of proposed household environmental levies for carbon emissions.

Example 7.1 Questions without Notice (11 March 2011: HoR Hansard, pp. 2422–3)

1	**Mr Abbott** – My question is to the Prime Minister. (…) So I ask the Prime Minister: how
2	does she propose to compensate first home buyers in Western Sydney, for instance, for this
3	$6,000-plus increase in the cost of housing?
4	**Ms GILLARD** (Prime Minister) – Predictably, the scare campaign continues with the made-
5	up facts and figures, and the Leader of the Opposition does what he always does, which is to
6	seek to cause fear amongst the Australian community, because he has no policies or plans
7	for the nation's future and he tries to hide that behind a never-ending series of fear
8	campaigns. Mr Speaker, do you recall the start of this parliamentary session, when the
9	Leader of the Opposition was trying to raise fear amongst the Australian community about
10	the government's proposed flood levy? Day after day in question time, we came in here and
11	questions were asked and answered about the flood levy. Fear was being raised—
12	**Dr Jensen** *interjecting* —
13	**The SPEAKER** – The member for Tangney is warned.
14	**Ms GILLARD** – the sense that somehow the future of the Australian nation would be
15	jeopardised if that legislation passed the parliament. We do not hear about that anymore,
16	do we? We do not hear about it.
17	**Mr Pyne** – Mr Speaker, on a point of order: in the minute since the Prime Minister has
18	started answering this question, it has been all argument. She was asked a very
19	straightforward factual question about compensation for housing costs. I would ask you to
20	draw her back to the question.
21	**The Speaker** – The Manager of Opposition Business has resumed his seat. He used the word
22	'argumentative'. I indicate that that is allowed by interpretations of the standing orders that
23	still stand, and I look forward to movements in that regard by the House. The requirement is
24	that the Prime Minister be directly relevant to the question. The Prime Minister has the call.
25	**Ms Gillard** – Thank you very much, Mr Speaker. I was making the simple point that already
26	this year we have seen a scare campaign answered and dealt with, and the Leader of the
27	Opposition is too embarrassed to even go back to that scare campaign now. So, of course he
28	has to start a new scare campaign, and we are seeing today's scare campaign on display. But
29	that is all it is: a scare campaign from the Leader of the Opposition, making up figures each
30	and every day—
31	**Mr Pyne** – Answer the question, you harridan.
32	**Ms Gillard** – making up figures in order to cause alarm in the Australian community. But the
33	Australian community are smarter than the Leader of the Opposition gives them credit for
34	(Turn continues 1 minute) Whether or not the Leader of the Opposition believes in climate
35	change depends on what day you catch him. As the member for Wentworth said, he is the
36	ultimate weathervane in Australian politics: no policies; no plans; no beliefs; no convictions;
37	just slogans and a scare campaign, and that is all we are seeing again today.
38	*Mr Pyne interjecting*—
39	**The Speaker** – Before calling the Leader of the Opposition, I say that, having consulted the
40	definition of the expression, I would have thought that the Manager of Opposition Business
41	would have thought twice about repeating the word. He will withdraw.
42	**Mr Pyne** – I withdraw the word 'harridan'.

Example 7.1 shows Gillard evading Abbott's rather straightforward question with an adversarial attack on the LO, using ethotic arguments that rest on veracity and 'made-up facts' (line 6) and that accuse him of a 'scare campaign' (lines 4–5). Her initial reaction is adversarial but what stands out from this example is the frequency with which she is interrupted and prevented from completing her response. First, on line 12, 'Dr Jensen' interrupts her response (although the contents of the intervention are not recorded) and it is sufficiently disruptive for the Speaker to intervene (naming him as 'The member for Tangney', line 13). Second, 'Mr Pyne' raises a 'Point of order'[2] to complain that Gillard is not answering the question by making a substantive 'argument' on an unrelated matter and thus contravening the QTs rules (lines 17–20). The Speaker rules in favour of Gillard and she continues until Payne says 'answer the question, you Harridan' (line 31). Surprisingly, neither Gillard nor the Speaker immediately react to this illegal intervention containing a directive and a sexist derogatory word meaning 'a strict, bossy or belligerent old woman'. It is only when Payne interrupts a further time (line 38) that the Speaker 'having consulted the definition' asks him to withdraw his comment, which he does on line 42.

There are therefore similarities between the adversarial language used in the HoC and Gillard's language to describe Abbott in this QT. Gillard certainly acts counter-stereotypically with respect to gender in her use of adversarial language. In Example 7.1 her language seems much more adversarial than Abbott's initial question, and her turn finishes by describing Abbott as a 'weathervane' with 'no beliefs, no plans, and no convictions' (lines 36–37). During the QT sessions with Gillard, Abbott only has 30 seconds to ask his question and this perhaps reduces opportunities for adversarial attacks. However, Abbott frequently interrupts Gillard illegally by shouting at her across the floor. This includes using the banned parliamentary word 'liar' repeatedly. On one occasion he interjected with this word so remorselessly that he was ejected from the chamber for doing so,[3] as shown in Example 7.2.

Example 7.2 Tony Abbott and illegal adversarial language (20 August 2012: HoR Hansard, p. 9114)

1   **Mr Champion** (Wakefield) (15:04): How is the government supporting communities across
2   Australia through the regional development –
3   **Mr Abbott** interjecting –
4   **Mr Albanese** – Madam Deputy Speaker, I raise a point of order. I hesitate to interrupt my
5   friend the member for Wakefield, but the Leader of the Opposition should withdraw the
6   interjections he persistently makes across the chamber along the lines on which you have
7   insisted they be withdrawn.
8   **The Deputy Speaker** – (Ms AE Burke): The Leader of the Opposition will withdraw without
9   qualification.
10   **Mr Abbott** – I withdraw.
11   **The Deputy Speaker** – I thank the Leader of the Opposition.

12   **Mr Abbott** – It is still an untrue statement.
13   **The Deputy Speaker** – The Leader of the Opposition will remove himself from the chamber
14   under standing order 94(a). The Leader of the Opposition has now been advised by the chair
15   on more than one occasion. I asked you, as you approached the dispatch box, to do it
16   without qualification. You could not help yourself. The Leader of the Opposition will leave
17   the chamber under 94(a).

The Hansard report of this incident shown in Example 7.2 does not reveal the full 'interjection' from Abbott (line 3), but it is clear from the context and from first-hand accounts that he directly called Julia Gillard a 'liar'. However, it is the contempt that he shows for the Speaker's directive to 'withdraw' the comment 'without qualification' (lines 8–9) that leads to his suspension from the proceedings. Although he initially withdraws the comment, he adds 'it is still an untrue statement' (line 12), leading the Speaker to observe that 'you could not help yourself' as she orders him to 'remove himself' from the chamber (lines 13–17). These actions are reminiscent of the rule-breaking behaviour in the HoC such as 'filibustering' – where contravening the rules directly and knowingly contests the authority of the institution – and in doing so, Abbott displays the strongest form of resistance to institutional regulation and authority.

Other accounts of Abbott's adversarial and sexist behaviour towards Gillard are given in her autobiography. These include incidents outside the chamber, including in one press conference when he says 'Are you suggesting to me that when it comes from Julia, no doesn't mean no' (Rehn 2010 cited in Gillard 2014: 106). On another occasion he refers to Gillard 'making an honest woman of herself' with respect to a political issue (the Carbon tax) (Gillard 2014: 106). As Gillard herself notes:

These words have entered our lexicon in the context of denying rape, of criticising unmarried, sexually active women. These words are in our lexicon alongside the words women have always shuddered to hear – 'she asked for it', 'slut'. Even if you are the single most powerful person in your country, if you are a woman, the images that are shadowed around you are of sex and rape'. (Gillard 2014: 106)

Gillard's sexist treatment more generally by both politicians and journalists during her time as PM was extreme. An example of this is Sydney radio presenter Alan Jones' comment that: 'It is absolutely laughable. The woman's off her tree and quite frankly they should shove her and Bob Brown in a chaff bag[4] and take them as far out to sea as they can and tell them to swim home' (Alan Jones, 6 July 2011 cited in ABC Media Watch 23 July 2012). Although this directive on public radio to drown the Prime Minister eventually elicited a full apology from Alan Jones, the extent of the violent and excessive comments against Gillard were consistent throughout her premiership. It has been noted that 'The figurations of woman, madness, liar, witch and water adhered to Gillard with a stickiness that conjured the hateful, humid, clammy body of

Figure 7.1 Image of Julia Gillard and Tony Abbott in Question Time in the House of Representatives, 5 February 2013. (Source: Stefan Postles/Stringer/Getty Images.)

female governance' (Varney 2017: 31). The opposing Liberal party were often at the forefront of these attacks, with one of the more extreme attacks coming at a Liberal party fundraising event where an option on the menu was 'Julia Gillard Kentucky Fried Quail – small breasts, huge thighs and a big red box' (Clune 2013, see Figure 7.1). In this way, Gillard's body is 'fetishized and cannibalized by her opponents, and rendered abject' (Varney 2017: 31).

For most of her time as PM, Gillard recognised what Donaghue (2015) describes as the 'conventional wisdom' that 'it is politically unwise to acknowledge directly – let alone confront – sexism' (2015: 162). Gillard herself refers to the explicit decision she took 'to tolerate all the sexist and gendered references and stereotyping, on the basis it was likely to swirl around for a while and then peter out' but that 'I was wrong. It actually worsened' (Gillard 2014: 113). After just over two years as PM, Gillard made her world-famous 'sexism and misogyny speech' in which she attacked Abbott and the opposition liberal party for the sexism and misogyny levelled at her, and as a particularly prescient example of a 'critical gendered moment', this is described in detail in the next section.

7.1.3   Julia Gillard: The 'Sexism and Misogyny Speech'

Julia Gillard's 'sexism and misogyny speech' occurred in the HoR on 9 October 2012. The parliamentary context of the speech was that the Speaker of the HoR, Peter Slipper, had been accused of sending another man MP explicit text messages about a woman. Gillard supported Slipper's appointment politically, and so she knew as she faced Tony Abbott at the QTs session that day he would berate and criticise her for supporting a sexist politician. As she says in her own words: 'my mind was shouting, *For Fuck's sake, after all the shit I have had to put up with, now I have to listen to Abbott lecturing me on sexism, for fuck's sake!*' (Gillard 2014: 110). Her speech is a direct and personal attack on Abbott as she responds to his calls for Slipper's resignation. The speech starts in Example 7.3.

Example 7.3 Beginning of Gillard's 'sexism and misogyny speech' (9 October 2012: HoR Hansard, p. 11581)

1	**Ms Gillard** I rise to oppose the motion moved by the
2	Leader of the Opposition, and in so doing I say to the Leader of the Opposition: I will not be
3	lectured about sexism and misogyny by this man. I will not. The government will not be
4	lectured about sexism and misogyny by this man – not now, not ever. The Leader of the
5	Opposition says that people who hold sexist views and who are misogynists are not
6	appropriate for high office. Well, I hope the Leader of the Opposition has a piece of paper
7	and he is writing out his resignation, because if he wants to know what misogyny looks like
8	in modern Australia he does not need a motion in the House of Representatives; he needs a
9	mirror. That is what he needs.

It has been noted that Gillard here effectively changes Abbott to the object position of the speech (Appleby 2015: 161), removing herself from the accusations he made about her in his proposal of the motion and positioning him as the morally dubious and sexist culprit. Her use of the first personal singular pronoun 'I' with 'the rhetorical emphasis of "I rise", "I will not", and, not now not ever' (Varney 2017: 33) underline her agency and determination to resist Abbott's accusations against her. She also names him as 'this man', which at once makes his gender salient and reduces his status. Gillard goes on to catalogue Abbott's comments about women, including that he had previously claimed it is 'not a bad thing' if men have more power than women or that women are under-represented in public life. She also quoted him as saying it is possible that 'men are by physiology or temperament more adapted to exercise authority or to issue command'. Then, as shown in Example 7.4, she catalogues further sexist comments from Abbott:

Example 7.4 Beginning of Gillard's 'sexism and misogyny speech', part 2 (9 October 2012: HoR Hansard, p. 11581)

1	I was very offended personally when the Leader of the Opposition as minister for health
2	said, 'Abortion is the easy way out.' I was very personally offended by those comments. He
3	said that in March 2004, and I suggest he check the records. I was also very offended on
4	behalf of the women of Australia when in the course of the carbon pricing campaign the
5	Leader of the Opposition said, 'What the housewives of Australia need to understand as

6   they do the ironing.' Thank you for that painting of women's roles in modern Australia!
7   Then, of course, I am offended by the sexism, by the misogyny, of the Leader of the
8   Opposition catcalling across this table at me as I sit here as Prime Minister, 'if the Prime
9   Minister wants to, politically speaking, make an honest woman of herself' – something that
10   would never have been said to any man sitting in this chair.

11   I was offended when the Leader of the Opposition went outside the front of the parliament
12   and stood next to a sign that said 'Ditch the witch'. I was offended when the Leader of the
13   Opposition stood next to a sign that described me as a man's bitch. I was offended by those
14   things. It is misogyny, sexism, every day from this Leader of the Opposition. Every day, in
15   every way, across the time the Leader of the Opposition has sat in that chair and I have sat
16   in this chair, that is all we have heard from him.

Here Gillard cites Abbott's comment that abortion is 'the easy way out' (line 2) and that she was 'personally offended' by his remarks. She then positions herself as representative for 'the women of Australia' and so moves from the highly individual response to that of 'tribune of the people' (Montgomery 2011: 38) who speaks on behalf of others. As suggested by Appleby (2015): 'In this pivotal speech Gillard identified *as* a woman and *with* women, but, at the same time, refused to conform to an oppressive gender regime that demands, amongst other behavioural norms, an essentialised, passive femininity' (2015: 161). Certainly, there is nothing passive about Gillard's performance. Her open physical stance and confrontational gestures – at times pointing directly at Abbott and at others moving her whole body towards him to emphasise her accusations – make her performance appear powerful, confident and assured. In her own words, Gillard refers to this ease of physical occupation of the space, saying she 'felt settled, loose limbed' and that 'I did not feel heated or angry. I felt powerful, forceful' (2014: 110). This was a watershed moment for Gillard, who, as mentioned earlier, had previously eschewed confronting every sexist comment and move against her as PM but who later confessed to being in a 'murderous rage' (Gillard and Summers 2013, cited in Appleby 2015: 160) as she replied to Abbott's motion to remove the Speaker for his sexism. This speech has been described as a 'breakthough performance' at a moment of 'realization of intolerable subjugation' (Varney 2017: 32). It is notable that most of the analyses of the speech focus on the way in which it was framed by the media (as discussed in Section 6.3.3) rather than the speech itself, and there is little comment on the immediate context of the speech. The analysis of the context of the speech, aided by Gillard's own accounts of the event (for example, Gillard 2014) also shed light on what might have triggered Gillard's 'rage' at this point. In fact, Gillard's famous speech must be read in context as a response to Abbott's twenty-minute speech immediately preceding it which functioned to propose the motion to remove the Speaker. Abbott's speech contained highly adversarial accusations, some of which are shown in Example 7.5a–c below:

Example 7.5a–c Abbott's accusations prior to Gillard's 'misogyny speech' (9 October 2012, HoR Hansard, p. 11574)

1   (a) Just as the Speaker has failed the character test, you, Prime Minister, are about to fail the
2   judgement test. And every day that you, Prime Minister, run a protection racket for the
3   current Speaker, just as you ran for months and years a protection racket for the member for
4   Dobell, you indicate your unfitness for high office as well.

5   (b) This is a government which is only too ready to detect sexism – to detect misogyny, no
6   less – until they find it in one of their own supporters, until they find it in someone upon
7   whom this Prime Minister relies to survive in her job. Then, of course, no fault can possibly
8   be found – no evil dare be spoken. Well, the Australian public are not mugs. They know what
9   is going on here; they know that this government is about to run a protection racket for
10 something, which is absolutely contemptible for attitudes and values, which are absolutely
11 and utterly indefensible.

12 (c) What this Prime Minister has done is shame this parliament. Should she now rise in this
13 place to try to defend the Speaker, to say that she retains confidence in the Speaker, she will
14 shame this parliament again. And every day the Prime Minister stands in this parliament to
15 defend this Speaker will be another day of shame for this parliament and another day of
16 shame for a government which should have already died of shame.

These examples show Abbott accusing Gillard of being dishonest in her appointment of Slipper to the position of Speaker for her own political gain. In Example 7.5a he says she has 'failed the judgement test' has run a 'protection racket' and is 'unfit for high office'. In Example 7.5b he accuses her of hypocrisy about sexism and misogyny, and being corrupt when it comes to 'attitudes and values' (line 10). In 15c his accusation that she has 'shamed' the parliament and that the government 'should have already died of shame' is particularly hard-hitting in ways that are not immediately obvious to a global audience because it refers to comments made about the death of Gillard's father. He had died only a month before this event (on 7 September 2012), and Alan Jones (the same radio 'shock jock' who had made the 'sack of chaff' comment mentioned above) said as part of a speech at a Liberal party event that: 'The old man recently died a few weeks ago of shame. To think that he had a daughter who told lies every time she stood for parliament' (Aston 2012). Therefore, Abbott is alluding to this earlier comment in his parliamentary speech and reinforcing the extremely personal and emotive idea that Gillard's father 'died of shame'. Gillard is not silenced by this implication however and incorporates a direct response to it as part of her speech. She quotes Abbott's words back to him before saying:

Example 7.6 Gillard's response to the 'died of shame' comment in her Sexism and Misogyny speech (9 October 2012, HoR Hansard, p. 11581)

Gillard: I indicate to the Leader of the Opposition that the government is not dying of
        shame – and my father did not die of shame. What the Leader of the Opposition
        should be ashamed of is his performance in this parliament and the sexism he
        brings with it.

There can scarcely be a more personal attack on a politician than to imply that the 'shame' they induced led to the death of a parent. It is an astonishingly cruel accusation and a measure of the adversarial lengths to which Abbott would go in order to confront Gillard. Gillard's speech gained millions of YouTube hits around the world (Gillard 2014) and has been held up as an exemplar of overt resistance to personal and institutional sexism. Close examination of the contexts around the speech reveal the extreme attacks she was subjected to immediately prior to the speech and show how she was directly responding to these adversarial and highly personal attacks. This is not a spontaneous outpouring, however, as the accuracy with which Gillard incorporates fairly obscure quotations word-for-word (see Example 7.4, lines 5–6) suggests that this was at least partly planned in advance. It has been noted that 'Some may say that PM Gillard was simply waiting for the right time to launch her anti-sexism speech for best political ends' (McLean and Maalsen 2013: 256). It is likely that the domestic political contexts had a bearing on the timing of the speech (in that one of Gillard's own party members in a minority government, the Speaker, was about to be forced to resign), but as shown in Section 7.1.4, the global interest in and the multiple and gendered framings of the speech could not have been predicted.

7.1.4   Julia Gillard: Gendered Mediation and the 'Gender Wars' Backlash

Although the immediate global reaction to Gillard's 'sexism and misogyny speech' was one of overwhelming support for a courageous stand against sexism, there was quite a different reaction from the Australian press (Donaghue 2015; Goldsworthy 2013; Ross 2017; Wright and Holland 2014). As a singular example of a Prime Minister accusing her main opponent of sexism within the national parliament, Gillard's speech has become an interesting and important test case for observing how accusations of gender inequality, sexism and misogyny are then subsequently dealt with and framed in the media. Linda Trimble incorporates an analysis of the gendered mediation of Gillard's speech in her book, *Mrs. Prime Minister* (2017). Like many other analysts, she notes that the media accused Gillard of starting a 'gender war' by launching her attack on Abbott. Unlike most, however, she notes that this accusation of the 'gender war' was in play before the speech, with Australian newspapers already framing Gillard's strategy as 'a concerted inflammatory and calculated gender war campaign' which hinged on the 'demonization' of Abbott and 'encouraging the view that Abbott is a misogynist' (Trimble 2017: 202). Into this context then, and at the national level, the 'misogyny speech' played into an already primed notion that accusations of sexism were disingenuous and they were fabricated for political gain: 'From the earliest moments of the media response, it was constructed as essential that the speech be only and entirely one thing or the other – authentic, and thus inspiring, or strategic, and thus worthless' (Donaghue 2015: 175). In other words, Gillard was represented as strategically 'playing the gender card' and this hid, negated or elided the accusations of sexism that she held against Abbott. The term 'playing the gender card' itself makes it possible to reduce complex, detailed arguments – in this case specific accusations of sexism – into something vague (Falk 2013; Worth et al. 2016). In their close analysis of 216 articles from the Australian print media published in the week following the speech, Worth et al. (2016) find that in most articles 'sexism was either constructed as irrelevant or ignored' (Worth et al. 2016: 58). They find that discourses oriented to the irrelevance of the issue of sexism to most Australians and that Gillard 'should rise above it', in spite of the acknowledgement that Gillard had been the victim of extreme sexist abuse (Worth et al. 2016: 58–61). Even in 'positive' representations of Gillard's speech, they find the act of resisting and speaking up against sexism is cast as an 'exceptional' act, to which not all women can aspire and thus 'subtly functions to maintain gender inequalities' (Worth et al. 2016: 62).

The impact of these types of media framings have been shown to have overwhelming negative consequences and costs (Donaghue 2015; Goldsworthy 2013; Holland and Wright 2017; Ross 2017; Trimble 2017; Worth et al. 2016; Wright and Holland 2014). These are elucidated as undermining the substance of the anti-sexist message; preventing the 'rallying cry' of the speech; casting Gillard as an outsider and an exception; and ultimately disassociating all women from leadership positions (Wright and Holland 2014). The media framings have also been found to reflect the 'double bind' inherent in all (western) women in leadership positions but at the same time in the specific context of Australian patriarchal norms (Holland and Wright 2017). This 'double oxymoronic ideal – of "women leader" and "women leader of Australia"' is shown to be pervasive in a context of exclusionary narratives of masculinity and 'mateship' running through the Australian National identity (Holland and Wright 2017).

Apart from media representations of Gillard immediately after her 'sexism and misogyny speech', more generally during the time of her premiership they invoke aspects of social class in addition to gender, in particular when she is described as a 'bogan'. This is a negative Australian English word for a working-class tasteless person, or 'a person of limited education or class' (Bongiorno 2012).[5] It is similar to the word 'chav' in British English, or 'trailer trash' in American English, although these are not synonymous and each have particular cultural connotations, with the British version being perceived as 'nastier' than the Australian one (Bongiorno 2012). The word is associated with Gillard from the outset of her premiership with Kevin Rudd, the outgoing PM in 2010, reportedly describing 'The Lodge' (the official Prime Minister's residence) as 'Boganville' after Gillard and her partner took up residence (Bongiorno 2012). Some commentaries view Gillard's 'bogan' characteristics as contributing to her lack of popularity or success as in the newspaper article titled 'PM must de-bogan to get attention' (Burnett 2011). However, this working-class characterisation is most closely associated with her voice, or as expressed in the same newspaper article 'the cause of her public image problem is simple. It's… that… accent' (Burnett 2011). Gillard's voice is described in extreme ways: 'Every time we hear her on the daily news, her voice makes the milk curdle, babies cry, dogs howl, flowers wilt and grandpa choke on his Weet Bix' (Burnett 2011). Her accent is thought of as embarrassingly lacking in culture and open for parody as the same journalist continues: 'the horror and shame of hearing Ms Gillard address an audience of world leaders and announce, with a smug grin, "Oi hope yous can pardun moi ratha strawng Orstrayan accent"' (Burnett 2011). Gillard's accent is variously described as regional: an 'Adelaide accent' (Frenkel 2011) or 'Victorian bogan' (Burnett 2011), or in terms of its sound: '"it's nasal", "I can't stand it", "it's twangy" are oft-heard comments' (Madill 2011). Like May, she also draws the 'robotic' characterisation: 'under pressure the PM's tone has become more robotic and less melodious' (Frenkel 2011). These assessments, whether about the origin of her accent or its sound, appear to be highly contradictory: 'So Gillard is deplored for sounding too much like a politician and criticised for sounding too much like a working-class suburbian, and all the while winning acclaim for being a good orator – which illustrates how subjective and driven by other motives the discussion on politicians' language can often be' (Gawne 2011). Gender does appear to be one such motive against which accents are judged. One research project found that when Australians were asked to evaluate speakers with regional and working-class Australian accents, men with these accents were rated as 'reliable, strong and trustworthy' while women with these accents were rated as untrustworthy and unlikely to be in professional positions' (Peck 2011). The analysis of the 'exclusionary narratives of masculinity' in Australian culture mentioned above, are also likely to have a bearing here, as these accents, like the figures of the 'Aussie Digger', the 'Larrikin' and 'Ocker'[6] overwhelmingly 'reproduce, celebrate and glorify working-class masculine qualities' (Holland and Wright 2017: 593).

It is also of note that criticisms of Gillard's voice and speaking style contain various directives and prescriptions about how she should act to rectify the perceived shortcomings. These prescriptions tend reflect the 'restrictive norms of linguistic femininity' (Cameron 1995: 211) or the gendered expectations that attend to the dissonance of women speaking with authority. This can be seen in an article by Dean Frenkel titled 'Drop the Gillard twang: it's beginning to annoy' where a list of 'improvements' are suggested, shown in Example 7.7.

Example 7.7 An excerpt from a newspaper article in *The Sunday Morning Herald* (Frenkel 2011)

1	How can she improve?

2 • Vowel articulation – 'e', 'i' and 'o' should be exercised in a far more understated way. No
3   over-articulating of vowels. She should consciously decide to drop the 'Gillard twang'. This
4   may well be the biggest-impact change she could make.

5 • More lightness – there's too much gravity in her voice. Add some occasional lightness that
6   taps into a greater range of melody and more frequent higher melody. This would raise her
7   energy and sound more natural.

8 • Speech rate – improve her 'skill control' at being able to work at different speech rates,
9   then raise the tempo of her 'stock speech rate' by a few notches.

10 • Balanced resonant placement – she should be a little less throaty and more resonantly
11   balanced between her throat and mouth.

12 • Energy/tone – it's time to think about the colour in her voice. Her tone is heavy and earthy.
13   But she could do with some lighter and brighter tones that introduce more melodious
14   qualities.

15 • Vocally – she appears to have little experience of singing and has not developed some vocal
16   subtlety skills that pass across to speech. Singing could greatly help – but not the gung-ho
17   footy anthem type.

These suggestions do little to elucidate what is meant by the 'Gillard twang' but do hold gendered connotations. Gillard is urged to adopt 'lightness', 'light and bright tones', to achieve a 'more resonantly balanced' style. This instruction would appear to read 'be more feminine'. At the same time, she is advised to drop the 'heavy and earthy', 'gung-ho footie anthem' and 'throaty' qualities associated with her perceived existing style, which appear to connote masculine voice qualities. It is also interesting to note that, if the advocated 'greater range' relates to the pitch of her voice, it is precisely the opposite directive that Margaret Thatcher undertook to change when she sought a 'steady', constant pitch over a variable one to 'drive through the noise' (see Section 5.5.2). These gendered directives therefore illustrate another series of double bind situations for women leaders: stereotypically 'feminine' features, such as higher pitch, draw negative evaluations of being 'shrill', 'weak', and lacking volume; stereotypical 'masculine' features, as in the case of Gillard, also attract criticism for having 'too much gravity' (Example 7.7, line 5). In addition to contradictory expectations about the sound of her voice, Gillard's fluency (she is thought to produce very few disfluency markers such as 'er' and 'um') is seen as a drawback which, along with other features shows 'a lack of spontaneity, a highly controlled delivery' that is 'likely to induce perceptions that Julia is being unnatural, rehearsed and disingenuous' (Madill 2011). However, if she produced more such disfluency markers, this would presumably add to the critique of her capabilities and lead to negative judgements about her 'inarticulacy' and unsuitability as a leader.

7.1.5   Summary

Julia Gillard ceased to be Prime Minister of Australia in June 2013 when she was deposed in a leadership challenge just 13 months after her famous 'sexism and misogyny speech'. This has led to speculation about the extent to which her overt resistance of sexist norms in a traditional, male-dominated parliament contributed to her political demise (Falk 2013; Hall and Donaghue 2013) and assertions that Tony Abbott 'won' (Donaghue 2015). Previous research has shown that orienting to gender in political interaction is problematic and requires careful management. Speaking up about sexism is therefore 'dangerous' (Worth et al. 2016) and is: 'constrained by the common sense understanding that women who rise above sexism are liked and respected, whereas those who speak up are perceived as extreme or aggressive "whingers". Certainly, her deposition was widely attributed to her "waning electoral popularity"' (Worth et al. 2016: 67–8). While it is impossible to say exactly how much of this dwindling popularity was a result of her resistance of sexism, it is possible to identify patterns of denigration that follow this type of resistance (Falk 2013; Hall and Donaghue 2013; Holland and Wright 2017; Worth et al. 2016).

The discursive space of resistance against sexism is shown to be quickly appropriated by discourses that suggest the protest is self-serving and manipulated, as in the claim that Gillard 'played the gender card' for her own gain. In making a stand against Abbott, Gillard made many enemies with one journalist observing at the time 'I suspect she will come to regret drawing such a nasty caricature of a man who resembles millions of Australian men' (Campbell 2012 cited in Holland and Wright 2017: 601). In a comparison of media framings of Gillard just after her misogyny speech with coverage in 2013 during the last four weeks of her government, the representation of her stand against sexism is found to become more sympathetic over time (Holland and Wright 2017). However, the analysts suggest that this is because as her tenure ended, she was not longer a threat to 'dominant narratives of the Australian national identity'; and because she started to escape the 'double binds' of women's leadership because she 'took up a new role in-line with gendered expectations, advocating for girls' rights' (Holland and Wright 2017: 599).

Gillard herself clearly attributes some of her demise to her position as a *woman* prime Minister, as in her resignation speech she says:

I've been a little bit bemused by those colleagues in the newspapers who have admitted that I have suffered more pressure as a result of my gender than other prime ministers in the past but then concluded that it had zero effect on my political position or the political position of the Labor Party. It doesn't explain everything, it doesn't explain nothing, it explains some things. And it is for the nation to think in a sophisticated way about those shades of grey. (Gillard 2013b)

These are fairly temperate words to describe the difficulties she faced given the outright sexism directed at her, let alone the personal attacks and misogynistic insults that were accepted and normalised as part of the political culture. I return to this discussion in Chapter 8 where I compare the performances and representation of May and Gillard with the final subject of the case study, Hillary Clinton.

7.2   Hillary Clinton

7.2.1   Introduction

The subject of the final case study, Hillary Clinton, has been included as she has possibly the highest international profile of all women leaders, and because she has attempted to occupy one of the most powerful political positions as US President. Clinton has had a long political career, as 'First Lady' of the US during her husband, Bill Clinton's government career (as governor of Arkansas and as US President), as Senator for New York, and as a potential candidate for democratic party nominee for president (in 2008–9). Finally, she became the Democratic Party Presidential Candidate in the 2016 election losing to Donald Trump (see Table 7.2 above).

Given her international profile and the shock of her defeat by Donald Trump in the 2016 US election, there have been many analyses of Clinton's language, political performances and representation in the media (Zulli 2018). As US parliamentary contexts are not comparable with those modelled on the Westminster parliament (described in detail in Chapters 3 and 4), this case study first examines 'critical gendered moments' in relation to gendered discourses in the US presidential debates of 2016. This allows an examination of Clinton's performance, linguistic style and the ways in which she confronts and resists Trump's sexist attitudes and behaviour. Then I give a selective overview of research into Clinton (mainly in the context of her two presidential bids in 2008 and 2016) that is most relevant to the barriers to women's participation in politics identified in Chapter 5 – specifically, Clinton's negotiation of gendered stereotypes, her representation in the media and finally, gendered representations of her speech and voice. In doing so I also draw upon Clinton's own reflections on the 2016 election published in her memoir *What Happened* in 2017.

7.2.2   Hillary Clinton: Critical Gendered Moments in the US Presidential TV Debates with Donald Trump, 2016

The 2016 US presidential campaign was characterised by unconventional and often unruly behaviour on the part of Donald Trump. This made him a unique political adversary for Clinton in the three televised debates leading

Table 7.2 *Timeline of significant events – Hillary Clinton 1993–2017*

Date	Event/Position held
1979–81	Attorney at Rose Law Firm; First Lady of Arkansas
1983–92	Attorney at Rose Law Firm; First Lady of Arkansas
1993–2001	First Lady of the USA (wife of president Bill Clinton)
2001–9	Senator of New York
2007–8	Campaign for the Democratic party's nomination for the US presidency (won by Obama in June 2008)
2009–13	Secretary of State (under President Obama)
2015–16	Presidential election campaign
26 September 2016	First televised debate with Donald Trump
4 October 2016	Second televised debate with Donald Trump
19 October 2016	Third televised debate with Donald Trump
8 November 2016	Defeated by Donald Trump in the US presidential election
2017	Publishes memoir *What Happened*

up to election day on 8 November 2016. Trump's behaviour in the televised debates has been described as a departure from 'long-held standards of politeness' and 'what has been considered appropriate behaviour in debate discourse' (Wicks et al. 2017: 55). The characteristics of televised debates are described in detail elsewhere (for example Adams 1992, 2015; Banwart and McKinney 2005; Cameron and Shaw 2016; Edelsky and Adams 1990) and pose particular challenges for the participants. They are prudent to rehearse their contributions in advance but must be careful to produce 'authentic talk' in which 'traces of scriptedness or rehearsal for performance are avoided, effaced or suppressed' (Montgomery 2001: 460) and must also appear 'confident but not self-satisfied, passionate but not zealous and confrontational but not aggressive' (Cameron and Shaw 2016: 29). Managing these competing demands from a vast overhearing audience (there were reportedly 85 million viewers for the first US televised debate [Nielson 2016]) means that the political stakes are exceptionally high with each participant only one wrong move or word away from a high-profile and potentially disastrous blunder. As Clinton says: 'A presidential debate is theater. It's a boxing match. It's high-stakes surgery' and an event that she prepared for well in advance: 'I practiced keeping my cool while my staff fired hard questions at me. They'd misrepresent my record. They'd impugn my character. Sometimes I'd snap back and feel better for getting it off my chest. I'd think to myself "Now that I've done that here, I don't have to do it on live TV." It worked' (Clinton 2017: 104). Clinton performed well in the televised debates and polls suggested that she had 'won' all three (Miller 2016). In contrast, Trump broke all the debate rules and conventions by blatant evasion of questions, interruptions, switching topic incoherently, repetition, and by using partial and incomplete utterances. A quantitative analysis of the linguistic performances of the politicians in the 2016 US primary debates (prior to the three presidential debates described in this section) illustrates how Trump's style departs from that of other politicians (Savoy 2018). In his study, Jaques Savoy found that Trump had the lowest score of nine candidates for 'mean sentence length' (MSL) and 'lexical density' (LD). Lexical density is a formula that expresses the 'informativeness' of a text (Biber et al. 2002) by calculating the number of 'function words' (grammatical words such as determiners, articles, modal and auxiliary verb forms) and 'lexical words' (nouns, names, adjectives, verbs, and adverbs). High lexical density indicates a more complex or more informative contribution and therefore Trump, with the lowest score (36.6) produces the least informative contributions. Trump also produces the smallest percentage of 'big words' (BW – or words of over six letters) and the lowest token to type ratio (TTR – the relationship between the vocabulary size and the number of word types). This value indicates that Trump prefers to reuse the same words and expressions, repeating his main ideas and convictions (Savoy 2018). Clinton's scores are much more moderate – but other (male) candidates score higher than her on all measures – although her scores for lexical density, big words and token to type ratio were above the mean. This indicates that, unlike Trump, her contributions reflect a more 'complex reasoning' (Savoy 2018: 157).

Example 7.8 is taken from the final part of the first televised debate (26 September 2016). Here, the moderator Lester Holt explicitly orients to gender in his question to Trump about Clinton as a 'first' woman presidential candidate and asks Trump about a comment he made in which he said that 'she didn't have the presidential look' (line 3).

Example 7.8 Trump questions Clinton's stamina in the first US televised debate in 2016[7] (Transcript)

LH = Lester Holt (moderator); HC = Hillary Clinton; DT = Donald Trump; Aud = Audience

1	LH:	Mr. Trump (.) this year secretary Clinton became the first woman nominated for
2		president by a major <u>party</u> (.) earlier this month you said she doesn't have quote (.) a
3		presidential <u>look</u> (.) she's <u>standing</u> here (.) right now (.) what did you <u>mean</u> by that
4	DT:	er she doesn't have the <u>look</u> (.) she doesn't have the <u>stam</u>ina (.) I said she doesn't have
5		the <u>STAM</u>ina (.) and (.) I <u>don't</u> believe she <u>does</u> have the <u>stam</u>ina (.) to be <u>pres</u>ident of
6		this country (.) you need tremendous <u>STAM</u>ina (.)
7	LH:	the quote [was I just don't think she has a presidential look]
8	DT:	[you have (.) WAIT a minute Lester you asked me] a question (.) <u>did</u> you ask
9		me a <u>question</u> (.) you have to be <u>able</u> (.) to ne<u>go</u>tiate (.) our <u>trade</u> deals (.) you have to be
10		able to ne<u>go</u>tiate (.) <u>that's</u> <u>right</u> (.) with Ja<u>pan</u> (.) with Saudi A<u>rab</u>ia (.) I mean can you
11		i<u>mag</u>ine we're defending Saudi A<u>rab</u>ia (.) and with <u>all</u> of the money they <u>have</u> (.) we're
12		defending them and they're not <u>pay</u>ing (.) all you have to do is <u>speak</u> to them (.) wait (.)
13		you have <u>so</u> <u>many</u> different things you have to be able to <u>do</u> (.) and <u>I</u> don't believe that

```
14              Hillary has the stamina
15     LH:      let's let her respond
16     HC:      well (.) as soon as he travels to a hundred and twelve countries and negotiates (.) a peace
17              deal (.) a cease-fire (.) a (.) release of dissidents (.) an opening of newer opportunities in
18              nations around the world or even spends eleven hours testifying (.) in front of a
19              congressional committee (.) he can talk to me about stamina (.)
20     AUD:                                                          [Applause/cheers 4 seconds]
21     DT:                                                          [the world]
22     DT:      let me tell you (.) let me tell you (.) Hillary has experience (.) but it's bad experience (.)
23              we have made so many bad deals during the last (.) [so she has got experience that I]
24     AUD:                                                    [Applause/ cheers 3 seconds
25              agree (.) but it's bad bad experience (.) whether it's the Iran deal that you're so in love
26              with where we gave them a hundred and fifty billion dollars back (.) whether it's the
27              Iran deal (.) whether it's uh anything you c (.) name (.) you almost can't name a good
28              deal I agree (.) she's got experience but it's bad experience (.) and this country can't
29              afford to have another four years of that kind of experience
30     AUD:     [CHEERS AND APPLAUSE 3 seconds]
```

This comment about Clinton not 'looking' presidential was made in an interview three weeks before the debate and had been criticised by pressure groups, such as Emily's List, who commented that Trump was 'playing the gender card' and that 'For every woman in America watching Trump lie, insult and divide his way through this election, saying a woman doesn't look "presidential" is one more reason why he is unfit to be president' (Parker 2016). The question is asked with these criticisms about Trump's attitude towards women in mind, but Trump responds by evading the question using the same grammatical structure as 'she doesn't have the look', but replacing the final word with 'she doesn't have the stamina' (lines 4–6). This has the effect of suggesting that 'stamina' and 'look' are indistinguishable when in fact they are completely unrelated concepts. When the moderator rejects and contests this evasion by explicitly stating 'The quote was "I don't think she has a presidential look"' (line 7), Trump resists this intervention by suggesting that he was not being allowed to answer the original question 'Wait a minute, Lester you asked me a question did you ask me a question' (line 8). This challenge, in the form of a question, breaks with canonical debate form in which the moderator asks the questions of the candidates and not the other way around. It serves to place Trump in the more powerful questioning role and allows him to steer the answer in a rather incoherent way to Clinton not having the 'stamina' to negotiate trade deals.

In contrast to Trump, Clinton formulates a direct and coherent response, starting with the discourse marker 'well' which seems to function more to emphasise the spontaneity of her answer than to buy time or show a 'dispreferred' response. This turn-initial 'well' is found to be the most frequent discourse marker in a selection of presidential primary debates (Sclafani 2017) although Trump is found to use this feature less than his opponents. It is suggested that the lack of 'well' at the beginning of Trump's speaking turns may help to construct him as a 'decisive' and 'straightforward' candidate (Sclafani 2017: 29). Conversely, use of 'well' by Trump's opponents may signal that they are attending to the structure of their responses in a way that signals evasion (Sclafani 2017: 29). It is notable that Clinton does not orient to the initial question (about her 'looks') but instead responds to Trump's tangential evasion that she does not have stamina (lines 15–19). In underlining her achievements as Secretary of State she shows her political and diplomatic accomplishments, and even refers to being questioned about her e-mails by a congressional committee (in October 2015). In doing so she not only displays her stamina, but also an ability to be open about potentially damaging events in her career. This response but is greeted well by the audience with applause and cheers. Trump responds with another non sequitur and shift in focus using the repetition of phrase 'let me tell you'. This time Trump creates a double topic shift from 'stamina' to 'experience' and from 'experience' to 'bad' political decisions and actions (lines 22–29). Trump repeats the adjective 'bad', a characteristic of his rhetorical style (Savoy 2018; Sclafani 2017).

Example 7.9 follows directly on from the previous example with Clinton again using the initial discourse-marker 'well' and confronting Trump.

Example 7.9 Clinton questions Trump in the first US televised debate (continued from Example 7.8; transcript)

```
31   HC:    well (.) one one thing (.) Lester is you know he tried to switch from from looks to
32          stamina (.) but this is a man who has called women pigs slobs and dogs (.) and someone
33          who has said (.) pregnancy is an inconvenience to employers (.) [who has said] women
34   DT:                                                                   [I never said that]
35   HC:    don't deserve equal pay unless they do as good [a job as men] (.)
36   DT:                                                    [didn't say that]
37   HC:    and one of the worst things he said (.) was about (.) a woman in a beauty contest (.) he
38          loves beauty contests supporting them and hanging around them (.) and he called this
39          woman Ms. Piggy (.) then he called her (.) Ms. Housekeeping because she was Latina (.)
40          Donald [she has a name (.) her name is Alicia Machado] and she has
41   DT:           [where did you find this (.) where did you find this (.) where did you find this]
42   HC:    become a U.S. citizen (.) and you [can bet she's going] to vote this November
43   DT:                                      [oh really (.) oh really] (.)
44          okay good let me just tell [you]
45   AUD:                              [Applause 1 second]
46   LH:                              [Mr. Trump] can you just take ten seconds and then we've got
47          the [final question]
48   DT:        [you know Hillary] is hitting me with tremendous commercials (.) er some of it's
49          said in entertainment (.) some of it's said (.) somebody who's been very vicious to me
50          Rosie O'Donnell (.) I said very tough things to her (.) and I think everybody would
51          agree (.) that she deserves it and nobody feels sorry for her (.) but you want to know the
52          truth (.) I was going to say (.) [something extremely] (.) rough (.) to Hillary to her
53   LH:                                     [please very quickly]
54   DT:    family and I said to myself (.) I can't do it I just can't do it (.) it's inappropriate (.) it's
55          not nice (.) but she's spent (.) hundreds of millions of dollars on negative ads on me (.)
```

56		many of which are absolutely untrue (.) they're untrue and they're misrepresentations
57		and I will tell you this Lester (.) it's not nice and I don't II don't deserve that but it's
58		certainly not a nice thing that she's done (.) it's hundreds of millions of ads and the
59		only gratifying thing is I saw the polls [come in today (.) and with all of that money]
60	LH:	[we have to move on to the final question]

First, she highlights his topic shift 'from looks to stamina' and then attacks him on his sexism. The accusation that he calls women 'pigs', 'slobs' and 'dogs' (line 2) is not new at this point, as at the first Republican debate on 6 August 2015 the journalist Megyn Kelly asked him a similar question: 'You've called women you don't like "fat pigs," "dogs," "slobs," and "disgusting animals." Does that sound to you like the temperament of a man we should elect as president?' (First Republican Primary Debate 2016). Trump responded to Kelly's question in that debate by saying that 'he didn't have time for political correctness' and that 'what I say is what I say'. He also retaliated by saying to Kelly 'I've been nice to you but I could easily not be nice to you'. This was subsequently borne out when he said of this episode that Kelly was angry, and 'had blood coming out of her eyes, blood coming out of her wherever', vilified her on Twitter and threatened to boycott further debates with her (Alter 2016). Clinton's repetition of Kelly's original question therefore interdiscursively shows support for Kelly's opposition of Trump in the previous debate and also serves to remind Trump of a previous occasion in which this line of questioning took him by surprise. Clinton continues by referring to his attitude towards pregnancy and women in the workplace. Trump responds by interrupting to repeatedly deny the accusation 'I never said that' (line 34) and 'didn't say that' (line 36). Clinton then adds to her accusations of sexism by referring to the way he described a named individual at a 'beauty pageant' which 'he loves … supporting them and hanging round them' by referring to her as 'Miss Housekeeping … Because she was Latina' thus charging Trump with racism in addition to sexism (line 39). Trump implies the claims are false by saying 'where did you find this?' (line 41). Trump then responds by saying 'Okay good', implying that he can answer the question but in a way that asserts his dominance and control over the topic using the imperative 'let me just tell you' (line 44). Then Trump completely changes the focus of Clinton's question by turning the accusation on her, that she 'is hitting me with tremendous commercials' before switching in the next moment to a partial defence of his behaviour by saying that the comments were made as 'entertainment' and as retaliation to Rosie O'Donnell, a comedian who has been 'very vicious to me' (line 49). He justifies 'saying tough things' to O'Donnell using the classic misogynistic victim-blaming phrase 'because she deserves it' (line 51) adding 'nobody feels sorry for her'. Then he attempts to vindicate himself by saying 'extremely rough to Hillary, to her family, but I just couldn't do it' (line 54). This implies that he could have been 'tougher' in his attacks on Clinton but he restrained himself, and that it was she who had done 'not a nice thing' for bringing out critical advertisements of him. This serves to allow Trump to dismiss the charges of sexism and racism by implying that they are part of a wider unfair campaign levelled against him.

The second debate took place on 9 October 2016, two days after the audio recording known as the 'Access Hollywood tape' was leaked to the press. In the recording, made in 2005, Trump says: 'when you're a star, they let you do it. You can do anything (...) grab'em by the pussy. You can do anything' and in reference to another woman saying he 'moved on her like a bitch' (Trump 2016c). This conversation in which Trump appeared to be casually referring to conducting sexual assault and in which he referred to women in demeaning and sexualised ways therefore formed part of the context of the whole of the second debate. There was widespread condemnation of the behaviour described by Trump on the tape which was described as 'illustrating rape culture' (Dirks 2016). Trump initially dismissed it as 'locker room banter', saying that 'Bill Clinton has said far worse to me on the golf course' (Trump 2016b), before issuing a video apology (Trump 2016a cited in Henderson 2016) which nevertheless maintained his relative innocence in comparison to that of Bill and Hillary Clinton: 'I've said some foolish things but there's a big difference between the words and actions of other people. Bill Clinton has actually abused women and Hillary has bullied, attacked, shamed and intimidated his victims' (Trump 2016a). In a move that was widely believed to be deflecting attention from his own sexual conduct, Trump brought women who claimed to have had affairs with Bill Clinton to the second presidential debate (Costa et al. 2016).

While a full analysis of Trump's language, attitudes and behaviour and the subsequent widespread reaction to these events falls outside the scope of this case study of Hillary Clinton (see for example Creedon 2018; Goldstein and Hall 2017; Grebelsky-Lichtman and Katz 2019; Jacobsen 2019; Maas et al. 2018; Sclafani 2017 for further analyses), it is necessary to examine how Clinton was positioned by these discourses and how she dealt with the extreme sexism and sexual aggression that they exhibit. Trump's conversation with Billy Bush is the enactment of hegemonic masculinity, as defined in Chapter 5, as a practice that shapes gender relations and strengthens fraternal networks by underlining men's dominance over women through homosocial bonding and sexual aggression. Trump attempted to defend the conversation by constructing a 'boys will be boys' discourse, downplaying the aggression to 'just' locker-room banter and disregarding or dismissing the effects on its victims. However, 'locker-room talk' itself has long been identified as a site of masculinist ideology that is conducive to sexual assault, violence against women and rape culture (Curry 1991, 1998; Kane and Disch 1993; Sanday 2007). As Deborah Cameron describes in a discussion of this episode: 'Banter is fraternal patriarchy's verbal glue. It strengthens the bonds of solidarity among male peers by excluding, Othering and dehumanising women; and in doing those things it also facilitates sexual violence' (Cameron 2016).

When Clinton faced Trump in the second debate she was therefore positioned by the context of Trump's taped conversation – as a woman and also as someone who is complicit within her own husband's sexual misconduct and her 'very large blind spot about his behaviour with other women' (Grant 2018: 107). Gender therefore figures large throughout the entire debate, but when specifically responding to a question about the 'Access Hollywood' recording in the second debate, Clinton's response broadens the discussion from the issue of the recording to a wider question about Trump's fitness to serve as President:

Example 7.10 Clinton's highlighting of Trump's attitude towards women in the second US Presidential Debate, 2016 (Transcript,[8] pronouns in bold)

1	HC:	…**we** have seen him in<u>sul</u>t women (.) **we** have seen him <u>rate</u> women (.) on their
2		appe<u>ar</u>ance (.) <u>rank</u>ing them from one to <u>ten</u> (.) **we**'ve seen him em<u>barr</u>ass women on
3		TV and on Twitter (.) **we** saw him after the first de<u>bate</u> spend nearly a <u>week</u> (.)
4		deni<u>gr</u>ating a former Miss Universe (.) in the <u>harsh</u>est most <u>person</u>al <u>terms</u> (.) so (.)
5		<u>yes</u> this <u>is</u> who Donald Trump is (.) but it's not only <u>wom</u>en and it's not only this
6		<u>vid</u>eo that raises questions about his (.) <u>fit</u>ness to be **our** President (.) because he has
7		<u>also</u> targeted immig<u>ran</u>ts (.) African-A<u>meri</u>cans (.) Lati<u>no</u>s (.) people with dis<u>abili</u>ties
8		(.) P-O-<u>W</u>s (.) <u>Mus</u>lims and so many others (.) so this is who Donald Trump is and the
9		question for **us (.)** the question (.) **our** <u>coun</u>try must answer (.) is that this is <u>not</u> who
10		**we** are (turn continues)

Although only a small extract from the full three-minute response, Example 7.10 shows Clinton's hard-hitting and direct resistance to and confrontation of Trump's sexist and racist behaviour. She uses the pronoun 'we' to include different groups within her perspective (for example 'we' women, 'we' the electorate), culminating in the final part of this extract in which she uses an inclusive pronoun three times 'the question for *us,* the question *our* country must answer is that this is not who *we* are' (lines 9–10). This use of plural, inclusive pronouns, together with collective nouns for groups of people (such as 'immigrants'; African-Americans and 'people with disabilities' (lines 7–8) contrasts with the repeated phrase 'this is who Donald Trump is' (lines 5 and 8). This serves to isolate Trump apart from the 'we' of Clinton's rhetoric, positioning him as a lone, aberrant individual and separating him entirely from the groups to which she alludes. For his part, Trump calls Clinton's response 'just

Figure 7.2 Image of Hillary Clinton and Donald Trump during the second presidential debate at Washington University in St. Louis, Missouri, 9 October 2016. (Source: Robyn Beck/Staff/Getty Images.)

words, folks' and simply reiterates the defence of the behaviour he has already given in official statements and interviews: that it was 'locker-room banter' and compares his own behaviour with that of Bill Clinton. This targeting of Bill Clinton undermines Hillary not only by the accusations themselves and her suggested complicity within them, but by excluding her and constructing her as peripheral to the masculinist networks of the golf course and the locker room in which they operate.

Trump also tried to dominate this debate physically, both with non-verbal communication as a commentary of shrugs and grimaces to accompany Clinton's contributions (Beattie 2016), and by his occupation of the space of the debating floor (see Figure 7.2). Clinton later describes Trump's actions in the debate: 'No matter where I walked, he followed me closely, staring at me. Making faces. It was incredibly uncomfortable. He was literally breathing down my neck. My skin crawled' (Clinton 2017: 136). Clinton also notes how constrained her options were in responding to Trump's invasive physical presence as 'a lot of people recoil from an angry woman, or even just a direct one' (Clinton 2017: 137). She was therefore constrained in her emotional response in a way that a man would not be (Goren 2018), and in a way that is limiting. While Clinton recognises that if she had confronted Trump about his physically dominating behaviour he would have 'gleefully' capitalised on it (Clinton 2017: 137), she still wonders if this is the appropriate response: 'Maybe I have overlearned the lesson of staying calm – biting my tongue, digging my fingernails into a clenched fist, smiling all the while, determined to present a composed face to the world' (Clinton 2017: 137). Clinton must therefore manage her opposition to Trump exceptionally carefully. Where she opposes him directly, it is in measured terms and in the strict confines of the conventional rhetoric of political debate. This is shown in the third and final debate when Trump uses hyperbolic and violent language to describe Clinton's position on later-term abortion, shown in Example 7.11.

Example 7.11 Extract from the Third Presidential Debate (19 October 2016, Nevada: Transcript, CNN 2016[9])

1	DT:	well I think it's terrible er if you <u>go</u> with what <u>Hill</u>ary is saying in the <u>ninth</u> month you
2		can take the baby (.) and <u>rip</u> (.) the baby (.) out of the <u>womb</u> (.) of the <u>moth</u>er (.) <u>just</u>
3		prior to the <u>birth</u> of the baby (.) <u>now</u> (.) <u>you</u> can say that that's ok<u>ay</u> (.) and <u>Hill</u>ary can
4		<u>say</u> that that's ok<u>ay</u> (.) but it's <u>not</u> okay with <u>me</u> (.) because <u>based</u> on what <u>she's</u>
5		saying and based on where she's going and where she's <u>been</u> (.) you can take the baby
6		and <u>rip</u> the baby out of the womb (.) in the <u>ninth</u> <u>month</u> (.) on the <u>final</u> <u>day</u> (.) and
7		that's not ac<u>cept</u>able
8	HC:	well that is <u>not</u> what happens in these cases and using that kind of er (.) <u>scare</u> rhetoric
9		is just <u>terribly</u> un<u>fortu</u>nate (.) you should <u>meet</u> with some of the women that I have
10		met with (.) women I have <u>known</u> over the course of my <u>life</u> (.) this is one of the
11		<u>worst</u> <u>possible</u> choices that <u>any</u> woman and her family has to <u>make</u> (.) and <u>I</u> do not
12		believe the government should be <u>making</u> it (turn continues)

Here Trump characterises Hillary's position as a brutal and violent one, repeating the phrase 'rip the baby out of the womb' (lines 2 and 6) and personalising this as her view 'based on what she's saying' and 'Hillary can say that's okay'. He positions himself as the person for who whom 'it is not okay' and for whom this is 'not acceptable'. Clinton responds, starting again with the discourse marker 'well' (line 8) before going on to contradict and refute his stance. She does so in a measured but direct way, alluding to his 'scare rhetoric' (line 8) and highlighting the experiences of women in that position. Her tame description of his rhetoric as 'terribly unfortunate' (line 9) contrasts strongly with Trump's violent imagery but can also be viewed as restraint borne out of the gender-based confines and constraints identified here.

7.2.3   Hillary Clinton: Gendered Stereotypes and Media Representation

Clinton has been described as straddling the line between masculinity and femininity in both the political issues she addresses and her traits as a politician (Zulli 2018). In her early career as a lawyer she has been described as displaying 'masculine' traits that did not conform to stereotypic notions of women's public speech styles, and this led to unconventional performances as US 'First Lady' when Bill Clinton became President in 1993 (Campbell 1998). Her performance at the 1996 Democratic Party Convention led to the following characterisation:

Clinton's style of public advocacy typically omits virtually all of the discursive markers by which women publicly enact their femininity. Her tone is usually impersonal, disclosing minimal information about herself; her ideas unfold deductively in the fashion of a lawyer's brief; all kinds of evidence are used, but personal examples rarely, if ever, appear, although she incorporates stories she has been told by others. She is impassioned but very rarely emotional. As she did in the congressional hearings, she may say that she speaks 'as a mother, a wife, a daughter, a sister, a woman,' but she does not assume those roles in speaking. Instead, she plays the roles for which she has been professionally trained, the roles of lawyer, advocate, and expert. She confronts adversaries and debates positions as she has done in the courtroom; she even attacks her opponents. In other words, she speaks forcefully and effectively, manifesting her competency in meeting rhetorical norms, but with few of the discursive markers that signal femininity. (Campbell 1998: 6)

Almost twenty years after this observation, Clinton still attests to 'walking a tightrope' and attempting to achieving 'balance' in respect to a number of these aspects (Clinton 2017). Yet these attempts have been largely unsuccessful with Clinton's behaviour and its subsequent representation giving textbook examples of political life on the gendered double bind. As she acknowledges:

In my experience, the balancing act women in politics have to master is challenging at every level, but it gets worse the higher you rise. If we are too tough, we're unlikeable. If we are too soft, we're not cut out for the big leagues. If we work too hard, we're neglecting our families. If we put family first, we're not serious about the work. If we have a career but no children, there's something wrong with us, and vice versa. If we want to compete for higher office, we're too ambitious. (Clinton 2017: 119)

As with May and Gillard and as identified as the 'master' gendered stereotype in Chapter 5, emotionalism figures large in representations of Clinton. She is represented as being at once 'unemotional' in some accounts (as described in the quotation from Campbell 1998) and in others she is over-emotional and displaying a lack of emotional control (Mavin et al. 2010). Clinton recognises this double bind, describing an occasion before the New Hampshire primary in 2008 as her 'famed tearful moment' when: 'I didn't even cry, not really. I was talking about how tough running for office can be (because it can be very tough), and my eyes glistened for a minute and my voice wavered for about one sentence. That was it. It became the biggest news story in America' (Clinton 2017: 123). She then continues by describing how her political opponents capitalised on this 'moment' by characterising her as a weak and ineffective leader. Clinton also recounts the impossible demands of the quest for 'authenticity' saying that: 'What could I do to be "more real"? Dance on a table? Swear a blue streak? Break down sobbing? That's not me, and if I had done any of those things, what would have happened? I'd have been ripped to pieces' (Clinton 2017: 122). It has been suggested that the demand for authenticity in politicians is a way of reinforcing gender and race boundaries. Obama received constant questions about whether he was 'authentically black' in his 2008–9 presidential campaign (Azari 2015). Sarah Palin[10] provides an interesting contrast with Clinton because she was viewed as authentic – 'feminine, maternal and folksy – but ultimately these qualities were held up as incompatible with the pursuit of higher office' (Azari 2015). In this way Palin experienced a different but similarly limiting aspect of authenticity's gendered double bind, which reduces 'both the candidate and the community in question to a narrow set of stereotypical characteristics' (Azari 2015).

The media coverage of Clinton's 2008–9 campaign was 'often hostile and the content trivialising' and 'more negative than Obama's coverage' (Ross 2017: 109). Further comparisons between the media framing of Clinton and Palin show how they were both objectified but in contrasting ways: 'Palin's attractiveness resulted in frequent and varied references to her "sexiness"; whereas, Clinton was viewed as not feminine enough in pantsuits that covered her "cankles" (thick ankles)' (Carlin and Winfrey 2009: 330). Similarly, Clinton's 2016 campaign was one in which 'discussion of her personal traits, policy positions, record of public service and health all skewed far more negative than positive' (Dolan et al. 2017). Many studies have shown how questions about her *likeability* have dominated media frames and representations of Clinton in both campaigns. In 2008, a US talk-show host said: 'Clinton reminds men of the worst characteristics of women they've encountered over their life: totally controlling, not soft and cuddly. Not sympathetic. Not understanding. Demanding, domineering, Nurse Ratched kind of thing' (Smith 2008). The archetype of the 'iron maiden' is evoked in this instance with the added horror of the character of the uncaring nurse from the film *One Flew over the Cuckoo's Nest*. In the 2016 campaign Clinton was described as being subject to 'utter evisceration by the press' (Grant 2018: 106) and 'likeability' was again brought to the fore:

Her likability continues to be an issue, and not just with Donald Trump – who called her 'such a nasty woman' during the final presidential debate – or his supporters, or establishment Republicans. She is famously disliked across party lines. A *New York Times* columnist once described her as looking 'less like a human being and more like an avatar from some corporate brand.' A *New York* magazine writer confessed she had, in the past, 'often compared [Hillary] to Darth Vader – more machine than woman' – and referenced the difficulty she 'has long had in coming across as, simply, a human being'. (Barrueco 2016)

Once again, the 'robot' or automaton metaphor comes into play and 'likeability' seems a thin smokescreen for more routine sexist ideas about women generally in authoritative positions and specifically about Clinton aspiring to the presidency and gaining toughness at the expense of her likeability. As

Clinton herself observes, the 'rightness' of a man for the role of US president is pervasive (see Chapter 1): 'It's not customary to have a woman lead or even to engage in the rough-and-tumble of politics. It's not normal – not yet. So when it happens, it often doesn't feel quite right' (Clinton 2017: 121). This 'rightness' of men and the 'wrongness' of women running for the 'top job' (also relating to Trump's claim that Clinton didn't 'look like' a president as discussed earlier) clearly has a bearing on perceptions of both authenticity and likeability: 'She has been despised and reviled not for any wrongs she has actually done but for accusations conjured to play into misogynist narratives of the unlikeable, power-hungry, conniving woman' (Grant 2018: 107). Like Gillard, Clinton has struggled to negotiate the perception that she is ambitious when 'according to deep-seated US cultural norms, ambition to professional political advancement by women in unseemly – even unwomanly' (Lawrence and Rose 2010: 93). It has also been suggested that the 'charge of unlikability did not come until she tried to get promoted to the highest office in the land' (Grant 2018: 109), and that until running for the office of president in 2015 she had ranked higher than Michelle Obama and Oprah Winfrey in the Gallup ranking of the most admired women in the world (Grant 2018: 109). Clinton's likeability was certainly challenged by Trump's crude and exaggerated displays of hyper-masculinity which presented particular challenges for her (Dolan et al. 2017). She needed to present herself as 'sufficiently masculine' in the face of Trump's macho displays without allowing voters 'to dismiss her as unladylike, as a woman who has lost touch with her more feminine side' (Dolan et al. 2017: xxiii). The level of vitriol and aggression levelled at her often centred on her morality, hence the Trump campaign slogans of 'Crooked Hillary' and 'Lock her up!'. This tapped into gendered notions of 'proper behaviour' as 'by tagging Hillary as "crooked" Trump could continuously prime voters to scrutinise and penalise her for falling short of "ladylike" behaviour while simultaneously engaging in more egregiously dishonest behaviour himself' (Dolan et al. 2017: xxv). In this way, Clinton is made a vulnerable target in what has been described as a paradox in American women's role as both 'moral guardians and suspect citizens' (Boryczka 2018: 123).

Other metaphorical characterisations of Clinton similarly express the aberrant nature of women in the political sphere, in particular that of Clinton as 'unruly woman' (Lim 2009). The unruly woman fails to be feminine in her duties as wife and mother, and also represents 'a threat to men because she aspires to be more than a Madonna or Beauty Queen' (Lim 2009: 260). Like Gillard, Clinton has been repeatedly referred to as 'bitch' and 'witch' which can be seen as types of the 'unruly woman' category (Lim 2009). The metaphor of the witch is often associated with the sound of her voice as a shrill, shrieking 'cackle', and this is a common description of Clinton's voice (Lim 2009; Romaniuk 2016). Tanya Romaniuk undertook research on the gendered framing of Hillary Clinton's laugh as a 'cackle' during her failed bid for the Democratic nomination in 2007–8. In the first part of her research, she analysed 'talk in-interaction' in order to establish the laughter patterns of politicians in broadcast interviews. She found that Clinton and all the politicians 'produce the same types of laughter (i.e. invited vs volunteered) and in the same sequential positions' (Romaniuk 2016: 542). In other words, laughter in these situations is a 'generic interactional practice, as opposed to one that only Clinton engages in' (2016: 543). In the second part of her research, Romaniuk analysed media representations of Clinton's laugh (or talk 'out-of interaction'). She found that Clinton's laugh was represented as a 'cackle' in a range of media representations, and suggests that: 'Both the negative semantic prosody of the term "cackle" and its indirect association with witches were simultaneously evoked by the term's use. For example, numerous representations alluded to or depicted Clinton as the Wicked Witch of the West (from *The Wizard of Oz*), a fictional character, but also a quintessential emblem of women politicians who occupy powerful leadership positions' (Romaniuk 2016: 543). Romaniuk shows that even though Clinton's laugh can be demonstrated to be a generic linguistic practice, it nevertheless is perceived and represented in gendered and sexist ways by the media (Clinton's image is in the first one to appear in a Google image search for the word 'cackle'). She concludes that there may be 'a range of other implicit and indirect processes through which women are culturally coded as gendered subjects, even when the practices they engage in and the actions they produce have little or nothing to do with gender' (2016: 547).

Clinton's voice also came under scrutiny from the time that her husband first ran for the Democratic nomination for president in 1992 when 'voters seemed put off by her high-powered Yale law school credentials, clipped Northern accent and her hippy wardrobe' (Stanley 1992). This continued throughout her political career, earning the nickname 'Shrillary' for what many perceived to be her loud, shrill 'yelling' voice (Khazan 2016). Some studies have contradicted this, however, showing that Clinton's pitch and loudness is average for her age and gender, and that she tends to lower her voice as her speech progresses, whereas Trumps raises his pitch as the speech progresses (Khazan 2016). The preoccupation with Clinton's voice was recognised by some as a sexist rather than a substantive criticism, and commentators were criticised for discussing Clinton's 'tone of voice' rather than 'what truly matters' because 'only a man's voice sounds like it tells important truths' (Ghitis 2016).

7.2.4   Summary

The amount of criticism and anger directed towards Hillary Clinton in the 2016 election appeared to be at odds with her successful performances and carefully managed campaign. As shown earlier, she managed the 'tightrope' of double binds relating to her emotionality, ambition, stamina and 'toughness' for the job and was said to have 'won' all three televised debates. Her linguistic performances in these events were measured and professional, adhering to expected discursive norms and containing the appropriate balance of confrontational and consensual rhetoric. She experienced no catastrophic media performances, avoided major gaffes and errors, and was prepared to face an unusual political adversary: Donald Trump.

> It quickly became evident that normal debate prep wouldn't work this time. Trump wouldn't answer any question directly. He was rarely linear in his thinking or speaking. He digressed into nonsense and then digressed even more. There was no point in refuting his arguments like it was a normal debate – it was almost impossible to identify what his arguments even were, especially since they changed minute-to-minute. (Clinton 2017: 105)

Despite the careful preparation, Clinton continued to receive negative judgements for all aspects of her appearance and behaviour. The representation of Clinton's voice as 'yelling' and 'shrill' and her laugh a witch's cackle, despite evidence that these qualities align within the normal ranges of volume and pitch, exemplify the workings of discriminative processes. After her 2008 loss to Barack Obama there was some criticism that she should have run a more 'feminine' campaign (Dolan et al. 2017; Lawrence and Rose 2010). In 2016 her campaign responded to this criticism by concentrating on her reputation which 'spoke to women's perceived strengths as natural collaborators', by focusing on policy issues that particularly affect women, and by underlining her potential position as the first woman president of the US (Dolan et al. 2017: xxiii). Despite these efforts, and against the expectations of many, Clinton failed win the election even though she secured almost three million more popular votes than Trump. She cannot therefore be configured straightforwardly as a loser, but it is likely that the way she negotiated her femininity played a part in her electoral loss, as one voter expresses it: 'She doesn't wear a dress ever … She'll probably show up in a pantsuit for the inaugural. She's not a typical woman – she's not soft. She's so power-hungry, which is not becoming of a woman' (Ball 2016 cited in Dolan et al. 2017: xxiii). Detailed research into voter attitudes in the 2016 US election suggests that sexism – particularly hostile sexism (displaying negative attitudes towards women who violate traditional norms) – played a role in voting outcomes of the election (Bock et al. 2017). Further, it appears that Clinton's accomplishments and experience in high-status roles made her the 'quintessential backlash candidate' who encountered discrimination for failing to act 'gender-normative manner' (Bock et al. 2017: 189–92). There is therefore some evidence to back up the opinion that: 'Had she been a man, I believe she would have won' (Grant 2018: 108). Further discussion of the issues raised by the case studies of Theresa May, Julia Gillard and Hillary Clinton is continued in the concluding chapter of this book (Chapter 8).

8 Women, Language and Politics
Gains and Losses

8.1 Introduction

In order to investigate the workings of gender and language in politics over a twenty-year period from 1998 to 2018, I have drawn from a wide range of linguistic data to explore the participation of women and men in political positions and institutions, mainly in the UK. In this chapter I return to the questions I posed in Chapter 1. Here I summarise the ways in which these questions have been addressed and present conclusions gained from analyses of data across the different chapters of this book. I also further these discussions by suggesting ways in which conditions for women in these political institutions (and more broadly in other political contexts) may have evolved by referring to more recent events, including those discussed in the case studies of Theresa May, Julia Gillard and Hillary Clinton in Chapters 6 and 7. In order to address these questions across all of the data covered in the book, I have organised the sections of this chapter into themes that were common across the different institutions and case studies.

8.2 Taking, Holding and Yielding the Floor

8.2.1 Turn-Taking on the Official or 'Legal' Debate Floor

One of the main questions addressed in the book is: how do women in politics participate in debate forums, particularly in those that are historically male-dominated, and in which women are still vastly under-represented and men over-represented? The analyses of the two different data sets discussed in Chapters 3 and 4 (the HoC in 1998–2001 and the devolved parliaments plus the HoC from 2009 to 2011) addressed this question by closely examining the debate floors and identifying the different rules and norms governing their operation. The progression of 'legal' debate turns (as recorded in the official reports of the institutions) offers opportunities for assessing participation according to these official turn-taking and floor-holding systems. Perhaps the most significant finding in these quantitative assessments was that women and men (in all but one of the institutions) spoke in proportion to their numbers overall. In other words, more or less across the board, women's and men's participation in the 'legal' progress of the debate floor reflected their proportional share of seats within the parliaments. This finding is surprising because the vast majority of research literature across other disciplines shows that routinely women lose their share of the floor to men and that this pattern is replicated across many different public and workplace contexts over time (for example Eakins and Eakins 1976; Edelsky 1981; Kathlene 1995; Karpowitz and Mendelberg 2014; Carter et al. 2018). It is not possible to make any strong claims against these other findings because the numbers in this study were only intended to give *qualitative impressions* of participation and so a much larger and more rigorous investigation would be necessary to show significance. Also, the finding does not attend to variation within groups (amongst talkative and silent women and men). However, when turns were classified and examined in more detail across the devolved parliaments and the HoC in Chapter 4, the pattern of proportional participation according to gender remained valid in nearly all of the turn-taking categories. This suggests that whether a politician is a man or a woman does not predict their share of the overall progression of legal debate turns, and indeed, the more detailed classification of debate turns in Chapter 4 points away from gender as a determining factor in institutional talking time. When turns were classified into 'allocated' and 'spontaneous' categories, the multiple factors affecting speaking turns became more apparent. Any of the interconnected factors listed in Table 8.1 can affect the uptake of speaking turns.

In addition to the factors represented in Table 8.1, more precise cultural, contextual and local factors can also play a part. For example, the rate at which MPs rebel against their party and how that rebellion relates to party discipline and individual participation can also be significant – here 'one might expect Members with high rebellion rates to participate more in a debate than those with low rebellion rates' (Catalano 2009: 56). Of course, gender may well play a part in the *likelihood* of MPs to rebel, or to be in more senior positions or elected to serve on committees and so on. So, while there does not appear to be a direct link between gender and participation in terms of the legal progression of debate turns, more indirect links are likely to operate through these other factors. It cannot be denied that gender is a structuring principle in political institutions, particularly those such as the HoC with historic and continued patterns of male domination. This underlines the need for research methods that are sensitive to contextual factors in order to capture and examine the complexity of gender within these interrelated aspects of participation.

One of the most interesting findings from this analysis involved the National Assembly for Wales (NAW), which has four main political parties. The NAW had the highest proportion of women representation across all the institutions (47 per cent in the 2009–11 term), yet women took only 32 per cent of all the

Table 8.1 *Possible factors affecting the uptake of speaking turns in political institutions*

Seniority	Roles as ministers, junior ministers, 'shadow' ministers determine speaking about particular areas of responsibility; junior or 'backbench' politicians have fewer chances to speak, apart from those types of debate or parts of debate interaction specifically designed to incorporate more junior members.
Leadership	Linked to seniority, but with specific speaking roles for the Prime Minister/First Ministers and Leaders of the Opposition.
Length of time in office	This factor is likely to affect familiarity with the official and unofficial rules, and long-standing MPs will have reputations and relationships built over time (e.g. with the Speaker) which may affect their ability to gain a speaking turn.
Committee membership	Roles as 'experts' on particular topics according to committee membership and involvement.
Incumbency	Politicians' positions as incumbents or as opposition parties affects the degree to which they oppose, scrutinise or support other members (for example, in PMQs).
Attendance rates	Members with high attendance rates may participate more than those with low attendance rates (Catalano 2009); many factors can affect attendance, including sick leave and parental leave.

speaking turns. What might account for the disparity in percentages? Section 4.4 suggests that women spoke less because of a combination of structural factors. The first factor was that the NAW has a high proportion of 'allocated turns' (turns with relatively fixed allocations according to party, seniority and role) and a low proportion of 'spontaneous' turns (turns that allow members to autonomously elect to speak). The second structural factor was that although the Welsh Conservative Party had thirteen members and occupied 21 per cent of assembly seats, it had only a single woman member. With four main parties present it might be expected that the Welsh Conservative Party would be assigned approximately 25 per cent of the allocated turns. The fact that the majority of turns are allocated, together with the lack of a proportional allocation of women AMs to one quarter of the Welsh Conservative turns accounted partially for the deficit. Combined with the fact that all of the presiding officers (moderators) in this sample of proceedings in the NAW were men[1] created the conditions in which the equal distribution of turns among men and women in the assembly was not achieved. This has ramifications for the 'critical mass theory' (Dahlerup 1988), which would predict that out of all the institutions investigated for the book, it would be the NAW – with its near parity of men and women – that would achieve the greater participation of women. I return to this discussion in Section 8.3 when considering possible factors that cause a political institution to be more egalitarian and encourages the participation of all its members.

Apart from the example in the NAW, the finding that in most categories of legal speaking turns men and women spoke in proportion to their numbers overall – despite recurrent findings to the contrary in several contexts – requires further discussion. It perhaps suggests the canonical form of the debate simply functions according to the ideals against which it was devised, to 'permit the equalization of turns' (Sacks et al. 1974: 730). Certainly, apart from the issues of distribution identified in the NAW and ruling out overt discrimination against members (for example, the moderator consistently refusing to call a particular speaker or group of speakers to take a turn), the legal floor of the debate turn-taking system seems to function in egalitarian ways. However, there were some smaller differences between different types of legal speaking turns with the most equitable type of turn being that of the straightforward 'giving a speech' variety. There was slight variation in asking questions across the institutions with men asking proportionately more questions than women across the different institutions in the 2009–11 data (by 10 per cent in the NAW; 5 per cent in the NIA; and 2 per cent in both the SP and the HoC, see Table 4.3), but not in the 1998–2001 HoC data (see Table 3.1). This possible difference should not be surprising, given that men have been found to be two and a half times more likely than women to ask questions in a sample of 250 academic seminars in twenty countries (Carter et al. 2018). However, as asking questions in parliament is not spontaneous and relies on allocation, the usefulness of parallels with other spontaneous contexts is limited. As noted in the descriptions of the debate floor, the legal floor can be impinged upon by rule-breaking and illegal interventions and this is discussed in Section 8.2.2.

8.2.2   Turn-Taking on the Unofficial or 'Illegal' Debate Floor

Making an illegal intervention in a debate can be thought of as an extremely powerful interactional move, where power is viewed as control over a scarce resource – the debate floor. In Chapter 3, I examined the illegal floor in detail to identify the different types of illegal interventions ranging from minimal (but nevertheless off-putting) interventions – including 'sledging', shouting out, heckling or 'barracking' a speaker – to the more invasive forms of illegal intervention. The most invasive form is a three-part structure comprised of an initial statement by the MP giving the speech, followed by an illegal challenge from an interrupting MP, and an immediate response from the initial MP. This type of illegal challenge directly impinges on the legal progression of debate turns because the interrupting MP manages to substantively occupy the legal debate floor (and this is marked officially by the recording of these interventions in the Official Reports). The most significant finding in relation to illegal interventions was in the 1998–2001 HoC data where it was found that men and not women made the vast majority of illegal interventions. This finding was repeated in the 2009–11 data when the HoC was included for comparative purposes with the devolved UK institutions. The close analysis of five debates in the 1998–2001 data showed that men made 90 per cent of the illegal interventions, and in the 2009–11 data men took 52 per cent of attributable illegal interventions, and women just 1 per cent (with 47 per cent not attributable to an identifiable speaker). This pattern was not replicated in the other UK institutions, with a much greater proportion of attributable illegal interventions made by women in all the devolved institutions than seen in the HoC (see Figure 4.7). When I analysed the debate floor more closely in each institution it was clear that women routinely took part in the most extreme forms of interactional rule-breaking in the NIA, the SP and the NAW – where they not only engaged in three-part illegal exchanges but also resisted and challenged the moderators when instructed to stop (see Examples 4.3–4.6) – but this was not the case in the HoC. Women in the HoC also seemed to eschew breaking rules relating to other practices such as filibustering which make much of ironic verbal play with the debate rules. I suggested that in the HoC a combination of factors, including sexist humour and its role in the reinforcement of fraternal networks (see Section 8.3) lead to women being involved only as peripheral members of the CoP. They are positioned as interlopers and bound to prove their worthiness by attention to symbolic capital through their adherence to the debate rules. The more recent analyses of Prime Minister Theresa May's parliamentary performances show her to be in a paradoxical position. Although ostensibly the most powerful individual in the parliament, she still seems to be positioned peripherally by collective responses (laughter and shouting) from her own party and the opposition, and particularly in relation to the more sexist humorous exchanges such as the 'Mrs Bone' example (see Example 6.10).

8.3 Adversarial Language and Ideological Beliefs about Gender and Speech Styles in Politics

The analysis of adversarial language in the HoC in Chapter 3 is central to the examination of women's performances in political contexts because of the strongly- and widely-held beliefs in the gendered 'different voice' ideology discussed in detail in Chapter 5. It has also been claimed that the adversarial political system reinforces the macho logic of appropriateness in parliaments, and that women are disadvantaged by this (Crewe 2014a: 677). The analysis of parliamentary data in Chapters 3 and 4, of Theresa May's performances in PMQs in Chapter 6, and the confrontational ways in which Julia Gillard and Hillary Clinton resist sexism in critical gendered moments in Chapter 7, all show that women and men both use the most adversarial features in these highly ritualised displays. In the HoC, there is some evidence to show that overall women MPs ask fewer adversarial questions than men, and that men ministers give more adversarial responses than women ministers. This is also borne out by other studies showing that women MPs in the HoC are less than half as likely to ask 'unhelpful' questions when they are in opposition than their male counterparts, although they were as likely to ask helpful questions when they are in government (Bates et al. 2014). Perhaps this is in part due to the different attendant risks for women performing publicly in counter-stereotypic ways and managing competing expectations linked to ideological beliefs about how women should use language. As mentioned in Chapter 5, negative assessments of women who behave in dominant, agentive or possibly 'unhelpful' ways can lead to any such behaviour being linked negatively to the 'master stereotype' of emotion (Brescoll 2016). Adversarial women can be thought of as over-emotional or too angry or aggressive when using the full range of strategies in the political repertoire and this could provide a disincentive for behaving in these ways. The ramifications of these actions are not easy to pin down, but as identified in Chapter 7, these actions are likely to have played a part in the political losses experienced by Julia Gillard and Hillary Clinton. Further, for some women in CoPs such as the HoC, behaving in adversarial ways constitutes a kind of gendered rule-breaking which can incur negative appraisals. Certainly, the dichotomous and essentialising range of behaviours associated with such clear-cut beliefs in competitive men and cooperative women do not fit the complexities of political situations in which all is strategic. Seemingly consensual moves (such as Corbyn using personal questions from the electorate in PMQs in Chapter 6) can function competitively, and personal attacks (such as on Michael Fabricant's hair in Example 3.4) can be used collaboratively to strengthen collective bonds. This was also found to be the case in our analysis of UK televised election debates in 2015 in which tactical collaboration between women leaders was combined with competitive and assertive moves (Cameron and Shaw 2016: 114).

Adversarial norms are stereotypically associated with men, as are the 'Punch and Judy' nature of speech events like televised debates and PMQs in the HoC. This connection between adversarial styles and masculinity certainly warrants more detailed research and investigation. I am aware that men in politics are rarely asked: why did you call Winterton a 'silly man'? (as in Example 3.2) or, why did you bray uncontrollably at the Prime Minister in PMQs? The lack of such questions contributes to the normalising of these behaviours to 'the way politics are done' and shifts the focus from men's aberrant behaviour to women's (possibly more reasonable) avoidance of the petty, name-calling aspects of these events. However, the devolved institutions of the UK were also found to be adversarial, yet they did not seem to operate in the same exclusionary ways as in Westminster, with men and women viewing these as shared norms. This was also found by Rosa Malley's ethnographic work in the SP and the HoC, noting that 'although behaviour may look similar in both parliaments, their

Members experience them differently' (2012: 716). In the SP, ritualised adversarial acts are traceable to a shared repertoire from the origin of the institution, rather than being associated with the 'historical dominance of upper-class white men' (Malley 2012: 716) as in the HoC.

Part of the difficulty in interrogating these adversarial norms is that they have multiple functions and forms. One of these is the democratic function of scrutiny: the ability to hold the prime minister and the government to account for their actions and policies. For example, to simply give an opposing view could be considered adversarial, but would fall on the respectful and logical side of the adversarial scale. We could also consider the rather impolite move of repeatedly asking politicians the same question in a way that exposes their evasion and puts pressure on them to answer. This also fulfils the scrutiny function, but perhaps falls on the more purposeful (and possibly more beneficial) side of the scale of adversarial behaviours. This approach is often associated with political interviews. Some in the HoC may feel the same function is being met by the theatrical eye-rolling, head-shaking and puerile insults hurled across the floor of the debating chamber at an opponent. These are the types of macho moves that normalise name-calling in ways that provide an atmosphere in which sexist comments can abound without censure (Collier and Raney 2018). To make a distinction between these sets of behaviours might enable the separation of one, in order to help identify the other as unproductive and unnecessary. Trudy Govier (1999) makes such a distinction between 'minimal adversariality' on the one hand, which she sees as a 'basic level' of 'respectful argumentation', and 'ancillary adversariality' on the other or the 'hostility, name-calling, rudeness, intolerance and quarrelsomeness that can infuse argument situations' (Govier 1999: 245). Govier's distinction has been criticised because her notion of 'minimal adversariality' ignores the gendered nature of what might be considered 'respectful' (Hundleby 2013; Rooney 2010). However, the idea of separating productive and destructive aspects of adversarial argumentation might be useful because it offers ways of hiving off the type of destructive adversariality that is particularly associated with hypermasculinity in some contexts. In doing so, it could open up more productive adversarial forms for a wider range of speakers.

8.4   Gender, Language and Institutional Change

8.4.1   *Progress and Change in the UK House of Commons*

The ideological belief in women's consensual and cooperative 'different voice' has led to expectations about the civilising difference that women will make when they enter male-dominated forums (Walsh 2001). The fact that overwhelming evidence suggests that no such monolithic style exists, and that women and men draw on a range of styles – some stereotypically coded masculine and some feminine – does not seem to diminish the strength of the prediction. Ethnographic interviews with politicians reflect this, with men and women politicians displaying a range of opinions about gendered differences in speech styles that conform to these stereotypes (see Chapters 3 and 4). In spite of these beliefs, there is no evidence to suggest that women civilise political forums when their numbers increase. For example, the work of Bates and colleagues (2014) shows that PMQs in the HoC have become more adversarial with time, and that even in 1997 when women's numbers rose at the sharpest rate ever, interruptions and adversarial questions also rose. Again, this is in the face of a continued *belief* in women's civilising influence – for example, Ed Milliband (a senior Labour politician and LO between 2010 and 2015) is quoted as saying that 'changing the composition of the HoC does help' and that PMQs are 'less bad than it was' (*The Telegraph* 2011, cited in Bates et al. 2014: 274) regardless of evidence to the contrary.

PMQs offer an intriguing test case for examining institutional change, even though successive leaders and senior parliamentarians have vowed to overcome the adversarial norms of the event, the highly ritualistic and formulaic performances of all the members persist over time. John Bercow, Speaker of the HoC from 2009 to 2014, wrote to all party leaders in 2014 asking them to put a stop to 'orchestrated barracking' and the 'yobbery and public school twittishness' associated with PMQs (Watt 2014). David Cameron (PM between 2010 and 2016 and LO from 2005 to 2010) confessed to failing in his aim to end 'Punch and Judy' politics, saying: 'The quieter tone I'd hoped we might be able to have, the better discussion of politics at Prime Minister's Questions, doesn't work' (Kirkup 2008). Recent research shows that LO Jeremy Corbyn's aim to 'do things differently' has led to more consensual exchanges (Bull and Waddle 2019; Fetzer and Weizman 2018; Waddle et al. 2019), and this is borne out by the analysis of May–Corbyn PMQs exchanges in Chapter 6. However, the longer term effects remain to be seen: (1) whether Corbyn becomes more adversarial over the course of his tenure – a common pattern in PMQs (Bates et al. 2014; Waddle et al. 2019); (2) whether these consensual moves have any lasting effects beyond his time in office as LO; and (3) whether exchanges will revert to the more characteristic 'Punch and Judy' norms with successive pairings.

Kanter's classic (1977) work 'Men and Women of the Corporation' describes this imperviousness to change in male-dominated institutions as linked to well-established power hierarchies that constitute 'self-perpetuating self-sealing systems – with links that can be broken only from outside' (1977: 249). Lovenduski (2014a: 19) notes that the 'well-established norms of appropriateness resist changes in the gender regime'. This certainly seems to be the case in the HoC with attempts to address the serious and pervasive atmosphere of sexism, sexual harassment and bullying, as discussed in Chapter 5. Some advances have been made in that a new parliament-wide behaviour code was agreed to in July 2018 and procedures for making complaints and obtaining support have been put in place (Kelly 2018). However, the subsequent report, on an 'Independent Inquiry into Bullying and Harassment of House of Commons Staff' by Dame Laura Cox was published in October 2018, and this found that there was 'pervasive abuse' amongst MPs and HoC staff in an institutional culture of 'deference, subservience, acquiescence and silence' (Cox 2018: 4). Other events also point to the institutional and political resistance to changing this culture and the failure to take such behaviour seriously. For example, two Conservative Party MPs who had been suspended from their party on allegations of sexually inappropriate conduct were reinstated in order to vote in a 'no confidence' ballot in Theresa May's leadership on 15 December 2018.

Despite these pervasive and seemingly immutable aspects of HoC culture, it should also be noted that there *have* been changes in the communicative norms of the HoC over time and some of these relate to gender. After the 2015 general election, the new intake of MPs (in particular fifty-six new SNP MPs) started to applaud in the chamber and although the Speaker forbid them from clapping at the time (Wheeler 2015), this behaviour still happens and is evident in Example 5.6 when the Speaker tells off Boris Johnson for being sexist. It is now (in 2019 – amid long, bitter and intractable debates on the UK leaving the EU) possible to hear women's voices amongst what used to be a distinctly male-only collective sound of jeers and shouts in more rowdy moments in the HoC chamber. It sounds incongruous to hear the 'braying' sound of 'hear hear' articulated in a woman's voice, because it so strongly connotes a masculine sound of approval or disapproval. Single-word heckling from women is also audible in the chamber and this has changed since the ethnographic observations were made for the projects presented in Chapters 3 and 4. We also know from recent personal accounts that women heckle and behave in these highly adversarial and stereotypically masculine ways. Hazarika and Hamilton's (2018) 'insiders' account of PMQs makes the point that 'women also shout' (2018: 218) and give examples of much more strategic and sustained attacks by women. For example, they quote Angela Eagle, a senior Labour woman MP, describing how she and other senior Labour MPs targeted David Cameron in PMQs:

'It's a pretty terrible thing to have as a Prime Minister, to have such a visible tell, but he would go red in the face.' Angela Eagle told us, 'The red used to go in a line all the way up, and you could see that he was losing it, and he would go bright red in a line, and so obviously you did your best to get him to do that.' (Hazarika and Hamilton 2018: 219)

It appears then, that women's participation in these more destructive or 'ancillary' and highly masculinised forms of adversarial discourse is apparent in

2019 in ways that it was not in 1999 or 2009. Rather than 'civilizing' male spaces it could be that women are adopting the discursive, masculinist norms of the institution. This could be a strategy adopted by women to negotiate their peripheral status as interlopers in this CoP, although this may position them in disempowered ways: 'The question for our times is how the "other" can exist without making the "other" the same. At the moment we have a situation which at best says you can enter and be promoted so long as you mimic and masquerade acceptable versions of femininity and "black" bodies' (Puwar 2004b: 77). It would be interesting to investigate whether women's participation extends to the other areas that have been identified as linguistic practices that are used exclusively or mainly by men in the HoC in Chapter 3. However, it does not appear from contemporary observations of HoC proceedings that women are collaborating with men to produce humour in ways that challenge the most authoritative members, or that they are ironically breaking and playing with the debate rules, as in the case of filibustering. As discussed in Chapters 5 and 6, these displays appear to have functions relating to homosocial bonding and the strengthening of fraternal networks, and there is nothing to suggest in the analysis of Theresa May's recent parliamentary performances in Chapter 6 that women – even the most powerful leaders – can break into this particular interactional game. In contrast, women in all the devolved institutions of the UK seem to participate in the full range of these practices, and there do not appear to be any that are performed exclusively by men – to the exclusion of women – as they are in the HoC.

8.4.2   Progress and Change in the UK's 'New' Devolved Institutions: What Makes an Institution More Egalitarian?

As discussed in detail in Chapter 4 and in Section 8.4.1, the examples of interaction in the SP, the NAW and the NIA show that women politicians in these institutions engage in the full range of discursive norms including using adversarial language, rule-breaking to gain the floor, challenging authoritative figures such as the First Minister or the presiding officer/Speaker; and engaging in sexualised humour with men (see Example 4.1). However, women in the assemblies are still subject to sexist comments and negative assessments by their peers for behaving in counter-stereotypic ways, as shown in the ethnographic interview data reported in Chapter 4, where women were viewed negatively for engaging in 'unladylike behaviour' such as barracking.

Although each of the three devolved institutions have distinct cultures, certain commonalities can be drawn between them to answer the question: what makes an institution more egalitarian? The first answer was evident from the outset: the more diverse an institution is from the start, the more likely it is to promote an egalitarian ethos, because there is no hierarchy of importance related to a sense of belonging or ownership for its members. This does seem to be the case in the devolved institutions in relation to gender as politicians in the SP and the NAW either characterised their institutions as gender neutral (in the NAW) or 'feminine' (in the SP). This is in sharp contrast to both the NIA and the HoC which were characterised by their members as highly masculinised spaces. While the devolved institutions exhibited diversity from the beginning in relation to gender (albeit minimally in the case of the NIA with only 17 per cent of women members), they all lack racial and ethnic diversity and this effectively excludes black, Asian and minority ethnic (BAME) politicians from being originators of the institutions. This is significant because it is likely to position BAME politicians in the same ways as women interlopers in the HoC, simply because there is no shared history of membership from the beginning.

The fact that the NIA is like the HoC in terms of the masculinised culture shows that there are many different dimensions to the gendering of institutions beyond different groups being present from the beginning. Gendered discourses about women and work were evident in the ethnographic interviews, with MLAs reporting comments such as 'My husband shouts at me as well and I don't take any notice of him either' (see Section 4.5). Similarly, a Sinn Féin woman MLA reported that the male leader of a Unionist party made directly sexist comments to her in the chamber, saying 'you should be home doing the dishes'. These gendered discourses of subservient women, domestic relationships and normalised male aggression were more prevalent in the NIA than in the other parliaments. The complex political sectarian landscape in Northern Ireland has been claimed to have played a part in women's political marginalisation. Women's equality has not been of political concern because of the 'primary focus on a movement for equal rights for Catholics' (Walsh 2001: 112). To attempt to counter this, 'transversal' grassroots feminist activism in such groups as the 'Northern Ireland Women's Coalition' (NIWC) aimed to suppress 'horizontal' differences, particularly according to religious allegiances 'in order to pursue common goals as *women*' in the run up to the Northern Ireland peace process in 1996 (Walsh 2001: 114). However, this type of feminist activism has been unable to flourish in the consociational political system put into place as part of the Good Friday Agreement of 1998. This system does not try to transcend divisions but 'operates from a realistic recognition of society's fragmentation and an appreciation of its dominant discourses of *nationalism, conflict* and *realism*' (Murtagh 2008: 22 italics in original). In this way, recognition of societal division is embedded into all areas of political life as part of the resolution of conflict, but this mitigates against the cross-community initiatives upon which previous grass-roots feminist activism was based.

Apart from these wider and regionally specific political and cultural concerns, other more tangible differences exist between the parliaments. The size of the institutions is a characteristic that seems to affect the behaviour of its members, with smaller chambers leading to more personalised but also more personally accountable interactions on the debate floor. As noted in Chapter 4, according to AMs, the 'human scale' of the NAW with its 60 members meant that 'you can't detach yourself from the person you are attacking'. This can have multiple effects however, with interviewees in the NAW claiming that the small size of the chamber made adversarial interaction less likely. Yet historically, some politicians (such as Winston Churchill) reportedly advocated small, compact chambers precisely to enact confrontation while seeing the 'whites of the opponents' eyes' (Goodsell 1988; Parkinson 2012: 111). However, this confrontational approach is thought to be rare, and it has been concluded that smaller chambers lead to 'good deliberation – respectful, mutual, rational' (Parkinson 2012: 112).

The NAW and the SP both had new purpose-built parliamentary premises for the new devolved institutions and with this came the opportunity to build political spaces that embodied the egalitarian ideals of the new institutions. It is a commonly held belief by politicians, academics and members of the public alike that the *shape* of a chamber is a causal factor in making an assembly confrontational or, indeed, more egalitarian. This belief holds that a 'horseshoe', circular or 'fan' shaped chamber is more conducive to consensual, fair debate, and the newly built NAW and the SP are both examples of this type of chamber (see images in Chapter 4). In contrast, chambers with rows of opposing straight benches where two sides face each other are thought to promote more pugilistic, confrontational interaction. The HoC and the NIA both inhabit this category of debating chamber. On the face of it then, the UK institutions that have been found to be less masculinised and to have a more egalitarian ethos (the NAW and the SP) are also those that have this circular style chamber. Those that have been found to be more masculinised and hostile to women's participation are those that have oppositional arrangements (the HoC and the NIA).

However, ethnographic observations and analyses of linguistic interaction challenge this rather simplistic notion of physical layout and its relation to political culture. As reported in Chapter 4, there is evidence in the SP that the First Minister adapted the physical layout of the chamber to fit the interactional needs of the speech event: he requested an additional microphone so that he could turn and face his opponents in the chamber in First Minister's Question Time. This suggests that the speech event and the pugilism inherent in its form and function – wholly inherited from Westminster – determined the behaviour. The form of the event dictated changes in the physical space rather than the 'circular' physical space overwhelming the adversarial conventions of the form. Academic literature, while not prolific on this subject, agrees that there is no systematic, but only anecdotal, evidence for a causal link between physical layout of a chamber and the consensual or confrontational ethos or culture of an assembly (Goodsell 1988; Parkinson 2012). John Parkinson (2012: 107) notes that the pursuit of evidence to support this 'form-behaviour nexus' is not worthwhile as 'parliamentary punch-ups' have only occurred in 'consensual', circular chambers (Parkinson 2012: 106). The fact that 'there is no evidence that merely changing the seating arrangement within a given assembly space will have an effect on behaviour in that space' (Parkinson 2012: 108) seems to consign this widely held and influential belief to the status of myth. This is supported by more recent observations of FMQs in the SP in that they appear, if anything, to be becoming *more* confrontational, more conventionalised and more like the Westminster events over time, in particular by using more formal forms of address. One interviewee observed that addressing each other using just a first name was prevalent at the beginning of the parliament in 1999 but seemed to becoming less frequent with MSPs increasingly using surnames and more formal address forms. The confrontational atmosphere in the NIA, including its hostility to women, is therefore not because of the layout of the chamber but rather due, at least in part, to the complex historic and divisive traditions that have marginalised concerns about women's equality. Unlike the other devolved assemblies, the NIA did not start with a political and cultural 'clean slate' in the same way as the NAW and the SP. Of course, they all have political and institutional traditions and histories, but none as complex and fraught as that of the NIA.

Given the lack of evidence for behavioural impacts due to the shape of parliamentary chambers, it is interesting that potentially much more relevant factors about debate interaction were all but ignored in the design of the new institutions. The close analysis of debate interaction and informal and formal institutional rules in Chapters 3 and 4 suggest that even small variations in the minutiae of debate proceedings can have unpredictable consequences on the equitable progression of debate turns. For example, the decision to *time* debate contributions in order to allow more speakers to contribute (a decision based on an egalitarian ethos) can lead to fewer give way interventions. Thus, speakers do not allow themselves to be held to account for fear of losing speaking time. Arguably this *reduces* both participation and accountability in debates. Another consequence of timing debate turns is the increase in bogus points of order (faux formal complaints made to the moderator during the proceedings) where politicians use this as a mechanism for getting their contributions onto the debate floor and into the official report, finding they had no time to do so given the restrictions. The act of pretending to have a complaint and demanding the cessation of the proceedings of the whole parliament to attend to it, falls into the category of authority-challenging and key-manipulating behaviours like 'filibustering' (see Section 3.4). These are precisely the types of moves where prior inequities hold sway and it is not all members, but only the most powerful and the most 'at home' that feel they can enact them. I am not making this point to conclude that debate turns should not be timed, but rather to illustrate how an entire dimension of political event design which acts as a mechanism for participation tends to be overlooked. In this way the inclusion of particular speech events – such as versions of PMQs – in the new devolved institutions casts a long shadow and transports Westminster culture along with the interactional conventions into these 'new' spaces. An 'ideal' parliament might therefore attend to the details of these interactional rules or 'standing orders' in ways that take these factors into account, including the ratio of 'allocated' to 'spontaneous' turns identified in Chapter 4 as affecting politicians' opportunities for participation. Research in political science on 'participatory spaces' (for example Asenbaum 2019b; Smith 2009) offer promising developments in this regard. Hans Asenbaum (2019b) suggests that physical, social and discursive aspects of spatiality should be considered together as 'assemblages' in order to understand their democratic function and potential for equality and participation. This seems to have the potential to be a model with which to address spatial relations in all their complexity.

8.5   Future Directions for Research into Gender, Language and Politics in Institutions

8.5.1   Interdisciplinary Research and Parliamentary Reform

Undertaking interdisciplinary research – in this case, sociolinguistics and politics – has certain benefits and constraints, and the constraints lie wholly in the practical difficulties of covering a vast amount of theoretical and empirical research across two different disciplines. The benefits are from the cross-fertilisation of ideas from one discipline to another, gaining a new perspective based on shared common ground. In this way, sociolinguists can view parliamentary institutions as just one context for examining power dynamics and gender in workplace interaction (along with business meetings, law courts, and emergency telephone calls to name a few examples). Yet for those working in political science, parliamentary institutions and their formal and informal workings are the main mechanism of democratic decision-making and therefore are the sole institutional focus of their enquiry. There are advantages to both approaches. Under the sociolinguistic approach, the findings from other institutional contexts (for example law courts) can give detailed insights into different aspects of parliamentary speech, such as asking questions (see Cotterill 2002; Eades 2000; Harris 1984). Under the political approach, a focus on parliamentary institutions and attendant formal mechanisms – such as quotas (Celis et al. 2014; Krook 2015; Murray 2014) or Early Day Motions[2] are possible (Childs and Withey 2004) – and give detailed insights into all aspects of the institutions. Transformation and change are at the core of much feminist work in both sociolinguistics and political science (see Mills and Mullany 2011 and Dovi 2018 respectively), and research into gender and politics has made an impact on political institutions in direct and practical ways (see Childs and Dhalerup 2018 for a full account). This is despite well-documented and continuing male-dominated patterns of participation and resistance to gendered change *inside* the academic discipline of political science (see Ahrens et al. 2018; Atchison 2018; Mügge et al. 2016; Randall and Lovenduski 2004). An example of research that has a direct impact on a political institution is Sarah Childs' 'The Good Parliament' report (Childs 2016). This report in the UK HoC identified forty-three recommendations for reforms that would transform the institution from a gender-insensitive institution to a 'diversity-sensitive' one. Some of these reforms have been put in place and others remain under consideration (Childs and Dhalerup 2018).

These reforms are likely to come into focus with the proposed movement of the HoC from its current premises in the Palace of Westminster which needs urgent refurbishment. It is thought that the HoC chamber will be relocated to alternative premises (this is likely to be Richmond House in Whitehall) by 2025 for about six years until the renovations are completed. It has been suggested that with this move come opportunities for institutional change, not just for the operation of the parliament in the interim accommodation, but for more significant long-term changes to be made to the renewed Palace of Westminster when MPs return (Maddox 2019). Inevitably, this will involve discussions about the size and physical layout of the chamber. Apart from the connotations of adversarial and consensual formations discussed earlier, the existing chamber is currently extremely cramped for the 647 MPs. Current plans indicate the relocated parliament will be an exact replica of the HoC chamber but given the significance of interactional norms and rules on the participation of MPs, it will be interesting to see if any changes are considered to the 'Standing Orders' in this respect. Whether or not more significant change takes place, the movement of parliament's premises will offer a unique opportunity to examine the possible effects of such radical spatial and potential cultural change to this institution's traditions, rituals and norms.

8.5.2   *Interdiscursivity and the Construction and Strengthening of Homosocial Bonds across Events*

One of the more fascinating aspects of undertaking research in the HoC relates to its *extremes* as a speech event. Every interactional move from the reinforcement of speaking turns with physical movements (from sedentary to standing positions), to the ritualised and rather extraordinary collective noises of agreement and disagreement and other rarefied and ritualised behaviours indicate that this is no ordinary communicative context. Displays of interactional power and dominance are also hyper-visible and stylised in this high-performance event on the political stage. Parliamentary forums such as the HoC therefore give extreme examples of closed-membership, elite behaviours. As such, these forums may seem rarefied and divorced from more everyday interactions. However, it is possible that in this extremity lies the opportunity to examine the source of some of the ingrained behaviours: how – for example, fraternal networks and homosocial bonds – are co-constructed in interaction, how these groups position women and how their behaviours are maintained and strengthened over time. These analyses in turn may allow us to further understand more subtle inequities and mechanisms by which one person can be suppressed and excluded by another – interrupted, silenced, belittled or derided – in more routine or 'everyday' encounters.

In this vein, a recurrent observation in the analysis of HoC data was the intertextual characteristics of the construction of fraternal networks through both humour and rule-breaking. For example, Mrs Bone (Example 6.10) became a figure of fun (mainly for Conservative men) over time, between 2011 and 2018.[3] Although Mr Bone MP initiated this running joke, it was taken up by David Cameron when he was Prime Minister, the Speaker (John Bercow) and numerous other MPs who were all men, with the exception of the awkward attempt of Theresa May's to join in (see Example 6.10). This is precisely the type of humour that excludes women and that appears so trivial and silly that any objection to it makes one appear humourless and unable to take a joke (as discussed in Chapter 5). However, the jokes about Mrs Bone sexually objectify her, make her the silent recipient of humour in her absence and place her squarely in a domestic, subservient role. It is therefore the type of humour that forges homosocial bonds. Example 8.1a and 8.1b give examples of the running joke at Mrs Bone's expense.

Example 8.1a Prime Minister's Question Time 28 March 2011 (Official Report)

1   Bone: Over the weekend, my wife was saying what a wonderful job the Prime Minister
2   was doing over the EU bail-outs, and that he was turning into a Mrs Thatcher. She
3   wondered if he could use his immense charm and ability to persuade the euro
4   countries not to ask us to participate in any bail-out? Will the Prime Minister satisfy
5   Mrs Bone?
6   Cameron: I am fast coming to the view that Mrs Bone is quite literally insatiable. I
7   will – [*Laughter.*] I will certainly do my best, but there are some things of which it is
8   quite difficult to persuade one's European colleagues. I take to heart the
9   compliments that Mrs Bone paid in the early part of my hon. Friend's question.
10   Speaker: I feel rather left out not to have met Mrs Bone

Example 8.1b Prime Minister's Questions Time. 27 June 2011 (Official Report)

1   Bone: Yesterday, I had a meeting with a constituent who I know can be very difficult at
2   times. She was exceptionally happy and was singing the praises of the Prime Minister

3	because we will not be involved in the Greek bail-out, and because after 2013 we
4	will not be involved in any bail-outs. However, Mrs Bone wanted to know whether, if
5	a bail-out came before 2013, Britain would vote no in any case, despite qualified
6	majority voting. She would be very happy if the Prime Minister gave that
7	undertaking, and it would be really helpful for the Bone household if he could.
8	Cameron: I feel that a very big part of my life is spent trying to give pleasure to Mrs
9	Bone. On this occasion, I can only so far.
10	Speaker: We note the admirable self-restraint that the Prime Minister has demonstrated
11	and we are grateful for it.

These running jokes about Mrs Bone rest on the Prime Minister being able to 'satisfy' her (Example 8.1a, lines 4–5), and on her being 'quite literally insatiable' (line 6). In Example 8.1b the humour lies with David Cameron claiming that 'a very big part of my life is spent trying to give pleasure to Mrs Bone' (lines 8–9). Both these examples are collusive, with the Speaker joining in with the jocularity although there is no need for him to intervene in his capacity as moderator. These jokes also fit a wider cultural genre of humour about the unseen nagging spouse or 'her indoors'. The question of how these jokes circulate across nearly ten years of parliamentary discourse and how they allow some to form bonds and others to be excluded can possibly be answered, or at least explored, through the concept of enregisterment (Agha 2003, 2007; Silverstein 2003). Interdiscursivity arises from: 'A perceived repetition and hence a seeming linkage (across encounters) of forms that are framed, reflexively, as being the "same thing, again" or as yet another instantiation of a recognised type in some cultural framework' (Gal 2018: 2). In this way, 'signs have the capacity to formulate identities, reputations, genres and publics' (Gal 2018: 2). The notion of interdiscursivity and the connections between events seems relevant to many of the examples of parliamentary discourse covered in this book. The 'Lady Nugee' examples in Chapters 5 and 6 reoccur over a period of two years between April 2016 and March 2018. The Speaker's admonition of Johnson discussed in Chapter 5 only comes after the sequence of events shown in Table 8.2.

   Table 8.2 illustrates that each time the address term (or the reference to Mrs Bone) is used it is also linked to the previous occasions and it can be viewed as a 'sign' that becomes 'recognized (and regrouped) as belonging to distinct, differentially valorized semiotic registers by a population' (Agha 2007: 81). In turn, registers are 'cultural models of action that link diverse behavioral signs to enactable effects, including images of persona, interpersonal relationship, and type of conduct' (Agha 2007: 145). This seems a particularly fruitful way of conceptualising future research into the process of creating and maintaining exclusive registers bound up with homosocial bonding in political discourse. As shown throughout this book, public displays which construct hegemonic masculinity are prevalent in politics – the 'Mrs Bone' example in the UK HoC,

Table 8.2 *An example of linked events over time (Lady Nugee)*

1: David Cameron calls Emily Thornberry 'Lady Nugee' 20 April 2016
2: Theresa May calls Emily Thornberry 'Lady Nugee' 6 February 2017 (Example 6.9a and b. Thornberry raises a 'Point of order')
3: Boris Johnson calls Emily Thornberry 'Lady Nugee' 17 October 2017
4: Boris Johnson calls Emily Thornberry 'Lady Nugee' 27 March 2018 (Examples 5.5–5.7. He is admonished by the Speaker and apologises)

the sexism directed at Gillard and Clinton, or Donald Trump's allusion to a conversation with Bill Clinton 'on the golf course' (see Section 7.2.2). These semiotic registers require more explication. This research could, in turn, elucidate the workings of exclusionary practices in a range of contexts outside political institutions and in more everyday events.

8.6   Case Studies of Women Leaders and Barriers to Political Participation

This final chapter has identified a set of barriers or obstacles to women's participation based on the institutional ethnographic and discourse analytic analyses in Chapters 3 and 4. These questions were asked: How do gender stereotypes constrain women's participation and give them additional burdens? What are the effects of sexism, fraternal networks, high visibility and gendered discourses of linguistic performance upon women politicians? With the case studies (Chapters 6 and 7) I addressed how successful women politicians like Theresa May, Julia Gillard and Hillary Clinton attempted to resist and counter these effects? These case studies of the three high-profile leaders sought to examine how they were constrained by and how they resisted these pressures by examining their use of language and their behaviour in 'critical gendered moments' when gender and/or gender relations were explicitly addressed.

Certain commonalities hold for all three women leaders. First, and perhaps unsurprisingly given the evidence from previous research and the parliamentary analyses earlier, all the women leaders speak in highly adversarial ways in parliamentary and televised performances. As shown in the analysis of 'gendered critical moments' in Chapter 7, both Gillard and Clinton face formidable sexist adversaries by confronting them directly. According to many descriptions, 'successful' leaders are those who display 'discourse competence' or the ability to draw on a combination of competitive and cooperative strategies (Mills 1992: 4). Gillard expresses this clearly when she says in an interview: 'If there is something I hope I have done for the image of women in public life is that we can go into an adversarial environment like parliament and we can dominate it and conquer it. I don't shy away from that. But that's not all of me' (Gillard 2013a).[4] In the case of Theresa May, there is more evidence of the 'toughness' of competition and confrontation than there is of the balance with more cooperative styles. As noted by Janet Holmes when describing a successful woman business leader: 'to achieve her goal of cultural change in the organisation, her talk is characterised by the adroit meshing of transactional and relational discourse features; she can be clear, direct and decisive when required, but she also encourages a cooperative style of interaction, using with humour skill to achieve this effect' (Holmes 2017: 37). Given the negative appraisals of Theresa May's approach to the Brexit negotiations in 2017–19 (see for example Glaze 2018), and her steadfast and stubborn refusal to show any flexibility in relation to compromising on her EU deal, she would arguably have been more successful if she had balanced her adversarial approach with more transactional, stereotypically feminine styles. However, May at this point was in a series of political paradoxes, caught between political rifts in her own party; across parliament more generally (as the opposition parties were also split on the issue); and between the EU and the UK, about if and how the UK should leave the EU. May's position on the 'glass cliff', described in Chapter 6, may be a useful reminder in future appraisals of her leadership that, although she had some stark failings as a leader, success at this precarious point in UK political history would have been difficult for any leader to achieve.

Perhaps the most noticeable features the three women leaders had in common were the exhaustive lengths to which they would go – and the tremendous energy they would expend – considering and weighing up every aspect of their public contributions and appearances. From Theresa May's controlled and highly rehearsed performances in PMQs; Gillard's careful negotiation of interview questions about her childlessness and her ambition; to Clinton's attention to every detail of her physical appearance. The sheer labour involved with their participation in the public sphere attests to the historical and cultural 'lack of fit' between women and the political roles that they fulfil. These can be seen as part of the 'historical burden of gendered expectations' (Biressi and Nunn 2017: 47) which, as noted in Chapter 1, centre on the dissonance of women performing the 'masculine voice of authority'. The excessive labour of women politicians, like domestic labour in the private sphere, seems to be overlooked in accounts of women in politics. Of course, men politicians also have to expend energy on impression-management, polishing performances and avoiding gaffes, but unlike women some high-ranking men do not appear to do so. Donald Trump and Boris Johnson in particular seem to perform their roles with unpreparedness as part of the construction of a particular type of masculinity: one that throws caution to the wind and is confident or arrogant enough to assume that any damage inflicted by these actions will be limited.

In her memoir, Hillary Clinton describes spending 'six hundred hours or twenty-five days' having her hair and make-up done during the 2016 campaign

(Clinton 2017: 87). She also confesses that: 'I'm not jealous of my male colleagues often, but I am when it comes to how they can just shower, shave, put on a suit, and be ready to go. The few times I've gone out without makeup, it's made the news' (Clinton 2017: 88). These expectations for women politicians are so normalised that they are rarely commented upon, unless they are transgressed, as Clinton notes. Yet they make up part of the burden of gendered expectations that are not only labour intensive but psychologically inhibiting: men can perform 'as they are', but women must put on an artificial mask to fit normative expectations of femininity in public. These labours also have linguistic equivalences, as the rehearsed style exemplified by Theresa May's parliamentary performances; Clintons detailed and stringent preparation for her debates with Trump; and Gillard's decision not to confront her sexist critics before her misogyny speech are all examples of women's 'silence or hyper-controlled language' which is imposed on some people, while others (mostly men) are allowed the 'liberties of a language that is securely established' (Bourdieu 1991: 82).

The psychological and emotional labour of the three women leaders is often couched in terms of *resilience*. Indeed, both Gillard (2014) and Clinton (2017) chose to use this word as a title for sections of their respective memoirs and Gillard describes her premiership as 'three years and three days of resilience' (Gillard 2014: 2). Theresa May's resilience is frequently alluded to by the UK press, particularly in the latter part of 2018 and early 2019 as she survived successive humiliating defeats and challenges to her premiership (see for example, Moir 2018). This common-sense notion of 'true grit', staying power and the ability to 'bounce back' has been denaturalised by scholars who note that the compunction for resilience is in fact part of the 'turn to character' (Bull and Allen 2018) that relies on conservative notions of the connection between 'character education' and life outcomes. This 'calls on people to be adaptable and positive, bouncing back from adversity and embracing a mindset in which negative experiences can – and must – be reframed in upbeat terms' (Gill and Orgad 2018: 477). Resilience is therefore a highly contested, flexible or 'sticky' concept (Ahmed 2004), which can be viewed as a psychological neo-liberal mechanism that is both classed and gendered (Gill and Orgad 2018). Into this discussion then, the elite women leaders who revel in their own resilience as a marker of their success and strength can be seen as being at the pinnacle of this self-improving endeavour. However, resilience is only achievable by *some* women who have economic and social privileges, and it is a mechanism by which the women leaders' psychological and emotional strain and suffering is reduced or entirely hidden.

Even given this intense physical, psychological and emotional labour, these endeavours are often not enough to mitigate or silence the criticism women leaders receive for their performances. Theresa May's control is 'unemotional' and turns her into a robotic 'Maybot' (and it is interesting that all three leaders experience this robotic characterisation to some degree); Clinton is still chastised for her appearance and for her 'pantsuits'; Gillard does not gain any ground by strategically staying silent about sexism for so long, and instead is accused of 'playing the gender card' when she eventually does confront it. The media analyses of the women leaders are predictable and (as identified in Chapters 6 and 7) often at once hostile and trivialising. Women in leadership positions also tend to be compared and likened to other women in similar positions, especially in relation to their appearance. May was not only compared with Thatcher but also with Angela Merkel – if only because they had both worn 'mint and turquoise outfits' (Freeman 2016). Similarly, on her first day as prime minister when she met Queen Elizabeth, rather than focusing on her new role, the media commented on May's 'acid yellow' outfit, which was compared with that of Hillary Clinton, who wore the same colour outfit on the same day (Cliff 2016). These are not straightforward comparisons however, as they are nearly always represented as competitions, with this May–Clinton outfit 'story' having the subtitle 'But who's Queen Bee?'. Another example of these comparisons is when Theresa May's haircut was said to be similar to that of Nicola Sturgeon (First Minister of the SP) with the headline 'Battle of the Haircuts!' (Tweedy 2017). In addition (as mentioned in Chapter 6), the legs of these same women were compared in the *Daily Mail* with the headline 'Never mind Brexit, who won legs-it' (Vine 2017). This trivialises both women leaders by diminishing their roles and activities and reducing their endeavours to petty a competition over their appearance. In this way, these comparisons often contain traces of the 'women beware women' discourse identified by Jane Sunderland as occurring when women are represented as being jealous and distrusting of other women (2004: 90).

Some positive aspects of women's representation and coverage have been observed. Linda Trimble notes that since Clinton's defeat in 2016 there has been a 'surge in interest' in women running for office claiming that 'when high-profile women politicians are in the news, ideologies of gender are on display, for better or for worse' (Trimble 2017: 6). Trimble's study of gender marking in the media coverage of women leaders also suggests that although pervasive during women's early years of service, after a woman has been in office for some time, gender marking decreases substantially (Trimble 2017: 71). In the case of Helen Clark, who was New Zealand Prime Minister for nine years and party leader for fifteen, she eventually became 'written into news stories as the prime minister, not the woman prime minister' (Trimble 2017: 70). Interestingly, Trimble points to the contradictory consequences for women of such gender marking: in some ways, gender marking of women politicians can highlight their expected differences from the unmarked normative male model of a successful politician, and this is often to women's detriment.

However, in other ways the marking of the first women to fulfil these roles can serve to 'make visible the assumption that politics is a male preserve' (Trimble 2017: 66).

This complexity is highlighted in more nuanced accounts of women's representation in particular contexts, with research into the Canadian elections finding that measures of 'candidate competitiveness' and 'novelty' were a more important determiner of media coverage than gender (Wagner et al. 2017). Similarly, Murphy and Rek (2018) find that women politicians received more coverage than men in the UK 2015 election in local news stories. Baxter's (2017, 2018) analyses of the representation of women leaders in the UK press finds that although Kanter's (1977) role traps are still dominant, some representations are more complex. As noted in Chapter 6, she finds that Theresa May is constructed according to the iron maiden and battle-axe stereotypes. Yet there are also 'traces' of positive representations of May including 'veiled admiration' of May's assertive actions and the suggested possibility that she will 'make an outstanding leader' (Baxter 2018: 48). Similarly, analyses of the media representation of Angela Merkel suggest that it is possible to gain positive recognition by the media, but only 'in the logic of a gendered system – emphasizing the possibility of a woman to act successfully *as a man*' (Lünenborg and Maier 2015: 287, italics in original).

It is certainly hard to see the positive side of media representations when the women leaders are subjected to particularly misogynistic attacks. As acknowledged in Chapter 7, both Clinton and Gillard have been the target of vitriol from their opponents (Trump and Abbott respectively) and from the wider media. The case studies suggest that Clinton and Gillard received more extreme levels of vitriol and abuse (for example, 'lock her up' and 'ditch the witch' respectively) than Theresa May. Violent comments were reportedly made about May from members of her own party in October 2018 (that she should 'bring a noose' to a party meeting and that 'she'll be dead soon', BBC News 2018), but this has never become part of mainstream media representations of May in the way that Clinton and Gillard were so publicly targeted. Gender therefore also appears to intersect with cultural and political factors in terms of the treatment of women politicians within the particular cultural and political contexts of Australia, the United States and the United Kingdom. It is also possible that conforming women like May on the right wing of the political spectrum are tolerated more because they align to traditional, conservative values (and in the case of US politician, Sarah Palin, to normative family values). Thus, they can be easily subsumed into the 'mother', 'nanny' or 'schoolmistress' role traps (Kanter 1977) by men even on their own side. This could also partly account for the fact that it is two right-wing women who have reached the highest role of prime minister whereas this has not been achieved by women on the left. Conservative women may therefore avoid attacks from anti-women elements of their own part of the political spectrum in ways that are not possible for women on the political left (such as Labour politicians Emily Thornberry, Harriet Harman and Dianne Abbott); or conservative women who do not conform by rebelling against their party (such as Theresa Gorman and Emma Nicholson referred to in Chapter 5, and more recently Anna Sourbry MP).

Despite these possible cultural and political differences, vitriol directed at women politicians can be seen as positioned on a cline (Kelly 1988) along which much extreme forms of behaviour and violence exist. In the United Kingdom the MP Jo Cox was murdered in 2017 and the conceptualising of violence against women on a continuum 'between which lie degrees of socio-cultural expectation, control, persuasion, pressure, threat and force' (Anitha and Gill 2009: 165) allows connections to be made between the more routine and everyday experiences of sexism and such extreme violent and criminal acts (Boyle 2019: 25). As noted in Chapter 1, violence against women in politics is globally on the increase and affects women in specific ways – including driving them out of politics or by deterring them from entering the political sphere in the first place. 'Nearly all participants in a program for aspiring women leaders in the United Kingdom stated that they had witnessed sexist abuse of women politicians online, and over 75 percent said that it weighed on their decision about whether to seek a role in public life' (Krook 2017: 84). Therefore, all different forms of sexism, misogyny and violence against women in politics on this continuum can be seen as anti-democratic and threatening to women's position in society.

Gillard and Clinton's resistance to sexist language and attacks described in Chapter 7 appeared to lead to substantial losses in each of their political contexts: Gillard lost a leadership challenge soon after her sexism and misogyny speech, and Clinton failed to be elected as the first woman US president. Clinton herself acknowledges this, but also identifies the contributory elements of her efforts to the overall advancement of women in politics: 'We did not win, but we made the sight of a woman nominee more familiar. We brought the possibility of a woman president closer' (Clinton 2017: 143). At the time of writing, in 2019, the gains and losses of women's political leadership have again come into focus. In the United States, Elizabeth Warren, the US senator whose example of 'persistence' in the face of silencing started this book, has announced that she will run for the US Democratic Party nomination for the US presidential election of 2020. This announcement was swiftly followed by media coverage about how 'unlikeable' Warren is and how 'unfavourably' she is viewed by the electorate. For Warren and other aspiring candidates like Sarah Huckabee and Kamala Harris, their political trajectories will surely be dogged by similar objections, abuse and misogyny as that of Hillary Clinton. The pervasive mixture of subtle and overt objections to women in the public sphere are often difficult to pin down, as Julia Gillard says: 'of all the experiences I had as Prime Minister, gender is the hardest to explain, to catch, to quantify' (2014: 98). Yet there *are* changes in the critical accounts of the sexist treatment of women in politics: the coverage of the 'problem' of Warren's likeability was swiftly followed by critical appraisals of this stance in ways that probably would have not been possible in previous times or perhaps even before Hillary Clinton's candidacy in 2016. Warren's 'unlikability' was 'called out' and identified as a smokescreen for objecting to her as a *woman* candidate by the mainstream media. For example, one such article called on journalists to approach criticisms of Warren in more sophisticated ways in order: 'to interpret these specific discomforts in light of the deeper discomfort that Americans again and again express with ambitious women' (Beinart 2019). It may be then, that although sexism and misogyny are still rife in the political landscape, and women candidates are still likely to face burdens and obstacles related to gender, a vigilant and unrelenting critique of the workings of these discourses may gradually stop women's voices being silenced in politics.

Appendix A: Description of the House of Commons Data Corpus 1998–2001

A.1.1 Description of Full Video Data Corpus of House of Commons Speech Events

Date	Description	Duration in minutes
21/01/98	#Prime Minister's Question Time	30
02/04/98	Departmental Questions: Trade and Industry	60
02/04/98	Mo Mowlam: Statement on Northern Ireland	5
06/04/98	Departmental Questions: Defence	30
06/04/98	Questions to Leader of the House (Anne Taylor) on Modernisation	30
06/04/98	Debate: Government Motion on Trade Union Recognition	10
29/04/98	Departmental Questions: International Development	5
29/04/98	Prime Minister's Question Time	30
02/06/98	Departmental Questions: Health	10
04/06/98	Business of the House (Anne Taylor)	20
22/06/98	Questions to Leader of the House (Anne Taylor) on Modernisation	30
22/06/98	Private Notice Question: Ian Paisley	10
22/06/98	Statement by Betty Boothroyd (Speaker)	5
22/06/98	Points of Order	5
22/06/98	Debate: Amendments to Crime and Disorder Bill: Clause 10	160
23/06/98	Departmental Questions: Scotland	30
01/07/98	Private Member's Debate: Gap Year Students (Nick St. Aubyn – Conservative).	95
01/07/98	Private Member's Debate: 50th Anniversary of the NHS	90
01/07/98	Private Member's Bill: Pedlars (Peter Brand – LibDem)	30
01/07/98	Private Member's Bill: Reefs at Risk (Tam Dalyell)	30

(Continued)

Date	Description	Duration in minutes
01/07/98	Private Member's Bill: Oxted Hospital (Peter Ainsworth – Conservative).	30
01/07/98	Departmental Questions: International Development	30
01/07/98	#Prime Minister's Question Time	30
01/07/98	Private Notice Question: Archie Kirkwood (LibDem)	30
01/07/98	Ten Minute Rule Bill: Young People and Local Government – Ashak Kumar (Lab)	10
01/07/98	Finance Bill No. 2. Amendments 48, 90, 15, 42. and Third Reading	270
01/07/98	Consideration of Lords' Amendments to the Teaching and Higher Education Bill	200
03/07/98	Consideration of Lords' Amendments to the Fireworks Bill	255
03/07/98	Adjournment Debate: North East London Probation Service	15
06/07/98	#Departmental Questions: Social Security	60
06/07/98	Statement by Harriet Harman on Child Support Agency Followed by Questions	60
06/07/98	*First Allotted Estimates Day Debate: Government's Proposals for Further Education.	180
13/07/98	Opposition debate on Manufacturing and Industrial Relations	130
15/07/98	Prime Minister's Question Time	30
21/10/98	#Prime Minister's Question Time	30
01/03/99	*Sexual Offences Bill Amendment 1: Age of Consent.	120
01/03/99	*Sexual Offences Bill Amendment 2: Position of Trust	120
02/03/99	#Departmental Questions: Health	60
02/03/99	Statement by Foreign Secretary Robin Cook	20
02/03/99	10 Minute Rule Bill: Teddy Taylor on Execution of UK Citizen in Calcutta	10
02/03/99	*Opposition Debate: Sierra Leone	180
02/03/99	Opposition Debate: Burden on Schools	80
03/03/99	Departmental Questions: Wales	30
03/03/99	#Prime Minister's Question Time	30
04/03/99	#Departmental Questions: Treasury	30
29/03/99	Prime Minister's Statement on Kosovo (+ questions)	30
29/03/99	New Writ (Southwark) – Fiona Jones Sacking	45
29/03/99	*Government debate on the Stephen Lawrence Inquiry	285

Date	Description	Duration in minutes
08/11/99	#Departmental Questions: Defence	30
12/04/00	Departmental Questions: Northern Ireland	30
12/04/00	Prime Minister's Question Time	30
03/04/00	Prime Minister's Question Time	30
10/05/00	Departmental Questions: Cabinet Office	30
10/05/00	#Prime Minister's Question Time	30
24/05/00	Prime Minister's Question Time	30
26/06/00	#Departmental Questions: Home	30
14/06/00	Departmental Questions: Cabinet Office	30
14/06/00	#Prime Minister's Question Time	30
10/01/01	Health and Social Care Bill (Second Reading)	120
	Total:	3535
		Hours:58.9

Key: * = Debates used in the analysis of floor apportionment (Section 3.2).
= Prime Minister's Question Times and Departmental Question Times used in the analysis of the adversarial linguistic style (Section 3.3).

A.1.2   Table Showing the Total Number of Prime Minister's Question Times; Departmental Question Times and All Other Speech Events (referred to as 'debates') and Their Duration in the Full Data Corpus (see Chapter 3)

Type of speech event	Number of events	Duration of all events (hours)
Debates	33	45.4
Prime Minister's Question Time	11	5.5
Departmental Question Time	15	8
Total Events/Duration in Full Corpus	59	58.9

A.1.3   Table Showing Details of the Ethnographic Interviews and the Interviewees (full interview transcripts in Shaw [2002])

Reference	Date	M/F	Party/seniority	First elected	Duration	Location
A	25/03/99	F	Labour Backbencher	1997	55 mins	MPs Office (Palace of Westminster)
B	13/04/99	F	Lib/Dem Senior	1997	45 mins	Corridor, Central Lobby
C	15/11/00	F	Labour Backbencher	1997	35 mins	MPs' Tea Rooms
D	04/04/01	F	Labour Senior	1983	50 mins	MPs Office Portcullis House
E	23/03/01	F	Labour Backbencher	1997	40 mins	MPs Office Portcullis House
F	09/07/01	M	Labour Backbencher	1997	35 mins	MPs' Tea Rooms

Appendix B: Description of the Devolved Parliaments Data Corpus 2009–11

A.2.1 Description of the Data for the Full Corpus of Events

A.2.1.1 List of Counted Events and Their Duration from the Northern Ireland Assembly

Date	Question time (minutes)	Plenary (minutes)	Total (minutes)
14/09/2009	30	210	240
09/11/2009	60	250	5310
10/11/2009	30	507	537
17/11/2009	30	230	260
07/12/2009	60	208	268
08/12/2009	30	171	201
22/02/2010	60	271	331
23/02/2010	30	330	360
08/03/2010	60	452	512
09/03/2010	30	296	326
22/03/2010	60	394	454
23/03/2010	30	267	297
Total minutes	510	3586	4096
Hours	8	60	68

A.2.1.2 List of Counted Events and Their Duration
        From the Scottish Parliament

Date	Question time (minutes)	Plenary (minutes)	Total (minutes)
16/09/2009	0	125	125
11/11/2009	0	171	171
12/11/2009	296	108	404
25/11/2009	30	175	205
09/12/2009	0	196	196
10/12/2009	81	280	361
24/02/2010	40	84	124
25/02/2010	99	312	411
03/03/2010	0	200	200
04/03/2010	90	265	355
10/03/2010	0	218	218
11/03/2010	100	313	413
24/03/2010	0	225	225
25/03/2010	91	330	421
Total minutes	827	3002	3829
Hours	14	50	64

A.2.1.3 List of Counted Events and Their Duration from the National
        Assembly for Wales

Date	Question times (minutes)	Plenary (minutes)	Total (minutes)
22/09/2009	180	30	210
10/11/2009	90	230	320
11/11/2009	100	196	296
08/12/2009	80	148	228
09/12/2009	70	205	275
23/02/2010	80	104	184
24/02/2010	90	252	342
02/03/2010	80	126	206
10/03/2010	140	317	457
17/03/2010	90	110	200
23/03/2010	140	219	359
24/03/2010	20	132	152
Total minutes	1160	2069	3229
Hours	19	35	54

A.2.1.4   List of Counted Events and Their Duration From the House of Commons

Date	Question Time (minutes)	Plenary (minutes)	Total (minutes)
14/10/2009	125	150	275
11/11/2009	63	337	400
12/11/2009	83	197	280
08/12/2009	60	403	463
09/12/2009	62	429	491
24/02/2010	68	307	375
25/02/ 2010	64	414	478
10/03/2010	62	422	484
11/03/2010	60	314	374
24/03/2010	62	424	486
25/03/2010	65	407	472
Total minutes	774	3,804	4,578
Hours	13	63	76

A.2.2   Table Showing Details of the Ethnographic Interviews and the Interviewees (anonymised)

A.2.2.1   List of interviews with Members of the Legislative Authority (MLAs) in Northern Ireland

Ref	Date	M/F	Party	Location	Duration (minutes)
MLA101	09/02/10	F	PUP	Stormont, Office	36
MLA102	09/02/10	M	DUP	Speaker's Rooms Stormont	30
MLA103	09/02/10	M	SF	Stormont, Office	20
MLA104	09/02/10	M	DUP	Stormont, Office	26
MLA105	09/02/10	M	UUP	Stormont, Tea Rooms	31
MLA106	10/02/10	M	UUP	Stormont, Office	37
MLA107	10/02/10	F	SF	Stormont, Tea Rooms	12
MLA108	10/02/10	F	Alliance	Stormont, Office	38
MLA109	10/02/10	F	SF	SF Offices, Falls Road	47
MLA201	22/06/10	M	SDLP	Stormont, Tea Rooms	31
MLA202	22/06/10	F	SDLP	Stormont, Office	36
MLA203	22/06/10	M	SF	Stormont, Office	30
MLA204	23/06/10	M	Alliance	Stormont, Office	20
MLA205	23/06/10	F	SF	Warrenpoint, St Mark's High School, classroom	26
MLA206	14/07/10	M	DUP	House of Commons	31

A.2.2.2 List of interviews with Members of the Scottish Parliament (MSPs)

Ref	Date	M/F	Party	Location	Duration (minutes)
MSP101	03/03/10	F	Labour	MSP's Office	35
MSP102	03/03/10	F	Labour	MSP's Office	38
MSP103	03/03/10	F	SNP	MSP's Office	13
MSP104	03/03/10	M	Labour	MSP's Office	18
MSP105	03/03/10	M	Labour	MSP's Office	40
MSP106	04/03/10	M	Conservative	MSP's Office	24
MSP107	04/03/10	F	Labour	MSP's Office	39
MSP108	04/03/10	M	Labour	MSP's Office	23
MSP109	04/03/10	M	Conservative	MSP's Office	33
MSP110	04/03/10	F	Labour	MSP's Office	25
MSP201	12/05/10	F	Conservative	MSP's Office	30
MSP202	12/05/10	F	Conservative	MSP's Office	25
MSP203	12/05/10	M	Green	MSP's Office	36
MSP204	12/05/10	F	SNP	MSP's Office	46
MSP205	13/05/10	M	SNP	MSP's Office	21

A.2.2.3 List of interviews with Assembly Members (AMs)
in the National Assembly for Wales

Ref	Date	M/F	Party	Location	Duration (minutes)
AM101	17/03/10	F	Lib Dem	Office, Tŷ Hywel	29
AM102	17/03/10	M	Conservative	Office, Tŷ Hywel	42
AM103	17/03/10	M	Labour	Office, Tŷ Hywel	25
AM104	17/03/10	M	PLC	Senedd public area	25
AM105	17/03/10	F	PLC	Senedd public area	32
AM106	18/03/10	F	PLC	Office, Tŷ Hywel	34
AM107	18/03/10	M	Conservative	Office, Tŷ Hywel	27
AM108	18/03/10	M	Conservative	Conservative public office	26
AM201	16/06/10	M	PLC	Office, Tŷ Hywel	22
AM202	16/06/10	M	LibDem	Office, Tŷ Hywel	52
AM203	16/06/10	M	Labour	Office, Tŷ Hywel	40
AM204	17/06/10	F	Labour	Senedd public area	32

Appendix C: Adversarial Language in the May–Corbyn Prime Minister's Question Times

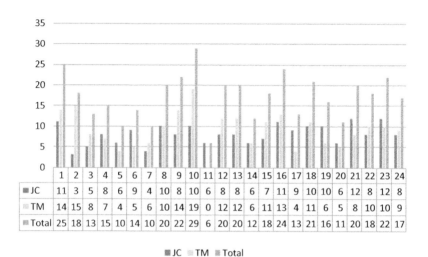

	1	2	3	4	5	6	7	8	9	10	11	12	13	14	15	16	17	18	19	20	21	22	23	24
JC	11	3	5	8	6	9	4	10	8	10	6	8	8	6	7	11	9	10	10	6	12	8	12	8
TM	14	15	8	7	4	5	6	10	14	19	0	12	12	6	11	13	4	11	6	5	8	10	10	9
Total	25	18	13	15	10	14	10	20	22	29	6	20	20	12	18	24	13	21	16	11	20	18	22	17

■ JC ☷ TM ▨ Total

Figure A.3.3.1 Showing the number of adversarial features used by May, Corbyn and in total over a sample of 24 sessions between 20 July 2016 and 18 July 2018.

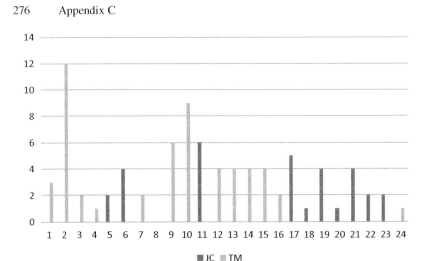

Figure A.3.3.2 Showing the difference in adversarial points between Corbyn and May in a sample of 24 sessions between 20 July 2016 and 18 July 2018.

Dates of the Prime Minister's Question Times used for the analysis: 20/07/2016; 07/09/2016; 19/10/2016; 23/11/2016; 14/12/2016; 18/01/2017; 01/02/2017; 01/03/2017; 22/03/2017; 26/04/2017; 28/06/2017; 19/07/2017; 06/09/2017; 18/10/2017; 22/11/2017; 13/12/2017; 17/01/2018; 07/02/2018; 07/03/2018; 28/03/2018; 02/05/2018; 23/05/2018; 20/06/2018; 18/07/2018.

Notes

Chapter 1

1. This can be found in the official Congressional Record – Senate(PDF). Congress. gov. 7 February 2017. p. S855. www.congress.gov/crec/2017/02/06/CREC-2017-02-06-bk2.pdf [accessed 20 October 2018].
2. Warren quoted Senator Ted Kennedy who had described Sessions as 'a disgrace', and read out a letter written at that time by another woman, Coretta Scott King, a human rights activist. King's letter was an objection to the appointment of Sessions in 1986 on the grounds that 'Mr. Sessions has used the awesome power of his office to chill the free exercise of the vote by black citizens'.
3. Rule XIX states that a senator may not ascribe 'to another senator or to other senators any conduct or motive unworthy or unbecoming a senator'. For further discussion see www.theatlantic.com/politics/archive/2017/02/a-brief-history-of-the-senate-rule-that-silenced-elizabeth-warren/516042/ [accessed 5 January 2019].
4. Senator Jeff Merkley of Oregon subsequently read the letter from Coretta Scott King without objection. Video available at: www.oregonlive.com/politics/index.ssf/2017/02/jeff_merkley_reads_coretta_scott_king_letter_about_jeff_sessions.html [accessed 2 February 2019].
5. The #MeToo movement (including 'hashtag feminism' in general) has many more complex effects than are represented here, including psychological consequences for participants who often pay an emotional 'tax' for their activism (Mendes et al. 2018).
6. The Greek is μῦθος δ' ἄνδρεσσι μελήσει πᾶσι where μῦθος is *muthos*.
7. The postcard is addressed to 'Miss C. Pankhurst, Women's Suffrage (illegible word), Clements Inn, The Strand, London W1'. In brackets next to the address is written 'or The Hotel Pentonville', threateningly alluding to the imprisonment of many suffragettes at the time, even though they were mostly imprisoned in Holloway prison rather than Pentonville, which was a male prison. With thanks to the Museum of London for allowing me to view the reverse of the postcard image.
8. The Church of England had allowed the ordination of women priests from November 1992 (Walsh 2001: 175).
9. Gina Miller is a UK businesswoman who forced the UK government to hold a parliamentary vote in order to trigger 'Article 50', the order to start the process of Britain leaving the European Union (Brexit) in November 2016.

Chapter 2

1. See www.hansard-corpus.org/x.asp
2. Standing orders: https://publications.parliament.uk/pa/cm201516/cmstords/0002/toc.htm
3. As noted in Section 3.2, overlaps between main 'legal' speakers are uncommon, but overlapping utterances between the MP giving the speech and other MPs speaking in the chamber (illegally) are common.

Chapter 3

1. A full list of all the events in the 1998–2001 data corpus can be found in Appendix A.1.1.
2. A 'give way' turn is the 'legal' means by which an MP can intervene on a legal speaker's turn. The MP who wishes to intervene stands and usually holds out their arm, saying 'Will the Right Honourable Lady/Gentleman give way?', and the current MP giving the speech either allows or refuses them a 'give way' intervention. After they have finished their intervention the 'current' speaking MP resumes their speech. The interactional turns such as the requests to give way are routinely omitted from the Hansard Official Report (Shaw 2018).
3. Full numbers for this summary can be seen in Shaw (2002, 114–55).
4. Referring to 'Dolly the sheep', the first animal ever to be cloned in 1998. The comment occurred on 13 July 1998.
5. Different ways of classifying personal attacks have been used in more recent studies of PMQs, with Waddle et al. (2019) producing a useful classification system which discounts some types of more generic attacks as part of the ritual of PMQs, and only counts attacks on 'enduring character traits' (2019: 67). This will certainly be considered in future assessments of PMQs.
6. See Appendix A for a full list of events in the 1998–2001 data corpus.

Chapter 4

1. The three devolved institutions had their first terms from 1998 (the NIA) and 1999 (the NAW and the SP) to 2003; the second term from 2003 to 2007; the third term from 2007 to 2011, within which the data for this project was collected between 2009–2011. Subsequent terms ran from 2011 to 2016; and from 2016.
2. An Economic and Social Research Council funded project: 'Gender and Linguistic Participation in the Devolved Parliaments of the UK' (RES 000223792) September 2009 and April 2011.
3. Standing orders of the NIA: www.niassembly.gov.uk/assembly-business/standing-orders/; History of and composition of the NIA: www.niassembly.gov.uk/about-the-assembly/general-information/history-of-the-assembly/#3
Standing orders of the SP: www.parliament.scot/parliamentarybusiness/17797.aspx; History and composition of the SP: www.parliament.scot/about-the-parliament.aspx
Standing orders of the NAW: www.assembly.wales/NAfW%20Documents/Assembly%20Business%20section%20documents/Standing_Orders/Clean_SOs.eng.pdf

History and Composition of the NAW: www.assembly.wales/en/bus-home/Pages/
Document-Library.aspx (all accessed on 10 January 2019).

4. See the NIA Committee for Culture, Arts and Leisure, briefing from the 'Ulster
Scots Agency' 11 February 2010 http://archive.niassembly.gov.uk/record/
committees2009/CAL/100211_BriefingfromUlsterScotsAgency.htm.

Chapter 5

1. Cameron's directive to Eagle can be found in the Hansard report for 27 April
2011, Vol 527, Column 170 or online here https://hansard.parliament.uk/
Commons/2011-04-27/debates/11042772000024/Engagements (accessed on 7
February 2020). There is no direct evidence for Bercow's alleged remarks, which
were reported by MPs to have taken place in the House of Commons Chamber on
16 May 2018.

2. Michael Fallon was Secretary of State for Defence, and resigned on 1 November
2017; Damian Green was First Secretary of State and Minister of the Cabinet
Office and resigned on 20 December 2017.

3. A 'whip' is an MP appointed by a political party to ensure that all members of the
party vote, and vote in line with party policy.

4. Helen Liddell and Dawn Primarolo.

5. www.fawcettsociety.org.uk/views-not-shoes (accessed on 2 August 2018).

6. The URLs for the articles, and authors are as follows (all written on 27/28 March 2018,
and accessed on 29 July 2018): (1) www.telegraph.co.uk/politics/2018/03/27/order-
boris-johnson-reprimanded-calling-emily-thornberry-noble/ by Harry Yorke; (2)
www.newstatesman.com/2018/03/watch-john-bercow-s-epic-rant-sexist-boris-
johnson-calling-emily-thornberry-lady-nugee by 'Media Mole'; (3) www.daily-
mail.co.uk/news/article-5549219/Speaker-rages-sexist-Boris-Johnson-Commons.html
by James Tapsfield; (4) www.thesun.co.uk/news/5912008/boris-johnson-is-accused-
of-sexism-in-the-commons-after-he-calls-corbyn-ally-emily-thornberry-by-her-
husbands-name/ by Hugo Gye; (5) www.mirror.co.uk/news/politics/boris-johnson-
forced-make-grovelling-12259100 by Mikey Smith; (6) www.express.co.uk/news/
politics/937728/Boris-Johnson-blunder-Theresa-May-sexist-Speaker-Bercow-Emily-
Thornberry by Holly Pyne; (7) www.bbc.co.uk/news/uk-politics-43557516 no author; (8)
www.theguardian.com/politics/2018/mar/27/johnson-apologises-for-sexist-reference-
to-emily-thornberry by Patrick Wintour; (9) www.independent.co.uk/news/uk/politics/
boris-johnson-sexist-emily-thornberry-husband-commons-lady-nugee-
apology-a8275866.html by Rob Merrick; (10)
www.huffingtonpost.co.uk/entry/boris-johnson-rebuked-for-sexist-behaviour-
towards-emily-thornberry_uk_5aba28e7e4b0decad04df7e2 by Ned Simons.

7. To make this more complicated, at the time of this incident, Bercow had been
accused of bullying members of his own staff, which was seen as 'a witch-hunt' to
'settle old scores' by some elements of the left-wing press (for example Elgot
2018). He had also been accused of sexism himself in calling Andrea Leadsom,
the Leader of the House of Commons, a 'stupid woman' (Cowburn 2018).

8. This is also similar to the justification of criticism of Mary Beard in *The
Spectator* 'It's not misogyny, Professor Beard, it's you' noted by Biressi and
Nunn (2017: 41).

Chapter 6

1. John Crace, sketch writer for *The Guardian* first used this term in a sketch on 8 November 2016 with the title 'May struggles to take back control – from her own Maybot'.
2. The 'Women2Win' campaign 'aims to increase the number of Conservative women in Parliament and in public life and is committed to identifying, training and mentoring female candidates for office' www.women2win.com/.
3. Theresa and Phillip May were interviewed on BBC1's 'The One Show' on 9 May 2017.
4. Comments made in an LBC radio phone-in on 10 October 2017.
5. The fire in Grenfell Tower, in North Kensington, London occurred on 14 June 2017 – a week after the 2017 General Election.
6. This is based on the analysis of only three PMQs sessions, but it is nevertheless indicative of a much more adversarial style between Hague and Blair. The sessions took place on 03/03/1999; 10/03/1999; and 19/01/2000.
7. He used this technique in eleven out of twenty-four sessions.
8. This alludes to an incident on 16 August 2016 in which Jeremy Corbyn claimed he had to sit on the floor of a train as there were no seats because of overcrowding.
9. Corbyn uses one of Thatcher's nicknames 'the Iron Lady' to make this pun. The source is – Hansard: 18 January 2017, Volume 619, Column 928.
10. The 100 year Anniversary of the Representation of the People Act was celebrated on 6 February 2018.
11. The video recording of this event can be viewed at: https://parliamentlive.tv/event/index/5c33f2dc-0892-4d70-84e3-a91b593fe67f (accessed on 28 September 2018) time of extract 16:13:38-16-14:05 or view the clip at: https://goo.gl/mUqHok .
12. This is the mechanism whereby MPs can raise infringements of the parliamentary rules or 'Standing Orders' with the Speaker, and they usually take place at the end of a debate or question time session.
13. *The Sun,* 12 July 2016.
14. The footage of Ken Clark making these remarks in the television studio before an interview, unaware the cameras were recording, was released by Sky News on 6 July 2016, just before Theresa May won the contest to become leader of the Conservative party.

Chapter 7

1. For further information see: www.aph.gov.au/About_Parliament/Senate (accessed on 15 October 2018).
2. As in the HoC Thornberry example, a Point of Order in the HoR is raised when a member believes that a parliamentary rule has been broken.
3. This happened in a QTs on 20 August 2012 and was the first time in 26 years that an Opposition Leader was thrown out of the parliament.
4. A 'Chaff-bag' is a large sack, used by framers to store and transport grain or 'chaff' the unwanted residue of a crop (such as the husks of seeds) that can be used for feeding livestock.

5. It should also be noted that 'bogan' can be used positively and self-referentially as a marker of Australian working-class culture and identity (for example 'Who will get my Bogan vote' [Badham 2013]). See also Moore (2019) and Nichols and Kolankiewicz (2017) for the origins and further connotations of the word.

6. See Holland and Wright (2017) for a discussion of these mythologised terms for Australian working-class men that celebrate 'mateship' and their 'laid back'; 'down-to-earth' and anti-authoritarian qualities (2017: 593).

7. The debate can be viewed at www.youtube.com/watch?v=855Am6ovK7s From 1:32:33–1:36:38.

8. The debate can be viewed at: www.youtube.com/watch?v=FRlI2SQ0Ueg from 09:23.

9. The debate can be viewed at: www.youtube.com/watch?v=smkyorC5qwc&t=5s from 15.00.

10. Governor of Alaska 2006–9, right-wing republican candidate for vice presidency in 2008–9 US election.

Chapter 8

1. This was because a woman Deputy Presiding Officer was on sick leave during this period.

2. An Early Day Motion is a single sentence motion put forward by any MP asking to be debates 'on an early day' but because they are unlikely to get parliamentary time they are mainly used to draw attention to a topic.

3. In January 2018 it was revealed that Mr Bone and his wife, Jenny Bone, had separated and had not lived together for two years (Southern and Spillett 2018).

4. Gillard then went on to explain in this interview for *Australian Weekly* that she enjoyed more domestic pursuits such as knitting and was then subjected to negative media accusations of cynically positioning herself in the domestic sphere.

References

Acton, E. K. and Potts, C., 2014. That straight talk: Sarah Palin and the sociolinguistics of demonstratives. *Journal of Sociolinguistics*, **18** (1), 3–31.

Adams, K. L., 1992. Accruing power on debate floors. In K. Hall, M. Bucholtz and B. Moonwomon, eds., *Locating Power: Proceedings of the Second Berkeley Women and Language Conference*. Berkeley: Berkeley Women and Language Group, 1–10.

Adams, K. L., 1999. Deliberate dispute and the construction of oppositional stance. *Pragmatics*, 9 (2), 231–248.

Adams, K. L., 2015. Governors debating: The role of situational, discourse and transportable identities. In J. Wilson and D. Boxer, eds., *Discourse, Politics and Women as Global Leaders*. Amsterdam: John Benjamins, 217–250.

Adcock, C., 2010. The politician, the wife, the citizen, and her newspaper. *Feminist Media Studies*, 10 (2), 135–159.

Adelswärd, V., 1989. Laughter and dialogue: The social significance of laughter in institutional discourse. *Nordic Journal of Linguistics*, 12 (2), 107–136.

Agha, A., 2003. The social life of cultural value. *Language and Communication*, 23 (3), 231–273.

Agha, A., 2007. *Language and Social Relations: Structure, Use and Social Significance*. Cambridge and New York: Cambridge University Press.

Ahmed, S., 2004. *The Cultural Politics of Emotion*. Edinburgh: Edinburgh University Press.

Ahrens, K., ed., 2009. *Politics, Gender and Conceptual Metaphors*. Basingstoke: Palgrave Macmillan.

Ahrens, P., Celis, K., Childs, S., Engeli, I., Evans, E., and Mügge, L., 2018. Editorial: Politics and gender: Rocking political science and creating new horizons. *European Journal of Politics and Gender*, 1 (1–2), 3–16.

Alexander, M., 2016. The metaphorical understanding of power and authority. In W. Anderson, E. Bramwell and C. Hough, eds., *Mapping English Metaphor through Time*. Oxford: Oxford University Press, 191–207.

Allen, P. and Childs, S., 2018. The grit in the oyster? Women's parliamentary organizations and the substantive representation of women. *Political Studies*. doi:10.1177/0032321718793080.

Alter, C., 2016. Trump faced his toughest opponent: Megyn Kelly. *Time Magazine*. http://time.com/4247405/donald-trump-megyn-kelly-debate-opponent/ [accessed 10 November 2018].

Angouri, J., 2011. 'We are in a masculine profession...': Constructing gender identities in a consortium of two multinational engineering companies. *Gender and Language*, 5 (2), 373–403.

Angouri, J., 2018a. *Culture, Discourse, and the Workplace*. London: Routledge.

Angouri, J., 2018b. Quantitative, qualitative, mixed or holistic research? Combining methods in linguistic research. In L. Litosseliti, ed., *Research Methods in Linguistics*. London: Bloomsbury, 35–55.

Anitha, S. and Gill, A., 2009. The illusion of protection? An analysis of forced marriage legislation and policy in the UK. *Journal of Social Welfare and Family Law*, 31 (3), 257–269.

Appleby, R., 2015. Julia Gillard: A murderous rage. In J. Wilson and D. Boxer, eds., *Discourse, Politics and Women as Global Leaders*. Amsterdam: John Benjamins, 149–168.

Archer, D., 2015. Slurs, insults, (backhanded) compliments and other strategic facework moves. *Language Sciences*, 52, 82–97.

Archer, D., 2018. Negotiating difference in political contexts: An exploration of Hansard. *Language Sciences*, 68 (July), 22–41.

Asenbaum, H., 2019a. Making a difference: Toward a feminist democratic theory in the digital age. *Politics & Gender*, 1–28. https://doi.org/10.1017/S1743923X18001010 [accessed 25 June 2019].

Asenbaum, H., 2019b. *Subject to Change: Anonymity and Democracy in the Digital Age*. London: University of Westminster.

Ashley, J., 2004. Bullied, patronised and abused – women MPs reveal the truth about life inside Westminster. *The Guardian*, 7 December. www.theguardian.com/politics/2004/dec/07/uk.gender [accessed 25 June 2018].

Asterhan, C. S. C., 2018. Exploring enablers and inhibitors of productive peer argumentation: The role of individual achievement goals and of gender. *Contemporary Educational Psychology*, 54 (July), 66–78.

Aston, H., 2012. Gillard's father died of shame: Alan Jones. *The Age*. www.theage.com.au/politics/federal/gillards-father-died-of-shame-alan-jones-20120929-26soa.html [accessed 24 October 2018].

Atanga, L. L., 2010. *Gender, Discourse and Power in the Cameroonian Parliament*. Oxford: African Books Collective.

Atchison, A. L., 2018. Towards the good profession: Improving the status of women in political science. *European Journal of Politics and Gender*, 1 (1–2), 279–298.

Atkinson, J. M., 1984. *Our Masters' Voices: Language and Body Language of Politics*. London: Methuen.

Atkinson, J. M. and Heritage, J., 1999. Jefferson's transcript notation. In A. Jaworski and N. Coupland, eds., *The Discourse Reader*. London: Routledge, 158–166.

Azari, J., 2015. Questions of authenticity are really questions about race, class, and democracy. *Vox*. www.vox.com/mischiefs-of-faction/2015/10/1/9431367/authenticity-race-gender-democracy [accessed 7 November 2018].

Bäck, H., Debus, M., and Müller, J., 2014. Who takes the parliamentary floor? The role of gender in speech-making in the Swedish Riksdag. *Political Research Quarterly*, 67 (3), 504–518.

Badham, V., 2013. Who will win my bogan vote? *The Guardian*, 27 May 2013. www.theguardian.com/commentisfree/2013/may/27/bogan-test-abbott-gillard [accessed 25 October 2018].

Ball, M., 2016. What kind of a man is Donald Trump? *The Atlantic*, 8 October 2016. www.theatlantic.com/politics/archive/2016/10/donald-trump-and-the-women/503402/ [accessed 10 October 2018].

Banwart, M. C. and McKinney, M. S., 2005. A gendered influence in campaign debates? Analysis of mixed-gender United States Senate and gubernatorial debates. *Communication Studies*, 56 (4), 353–373.

Barrueco, J., 2016. The real reason people question if Hillary Clinton is human. *Cosmopolitan*. www.cosmopolitan.com/politics/a6963161/hillary-clinton-unlikable-human-robotic/ [accessed 7 November 2018].

Bates, S. R., Kerr, P., Byrne, C., and Stanley, L., 2014. Questions to the Prime Minister: A comparative study of PMQs from Thatcher to Cameron. *Parliamentary Affairs*, 67 (2), 253–280.

Baxter, J., 1999. Teaching girls to speak out: An investigation of the extent to which gender is a pertinent discourse for describing and assessing girls' and boys' speech in public contexts. Unpublished PhD thesis. University of Reading.

Baxter, J., 2006. *Speaking Out: The Female Voice in Public Contexts*. Basingstoke: Palgrave Macmillan.

Baxter, J., 2010. *The Language of Female Leadership*. Basingstoke: Palgrave Macmillan and Springer.

Baxter, J., 2017. Freeing women political leaders from their gender stereotypes. In C. Ilie and S. Schnurr, eds., *Challenging Leadership Stereotypes through Discourse*. Singapore: Springer, 173–194.

Baxter, J., 2018. *Women Leaders and Gender Stereotyping in the UK Press: A Poststructuralist Approach*. Basingstoke and New York: Palgrave Macmillan.

BBC, 2015. BBC Two – Inside the commons. www.bbc.co.uk/programmes/b0522z48 [accessed 25 June 2018].

BBC News, 2018. MPs condemn 'vile' abuse of Theresa May. *BBC News Website*. www.bbc.com/news/uk-politics-45938754 [accessed 22 October 2018].

Beal, F. M., 2008. Double Jeopardy: To be black and female. *Meridians*, 8 (2), 166–176.

Beard, M., 2017. *Women and Power: A Manifesto*. London: Liveright Publishing Corporation.

Beattie, G., 2016. How Donald Trump bullies with his body language. *The Conversation*. http://theconversation.com/how-donald-trump-bullies-with-his-body-language-66468 [accessed 10 November 2018].

Beckwith, K., 2007. Numbers and newness: The descriptive and substantive representation of women. *Canadian Journal of Political Science/Revue canadienne de science politique*, 40 (1), 27–49.

Beinart, P., 2019. There's a reason many voters have negative views of Warren – But the press won't tell you why. *The Atlantic*, 2 January. www.theatlantic.com/ideas/archive/2019/01/elizabeth-warren-unpopular-it-depends-who-you-ask/579247/ [accessed 28 January 2019].

Bejarano, C. E., 2013. *The Latina Advantage: Gender, Race, and Political Success*. Austin: University of Texas Press.

Bennister, M., 2016. The oratory of Hillary Clinton. In A. Crines and D. Moon, eds., *Democratic Orators from JFK to Barack Obama*. London: Palgrave Macmillan, 239–260.

Bergvall, V., 1999. Towards a comprehensive theory of language and gender. *Language in Society*, 28 (2), 273–293.

Bicquelet, A., Weale, A., and Judith, B., 2012. In a different parliamentary voice? *Politics & Gender*, 8 (1), 83–121.

Biber, D., Conrad, S., and Leech, G., 2002. *Longman Student Grammar of Spoken and Written English*. Harlow: Longman.

Billig, M., 2000. Towards a critique of the critical. *Discourse & Society*, 11 (3), 291–292.

Bird, K., 2005. Gendering parliamentary questions. *The British Journal of Politics & International Relations*, 7 (3), 353–370.

Bird, S., 1996. Welcome to the men's club: Homosociality and the maintenance of hegemonic masculinity. *Gender and Society*, 10 (2), 120–132.

Biressi, A. and Nunn, H., 2017. Transforming the politics of gender and voice: Strategies of expertise and experience. In R. S. Sabido, ed., *Representing Communities: Discourse and Contexts*. Basingstoke: Palgrave Macmillan, 35–53.

Bjarnegård, A. P. E., 2013. *Gender, Informal Institutions and Political Recruitment: Explaining Male Dominance in Parliamentary Representation*. New York: Palgrave Macmillan.

Bjarnegård, E. and Murray, R., 2018a. Critical perspectives on men and masculinities in politics: Introduction. *Politics & Gender*, 14 (2), 264–265.

Bjarnegård, E. and Murray, R., 2018b. Revisiting forms of representation by critically examining men. *Politics & Gender*, 14 (2), 265–270.

Blair, T., 2011. *A Journey*. London: Arrow Books.

Blaxill, L. and Beelen, K., 2016. A feminized language of democracy? The representation of women at Westminster since 1945. *Twentieth Century British History*, 27 (3), 412–449.

Bock, J., Byrd-Craven, J., and Burkley, M., 2017. The role of sexism in voting in the 2016 presidential election. *Personality and Individual Differences*, 119 (December), 189–193.

Bongiorno, F., 2012. What we talk about when we talk about bogans. *Inside Story*. https://insidestory.org.au/what-we-talk-about-when-we-talk-about-bogans/ [accessed 25 October 2018].

Bortoluzzi, M. and Semino, E., 2016. Face attack in Italian politics. *Journal of Language Aggression and Conflict*, 4 (2), 178–201.

Boryczka, J. M., 2018. WANTED: Hillary Clinton, suspect citizen. *Politics & Gender*, 14 (1), 121–127.

Bourdieu, P., 1991. *Language and Symbolic Power*. Cambridge: Polity Press.

Boxer, D., Jones, L. M., and Cortés-Conde, F., 2017. Cracking the concrete ceiling in male-dominated societies: A tale of three 'Presidentas'. In C. Ilie and S. Schnurr, eds., *Challenging Leadership Stereotypes through Discourse*. Singapore: Springer, 195–219.

Boyd, M. S., 2012. Reframing the American dream: Conceptual metaphor and personal pronouns in the 2008 US presidential debates. In P. Cap and U. Okulska, eds., *Analyzing Genres in Political Communication*. Amsterdam: John Benjamins, 297–320.

Boyle, K., 2019. What's in a name? Theorising the inter-relationships of gender and violence. *Feminist Theory*, 20 (1), 19–36.

Bradley-Geist, J. C., Rivera, I., and Geringer, S. D., 2015. The collateral damage of ambient sexism: Observing sexism impacts bystander self-esteem and career aspirations. *Sex Roles*, 73 (1), 29–42.

Brescoll, V. L., 2011. Who takes the floor and why: Gender, power, and volubility in organizations. *Administrative Science Quarterly*, 56 (4), 622–641.

Brescoll, V. L., 2016. Leading with their hearts? How gender stereotypes of emotion lead to biased evaluations of female leaders. *The Leadership Quarterly*, 27 (3), 415–428.

Brewis, J., 2001. 'Telling it like it is?' Gender, language and organizational theory. In R. Westwood and S. Linstead, eds., *The Language of Organization*. London: Sage, 283–309.

Brown, A., 2000. Designing the Scottish parliament. *Parliamentary Affairs*, 53 (3), 542–556.

Brown, A., 2005. Women and the new Scottish parliament: Making a difference? (Research Summary) ESRC *End of Award Report*. R000223281 Swindon: ESRC.

Brown, P. and Levinson, S., 1987. *Politeness: Some Universals in Language Usage*. Cambridge: Cambridge University Press.

Browning, B. C., Wright, P. E., and Fowler, A. R., eds., 2018. *House of Representatives Practice*. 7th ed. Canberra: Australian Government Publishing Service. www.aph.gov.au/About_Parliament/House_of_Representatives/Powers_practice_and_procedure/Practice7 [accessed 15 October 2018].

Bull, P., 2013. The role of adversarial discourse in political opposition: Prime Minister's questions and the British phone-hacking scandal. *Language and Dialogue*, 3 (2), 254–272.

Bull, P., 2016. Theresa May has a very special technique for avoiding questions. *The Conversation*. http://theconversation.com/theresa-may-has-a-very-special-technique-for-avoiding-questions-67424 [accessed 24 September 2018].

Bull, A. and Allen, K., 2018. Introduction: Sociological interrogations of the turn to character. *Sociological Research Online*, 23 (2), 392–398.

Bull, P. and Mayer, K., 1988. Interruptions in political interviews: A study of Margaret Thatcher and Neil Kinnock. *Journal of Language and Social Psychology*, 7 (1), 35–46.

Bull, P. and Strawson, W., 2019. Can't answer? won't answer? An analysis of equivocal responses by Theresa May in Prime Minister's questions. *Parliamentary Affairs*, Online First. http://academic.oup.com/pa/advance-article/doi/10.1093/pa/gsz003/5307955 [accessed 12 February 2019].

Bull, P. and Waddle, M., 2019. Let me now answer, very directly, Marie's question. *Journal of Language Aggression and Conflict*, 7 (1), 56–78.

Bull, P. and Wells, P., 2012. Adversarial discourse in Prime Minister's questions. *Journal of Language and Social Psychology*, 31 (1), 30–48.

Burnett, D., 2011. PM must de-bogan to get attention. *Sunshine Coast Daily*, 19 July. www.sunshinecoastdaily.com.au/news/pm-must-de-bogan-her-accent-to-get-us-listening/909174/ [accessed 25 October 2018].

Butler, J., 1990. *Gender Trouble: Feminism and the Subversion of Identity*. London: Routledge.

Cameron, D., 1990. *The Feminist Critique of Language: A Reader*. London: Routledge.

Cameron, D., 1992. 'Not gender difference but the difference gender makes' – Explanation in research on sex and language. *International Journal of the Sociology of Language*, 94 (1), 13–26.

Cameron, D., 1995. *Verbal Hygiene*. London: Routledge.

Cameron, D., 1996. The language-gender interface: Challenging co-optation. In V. Bergvall and J. M. Bing, eds., *Rethinking Language and Gender Research: Theory and Practice*. New York: Longman, 31–55.

Cameron, D., 1997a. Performing gender identity: Young men's talk and the construction of heterosexual masculinity. In S. Johnson and U. H. Meinhof, eds., *Language and Masculinity*. Oxford: Blackwell, 47–64.

Cameron, D., 1997b. Theoretical debates in feminist linguistics: Questions of sex and gender. In R. Wodak, ed., *Gender and Discourse*. London: Sage, 21–37.

Cameron, D., 2000. *Good to Talk? Living and Working in a Communication Culture*. London: Sage.

Cameron, D., 2003. Gender and language ideologies. In J. Holmes and M. Meyerhoff, eds., *The Handbook of Language and Gender*. Oxford: Blackwell, 447–467.

Cameron, D., 2006. *On Language and Sexual Politics*. London: Routledge.

Cameron, D., 2007. *The Myth of Mars and Venus: Do Men and Women Really Speak Different Languages?* Oxford: Oxford University Press.

Cameron, D., 2016. On banter, bonding and Donald Trump. Language: A feminist guide. https://debuk.wordpress.com/2016/10/09/on-banter-bonding-and-donald-trump/ [accessed 11 November 2018].

Cameron, D., Frazer, E., Harvey, P., Rampton, B., and Richardson, K., 1992. *Researching Language: Issues of Power and Method*. London and New York: Routledge.

Cameron, D., McAlinden, F., and O'Leary, K., 1988. Lakoff in context: The social and linguistic functions of tag questions. In J. Coates and D. Cameron, eds., *Women in Their Speech Communities*. Harlow: Longman, 74–93.

Cameron, D. and Shaw, S., 2016. *Gender, Power and Political Speech: Women and Language in the 2015 UK General Election*. Basingstoke: Palgrave Macmillan.

Cameron, D. and Shaw, S., 2020. Constructing women's "different voice": Gendered Mediation in the 2015 UK General Election. *Journal of Language and Politics*, 19 (1), 143–159.

Campbell, A., 2011. *The Alastair Campbell Diaries. Vol. 2: Power to the People 1997–99*. London: Hutchinson.

Campbell, J., 2012. Warning women: Don't read this. *The Sydney Morning Herald*, 14 October.

Campbell, K. K., 1989. *Man Cannot Speak for Her: A Critical Study of Early Feminist Rhetoric*. New York: Praeger.

Campbell, K. K., 1998. The discursive performance of femininity: Hating Hillary. *Rhetoric & Public Affairs*, 1 (1), 1–20.

Carlin, D. B. and Winfrey, K. L., 2009. Have you come a long way, baby? Hillary Clinton, Sarah Palin, and sexism in 2008 campaign coverage. *Communication Studies*, 60 (4), 326–343.

Carter, A., Croft, A., Lukas, D., and Sandstrom, G., 2018. Women's visibility in academic seminars: Women ask fewer questions than men. *PLOS ONE*, 13 (9), e0202743. http://arxiv.org/abs/1711.10985 [accessed 3 January 2019].

Catalano, A., 2009. Women acting for women: An analysis of gender and debate participation in the British House of Commons 2005–2007. *Politics & Gender*, 5 (1), 45–68.

Celis, K. and Childs, S., 2018. Conservatism and women's political representation. *Politics & Gender*, 14 (1), 5–26.

Celis, K., Childs, S., Kantola, J., and Krook, M. L., 2008. Rethinking women's substantive representation. *Representation*, 44 (2), 99–110.

Celis, K. and Erzeel, S., 2015. Beyond the usual suspects: Non-Left, male and non-feminist MPs and the substantive representation of women. *Government and Opposition*, 50 (1), 45–64.

Celis, K., Erzeel, S., Mügge, L., and Damstra, A., 2014. Quotas and intersectionality: Ethnicity and gender in candidate selection. *International Political Science Review*, 35 (1), 41–54.

Celis, K. and Lovenduski, J., 2018. Power struggles: Gender equality in political representation. *European Journal of Politics and Gender*, 1 (1–2), 131–147.

Chaney, P., 2004. The post-devolution equality agenda: The case of the Welsh assembly's statutory duty to promote equality of opportunity. *Policy and Politics*, 32 (1), 63–77.

Chappell, L., 2006. Comparing political institutions: Revealing the gendered 'logic of appropriateness'. *Politics & Gender*, 2 (2), 223–235.

Chappell, L. and Waylen, G., 2013. Gender and the hidden life of institutions. *Public Administration*, 91 (3), 599–615.

Charteris-Black, J., 2009. Metaphor and gender in British parliamentary debates. In K. Ahrens, ed., *Politics, Gender and Conceptual Metaphors*. Basingstoke: Palgrave Macmillan, 139–165.

Charteris-Black, J., 2014. *Analysing Political Speeches: Rhetoric, Discourse and Metaphor*. Basingstoke: Palgrave Macmillan.

Charteris-Black, J., 2017. Competition metaphors and ideology: Life as a race. In R. Wodak and B. Forchtner, eds., *The Routledge Handbook of Language and Politics*. Oxford: Routledge, 202–217.

Childs, S., 2000. The new labour women MPs in the 1997 British parliament: Issues of recruitment and representation. *Women's History Review*, 9 (1), 55–73.

Childs, S., 2004. *New Labour's Women MPs: Women Representing Women*. London and New York: Routledge.

Childs, S., 2016. The good parliament. University of Bristol/ESRC. www.bristol.ac.uk/media-library/sites/news/2016/july/20%20Jul%20Prof%20Sarah%20Childs%20The%20Good%20Parliament%20report.pdf [accessed 23 July 2018].

Childs, S. and Dahlerup, D., 2018. Increasing women's descriptive representation in national parliaments: The involvement and impact of gender and politics scholars. *European Journal of Politics and Gender*, 1 (1–2), 185–204.

Childs, S. and Krook, M. L., 2006. Should feminists give up on critical mass? A contingent yes. *Politics & Gender*, 2 (4), 522–530.

Childs, S. and Webb, P., 2011. *Sex, Gender and the Conservative Party: From Iron Lady to Kitten Heels*. Basingstoke: Palgrave Macmillan.

Childs, S. and Withey, J., 2004. Women representatives acting for women: Sex and the signing of early day motions in the 1997 British parliament. *Political Studies*, 52 (3), 552–564.

Chilton, P. A., 2004. *Analysing Political Discourse: Theory and Practice*. London: Routledge.

Christie, C., 2003. Politeness and the linguistic construction of gender in parliament: An analysis of transgressions and apology behaviour. Sheffield Hallam Working Papers: Linguistic Politeness and Context. http://extra.shu.ac.uk/wpw/politeness/christie.htm [accessed 27 August 2015].

Cliff, M., 2016. Theresa May and Hillary Clinton wear matching outfits. *Mail Online*, 13 July. www.dailymail.co.uk/femail/article-3688798/Theresa-wears-yellow-black-ensemble-just-like-Hillary-Clinton.html [accessed 13 February 2019].

Clinton, H. R., 2017. *What Happened*. London: Simon & Schuster.

Clune, B., 2013. Playing the 'gender card'? As if Julia Gillard has a choice. *The Guardian*, 12 June. www.theguardian.com/commentisfree/2013/jun/12/menu-quail-julia-gillard-liberal [accessed 16 October 2018].

CNN, 2016. Full 3rd presidential debate. https://edition.cnn.com/videos/politics/2016/10/20/trump-clinton-entire-las-vegas-debate-sot.cnn [accessed 12 November 2018].

Coates, J., 1989. Gossip revisited: Language in all-female groups. In J. Coates and D. Cameron, eds., *Women in Their Speech Communities*. Harlow: Longman, 94–121.

Coates, J., 1994. The language of the professions: Discourse and career. In J. Evetts, ed., *Women and Career: Themes and Issues In Advanced Industrial Societies*. London: Routledge, 72–86.

Cockcroft, R., Cockcroft, S., Hamilton, C., and Downing, L. H., 2014. *Persuading People: An Introduction to Rhetoric*. 3rd ed. Basingstoke: Palgrave Macmillan.

Cole, H., 2017. PM-snooze: Theresa May and Jeremy Corbyn bore everyone to tears with another repetitive PMQs squabble on the NHS. 22 February. www.thesun.co.uk/news/2927654/theresa-may-and-jeremy-corbyn-bore-everyone-to-tears-with-another-repetitive-pmqs-squabble-on-the-nhs/ [accessed 21 September 2018].

Collier, C. N. and Raney, T., 2018. Understanding sexism and sexual harassment in politics: A comparison of Westminster parliaments in Australia, the United Kingdom, and Canada. *Social Politics: International Studies in Gender, State & Society*, 25 (3), 432–455.

Collins, P. H., 1990. *Black Feminist Thought: Knowledge, Consciousness, and the Politics of Empowerment*. New York: Routledge.

Collins, P. H. and Bilge, S., 2016. *Intersectionality*. Cambridge and Malden: Polity Press.

Commonwealth Parliament, 2018. Infosheet 1 – Questions. Parliament of Australia. www.aph.gov.au/About_Parliament/House_of_Representatives/Powers_practice_and_procedure/00_-_Infosheets/Infosheet_1_-_Questions [accessed 15 October 2018].

Connell, R. W., 1987. *Gender and Power: Society, the Person, and Sexual Politics*. Stanford: Stanford University Press.

Connell, R. W., 1995. *Masculinities*. Oxford: Polity Press.

Connell, R. W. and Messerschmidt, J. W., 2005. Hegemonic masculinity: Rethinking the concept. *Gender & Society*, 19 (6), 829–859.

Copland, F. and Creese, A., 2015. *Linguistic Ethnography: Collecting, Analysing and Presenting Data*. London: Sage.

Cortès-Conde, F. and Boxer, D., 2015. Breaking the glass and keeping the ceiling: Women presidentas' discursive practices in Latin America. In J. Wilson and D. Boxer, eds., *Discourse, Politics and Women as Global Leaders*. Amsterdam: John Benjamins, 43–66.

Coser, R. L., 1960. Laughter among colleagues. *Psychiatry*, 23 (1), 81–95.

Costa, R., Balz, D., and Rucker, P., 2016. Donald Trump wanted to put Bill Clinton's accusers in his family box. Debate officials said no. *The Independent*, 10 October. www.independent.co.uk/news/world/americas/us-elections/presidential-debate-donald-trump-tried-to-get-the-woman-accusing-bill-clinton-of-sex-abuse-sat-in-a7353466.html [accessed 10 November 2018].

Cotter, C., 2011. Women's place at the Fourth Estate: Constraints on voice, text, and topic. *Journal of Pragmatics*, 43 (10), 2519–2533.

Cotterill, J., 2002. *Language in the Legal Process*. Basingstoke: Palgrave Macmillan.

Coupland, N., 2007. *Style: Language Variation and Identity*. Cambridge: Cambridge University Press.

Cowburn, A., 2018. Speaker John Bercow accused of calling Andrea Leadsom a 'stupid woman'. *Independent*, 18 May. www.independent.co.uk/news/uk/politics/ john-bercow-andrea-leadsom-stupid-woman-house-of-commons-bullying-accusations-a8357071.html [accessed 29 July 2018].

Cox, L., 2018. The bullying and harassment of house of commons staff: Independent inquiry report. *Independent Inquiry Report*. www.cloisters.com/images/Bullying-Harassment-HOC-Staff-Oct-2018.pdf [accessed 5 January 2019].

Crace, J., 2016. Theresa struggles to take back control – from her Maybot. *The Guardian*, 8 November. www.theguardian.com/politics/2016/nov/08/theresa-may-struggles-take-back-control-maybot-india-brexit [accessed 25 September 2018].

Crace, J., 2018. *I, Maybot: The Rise and Fall*. 2nd ed. London: Guardian Faber Publishing.

Cracknell, R. and Keen, R., 2014. Women in parliament and government – Commons library standard note. *UK Parliament*. www.parliament.uk/business/publications/ research/briefing-papers/SN01250/women-in-parliament-and-government [accessed 18 March 2015].

Crawford, M., 1995. *Talking Difference: On Gender and Language*. London: Sage.

Creedon, P., 2018. Media narratives of gender in the contentious conservative age of Trump. In R. E. Gutsche, Jr., ed., *The Trump Presidency, Journalism, and Democracy*. New York: Routledge, 156–178.

Crenshaw, K., 1989. Demarginalizing the intersection of race and sex: A black feminist critique of antidiscrimination doctrine, feminist theory and antiracist politics. *The University of Chicago Legal Forum*, 1989, 140, 139–167.

Crenshaw, K., 1991. Mapping the margins: Intersectionality, identity politics, and violence against women of color. *Stanford Law Review*, 43 (6), 1241–1299.

Crewe, E., 2005. *Lords of Parliament: Manners, Rituals and Politics*. Manchester: Manchester University Press.

Crewe, E., 2010. An anthropology of the house of lords: Socialisation, relationships and rituals. *The Journal of Legislative Studies*, 16 (3), 313–324.

Crewe, E., 2014a. Ethnographic research in gendered organizations: The case of the Westminster parliament. *Politics & Gender*, 10 (4), 673–678.

Crewe, E., 2014b. Westminster parliamentarians: Performing politics. In S. M. Rai and R., E. Johnson, eds., *Democracy in Practice: Ceremony and Ritual in Parliament*. Basingstoke: Palgrave Macmillan, 40–59.

Crewe, E., 2015. *The House of Commons: An Anthropology of MPs at Work*. London and New York: Bloomsbury Academic.

Culpeper, J., 1996. Towards an anatomy of impoliteness. *Journal of Pragmatics*, 25 (3), 349–367.

Cunningham, C. M., Crandall, H. M., and Dare, A. M., eds., 2017. *Gender, Communication, and the Leadership Gap*. Charlotte: Information Age Publishing, Inc.

Curry, T. J., 1991. Fraternal bonding in the locker room: A profeminist analysis of talk about competition and women. *Sociology of Sport Journal*, 8 (2), 119–135.

Curry, T. J., 1998. Beyond the locker room: Campus bars and college athletes. *Sociology of Sport Journal*, 15 (3), 205–215.

Dahlerup, D., 1988. From a small to a large minority: Women in Scandinavian politics. *Scandinavian Political Studies*, 11 (4), 275–298.

Daly, M., 1977. *Beyond God the Father: Toward a Philosophy of Women's Liberation.* Boston: Beacon Press.

Davis, K., 2008. Intersectionality as buzzword: A sociology of science perspective on what makes a feminist theory successful. *Feminist Theory*, 9 (1), 67–85.

De Smet, H., 2016. How gradual change progresses: The interaction between convention and innovation. *Language Variation and Change*, 28 (1), 83–102.

De Swert, K. and Hooghe, M., 2010. When do women get a voice? Explaining the presence of female news sources in Belgian news broadcasts (2003–5). *European Journal of Communication*, 25 (1), 69–84.

Deacon, D., Downey, J., Smith, D., Stanyer, J., and Wring, D., 2017. A tale of two leaders: News media coverage of the 2017 general election. In E. Thorsen, D. Jackson and D. Lilleker, eds., *UK Election Analysis 2017: Media, Voters and the Campaign*. Bournemouth: PSA/Bournemouth University, 40–41.

Deacon, M., 2017. The real reason Tories call Emily Thornberry 'Lady Nugee'... and it isn't sexist. *The Telegraph*, 12 July. www.telegraph.co.uk/news/2017/07/12/real-reason-tories-call-emily-thornberry-lady-nugee-isnt-sexist/ [accessed 29 June 2018].

DeFrancisco, V. L., 1991. The sounds of silence: How men silence women in marital relations. *Discourse and Society*, 2 (4), 413–424.

Demmen, J., Jeffries, L., and Walker, B., 2018. Charting the semantics of labour relations in House of Commons debates spanning two hundred years. In M. Kranert and G. Horan, eds., *Doing Politics: Discursivity, Performativity and Mediation in Political Discourse*. Amsterdam: John Benjamins, 81–104.

Derks, B., Van Laar, C., and Ellemers, N., 2016. The queen bee phenomenon: Why women leaders distance themselves from junior women. *The Leadership Quarterly*, 27 (3), 456–469.

Dionne, A. M., 2010. *Women, Men and the Representation of Women in the British Parliaments: Magic Numbers?* Manchester: Manchester University Press.

Dirks, D., 2016. Progress would be accepting that Trump's 'locker room talk' illustrates 'rape culture'. *New York Times*, 13 October. www.nytimes.com/roomfordebate/2016/10/13/what-did-donald-trump-reveal-about-progress-for-women/progress-would-be-accepting-that-trumps-locker-room-talk-illustrates-rape-culture [accessed 11 November 2018].

Dodson, D. L., 2006. *The Impact of Women in Congress*. Oxford: Oxford University Press.

Dolan, J., Deckman, M. M., and Swers, M. L., 2017. *Women and Politics: Paths to Power and Political Influence*. Updated 3rd ed. Lanham: Rowman & Littlefield Publishers.

Donaghue, N., 2015. Who gets played by 'the gender card'? *Australian Feminist Studies*, 30 (84), 161–178.

Dörnyei, Z., 2007. *Research Methods in Applied Linguistics: Quantitative, Qualitative, and Mixed Methodologies*. Oxford and New York: Oxford University Press.

Dovi, S., 2018. Misogyny and transformations. *European Journal of Politics and Gender*, 1 (1–2), 131–147.

Duff, P. A., 2018. Case study research in Applied Linguistics. In L. Litosseliti, ed., *Research Methods in Linguistics*. London: Bloomsbury, 305–330.

Eades, D., 2000. I don't think it's an answer to the question: Silencing Aboriginal witnesses in court. *Language in Society*, 29 (2), 161–195.

Eagly, A. H. and Carli, L. L., 2007. *Through the Labyrinth: The Truth about How Women Become Leaders*. Boston: Harvard Business Press.

Eagly, A. H. and Heilman, M. E., 2016. Gender and leadership: Introduction to the special issue. *The Leadership Quarterly*, 27 (3), 349–353.

Eagly, A. H. and Steffen, V., 1986. Gender and aggressive behavior: A meta-analytic review of the social psychological literature. *Psychological Bulletin*, 100 (3), 309–330.

Eakins, B. and Eakins, R. G., 1976. Verbal turn-taking and exchanges in faculty dialogue. In B. L. Dubois and I. Crouch, eds., *The Sociology of the Languages of American Women*. San Antonio: Trinity University, 53–62.

Eberhardt, L. and Merolla, J. L., 2017. Shaping perceptions of Sarah Palin's charisma: Presentations of Palin in the 2008 presidential election. *Journal of Women, Politics & Policy*, 38 (2), 103–127.

Eckert, P., 1998. Gender and sociolinguistic variation. In J. Coates, ed., *Language and Gender: A Reader*. Oxford: Blackwell, 64–75.

Eckert, P. and McConnell-Ginet, S., 1992a. Communities of Practice: Where language, gender and power all live. In K. Hall, M. Bucholtz and B. Moonwomon, eds., *Locating Power: Proceedings of the Second Berkeley Women and Language Group*. Berkeley: Berkeley Women and Language Group, 88–89.

Eckert, P. and McConnell-Ginet, S., 1992b. Think practically and look locally: Language and gender as community-based practice. *Annual Review of Anthropology*, 21 (1), 461–488.

Eckert, P. and McConnell-Ginet, S., 2013. *Language and Gender*. 2nd ed. Cambridge: Cambridge University Press.

Edelsky, C., 1981. Who's got the floor? *Language in Society*, 10 (3), 383–421.

Edelsky, C. and Adams, K., 1990. Creating inequality: Breaking the rules in debates. *Journal of Language and Social Psychology*, 9 (3), 171–190.

Edmondson, C. and Lee, J. C., 2019. Meet the new freshmen in congress. *New York Times*, 3 January. www.nytimes.com/interactive/2018/11/28/us/politics/congress-freshman-class.html [accessed 14 January 2019].

Eggins, S. and Slade, D., 1997. *Analysing Casual Conversation*. London: Equinox.

Elgot, J., 2018. Bercow bullying claims are a witch-hunt, says serjeant at arms. *The Guardian*, 13 June. www.theguardian.com/politics/2018/jun/13/bercow-bullying-claims-are-a-witch-hunt-says-serjeant-at-arms [accessed 29 July 2018].

Elgot, J. and Walker, P., 2018. Jeremy Corbyn to MPs: I did not call Theresa May a 'stupid woman'. *The Guardian*, 19 December. www.theguardian.com/politics/2018/dec/19/jeremy-corbyn-accused-of-calling-theresa-may-a-stupid-woman [accessed 30 December 2018].

Enli, G., 2015. *Mediated Authenticity: How the Media Constructs Reality*. New York: Peter Lang Publishing Inc.

Erskine May, T., 2015. *A Treatise upon the Law, Privileges, Proceedings and Usage of Parliament*. Cambridge: Cambridge University Press.

Ervin-Tripp, S. and Lampert, M. D., 1992. Gender differences in the construction of humorous talk. In K. Hall, M. Bucholtz and B. Moonwomon, eds., *Locating Power: Proceedings of the Second Berkeley Women and Language Conference*. Berkeley: Berkeley Women and Language Group, 108–117.

Esposito, E., 2017. The mother's picong: A discursive approach to gender, identity and political leadership in Trinidad and Tobago. *Discourse & Society*, 28 (1), 24–41.

Evans, E., 2016. Diversity matters: Intersectionality and women's representation in the USA and UK. *Parliamentary Affairs*, 69 (3), 569–585.

Fairclough, N., 1989. *Language and Power*. Harlow: Longman.

Fairclough, N., 1992. Discourse and text: Linguistic and intertextual analysis within discourse analysis. *Discourse & Society*, 3 (2), 193–217.

Fairclough, N., 1995. *Critical Discourse Analysis: The Critical Study of Language*. London: Longman.

Fairclough, N., 2000. *New Labour, New Language?* London: Routledge.

Fairclough, N. and Fairclough, I., 2012. *Political Discourse Analysis: A Method for Advanced Students*. London: Routledge.

Fairclough, N. and Wodak, R., 1997. Critical discourse analysis. In: T. A. van Dijk, ed., *Discourse as Social Interaction*. London: Sage, 258–284.

Falk, E., 2010. *Women for President: Media Bias in Nine Campaigns*. Champaign: University of Illinois Press.

Falk, E., 2013. Clinton and the playing-the-gender-card metaphor in campaign news. *Feminist Media Studies*, 13 (2), 192–207.

Fawcett Society, 2015. Views not shoes. *Fawcett Society*. www.fawcettsociety.org.uk/views-not-shoes [accessed 2 August 2018].

Feld, V., 2000. A new start in Wales: How devolution is making a difference. In A. Coote, ed., *New Gender Agenda: Why Women Still Want More*. London: Institute for Public Policy Research, 74–80.

Felice, R. D. and Garretson, G., 2018. Politeness at work in the Clinton email Corpus: A first look at the effects of status and gender. *Corpus Pragmatics*, 2 (3), 1–22.

Feng, W. and Wu, D., 2015. Discourses of female leaders in postcolonial Hong Kong. In J. Wilson and D. Boxer, eds., *Discourse, Politics and Women as Global Leaders*. Amsterdam: John Benjamins, 251–274.

Fenton-Smith, B., 2008. Discourse structure and political performance in adversarial parliamentary questioning. *Journal of Language and Politics*, 7 (1), 97–118.

Fetzer, A. and Weizman, E., 2018. 'What I would say to John and everyone like John is...': The construction of ordinariness through quotations in mediated political discourse. *Discourse & Society*, 29 (5), 495–513.

Fetzer, A., Weizman, E., and Berlin, L. N., eds., 2015. *The Dynamics of Political Discourse: Forms and Functions of Follow-Ups*. Amsterdam: John Benjamins.

First Republican Primary Debate, 2016. Cleveland: Fox News Channel: Quicken Loans Arena. https://video.foxnews.com/v/4406746003001/?#sp=show-clips [accessed 10 November 2018].

Fisher, V. and Kinsey, S., 2014. Behind closed doors! Homosocial desire and the academic boys club. *Gender in Management: An International Journal*, 29 (1), 44–64.

Formato, F., 2014. Language use and gender in the Italian parliament. PhD thesis. Lancaster: Lancaster University. http://eprints.lancs.ac.uk/71736/ [accessed 30 April 2018].

Formato, F., 2019. *Gender, Discourse and Ideology in Italian*. London: Palgrave Macmillan.

Foucault, M., 1972. *The Archaeology of Knowledge*. New York: Pantheon Books Inc.

Fracchiolla, B., 2011. Politeness as a strategy of attack in a gendered political debate – The Royal–Sarkozy debate. *Journal of Pragmatics*, 43 (10), 2480–2488.

Franceschet, S., 2011. Gendered institutions and women's substantive representation: Female legislators in Argentina and Chile. In M. L. Krook and F. Mackay, eds., *Gender, Politics and Institutions: Towards a Feminist Institutionalism*. Basingstoke and New York: Palgrave Macmillan, 58–78.

Franklin, M. N. and Norton, P., eds., 1993. *Parliamentary Questions*. Oxford and New York: Clarendon Press.

Freed, A. F., 1996. Language and gender in an experimental setting. In V. Bergvall and J. M. Bing, eds., *Rethinking Language and Gender Research: Theory and Practice*. New York: Longman, 55–76.

Freeman, H., 2016. Theresa May, Margaret Thatcher: Spot the difference – and the sexism. *The Guardian*, 23 July. www.theguardian.com/lifeandstyle/commentisfree/2016/jul/23/theresa-may-margaret-thatcher-spot-the-difference-uk-politics-hadley-freeman [accessed 8 April 2018].

Frenkel, D., 2011. Drop the Gillard twang: It's beginning to annoy. *The Sydney Morning Herald*, 20 April. www.smh.com.au/politics/federal/drop-the-gillard-twang-its-beginning-to-annoy-20110420-1dosf.html [accessed 11 October 2018].

Friedman, A., 2013. Hey 'ladies'. *The New Republic*. https://newrepublic.com/article/112188/how-word-lady-has-evolved [accessed 30 September 2018].

Gains, F. and Lowndes, V., 2014. How is institutional formation gendered, and does it make a difference? A new conceptual framework and a case study of police and crime commissioners in England and Wales. *Politics & Gender*, 10 (4), 524–548.

Gal, S., 1991. Between speech and silence: The problematics of research on language and gender. In M. di Leonardo, ed., *Gender at the Crossroads of Knowledge: Feminist Anthropology in the Postmodern Era*. Berkeley: University of California Press, 175–203.

Gal, S., 1995. Language, gender and power: An anthropological review. In K. Hall and M. Bucholtz, eds., *Gender Articulated: Language and the Socially Constructed Self*. London: Routledge, 170–182.

Gal, S., 2018. Registers in circulation: The social organization of interdiscursivity. *Signs and Society*, 6 (1), 1–24.

Galea, N. and Gaweda, B., 2018. (De)constructing the masculine blueprint: The institutional and discursive consequences of male political dominance. *Politics & Gender*, 14 (2), 276–282.

Gardner, B., 2014. From 'shrill' housewife to Downing Street: The changing voice of Margaret Thatcher, 25 November. www.telegraph.co.uk/news/politics/11251919/From-shrill-housewife-to-Downing-Street-the-changing-voice-of-Margaret-Thatcher.html [accessed 31 July 2018].

Gawne, L., 2011. Accent on politicians' speech misses the point. *The Sydney Morning Herald*, 28 November. www.smh.com.au/politics/federal/accent-on-politicians-speech-misses-the-point-20111128-1o360.html [accessed 25 October 2018].

Gershon, S., 2012. When race, gender, and the media intersect: Campaign news coverage of minority congresswomen. *Journal of Women, Politics & Policy*, 33 (2), 105–125.

Ghitis, F., 2016. The 'shrill' smear against Hillary Clinton. *CNN*. www.cnn.com/2016/02/08/opinions/hillary-clinton-sexism-ghitis/index.html [accessed 13 November 2018].

Gill, R., 2011. Sexism reloaded, or, it's time to get angry again! *Feminist Media Studies*, 11 (1), 61–71.

Gill, R. and Orgad, S., 2018. The amazing bounce-backable woman: Resilience and the psychological turn in neoliberalism. *Sociological Research Online*, 23 (2), 477–495.

Gillard, J., 2013a. Interview with Julia Gillard. www.nowtolove.com.au/celebrity/celeb-news/julia-gillard-why-shes-knitting-for-the-royal-baby-9786 [accessed 12 June 2018].

Gillard, J., 2013b. Julia Gillard's resignation speech. http://rescu.com.au/julia-gillards-speech-video-transcript/ [accessed 5 January 2019].

Gillard, J., 2014. *My Story*. Sydney: Random House.

Gillard, J., and Summers, A., 2013. "Julia Gillard and Anne Summers." *Big Ideas, ABC Radio National*. www.abc.net.au/radionational/programs/bigideas/Julia-gillard-26-anne-summers/4978214 [accessed 7 February 2020]

Gilligan, C., 1982. *In a Different Voice: Psychological Theory and Women's Development*. Harvard: Harvard University Press.

Glaze, B., 2018. How stubborn May stumbled into leadership fight thanks to blunder after blunder. *Daily Mirror*. www.mirror.co.uk/news/politics/how-stubborn-theresa-ploughed-no-13724406 [accessed 15 February 2019].

Gleason, S. A., 2019. Beyond Mere presence: Gender norms in oral arguments at the U.S. supreme court. *Political Research Quarterly*. doi:10.1177/1065912919847001.

Gobo, G., 2008. *Doing Ethnography*. London: Sage.

Goldstein, D. M. and Hall, K., 2017. Postelection surrealism and nostalgic racism in the hands of Donald Trump. *HAU: Journal of Ethnographic Theory*, 7 (1), 397–406.

Goetz, A. M., 2003. Women's political effectiveness: A conceptual framework. In A. M. Goetz and S. Hassim, eds., *No Shortcuts to Power: African Women in Politics and Policy Making*. London: Zed Books, 29–80.

Goffman, E., 1959. *The Presentation of Self in Everyday Life*. Harmondsworth: Penguin.

Goffman, E., 1981. *Forms of Talk*. Philadelphia: University of Pennsylvania Press.

Goldsworthy, A., 2013. Unfinished business: Sex, freedom and misogyny. *Quarterly Essay*, 50 (1), 1–79.

Goodsell, C. T., 1988. The architecture of parliaments: Legislative houses and political culture. *British Journal of Political Science*, 18 (3), 287–302.

Goodwin, M. H., 2006. *The Hidden Life of Girls: Games of Stance, Status, and Exclusion*. Malden: Wiley-Blackwell.

Gordon, K., Gordon, R., and Nabor, A., 2017. The reinforcement of hegemonic masculinity through gender frames during the 2016 election. *Global Tides*, 11 (8), 1–16.

Goren, L. J., 2018. Authenticity and emotion: Hillary Rodham Clinton's dual constraints. *Politics & Gender*, 14 (1), 111–115.

Gorman, T., 1993. *The Bastards: Dirty Tricks and the Challenge to Europe*. London: Pan.

Govier, T., 1999. *The Philosophy of Argument*. Newport News: Vale Press.

Graddol, D. and Swann, J., 1989. *Gender Voices*. Oxford: Wiley-Blackwell.

Graham, K., Bernards, S., Abbey, A., Dumas, T. M., and Wells, S., 2017. When women do not want it: Young female Bargoers' experiences with and responses to sexual harassment in social drinking contexts. *Violence Against Women*, 23 (12), 1419–1441.

Graham, R., 2019. The users of unparliamentary language in the New Zealand House of Representatives 1890 to 1950: A community of practice perspective. *Journal of Pragmatics*, 149 (August), 14–24.

Grant, J., 2018. A left feminist comment on supporting Hillary Clinton. *Politics & Gender*, 14 (1), 106–111.

Grebelsky-Lichtman, T. and Katz, R., 2019. When a man debates a woman: Trump vs. Clinton in the first mixed gender presidential debates. *Journal of Gender Studies*. doi:10.1080/09589236.2019.1566890.

Green, J. and Bloome, D., 1997. Ethnography and ethnographers of and in education: A situated perspective. In J. Flood, S. Heath and D. Lapp, eds., *A Handbook for Literacy Educators*. New York: Macmillan, 181–202.

Greene, J. C. and Caracelli, V. J., 2003. Making paradigmatic sense of mixed-method practice. In A. Tashakkori and C. Teddlie, eds., *Handbook of Mixed Methods in Social and Behavioral Research*. Thousand Oaks: Sage, 91–110.

Grey, J., 1992. *Men Are from Mars, Women Are from Venus*. New York: Harper Collins.

Grimshaw, J., 1987. Philosophy and aggression. *Radical Philosophy*, 47 (Autumn), 18–20.

Gumperz, J. J. and Hymes, D. H., 1972. *Directions in Sociolinguistics: Ethnography of Communications*. New York: Holt McDougal.

Haack, S., 2003. Truth, truths, 'truth', and 'truths' in the law. *Harvard Journal of Law & Public Policy*, 26 (1), 17–21.

Hall, L. J. and Donaghue, N., 2013. 'Nice girls don't carry knives': Constructions of ambition in media coverage of Australia's first female prime minister. *British Journal of Social Psychology*, 52 (4), 631–647.

Hall, R. M. and Sandler, B. R., 1982. The classroom climate: A chilly one for women? Washington, DC: Project on the Status and Education of Women, Association of American Colleges. https://eric.ed.gov/?id=ED215628 [accessed 4 July 2018].

Haraldsson, A. and Wängnerud, L., 2019. The effect of media sexism on women's political ambition: Evidence from a worldwide study. *Feminist Media Studies*, 19 (4), 525–541.

Harman, H., 2017. *A Woman's Work*. London: Allen Lane/Penguin Random House.

Harmer, E., 2017. Online election news can be bloody difficult (for a) woman. In E. Thorsen, D. Jackson, and D. Lilleker, eds., *UK Election Analysis 2017: Media Voters and the Campaign*. Poole: Bournemouth University, Political Studies Association/Centre for Politics and Media Research, 39.

Harrington, K., Litosseliti, L., Sauntson, H., and Sunderland, J., eds., 2008. *Gender and Language Research Methodologies*. Basingstoke and New York: Palgrave Macmillan.

Harris, S., 1984. Questions as a mode of control in magistrates' courts. *International Journal of the Sociology of Language*, 1984 (49), 5–28.

Harris, S., 2001. Being politically impolite: Extending politeness theory to adversarial political discourse. *Discourse & Society*, 12 (4), 451–472.

Haywood, C., Johansson, T., Hammarén, N., Herz, M., and Ottemo, A., 2018. *The Conundrum of Masculinity: Hegemony, Homosociality, Homophobia and Heteronormativity*. Oxon: Routledge.

Hazarika, A. and Hamilton, T., 2018. *Punch and Judy Politics: An Insiders' Guide to Prime Minister's Questions*. London: Biteback Publishing.

Hearn, J., 1992. *Men in the Public Eye*. London: Routledge.

Heilman, M. E., 1983. Sex bias in work settings: The lack of fit model. *Research in Organizational Behavior*, 5, 269–298. https://nyuscholars.nyu.edu/en/publications/sex-bias-in-work-settings-the-lack-of-fit-model.

Heller, M., Pietikäinen, S., and Pujolar, J., 2018. *Critical Sociolinguistic Research Methods: Studying Language Issues That Matter*. London: Routledge.

Hellinger, M., 1990. *Kontrastive Feministische Linguistik*. Ismaning: Hueber.

Helmke, G. and Levitsky, S., 2004. Informal institutions and comparative politics: A research agenda. *Perspectives on Politics*, 2 (4), 725–740.

Henderson, B., 2016. Donald Trump makes rare apology after video emerges of him making sexually aggressive comments about women. *The Telegraph*, 7 October. www.telegraph.co.uk/news/2016/10/07/donald-trump-on-groping-and-kissing-women-when-youre-a-star-they/ [accessed 11 November 2018].

Hewitt, R., 1997. 'Boxing out' and 'taxing'. In S. Johnson and U. H. Meinhof, eds., *Language and Masculinity*. Oxford: Blackwell, 27–46.

Holland, J. and Wright, K. A., 2017. The double delegitimatisation of Julia Gillard: Gender, the media, and Australian political culture. *Australian Journal of Politics and History*, 63 (4), 588–602.

Holmes, J., 1992. Women's talk in public contexts. *Discourse and Society*, 3 (2), 121–150.

Holmes, J., 1995. *Women, Men and Politeness*. London: Longman.

Holmes, J., 2006. *Gendered Talk at Work: Constructing Gender Identity Through Workplace Discourse*. Oxford: Blackwell.

Holmes, J., 2017. Leadership and change management: Examining gender, cultural and 'hero leader' stereotypes. In C. Ilie and S. Schnurr, eds., *Challenging Leadership Stereotypes through Discourse*. Singapore: Springer, 15–43.

Holmes, J. and Marra, M., 2002. Having a laugh at work: How humour contributes to workplace culture. *Journal of Pragmatics*, 34 (12), 1683–1710.

Holmes, J. and Meyerhoff, M., 1999. The community of practice: Theories and methodologies in language and gender research. *Language in Society*, 28 (2), 173–183.

Holmes, J. and Stubbe, M., 2003. 'Feminine' workplaces: Stereotype and reality. In J. Holmes and M. Meyerhoff, eds., *The Handbook of Language and Gender*. Oxford: Blackwell, 573–600.

Homer, 1980. *The Odyssey*. Oxford: Oxford University Press.

Hoyt, C. L. and Murphy, S. E., 2016. Managing to clear the air: Stereotype threat, women, and leadership. *The Leadership Quarterly*, 27 (3), 387–399.

Hughes, R., 1996. *English in Speech and Writing: Investigating Language and Literature*. London: Routledge.

Hundleby, C., 2013. Aggression, politeness and abstract adversaries. *Informal Logic*, 33 (2), 238–262.

Hyde, J. S., 2005. The gender similarity hypothesis. *American Psychologist*, 60 (6), 581–592.

Hymes, D. H., 1972a. Models of the interaction of language and social life. In J. Gumperz and D. H. Hymes, eds., *Directions in Sociolinguistics: The Ethnography of Communication*. Oxford: Blackwell, 35–71.

Hymes, D. H., 1972b. Toward ethnographies of communication: The analysis of communicative events. In P. Giglioli, ed., *Language and Social Context.* Harmondsworth: Penguin, 21–44.

Hymes, D. H., 1974. *Foundations in Sociolinguistics: An Ethnographic Approach.* Philadelphia: University of Pennsylvania Press.

Ilie, C., 2010. Strategic uses of parliamentary forms of address: The case of the U.K. Parliament and the Swedish Riksdag. *Journal of Pragmatics*, 42 (4), 885–911.

Ilie, C., 2013. Gendering confrontational rhetoric: Discursive disorder in the British and Swedish parliaments. *Democratization*, 20 (3), 501–521.

Ilie, C., 2015. Follow-ups as multifunctional questioning and answering strategies in Prime Minister's Questions. In A. Fetzer, E. Weizman and L. N. Berlin, eds., *The Dynamics of Political Discourse: Forms and Functions of Follow-Ups.* Amsterdam: John Benjamins, 195–218.

Ilie, C., 2018. Behave yourself, woman! *Journal of Language and Politics*, 17 (5), 594–616.

Ilie, C. and Schnurr, S., eds., 2017. *Challenging Leadership Stereotypes through Discourse: Power, Management and Gender.* Singapore: Springer.

Inside the Commons, 2015. Episode 1, lifting the lid, inside the commons – BBC Two. *Open University and BBC.* www.open.edu/openlearn/tv-radio-events/tv/inside-the-commons?episode=18178#episode-details [accessed on 4 February 2015].

Jacobson, L., 2017. Did Elizabeth Warren break the rules? Plus 5 other questions about Rule 19. *PolitiFact.* www.politifact.com/truth-o-meter/article/2017/feb/08/did-elizabeth-warren-break-rules-plus-5-other-ques/ [accessed 22 December 2018].

Jacobsen, R. R., 2019. Interruptions and co-construction in the First 2016 Trump–Clinton US presidential debate. *Journal of Pragmatics*, 148 (July), 71–87.

Jamieson, K. H., 1995. *Beyond the Double Bind: Women and Leadership.* New York: Oxford University Press.

Jenkins, M. M., 1985. 'What's so funny?' Joking among women. In S. Bremner, N. Caskey and B. Moonwomon, eds., *Proceedings of the First Berkeley Women and Language Conference.* Berkeley: Berkeley Women and Language Group, 135–151.

Johnson, S. K., Murphy, S. E., Zewdie, S., and Reichard, R. J., 2008. The strong, sensitive type: Effects of gender stereotypes and leadership prototypes on the evaluation of male and female leaders. *Organizational Behavior and Human Decision Processes*, 106 (1), 39–60.

Jones, A. R., 1987. Nets and bridles: Early modern conduct books and sixteenth century women's lyrics. In N. Armstrong and L. Tennenhouse, eds., *The Ideology of Conduct: Essays on Literature and the History of Sexuality.* New York: Methuen, 39–72.

Jones, J. J., 2016. Talk 'like a man': The linguistic styles of Hillary Clinton, 1992–2013. *Perspectives on Politics*, 14 (3), 625–642.

Jones, L. M., 2015. Ellen Johnson Sirleaf: Media's 'Ma Ellen' or the 'Iron Lady' of West Africa? Textual discourse and the brand of a leader. In J. Wilson and D. Boxer, eds., *Discourse, Politics and Women as Global Leaders.* Amsterdam: John Benjamins, 315–344.

Kammoun, R., 2015. Gender and political discourse in Tunisia. In J. Wilson and D. Boxer, eds., *Discourse, Politics and Women as Global Leaders.* Amsterdam: John Benjamins, 121–148.

Kane, M. J. and Disch, L. J., 1993. Sexual violence and the reproduction of male power in the locker room: The 'Lisa Olson incident'. *Sociology of Sport Journal*, 10 (4), 331–352.

Kanter, R. M., 1977. *Men and Women of the Corporation*. New York: Basic Books.

Karpowitz, C. F. and Mendelberg, T., 2014. *The Silent Sex: Gender, Deliberation, and Institutions*. Princeton: Princeton University Press.

Kathlene, L., 1994. Power and influence in state legislative policy making: The interaction of gender and position in committee hearing debates. *American Political Science Review*, 88 (3), 560–576.

Kathlene, L., 1995. Position power versus gender power: Who holds the floor? In G. Duerst-Lahti and R. Kelly, eds., *Gender, Power, Leadership and Governance*. Ann Arbor: University of Michigan Press, 167–193.

Kelly, L., 1988. *Surviving Sexual Violence*. Oxford: Polity Press.

Kelly, R., 2018. Independent complaints and grievance scheme. https://researchbriefings.parliament.uk/ResearchBriefing/Summary/CBP-8369 [accessed 19 January 2019].

Khazan, O., 2016. What criticisms of Hillary's voice say about our hidden biases. *The Atlantic*. www.theatlantic.com/science/archive/2016/08/hillarys-voice/493565/ [accessed 13 November 2018].

King, M., 2005. A critical assessment of Steenbergen et al's Discourse Quality Index. *Roundhouse: A Journal of Critical Theory and Practice*, 1 (1), 1–8.

Kirkup, J., 2008. David Cameron fails to end 'Punch and Judy' politics. www.telegraph.co.uk/news/politics/conservative/1908155/David-Cameron-fails-to-end-Punch-and-Judy-politics.html [accessed 19 January 2019].

Klofstad, C. A., Anderson, R. C., and Peters, S., 2012. Sounds like a winner: Voice pitch influences perception of leadership capacity in both men and women. *Proceedings of the Royal Society of London B: Biological Sciences*, 279 (1738), 2698–2704.

Klofstad, C. A., Nowicki, S., and Anderson, R. C., 2016. How voice pitch influences our choice of leaders. *American Scientist; Research Triangle Park*, 104 (5), 282–287.

Knight, H. M., 1992. Gender interference in transsexuals' speech. In K. Hall, M. Bucholtz and B. Moonwomon, eds., *Locating Power: Proceedings of the Second Berkeley Women and Language Conference*. Berkeley: Berkeley Women and Language Group, 312–317.

Koller, V. and Semino, E., 2009. Metaphor, politics and gender: A case study from Germany. In K. Ahrens, ed., *Politics, Gender and Conceptual Metaphors*, Basingstoke: Palgrave Macmillan, 9–35.

Kram, K. and Hampton, M. M., 2003. When women lead: The visibility-vulnerability spiral. In R. J. Ely, E. G. Foldy and M. A. Scully, eds., *Reader in Gender, Work and Organization*. Oxford: Blackwell, 211–223.

Krook, M. L., 2015. Empowerment versus backlash: Gender quotas and critical mass theory. *Politics, Groups, and Identities*, 3 (1), 184–188.

Krook, M. L., 2017. Violence against women in politics. *Journal of Democracy*, 28 (1), 74–88.

Krook, M. L., 2018. Westminster too: On sexual harassment in British politics. *The Political Quarterly*, 89 (1), 65–72.

Krook, M. L. and Mackay, F., 2011. *Gender, Politics and Institutions: Towards a Feminist Institutionalism*. Basingstoke and New York: Palgrave Macmillan.

Kulick, D., 1993. Speaking as a woman: Structure and gender in domestic arguments in a New Guinea village. *Cultural Anthropology*, 8 (4), 510–541.

Lakoff, R. T., 1990. *Talking Power: The Politics of Language*. New York: Basic Books.

Larson, B. N., 2016. Gender/genre: The lack of gendered register in texts requiring genre knowledge. *Written Communication*, 33 (4), 360–384.

Lawrence, R. G. and Rose, M., 2010. *Hillary Clinton's Race for the White House: Gender Politics and the Media on the Campaign Trail*. Boulder: Lynne Rienner Publishers.

Lazar, M. M., 2005. *Feminist Critical Discourse Analysis: Gender, Power and Ideology in Discourse*. Basingstoke: Palgrave Macmillan.

Legman, G., 2006. *Rationale of the Dirty Joke: An Analysis of Sexual Humor*. 2nd ed. New York: Simon & Schuster.

Levon, E., 2015. Integrating intersectionality in language, gender, and sexuality research. *Language and Linguistics Compass*, 9 (7), 295–308.

Lim, E. T., 2009. Gendered metaphors of women in power: The case of Hillary Clinton as Madonna, unruly woman, bitch and witch. In K. Ahrens, ed., *Politics, Gender and Conceptual Metaphors*. Basingstoke: Palgrave Macmillan, 254–269.

Loke, J., Harp, D., and Bachmann, I., 2011. Mothering and governing: How news articulated gender roles in the cases of Governors Jane Swift and Sarah Palin. *Journalism Studies*, 12 (2), 205–220.

Lovenduski, J., 2005. *Feminizing Politics*. Cambridge and Malden: Polity Press.

Lovenduski, J., 2014a. The institutionalisation of sexism in politics. *Political Insight*, 5 (2), 16–19.

Lovenduski, J., 2014b. Prime Minister's questions as political ritual at Westminster. In S. M. Rai and R. E. Johnson, eds., *Democracy in Practice: Ceremony and Ritual in Parliament*. Basingstoke: Palgrave Macmillan, 132–162.

Luff, D., 1999. Dialogue across the divides: 'Moments of rapport' and power in feminist research with anti-feminist women. *Sociology*, 33 (4), 687–703.

Lünenborg, M. and Maier, T., 2015. Governing in the gendered structure of power: The media discourse on Angela Merkel and her power-driven leadership style. In J. Wilson and D. Boxer, eds., *Discourse, Politics and Women as Global Leaders*. Amsterdam: John Benjamins, 275–292.

Maas, M. K., McCauley, H. L., Bonomi, A. E., and Leija, S. G., 2018. 'I was grabbed by my pussy and its #NotOkay': A Twitter backlash against Donald Trump's degrading commentary. *Violence Against Women*, 24 (14), 1739–1750.

Mackay, F., 2004. Gender and political representation in the UK: The state of the 'discipline'. *British Journal of Politics and International Relations*, 6 (1), 99–100.

Mackay, F., 2010. Gendering constitutional change and policy outcomes: Substantive representation and domestic violence policy in Scotland. *Policy and Politics*, 38 (3), 369–388.

Mackay, F., 2014. Nested newness, institutional innovation, and the gendered limits of change. *Politics & Gender*, 10 (4), 549–571.

Mackay, F. and McAllister, L., 2012. Feminising British politics: Six lessons from devolution in Scotland and Wales. *The Political Quarterly*, 83 (4), 730–734.

Mackay, F., Myers, F., and Brown, A., 2003. Towards a new politics? Women and constitutional change in Scotland. In A. Dobrowolsky and V. Hart, eds., *Women Making Constitutions: New Politics and Comparative Perspectives*. Basingstoke: Palgrave Macmillan, 84–98.

Mackay, F. and Waylen, G., 2014. Introduction: Gendering 'new' institutions. *Politics & Gender*, 10 (4), 489–494.

Maddox, B., 2019. UK parliament should use renovation to rethink its ways. *Financial Times*, 6 January. www.ft.com/content/80012468-101a-11e9-b2f2-f4c566a4fc5f [accessed 27 January 2019].

Madill, C., 2011. Nervous not nasal, misunderstood not misleading – Julia's just trying too hard. *The Conversation*. http://theconversation.com/nervous-not-nasal-misunderstood-not-misleading-julias-just-trying-too-hard-1301 [accessed 25 October 2018].

Malley, R., 2012. Feeling at home: Inclusion at Westminster and the Scottish Parliament. *The Political Quarterly*, 83 (4), 714–716.

Mansbridge, J. J., 1983. *Beyond Adversary Democracy*. Chicago: University of Chicago Press.

Mansbridge, J. J., 1999. Should blacks represent blacks and women represent women? A contingent 'yes'. *The Journal of Politics*, 61 (3), 628–657.

Marra, M., Holmes, J., and Kidner, K., 2017. Transitions and interactional competence: Negotiating boundaries through talk. In S. P. Doehler, A. Bangerter, G. de Weck, L. Filliettaz, E. González-Martínez, and C. Petitjean, eds., *Interactional Competences in Institutional Settings*. Cham: Palgrave Macmillan, 227–251.

Martin, J., 2014. *Politics and Rhetoric: A Critical Introduction*. London: Routledge.

Mavin, S., 2006. Venus envy: Problematizing solidarity behaviour and queen bees. *Women in Management Review*, 21 (4), 264–276.

Mavin, S., Bryans, P., and Cunningham, R., 2010. Fed-up with Blair's babes, Gordon's gals, Cameron's cuties, Nick's nymphets: Challenging gendered media representations of women political leaders. *Gender in Management: An International Journal*, 25 (7), 550–569.

May, T., 2009. Theresa May: My life as a female MP. *BBC News*, 17 June. http://news.bbc.co.uk/1/hi/business/8033607.stm [accessed 13 February 2019].

May, T., 2017a. Theresa May BBC interview with Laura Kuenssberg. www.bbc.co.uk/news/uk-politics-39784170 [accessed 2 June 2018].

May, T., 2017b. Theresa May defends temporary exclusion orders and her record on security. *TV*. www.itv.com/news/2017-06-06/theresa-may-defends-temporary-exclusion-orders-and-her-record-on-security/ [accessed 15 February 2019].

May, T., 2018a. PM's vote 100 speech: 6 February 2018. *GOV.UK*. www.gov.uk/government/speeches/pms-vote-100-speech-6-february-2018 [accessed 13 February 2019].

May, T., 2018b. Theresa May BBC interview with Laura Kuenssberg. *TV*. www.bbc.co.uk/news/uk-politics-39784170 [accessed 9 October 2018].

May, T., 2018c. Theresa May's speech to the 2018 conservative party conference. www.politicshome.com/news/uk/political-parties/conservative-party/news/98760/read-full-theresa-mays-speech-2018 [accessed 9 October 2018].

McDougall, L., 1998. *Westminster Women*. London: Vintage.

McElhinny, B., 1998. I Don't smile much anymore: Affect, gender, and the discourse of Pittsburgh police officers. In J. Coates, ed., *Language and Gender: A Reader*. Oxford: Blackwell Publishers, 309–327.

McElhinny, B., 2003. Theorizing gender in sociolinguistics and linguistic anthropology. In J. Holmes and M. Meyerhoff, eds., *The Handbook of Language and Gender*. Oxford: Blackwell, 21–42.

McGlone, M. S. and Pfiester, R. A., 2015. Stereotype threat and the evaluative context of communication. *Journal of Language and Social Psychology*, 34 (2), 111–137.

Mclean, J. and Maalsen, S., 2013. Destroying the joint and dying of shame? A geography of revitalised feminism in social media and beyond. *Geographical Research*, 51 (3), 243–256.

Medeiros, M., Forest, B., Shah, P., and Juenke, E. G., 2019. Still not there: Continued challenges to women's political representation. *Politics, Groups, and Identities*, 7 (2), 386–388.

Media Watch 'Alan Jones's chaff bag is filling up fast', 2012. Australian Broadcasting Corporation. www.abc.net.au/mediawatch/episodes/alan-joness-chaff-bag-is-filling-up-fast/9973982 [accessed 23 October 2018].

Mellgren, C., Andersson, M., and Ivert, A.-K., 2018. 'It happens all the time': Women's experiences and normalization of sexual harassment in public space. *Women & Criminal Justice*, 28 (4), 262–281.

Mendes, K., Ringrose, J., and Keller, J., 2018. #MeToo and the promise and pitfalls of challenging rape culture through digital feminist activism. *European Journal of Women's Studies*, 25 (2), 236–246.

Meyjes, T., 2016. Theresa May turned into Margaret Thatcher right before our eyes during first PMQs. *Metro*. https://metro.co.uk/2016/07/20/theresa-may-turned-into-margaret-thatcher-right-before-our-eyes-during-first-pmqs-6018209/ [accessed 24 September 2018].

Millar, S., Wilson, J., and Boxer, D., 2015. Under fire: Pronominal use and leadership in the discourse of Helle Thorning-Schmidt. In J. Wilson and D. Boxer, eds., *Discourse, Politics and Women as Global Leaders*. Amsterdam: John Benjamins, 67–92.

Miller, J., 2016. Polls say Hillary Clinton won the debates – will it matter? *CBS News: Face the Nation*. www.cbsnews.com/news/polls-hillary-clinton-won-debates-election-2016-donald-trump/ [accessed 10 November 2018].

Mills, S., 1992. Discourse competence: Or how to theorize strong women speakers. *Hypatia*, 7 (2), 4–17.

Mills, S., 2003. Caught between sexism, anti-sexism and 'political correctness': Feminist women's negotiations with naming practices. *Discourse & Society*, 14 (1), 87–110.

Mills, S., 2008. *Language and Sexism*. Cambridge: Cambridge University Press.

Mills, S. and Mullany, L., 2011. *Language, Gender and Feminism: Theory, Methodology and Practice*. London: Routledge.

Mitchell, J., 2010. The narcissism of small differences: Scotland and Westminster. *Parliamentary Affairs*, 63 (1), 98–116.

Mohammed, D., 2018. *Argumentation in Prime Minister's Question Time: Accusation of Inconsistency in Response to Criticism*. Amsterdam: John Benjamins.

Moir, 2018. You have to admire Theresa May's resilience and grit. *Daily Mail*, 17 November. www.dailymail.co.uk/debate/article-6399497/JAN-MOIR-admire-Theresa-Mays-resilience-grit-fire.html [accessed 22 February 2019].

Mollin, S., 2007. The Hansard hazard: Gauging the accuracy of British parliamentary transcripts. *Corpora*, 2 (2), 187–210.

Montgomery, M., 2001. The uses of authenticity: 'Speaking from experience' in a U.K. election broadcast. *The Communication Review*, 4 (4), 447–462.

Montgomery, M., 2011. The accountability interview: Politics and change in UK public service broadcasting. In M. Ekström and M. Patrona, eds., *Talking Politics in Broadcast Media: Cross Cultural Perspectives on Political Interviewing, Journalism and Accountability*. Amsterdam: John Benjamins, 33–56.

Moore, B., 2019. A new twist in the elusive quest for the origins of the word 'bogan' leads to Melbourne's Xavier College. *The Conversation*. http://theconversation.com/a-new-twist-in-the-elusive-quest-for-the-origins-of-the-word-bogan-leads-to-melbournes-xavier-college-113755 [accessed 27 June 2019]

Mouffe, C., 2013. *Agonistics: Thinking the World Politically*. London: Verso Books.

Moulton, J., 1983. A paradigm of philosophy: The adversary method. In S. Harding and M. B. Hintikka, eds., *Discovering Reality: Feminist Perspectives on Epistemology, Metaphysics, Methodology, and Philosophy of Science*. Dordrecht: Springer, 149–164.

Mower, S., 2016. Theresa May's style is more than just her shoes. *Daily Mail Online*, 1 August. www.dailymail.co.uk/femail/article-3717301/How-dress-like-grown-s-Theresa-s-style-striking-shoes-fashion-expert-SARAH-MOWER-says.html [accessed 19 November 2018].

Mügge, L., Evans, E., and Engeli, I., 2016. Introduction: Gender in European political science education – taking stock and future directions. *European Political Science*, 15 (3), 281–291.

Mügge, L., Montoya, C., Emejulu, A., and Weldon, S. L., 2018. Intersectionality and the politics of knowledge production. *European Journal of Politics and Gender*, 1 (1–2), 17–36.

Mulkay, M., 1988. *On Humor: Its Nature and Its Place in Modern Society*. London: Polity Press.

Mullany, L., 2007. *Gendered Discourse in the Professional Workplace*. Basingstoke: Palgrave Macmillan.

Mullany, L., 2012. Discourse, gender and professional communication. In J. P. Gee and M. Handford, eds., *The Routledge Handbook of Discourse Analysis*. London: Routledge, 509–522.

Murphy, J., 2014. (Im)politeness during Prime Minister's Questions in the U.K. Parliament. *Pragmatics and Society*, 5 (1), 76–104.

Murphy, J. and Rek, B., 2018. Candidate gender and the media attention in the 2015 UK general election. *Parliamentary Affairs*. https://academic.oup.com/pa/advance-article/doi/10.1093/pa/gsy019/4963368 [accessed 31 July 2018].

Murray, R., 2014. Quotas for men: Reframing gender quotas as a means of improving representation for all. *American Political Science Review*, 108 (3), 520–532.

Murtagh, C., 2008. A transient transition: The cultural and institutional obstacles impeding the Northern Ireland Women's Coalition in its progression from informal to formal politics. *Irish Political Studies*, 23 (1), 21–40.

Museum of London. Anti-suffrage postcard sent to Christabel Pankhurst in 1909. https://collections.museumoflondon.org.uk/online/object/289813.html [accessed 30 November 2018].

Nichols, D. and Kolankiewicz, V., 2017. Bogan in the eye of the beholder: The curious case of Rebel Wilson. *The Conversation*. http://theconversation.com/bogan-in-the-eye-of-the-beholder-the-curious-case-of-rebel-wilson-78259 [accessed 27 June 2019].

Nicholson, E., 1996. *Secret Society: Inside – and Outside – the Conservative Party*. London: Indigo.

Nielson, 2016. First Presidential Debate of 2016 Draws 84 Million Viewers. www.nielsen.com/us/en/insights/news/2016/first-presidential-debate-of-2016-draws-84-million-viewers [accessed 8 November 2018].

Norris, P., 1997. *Women, Media, and Politics*. New York: Oxford University Press.

Ochs, E., 1992. Indexing gender. In A. Duranti and C. Goodwin, eds., *Rethinking Context: Language as an Interactive Phenomenon*. Cambridge: Cambridge University Press, 335–359.

Okimoto, T. G. and Brescoll, V. L., 2010. The price of power: Power seeking and backlash against female politicians. *Personality and Social Psychology Bulletin*, 36 (7), 923–936.

Parker, A., 2016. Donald Trump says Hillary Clinton doesn't have 'a presidential look'. *The New York Times*, 6 September. www.nytimes.com/2016/09/07/us/politics/donald-trump-says-hillary-clinton-doesnt-have-a-presidential-look.html [accessed 8 November 2018].

Parkinson, J. R., 2012. *Democracy and Public Space: The Physical Sites of Democratic Performance*. Oxford: Oxford University Press.

Parliament UK, 2010. Equality act 2010. www.legislation.gov.uk/ukpga/2010/15 [accessed 27 June 2018].

Parliamentary Report, 2018. Report on an independent complaints and grievance policy. Westminster: Parliament UK. Cross Party Working Group on an Independent Complaints and Grievance Policy. https://researchbriefings.parliament.uk/ResearchBriefing/Summary/CDP-2018-0049 [accessed 27 June 2018].

Pauwels, A., 1998. *Women Changing Language*. London: Longman.

Pavlenko, A. and Blackedge, A., 2004. Introduction: New theoretical approaches to the study of negotiation of identities in multilingual contexts. In A. Pavlenko and A. Blackedge, eds., *Negotiations of Identity in Multilingual Contexts*. Clevedon: Multilingual Matters, 1–33.

Peck, J., 2011. When Julia talks, does her gender speak louder? *The Conversation*. http://theconversation.com/when-julia-talks-does-her-gender-speak-louder-1342 [accessed 25 October 2018].

Penny, L., 2016. A Tory leadership race between two women is not a feminist revolution. *New Statesman*, 7 July. www.newstatesman.com/politics/feminism/2016/07/tory-leadership-race-between-two-women-not-feminist-revolution [accessed 9 October 2018].

Phillips, A., 1995. *The Politics of Presence*. Oxford: Clarendon Press.

Phillips, J., 2017. *Everywoman: One Woman's Truth about Speaking the Truth*. London: Hutchinson.

Pitkin, H. F., 1967. *The Concept of Representation*. Berkeley: University of California Press.

Pizzini, F., 1991. Communication hierarchies in humour: Gender differences in the obstetrical/gynaecological setting. *Discourse & Society*, 2 (4), 477–488.

Puwar, N., 1997. Reflections on interviewing women MPs. http://socresonline.org.uk/2/1/4.html [accessed 28 August 2017].

Puwar, N., 2004a. *Space Invaders: Race, Gender and Bodies Out of Place*. Oxford: Berg.

Puwar, N., 2004b. Thinking about making a difference. *The British Journal of Politics and International Relations*, 6 (1), 65–80.

Ramazanoglu, C. and Holland, J., 2002. *Feminist Methodology: Challenges and Choices*. London: Sage.

Rampton, B., 2007. Neo-Hymsian linguistic ethnography in the United Kingdom. *Journal of Sociolinguistics*, 11 (5), 548–607.

Randall, V. and Lovenduski, J., 2004. Gender in contemporary British politics. *The British Journal of Politics & International Relations*, 6 (1), 1–2.

Rehn, A., 2010. Abbott's no means no gaffe. *The Daily Telegraph*, 3 August 2010. www.dailytelegraph.com.au/abbotts-no-means-no-gaffe/news-story/c61d44cfa 2e5f40744cc9fcc6628b375 [accessed 22 October 2018].

Reid Boyd, E., J., 2012. Lady: Still a feminist four letter word? *Women and Language*, 35 (2), 35–52.

Reid, C., 2014. Rhetoric and parliamentary leadership - Prime Minister's questions. In J. Atkins, A. Finlayson, J. Martin, and N. Turnbull, eds., *Rhetoric in British Politics and Society*. Basingstoke and New York: Palgrave Macmillan, 45–57.

Reingold, B., 2000. *Representing Women: Sex, Gender and Legislative Behavior in Arizona and California*. Chapel Hill: The University of North Carolina Press.

Reisigl, M., 2010. Rhetoric of political speeches. In R. Wodak and V. Koller, eds., *Handbook of Communication in the Public Sphere*. Berlin and New York: Mouton de Gruyter, 243–270.

Rhodes, R. A. W., 2005. Everyday life in a ministry: Public administration as anthropology. *The American Review of Public Administration*, 35 (1), 3–25.

Robinson, S. and Kerr, R., 2018. Women leaders in the political field in Scotland: A socio-historical approach to the emergence of leaders. *Leadership*, 14 (6), 662–686.

Romaniuk, T., 2016. On the relevance of gender in the analysis of discourse: A case study from Hillary Rodham Clinton's presidential bid in 2007–2008. *Discourse & Society*, 27 (5), 533–553.

Rooney, P., 2010. Philosophy, adversarial argumentation and embattled reason. *Informal Logic*, 30 (3), 203–234.

Ross, K., 2017. *Gender, Politics, News: A Game of Three Sides*. Chichester: Wiley-Blackwell.

Ross, K. and Carter, C., 2011. Women and news: A long and winding road. *Media, Culture & Society*, 33 (8), 1148–1165.

Ross, K. and Comrie, M., 2012. The rules of the (leadership) game: Gender, politics and news. *Journalism*, 13 (8), 969–984.

Rubtcova, M., Butorina, Y., Nakopia, L., Stepanova, E., and Gallina, S., 2018. The analysis of Theresa May and Justin Trudeau's Twitter accounts media constituent. Rochester: Social Science Research Network. SSRN Scholarly Paper No. ID 3116711. https://papers.ssrn.com/abstract=3116711 [accessed 4 June 2018].

Rudman, L. A. and Fairchild, R., 2004. Reactions to counterstereotypic behaviour: The role of backlash in cultural stereotype maintenance. *Journal of Personality and Social Psychology*, 87 (2), 157–176.

Rudman, L. A., Moss-Racusin, C. A., Phelan, J. E., and Nauts, S., 2012. Status incongruity and backlash effects: Defending the gender hierarchy motivates prejudice against female leaders. *Journal of Experimental Social Psychology*, 48 (1), 165–179.

Ryan, M. K. and Haslam, S. A., 2005. The glass cliff: Evidence that women are over-represented in precarious leadership positions. *British Journal of Management*, 16 (2), 81–90.

Ryan, M. K., Haslam, S. A., Morgenroth, T., Rink, F., Stoker, J., and Peters, K., 2016. Getting on top of the glass cliff: Reviewing a decade of evidence, explanations, and impact. *The Leadership Quarterly*, 27 (3), 446–455.

Saalfeld, T., 2011. Parliamentary questions as instruments of substantive representation: Visible minorities in the UK House of Commons, 2005–10. *The Journal of Legislative Studies*, 17 (3), 271–289.

Sacks, H., Schegloff, E. A., and Jefferson, G., 1974. A simplest systematics for the organization of turn-taking for conversation. *Language*, 50 (4), 696–735.

Sanday, P. R., 2007. *Fraternity Gang Rape: Sex, Brotherhood, and Privilege on Campus*. 2nd ed. New York: New York University Press.

Savigny, H., 2014. Women, know your limits: Cultural sexism in academia. *Gender and Education*, 26 (7), 794–809.

Saville-Troike, M., 2003. *The Ethnography of Communication: An Introduction*. 3rd ed. Malden: Blackwell Pub.

Savoy, J., 2018. Analysis of the style and the rhetoric of the 2016 US presidential primaries. *Digital Scholarship in the Humanities*, 33 (1), 143–159.

Sawer, M., 2013. Misogyny and misrepresentation. *Political Science*, 65 (1), 105–117.

Sawer, P., 2012. How Maggie Thatcher was remade. 8 January. www.telegraph.co.uk/news/politics/margaret-thatcher/8999746/How-Maggie-Thatcher-was-remade.html [accessed 31 July 2018].

Schreiber, R., 2016. Gender roles, motherhood, and politics: Conservative women's organizations frame Sarah Palin and Michele Bachmann. *Journal of Women, Politics & Policy*, 37 (1), 1–23.

Schreiber, R., 2018. Is there a conservative feminism? An empirical account. *Politics & Gender*, 14 (1), 56–79.

Sclafani, J., 2017. *Talking Donald Trump: A Sociolinguistic Study of Style, Metadiscourse, and Political Identity*. London: Routledge.

Sealey, A. and Bates, S., 2016. Prime ministerial self-reported actions in Prime Minister's Questions 1979–2010: A corpus-assisted analysis. *Journal of Pragmatics*, 104 (October), 18–31.

Searle, J. R., 1969. *Speech Acts: An Essay in the Philosophy of Language*. Cambridge: Cambridge University Press.

Second Presidential Debate, 2016. Washington University in St. Louis. www.nytimes.com/video/us/politics/100000004696519/watch-live-second-presidential-debate.html [accessed 12 November 2018].

Sedgwick, E. K., 1985. *Between Men: English Literature and Male Homosocial Desire*. New York: Columbia University Press.

Segal, L., 2006. Men at Bay: The contemporary 'crisis' of masculinity. In S. Whitehead, ed., *Men and Masculinities: Critical Concepts in Sociology*. London: Routledge, 272–281.

Sensales, G. and Areni, A., 2017. Gender biases and linguistic sexism in political communication: A comparison of press news about men and women Italian ministers. *Journal of Social and Political Psychology*, 5 (2), 512–536.

Shaw, S., (In Press). Gender, language and elite ethnographies in political institutions. In J. Angouri and J. Baxter, eds., *The Routledge Handbook of Language, Gender and Sexuality*. London: Routledge.

Shaw, S., 2000. Language, gender and floor apportionment in political debates. *Discourse & Society*, 11 (3), 401–418.

Shaw, S., 2002. Language and gender in the house of commons. PhD thesis. The Institute of Education, University of London.

Shaw, S., 2006. Governed by the rules? The female voice in parliamentary debates. In J. Baxter, ed., *Speaking Out: The Female Voice in Public Contexts*. Basingstoke: Palgrave Macmillan, 81–102.

Shaw, S., 2011. 'I am not an Honourable Lady!': Gender and language in the National Assembly for Wales. *Journal of Applied Linguistics and Professional Practice*, 8 (3), 275–294.

Shaw, S., 2013. An ethnographic investigation into gender and language in the Northern Ireland Assembly. In I. Poggi, F. D'Errico, L. Vincze and A. Vinciarelli, eds., *Multimodal Communication in Political Speech. Shaping Minds and Social Action*. Berlin: Springer, 39–53.

Shaw, S., 2018. Off the record: The transcription of parliamentary debates for political discourse analysis. In M. Kranert and G. Horan, eds., *Doing Politics: Discursivity, Performativity and Mediation in Political Discourse*. Amsterdam: John Benjamins, 105–126.

Sheldon, A., 2015. 'Thank you for Heckling me' Hillary Rodham Clinton's discursive management of her public persona, her political message and the 'Iron my shirt' hecklers in the 2008 presidential election campaign. In J. Wilson and D. Boxer, eds., *Discourse, Politics and Women as Global Leaders*. Amsterdam: John Benjamins, 195–216.

Shibamoto-Smith, J. S., 2011. Honorifics, 'politeness,' and power in Japanese political debate. *Journal of Pragmatics*, 43 (15), 3707–3719.

Shor, E., Rijt, A. van de, Ward, C., Blank-Gomel, A., and Skiena, S., 2014. Time trends in printed news coverage of female subjects, 1880–2008. *Journalism Studies*, 15 (6), 759–773.

Silverstein, M., 2003. Indexical order and the dialectics of sociolinguistic life. *Language & Communication*, 23 (3), 193–229.

Sinclair, J. and Coulthard, M., 1975. *Towards an Analysis of Discourse: The English Used by Teachers and Pupils*. Oxford: Oxford University Press.

Slembrouck, S., 1992. The parliamentary Hansard 'verbatim' report: The written construction of spoken discourse. *Language and Literature*, 1 (2), 101–120.

Smith, A., 2008. Limbaugh returned to 'testicle lockbox'; claimed Clinton 'reminds men of the worst characteristics of women'. *Media Matters for America*. www.mediamatters.org/research/2008/02/15/limbaugh-returned-to-testicle-lockbox-claimed-c/142573 [accessed 7 November 2018].

Smith, G., 2009. *Democratic Innovations: Designing Institutions for Citizen Participation*. Cambridge: Cambridge University Press.

Smith, P., Caputi, P., and Crittenden, N., 2012. A maze of metaphors around glass ceilings. *Gender in Management: An International Journal*, 27 (7), 436–448.

Smooth, W., 2006. Intersectionality in electoral politics: A mess worth making. *Politics & Gender*, 2 (3), 400–414.

Sones, B., Moran, M., and Lovenduski, J., 2005. *Women in Parliament: The New Suffragettes*. London: Politico's Publishing Ltd.

Sorrentino, J. and Augoustinos, M., 2016. 'I don't view myself as a woman politician, I view myself as a politician who's a woman': The discursive management of gender identity in political leadership. *British Journal of Social Psychology*, 55 (3), 385–406.

Southern, K. and Spillett, R., 2018. Tory MP allegedly leaves his wife for woman 20 years his junior. *Mail Online*, 11 January. www.dailymail.co.uk/news/article-5260677/Tory-MP-leaves-wife-woman-20-years-junior.html [accessed 28 January 2019].

Sparrow, A., 2016. PMQs verdict: Has Theresa May got a new gag writer? *The Guardian*, 7 September. www.theguardian.com/global/2016/sep/07/pmqs-verdict-theresa-may-new-gag-writer [accessed 25 September 2018].

Sreberny-Mohammadi, A. and Ross, K., 1996. Women MPs and the media: Representing the body politic. *Parliamentary Affairs*, 49 (1), 103–115.

Stanley, A., 1992. Democrats in New York; A softer image for Hillary Clinton. *The New York Times*, 13 July. www.nytimes.com/1992/07/13/news/democrats-in-new-york-a-softer-image-for-hillary-clinton.html [accessed 13 November 2018].

Steenbergen, M. R., Bächtiger, A., Spörndli, M., and Steiner, J., 2003. Measuring political deliberation: A discourse quality index. *Comparative European Politics*, 1 (1), 21–48.

Steiner, J., Bächtiger, A., Spörndli, M., and Steenbergen, M. R., 2004. *Deliberative Politics in Action: Analyzing Parliamentary Discourse*. Cambridge: Cambridge University Press.

Stopfner, M., 2018. Put your 'big girl' voice on. *Journal of Language and Politics*, 17 (5), 617–635.

Stubbe, M., Lane, C., Hilder, J., Vine, E., Vine, B., Marra, M., Holmes, J., and Weatherall, A., 2003. Multiple discourse analyses of a workplace interaction. *Discourse Studies*, 5 (3), 351–388.

Stubbs, M., 1983. *Discourse Analysis: The Sociolinguistic Analysis of Natural Language*. Chicago and London: University of Chicago Press.

Suleiman, C. and O'Connell, D. C., 2008. Gender differences in the media interviews of Bill and Hillary Clinton. *Journal of Psycholinguistic Research*, 37 (1), 33–48.

Sunderland, J., 2004. *Gendered Discourses*. Basingstoke: Palgrave Macmillan.

Sunderland, J., 2007. Contradictions in gendered discourses: Feminist readings of sexist jokes? *Gender and Language*, 1 (2), 207–228.

Sunderland, J. and Litosseliti, L., 2008. Current research methodologies in gender and language studies: Key issues. In K. Harrington, L. Litosseliti, H. Sauntson and J. Sunderland, eds., *Gender and Language Research Methodologies*. Basingstoke: Palgrave Macmillan, 1–20.

Swann, J., 1992. *Girls, Boys and Language*. Oxford: Wiley-Blackwell.

Swann, J., 2002. Yes, but is it gender? In L. Litosseliti and J. Sunderland, eds., *Gender Identity and Discourse Analysis*. Amsterdam: Benjamins, 43–67.

Swift, D., 2019. From 'I'm not a feminist, but…' to 'Call me an old-fashioned feminist…': Conservative women in parliament and feminism, 1979–2017. *Women's History Review*, 28 (2), 317–336.

Tamale, S., 1998. *When Hens Begin to Crow: Gender and Parliamentary Politics in Uganda*. London: Routledge.

Tannen, D., 1984. *That's Not What I Meant! How Conversational Style Makes or Breaks Relationships*. New York: William Morrow & Company.

Tannen, D., 1990. *You Just Don't Understand: Men and Women in Conversation*. New York: Ballantine.

Taylor, E. A., Smith, A. B., Welch, N. M., and Hardin, R., 2018. 'You should be flattered!': Female sport management faculty experiences of sexual harassment and sexism. *Women in Sport and Physical Activity Journal*, 26 (1), 43–53.

Thompson, S. and Yates, C., 2017. Maybot, Mummy or Iron Lady? Loving and loathing Theresa May. In E. Thorsen, D. Jackson and D. Lilleker, eds., *UK Election Analysis 2017: Media, Voters and the Campaign*. Bournemouth: PSA/Bournemouth University, 131. www.electionanalysis.uk/uk-election-analysis-2017/section-8-personality-politics-and-popular-culture/maybot-mummy-or-iron-lady-loving-and-loathing-theresa-may/ [accessed 26 June 2017].

Thornborrow, J., 2002. *Power Talk: Interaction in Institutional Settings*. London: Longman, Pearson Education.

Thorne, B., Kramarae, C., and Henley, N., eds., 1983. *Language, Gender, and Society*. Rowley: Newbury House.

Tigue, C. C., Borak, D. J., O'Connor, J. J. M., Schandl, C., and Feinberg, D. R., 2012. Voice pitch influences voting behavior. *Evolution and Human Behavior*, 33 (3), 210–216.

Trimble, L., 2016. Julia Gillard and the Gender Wars. *Politics & Gender*, 12 (2), 296–316.

Trimble, L., 2017. *Ms. Prime Minister: Gender, Media and Leadership*. Toronto: University of Toronto Press.

Trimble, L., Wagner, A., Sampert, S., Raphael, D., and Gerrits, B., 2013. Is it personal? Gendered mediation in newspaper coverage of Canadian national party leadership contests, 1975–2012. *The International Journal of Press/Politics*, 18 (4), 462–481.

Troemel-Ploetz, S., 1991. Selling the apolitical. *Discourse and Society*, 2 (4), 489–502.

Trump, D., 2016a. Donald Trump apologizes for controversial video remarks. *Fox News*. www.youtube.com/watch?v=eA597Kn5iPk [accessed 10 November 2018].

Trump, D., 2016b. Statement from Donald J. Trump. Trump-Pence: Make America Great Again. https://web.archive.org/web/20161007210105/https://www.donaldjtrump.com/press-releases/statement-from-donald-j.-trump [accessed 11 November 2018].

Trump, D., 2016c. Transcript: Donald Trump's taped comments about women. 8 October. www.nytimes.com/2016/10/08/us/donald-trump-tape-transcript.html [accessed 10 November 2018].

Tweedy, J., 2017. PM Theresa May unveils new shorter hair style. *Mail Online*, 20 March. www.dailymail.co.uk/~/article-4331920/index.html [accessed 13 February 2019].

Uchida, A., 1992. When 'difference' is 'dominance': A critique of the 'anti-power-based' cultural approach to sex differences. *Language in Society*, 21 (4), 547–568.

van Dijk, T. A., 2000. On the analysis of parliamentary debates on immigration. In M. Reisigl and R. Wodak, eds., *The Semiotics of Racism: Approaches to Critical Discourse Analysis*. Vienna: Passagen Verlag, 85–103.

van Dijk, T. A., 2004. Text and context of parliamentary debates. In P. Bayley, ed., *Cross-Cultural Perspectives on Parliamentary Discourse*. Amsterdam: John Benjamins, 339–372.

van Dijk, T. A., 2008. *Discourse and Power.* 2008th ed. Basingstoke: Palgrave.

van Dijk, T. A., 2016. Critical discourse studies: A sociocognitive approach. In R. Wodak and M. Meyer, eds., *Methods of Critical Discourse Studies.* London: Sage, 62–85.

Varney, D., 2017. 'Not now, not ever': Julia Gillard and the performative power of affect. In E. Diamond, D. Varney and C. Amich, eds., *Performance, Feminism and Affect in Neoliberal Times.* New York: Palgrave Macmillan, 25–38.

Vial, A. C., Napier, J. L., and Brescoll, V. L., 2016. A bed of thorns: Female leaders and the self-reinforcing cycle of illegitimacy. *The Leadership Quarterly,* 27 (3), 400–414.

Vine, S., 2017. Never mind Brexit. Who won legs-it? *The Daily Mail,* 28 March.

Vinkenburg, C. J., van Engen, M. L., Eagly, A. H., and Johannesen-Schmidt, M. C., 2011. An exploration of stereotypical beliefs about leadership styles: Is transformational leadership a route to women's promotion? *The Leadership Quarterly,* 22 (1), 10–21.

Waddle, M., Bull, P., and Böhnke, J. R., 2019. 'He is just the nowhere man of British politics': Personal attacks in Prime Minister's questions. *Journal of Language and Social Psychology,* 38 (1), 61–84.

Wagner, A., Trimble, L., Sampert, S., and Gerrits, B., 2017. Gender, competitiveness, and candidate visibility in newspaper coverage of Canadian party leadership contests. *The International Journal of Press/Politics,* 22 (4), 471–489.

Wagner, I. and Wodak, R., 2006. Performing success: Identifying strategies of self-presentation in women's biographical narratives. *Discourse & Society,* 17 (3), 385–411.

Wahl-Jorgensen, K., 2017. The battle for authenticity. In E. Thorsen, D. Jackson, and D. Lilleker, eds., *UK Election Analysis 2017: Media, Voters and the Campaign.* Bournemouth: PSA/Bournemouth University, 69.

Walker, J., 2016. Mom or mum? MP Jess Phillips makes Hansard spell it the Brummie way. *birminghammail.* www.birminghammail.co.uk/news/midlands-news/mom-mum-mp-jess-phillips-12308391 [accessed 5 January 2019].

Walsh, C., 2001. *Gender and Discourse: Language and Power in Politics, the Church and Organisations.* Harlow: Longman.

Walsh, C., 2015. Media capital or media deficit? *Feminist Media Studies,* 15 (6), 1025–1034.

Walter, J., 2017. 'No loans for ladies': Julia Gillard and capital denied. In M. Bennister, B. Worthy and P. t' Hart, eds., *The Leadership Capital Index: A New Perspective on Political Leadership.* Oxford: Oxford University Press, 45–62.

Walton, D. N., 2009. *Ad Hominem Arguments.* Tuscaloosa: The University of Alabama Press.

Wang, V., 2014. Tracing gender differences in parliamentary debates: A growth curve analysis of Ugandan MPs' activity levels in plenary sessions, 1998–2008. *Representation,* 50 (3), 365–377.

Wängnerud, L., 2009. Women in parliaments: Descriptive and substantive representation. *Annual Review of Political Science,* 12 (1), 51–69.

Wapshott, N. and Brock, G., 1983. *Thatcher.* London: Futura Publications.

Ward, O., 2017. Intersectionality and press coverage of political campaigns: Representations of Black, Asian, and Minority Ethnic Female Candidates at the U.K. 2010 General Election. *The International Journal of Press/Politics,* 22 (1), 43–66.

Wasburn, P. C. and Wasburn, M. H., 2011. Media coverage of women in politics: The curious case of Sarah Palin. *Media, Culture & Society*, 33 (7), 1027–1041.

Watt, N., 2014. John Bercow calls for end to 'orchestrated barracking' at PMQs. *The Guardian*, 18 February. www.theguardian.com/politics/2014/feb/18/john-bercow-pmqs-letter-party-leaders [accessed 19 January 2019].

Waylen, G., 2008. Feminist perspectives on transforming global governance: Challenges and opportunities. In S. M. Rai and G. Waylen, eds., *Global Governance: Feminist Perspectives*. London: Palgrave, 254–275.

Waylen, G., ed., 2017. *Gender and Informal Institutions*. London: Rowman and Littlefield.

Webster, W., 1990. *Not a Man to Match Her: The Marketing of a Prime Minister*. London: The Women's Press.

Wenger, E., 1998. *Communities of Practice*. Cambridge: Cambridge University Press.

West, C., 2012. Mammy, Jezebel, Sapphire, and their homegirls: Developing an 'oppositional gaze' toward the images of Black women. In J. C. Chrisler, C. Golden, and P. D. Rozee, eds., *Lectures on the Psychology of Women*. Long Grove: Waveland Press, Inc, 286–299.

Wheeler, B., 2015. Why are MPs banned from clapping? 28 May. www.bbc.com/news/uk-politics-32913113 [accessed 27 January 2019].

Whiting, S. and Braniff, M., 2016. 'There is no point having a token woman': Gender and representation in the 'new' Northern Ireland. *Democratic Audit UK*. www.democraticaudit.com [accessed 3 January 2019].

Wicks, R. H., Eubanks, A. D., Dye, R. G., Stewart, P. A., and Eidelman, S., 2017. The 2016 US Presidential debates. Perceptions of Donald Trump and Hillary Clinton based on presentation style. In A. Cavari and R. J. Powell, eds., *The 2016 Presidential Election: The Causes and Consequences of a Political Earthquake*. Lanham: Lexington Books, 43–57.

Williams, M. J. and Tiedens, L. Z., 2016. The subtle suspension of backlash: A meta-analysis of penalties for women's implicit and explicit dominance behavior. *Psychological Bulletin*, 142 (2), 165–197.

Williams, P. M., 1980. Interviewing politicians: The life of Hugh Gaitskell. *Political Quarterly*, 51 (3), 303–316.

Williamson, J., 2003. Comment: Sexism with an alibi. *The Guardian*, 31 May. www.theguardian.com/media/2003/may/31/advertising.comment [accessed 16 November 2018].

Willis, R., 2017. Taming the Climate? Corpus analysis of politicians' speech on climate change. *Environmental Politics*, 26 (2), 212–231.

Wilson, J., 1990. *Politically Speaking: The Pragmatic Analysis of Political Language*. London: Blackwell.

Wilson, J. and Irwin, A., 2015. 'Why can't a woman be more like a man?' Margaret Thatcher and the discourse of leadership. In J. Wilson and D. Boxer, eds., *Discourse, Politics and Women as Global Leaders*. Amsterdam: John Benjamins, 21–42.

Winters, K. and Carvalho, E., 2015. Why did Nicola and Nigel do so well out of the debates? They are authentic and articulate, that's why. *QESB 2015 Blog/The Qualitative Election Study of Britain*. https://qesb.info/media-coverage/blog-articles/ [accessed 5 July 2018].

Wodak, R., 1997. Introduction: Some important issues in the research of gender and discourse. In R. Wodak, ed., *Gender and Discourse*. London: Sage, 1–20.

Wodak, R., 2003. Multiple Identities: The role of female parliamentarians in the EU parliament. In J. Holmes and M. Meyerhoff, eds., *The Handbook of Language and Gender*. Oxford: Blackwell, 671–698.

Wodak, R., 2009. *The Discourse of Politics in Action: Politics as Usual*. Basingstoke: Palgrave Macmillan.

Wodak, R., 2014. Political discourse analysis: Distinguishing frontstage and backstage contexts. A discourse-historical approach. In J. Flowerdew, ed., *Discourse in Context: Contemporary Applied Linguistics*. London: Bloomsbury, 321–345.

Worth, A., Augoustinos, M., and Hastie, B., 2016. 'Playing the gender card': Media representations of Julia Gillard's sexism and misogyny speech. *Feminism & Psychology*, 26 (1), 52–72.

Wortham, S. and Reyes, A., 2015. *Discourse Analysis Beyond the Speech Event*. London: Routledge.

Wright, K. A. M. and Holland, J., 2014. Leadership and the media: Gendered framings of Julia Gillard's 'sexism and misogyny' speech. *Australian Journal of Political Science*, 49 (3), 455–468.

Yoder, J. D., 1991. Rethinking tokenism: Looking beyond numbers. *Gender & Society*, 5 (2), 178–192.

Yoong, M., 2019. 'Where's our #30peratus': A feminist critical discourse analysis of Twitter debates on women's political representation. In S. Lemiere, ed., *Minorities Matter: Malaysian Politics and People*. Selangor: Strategic Information and Research Development Centre, 21–35.

Yu, B., 2014. Language and gender in congressional speech. *Literary and Linguistic Computing*, 29 (1), 118–132.

Zimmerman, D. H. and West, C., 1975. Sex roles, interruptions and silences in conversation. In B. Thorne and N. Henley, eds., *Language and Sex: Difference and Dominance*. Rowley: Newbury House Publishers, 105–129.

van Zoonen, L., 2006. The personal, the political and the popular: A woman's guide to celebrity politics. *European Journal of Cultural Studies*, 9 (3), 287–301.

Zulli, D., 2018. The changing norms of gendered news coverage: Hillary Clinton in the *New York Times*, 1969–2016. *Politics & Gender*, 1–23. doi:10.1017/s1743923x18000466.

Index